The Next Great War?

The BELFER CENTER STUDIES IN INTERNATIONAL SECURITY book series is edited at the Belfer Center for Science and International Affairs at the Harvard Kennedy School and is published by the MIT Press. The series publishes books on contemporary issues in international security policy, as well as their conceptual and historical foundations. Topics of particular interest to the series include the spread of weapons of mass destruction, internal conflict, the international effects of democracy and democratization, and U.S. defense policy.

A complete list of Belfer Center Studies appears at the back of this volume.

The Next Great War?

The Roots of World War I and the
Risk of U.S.-China Conflict

Richard N. Rosecrance and Steven E. Miller, editors

Belfer Center Studies in International Security
The MIT Press
Cambridge, Massachusetts
London, England

The MIT Press, One Rogers Street, Cambridge, MA 02142-1209, USA

This book was typeset in Minion Pro and Scala Sans by Rex Horner.
Printed and bound in the United States of America.

Library of Congress Cataloging-in-Publication Data

The next great war? : the roots of World War I and the risk of U.S.-
China conflict / edited by Richard Rosecrance and Steven E. Miller.
pages   cm.— (Belfer Center studies in international security)
Includes bibliographical references and index.
ISBN 978-0-262-02899-8 (hardcover : alk. paper)
1. World War, 1914–1918—Causes. 2. United States—Foreign
relations—China. 3. China—Foreign relations—United States.
I. Rosecrance, Richard N., editor of compilation. II. Miller, Steven E.,
editor of compilation.
D511.N485   2015
940.3'11—dc23   2014033728

10 9 8 7 6 5 4 3 2 1

To Barbara

Contents

A Century after Sarajevo: Taking Stock and Looking Forward

Introduction

The Sarajevo Centenary—1914 and the Rise of China

Steven E. Miller

I N THE GOLDEN summer of 1914, the assassination of the heir to the Austro-Hungarian throne in Vienna's distant Balkan province of Bosnia-Herzegovina triggered a sequence of events that within weeks had plunged Europe's major powers into war. What followed was a disaster of immense proportions. The costs of this war were vast; for more than four cruel years, the great powers spent lavishly in blood and treasure. Men were cut down in the millions and treasuries were emptied. The consequences of this war were enormous and lasting. By war's end, four empires—the German, Russian, Austrian, and Ottoman—had been destroyed. The map of Europe and the Middle East had been redrawn. Germany and Russia had been wracked by internal revolutions, with fateful long-term implications for both those countries and for the world. Even the European victors, France and Britain, had been weakened by a savage depletion that hastened their declines as major powers. Out of the wreckage of World War I flowed developments that were central to international politics for the remainder of the twentieth century: the rise of Nazism, a second global war, and the Cold War rivalry that pitted the heirs to the Russian Revolution of 1917 against the one power that emerged from World War I unscathed and strengthened, the United States. In the summer of 1914, history pivoted: the previous world would be destroyed and the path that opened up was dark and dangerous. This was one of the formative turning points in modern history.

It is not surprising, then, that even after the passage of one hundred years, the events of 1914 remain compelling. Remarkably, controversy over the war's origins has continued unabated. Basic facts remain in dispute.[1] There has been endless debate about assigning responsibility for the war. There have been waves of reinterpretation as new evidence has been discovered or new theoretical understandings of international politics have been explored.[2] As the academic field of international relations has evolved over recent decades—with new work on nationalism, militarism, interdependence, preventive war, offense-defense theory, signaling and bargaining, perceptions and misperceptions, deterrence, and deterrence failure, among other conceptual developments—1914 has been reexamined through a variety of intellectual lenses. The great animating questions have remained constant, however, shaped by the full retrospective understanding of the unprecedented disaster that the elites of 1914 brought upon their countries: How could this catastrophe have happened? What explains the events of 1914? An enormous literature has sought to answer these questions.[3]

The drama of 1914 draws our gaze backward, but an equally haunting question arises if we look ahead: Could 1914 happen again? Could the forces and factors that put the great powers on what turned out to be an unstoppable path to war in 1914 operate in our own time? Can we see any indications that conditions present in 1914 might be replicated in the contemporary setting?

The aim of this volume is to look back in order to look ahead. The contributors have been asked to probe the origins of World War I seeking warning signs, lessons, cautionary tales, or causal conclusions that are (or might be) applicable to the current international order. What can we learn from the 1914 case that will help us better to understand and, more importantly, to help shape international politics today? Can we identify tragic mistakes that should be avoided? Can we reduce the likelihood of great power conflict in the future by understanding what led to it in the past? Because the issue at hand is the violent collision of great powers, in today's world these questions lead directly to consideration of China's relations with the United States. If there is to be great power conflict in the era ahead, it seems most likely that this will involve a rising China challenging a predominant America. Could there be a 1914 redux between these two powerful states? Rivalry seems inevitable, but can this rivalry be managed in a way that avoids war? Are there factors at play in U.S.-China relations that, as in 1914, could trigger an escalation to war? Our contributors have sought to draw upon their understandings of 1914 to assess the evolving relationship between Washington and Beijing, to note similarities and differences with 1914, and to highlight possible dangers as well as potential opportunities.

Looking Back: What Caused the Disaster of 1914?

The historiography on the deep and proximate causes of war in 1914 does not lead to single or simple explanations. The chapters that follow reflect the multidimensional character of the literature on 1914. The chapters in this volume draw on multiple layers of explanation, some focusing on a particular dimension of the drama in 1914 and others employing clusters of causal factors in their analyses.

Bad Ideas

A running theme throughout many of the chapters that follow, and the subject of some of them, is the importance of the ideational context that existed in 1914. Put simply, many of those making fateful choices in 1914 (as well as the elites around them and the publics they governed) were influenced by a toxic stew of pernicious beliefs. To a degree that may now be impossible to fully fathom, for example, war was glorified. It was widely regarded as noble, purifying, desirable, a healthy test of men and institutions, a promoter of civilization, and a source of progress. As Stephen Van Evera notes in his chapter, the outbreak of war was accordingly greeted with "ecstasy" in many quarters. Kevin Rudd reminds us that cheering crowds in the world's great cities jubilantly hailed their countries' declarations of war. This was a perspective, however, that did not survive the carnage of 1914–18.

War was not only desirable; it was also viewed as inevitable by many, especially in Europe's militaries. As Joseph Nye warns in his chapter, the premise of inevitability—generally unwarranted, in Nye's view—is extremely "corrosive" in international politics. Once war is assumed to be unavoidable, the calculations of leaders and militaries change. The question is no longer whether there will or should be a war, but when the war can be fought most advantageously. Even those neither eager for nor optimistic about war may opt to fight when operating in the framework of inevitability. Jack Snyder notes that one of the distinctive features of 1914 is that all of the continental great powers believed that it was an opportune time to fight; as many key figures across Europe judged it, better war now than war later. In a time of shifting power balances, preventive war logics were evident among the ranks of decisionmakers.

As Van Evera, Snyder, Nye, and others emphasize, Europe's militaries were marked by a "cult of the offensive," a deep (but flawed) belief that attack was the superior mode of fighting and that first-strike advantages were large and potentially decisive. By 1914 all of the continental powers had adopted offensive military doctrines, producing instability that contributed to the outbreak of war. In an offense-dominant world, conquest is thought to be easy, waiting for diplomacy can be dangerous, hesitation can mean defeat, and mobilization means war. Although some gloomy but farsighted individuals feared a protracted struggle, the belief in decisive offensive action led to a more common view that the war would be over quickly, that someone would achieve the knockout blow. Why avoid war if it is to be short, glorious, and triumphant? Richard Cooper observes in his chapter that had the leaders of 1914 more accurately understood the staggering costs the war would impose, they would have made a more strenuous effort to avoid it. But they were operating on a set of premises that led them to expect more or less the opposite of what happened.

These military predispositions were wedded to a set of beliefs that, particularly in Germany, led to aggressive foreign policies. Social Darwinist interpretations saw international politics as a fierce struggle in which all were tested and only the fittest survived and ascended the hierarchy of power. "Expand or die" philosophies induced greed for additional territories or colonies; empires were seen as a great source and symbol of strength. "Win through intimidation" strategies reflected a deep commitment to coercive models of international politics; it was thought vital to stand tough, keep firm, look strong, and avoid compromises that signaled weakness and surrender. Many of the elites in 1914 saw themselves involved in a mortal contest that would determine their fates, that would establish the upward or downward trajectories of their countries, that would augment or undermine their relative power. In this contest, it was essential to assert and defend their place in the hierarchy, to marshal and employ the power that would guarantee their appropriate place in the sun. For rising powers such as Germany and Russia, this meant demanding or seizing a greater role for themselves on the world stage; for states worried about relative decline—notably, Britain and France—it meant doing whatever necessary to protect their international positions from the new contenders.

Europe's leaders might have looked back on the sequence of wars starting with the American Civil War and concluded that defensive postures were advantageous, that well-prepared defenses could thwart attacking forces while inflicting severe casualties, and that it was possible to effectively defend one's territory from a defensive crouch. As Van Evera notes in his chapter, there was ample evidence to this effect. Further, with different expectations about the near future, Europe's leaders might have sought to preserve peace rather than optimize for the war they thought inevitable. Similarly, they might have avoided zero-sum interpretations of their relations with one another, harkening back to earlier periods when, as Alan Alexandroff points out, Europe's great powers collaborated in a concert system that enabled them to effectively manage their affairs for long periods or when, as in the Bismarckian era, restraint was sometimes valued over aggressiveness. Under these circumstances, the Sarajevo crisis could have been resolved peacefully, mobilization would have been unnecessary, and the disaster of 1914 could have been averted.

Instead, the collection of what Van Evera terms "bellicist" ideas—glorious war, inevitable war, short war, offensive war, triumphant war, all in the service of aggressive Social Darwinist foreign policies—colored the choices and expectations of many of Europe's key leaders.[4] This helps to explain why the spark at Sarajevo set Europe ablaze.

Dysfunctional Internal Politics

A second layer of explanation for the events of 1914 lies in the domestic politics of Europe's great powers. Several broad points emerge from the analyses that follow in this volume.

First, the domestic coalitions that dominated internal politics in several of the key countries—notably, in Germany, Russia, and Austria-Hungary—embraced the bellicist ideas so prevalent in 1914. As Etel Solingen points out in her chapter, there are always alternative forces and alternative views that vie for power and influence in domestic settings. Internationalist domestic coalitions that privilege economic growth and seek to promote exports in an open trading system, she argues, are more averse to war because they prosper from wider engagement with the world economy. Similarly, peace groups and advocates of international law and arbitration sought to contest the ideas and preferences of those with a more martial mentality. Policy in Germany, Russia, Austria-Hungary, and Serbia, however, was in the hands of forces who were inward-looking, militarized, and imbued with the bellicist mentality. The impact of these ideas was so great because they had prevailed in the political contestation between coalitions within major powers.

Two factors magnified the effect of the internal triumph of bellicist coalitions. One was the existence of virulent nationalisms—labeled "hypernationalism" by Solingen—that mobilized masses, whipped up nationalist fervor, incited hatred of other countries, and promoted support for aggressive policies. The other was the prevalence of militarism, marked by a passionate reverence for and a deference to the military. This factor guaranteed that the military had a large and disproportionately influential voice in national policymaking. Thus the institution that most strongly and loudly advocated for war and for war-causing ideas had unusual status and great capacity to advance its views, both within the elite and with the public. Hypernationalism and militarism traveled together like inseparable twins, with nationalist ideologies exalting the military and absorbing its ideas.

Second, Europe faced what T.G. Otte describes as a continent-wide crisis of governance. Each capital had its own unique tale but the government of every major power in Europe was deeply troubled. The imperial powers were seeking, without great skill or success, to suppress or adapt to the rise of mass politics and the demise of monarchical legitimacy. Germany, Otte says, was in the midst of a "permanent crisis of state," its government disorganized and indecisive, its finances is disarray. Austria-Hungary, that doomed agglomeration of territories, peoples, languages, and religions, was deeply divided and confronted insuperable structural problems that made it impossible to achieve national cohesion. Russia was torn by endless machinations in the upper reaches of its government and in the court of the tsar; by 1914 it had achieved "a state of permanent confusion." Meanwhile, the Western democracies, Britain and France, were riven with party cleavages, personal animosities among political leaders, and constitutional crises—these governments were "beleaguered" and "besieged," and stalemate was the order of the day. Some of the most consequential decisions of the twentieth century were made by men and governments handicapped—in some cases, crippled—by the dysfunctional domestic settings in which they operated.

The effect of this widespread blight of domestic crisis was not that governments or leaders sought war as a diversionary tactic; on the contrary, Otte argues that the internal fragility of Europe's major powers was a restraining factor. Governments were uncertain, unconfident, indecisive, incompetent, paralyzed, in some cases distracted until far too late, incapable of coherent strategy, unable to coordinate policy. Momentum toward war went unchecked, while moderating forces were weakened. Confident, effective, strategically sound governance capable of interrupting the march to war was simply lacking. Weak governments in domestic crisis, led by coalitions steeped in war-promoting ideas, made the choices that led to war in the summer of 1914. As Otte concludes, "The decisions for war in 1914 reflected the political paralysis in some countries and a crisis of governance in others."[5]

A final domestic factor that figures in the analyses that follow focuses on the quality of the men at the apex of power. It was Europe's misfortune that at this moment of supreme danger it was ruled by a collection of unimpressive and eccentric figures. The three emperors whose decisions guaranteed war in 1914 were particularly unfortunate, as reflected in Nye's characterization of them: the kaiser, a "weak, emotional blusterer" who operated without skill; Franz Josef of Austria, "a tired old man who was putty in the hands" of the war faction; and the tsar, an "isolated autocrat" surrounded by incompetent ministers. The deficiencies of Europe's leaders, however, were not limited to the emperors. German Chancellor Theobald Bethmann Hollweg was, Otte notes, a flawed, technocratic bureaucrat. The French leader René Viviani, who was both prime minister and foreign minister, was "utterly ignorant" of international affairs.

No one involved in this crisis was touched with greatness; no one possessed a modicum of Bismarckian wisdom or Kissingerian skill; no statesman arose in the press of acute crisis to save Europe from itself.

As David Richards points out, the three emperors at the center of the crisis represented the fading vestiges of hereditary monarchy. Their "atavistic" form of government conferred vast power on designated successors regardless of qualifications or aptitude. Their regimes were increasingly unpopular, increasingly illegitimate, ill-suited for the times, and unable to adapt in response to powerful social and economic forces. This waning trio of erratic and unwise men helped to set Europe on fire. Richards suggests that "stronger sovereigns might have said no to the generals when they urged mobilization."[6] But such sovereigns did not exist in 1914.

Bad ideas fed bad decisions, which led to war in 1914. The bad ideas flourished in various domestic settings and were incorporated into the worldview of dominant domestic coalitions in several key countries. The bad decisions were rendered by national governments, which at every step had alternatives and a capacity for choice, however imperfect their decisionmaking. Hence the politics and processes within states are an integral part of the story of 1914—and they figure prominently in the chapters that follow.

An International Stage for War

A third level of explanation focuses on those factors, forces, and developments in the international order that contributed to the outbreak of war. A number of attributes of the international situation in 1914 combined to facilitate the slide to war, but two figure particularly prominently in the discussions in this volume.

First, the European system was marked by significant shifts in the balance of power, producing tension and dislocation in relations between rising and declining powers. In 1914 the successes of Serbia in the Balkans alarmed Austria; the growth of Russian power as it recovered from defeat and revolution in 1905 alarmed Germany and Austria; the growth of German power alarmed France and Britain; and the resulting fears of adverse shifts in the balance contributed, as Jack Snyder demonstrates, to the judgment among the continental powers that it was better to fight now than later. Thucydides, in his account of the Peloponnesian War, identified this causal dynamic: it was the rise of Athens's power, he said, and the fear this produced in Sparta, that caused the war—a phenomenon now labeled the Thucydides Trap, assessed by Graham Allison, David Richards, Charles Maier, and Joseph Nye in this volume. The year 1914 witnessed the Thucydides Trap in action: fearful responses to shifts in the balance of power, leading to conflict. The Thucydides Trap does not make war inevitable, but it does produce friction and introduce preventive war incentives—and in 1914 these did contribute to war.

Second, the European order was structured around two great alliances pitted against one another, linking fates and raising the possibility that local conflict could flare into a European conflagration—as happened in 1914. If there is one strong theme to emerge from this volume, it is that alliance dynamics represent a great danger and can be a source of unwanted conflict. Allison, Nye, Rosecrance, Cooper, Rudd, and Maier all issue warnings to beware the adverse consequences of alliances. In the crisis of 1914, Russia's support of Serbia, Germany's support of Austria, and France's commitment to Russia helped to transform an assassination in Sarajevo into a world war. Richard Rosecrance puts it plainly: "World War I happened because allies had to be bailed out."[7] Maier highlights the "excruciating choices" that alliance dynamics can impose on leaders: weaken one's position and credibility by abandoning allies or risk war by supporting them. Concerns about preserving allies and offering credible commitments to them cause states to run such risks, but the resulting entanglements can be costly or even disastrous.

These two features of the international order provided the foundation for the world war: the shifting balance of power created the preventive incentives to fight; the alliance system made it likely that a war, once started, would engulf all of the great powers of Europe. But several other features of the international landscape contributed to the environment that led to war. The great alliances of 1914 were relatively evenly matched. This balance of power allowed both sides to hope that victory would be possible and each could calculate that war was worth the risk. Had one side possessed a clear preponderance—an "over-balance," as Rosecrance calls it—avoiding would have been easier because the weaker side would have little incentive to pick a fight it would lose.

Great power concerns about the evolution of the balance of power were exacerbated by arms racing. Several of the countries were in the midst of buildups, creating anxieties in other capitals and providing another source of preventive war incentive. Why not fight before an opponent's military modernization is complete? Expectations of war were further compounded by the pace of technological change. The growth of railroads, the mechanization of military forces, and advances in gunnery were altering the logistics and lethality of war. It was clear in 1914 that Europe's leaders and militaries had not fully comprehended the implications of technological change, but they were aware that arms racing and technological change could disrupt the international hierarchy and affect their international standing, for better or worse.

The years before the outbreak of war were marked by recurrent crises in the Balkans and North Africa. These involved serious confrontations between major powers, serious collisions of interest. But in the end, each of the big crises was managed successfully and resolved peacefully. As Arthur Stein suggests, this produced a kind of complacency in Europe; the great powers knew how to handle such crises and were experienced at doing so. At least initially, the diplomatic imbroglio in 1914 was just another Balkan crisis. Stein notes, however, that recurrent crises can grow more difficult to control across time because states change their behavior, seeking better outcomes for themselves and because they worry about the reputational effects of repeatedly backing down. Having been rebuffed in earlier crises, for example, the kaiser vowed in 1914 that this time he would not give in. A pattern of crises can thus have a reinforcing double effect: producing complacency that peace will be preserved while making peace more difficult to preserve. This was an element of the landscape in 1914.

There were a number of international factors that made 1914 a dangerous time, but still war was not inevitable. One further feature of this time, however, put Europe on a short fuse. This was the instability of the military arrangements on the Continent, reflecting the cult of the offensive and other bellicist mentalities. Militaries were fearful of losing competitive mobilization races, and war planners sought to move fast and strike the first blow. There was a premium on haste, once war seemed in prospect, because delay was thought to be potentially fatal. Once mobilization began, diplomacy was crowded out by logistical imperatives. Railway tables were not a major cause of the war, as Nye observes, but at the climax of the crisis they made it impossible to avert the war because there was no time left for negotiation, and almost instantly large armies were hurled across borders. The diplomats were bystanders once the slaughter had begun.

Looking Ahead: Could 1914 Happen Again?

What can we learn about the prospects for U.S.-China relations from this series of explorations of 1914? There is much that is reassuring in this volume. The analyses that follow highlight or reveal at least as many differences as similarities; 2014 does not wholly resemble 1914. But this does not mean that there are not grounds for concern. Some of the structural features present in 1914 exist today. And when one credits the role of agency and accident in 1914—the contingent nature of events, as Rosecrance puts it—it is possible that China and the United States could find their own way to war.

Reassuring Comparisons

Some prominent features of the environment in 1914 are absent today. The glorification of war has largely disappeared in the aftermath of two gruesome world wars. Although many expect the United States and China to be rivals and believe that there will be points of friction in the relations between them, there is little indication that either side is influenced by the thought that war is inevitable. (Indeed, one of China's core strategic concepts is the notion of "peaceful development.") While offensive operations figure in the military doctrines of today's powers, nothing like the pervasive cult of the offensive presently exists. Although nationalism remains a potent force in both countries, the virulent hypernationalism visible before World War I is not in evidence. While both countries have large and influential militaries, there is, as Van Evera concludes, little sign of the extreme militarism that marked some societies in the lead-up to war. In 1914 the domestic politics of the most significant rising power, Germany, were dominated by a militarized, nationalist coalition, whereas the predominant faction in China today, Solingen suggests, is a war-averse internationalizing coalition deeply connected to the world economy and prospering from the rapid rise in gross domestic product made possible by export-led growth. If one is persuaded by Solingen's argument about the fundamental importance of the character of the dominant internal coalition, then this is a decisive point. In short, many of the factors that are thought to have contributed to war in 1914 are not present in the contemporary era.

There are also significant differences in international context. Europe's continental powers shared borders, had a history of direct conflict, and had territorial grievances against one another. When great powers are both neighbors and potential adversaries, the result can be unstable and potentially treacherous because both will be highly sensitive to any perceived shift in the military balance. In stark contrast, the United States and China are separated by the world's largest ocean. Although they clearly have conflicts of interest in Asia and have fought one another in the past (notably, during the Korean War), they do not have an equivalent history of direct conflict with each other. Washington and Beijing are certainly wary of the military capabilities and modernizations on the other side, but neither is worried about a large-scale invasion of the homeland nor do they fear sudden catastrophic defeat by an invading army.

Europe's elites were managing a multipolar system of five great powers (six if one includes the Ottomans) in which shifts in patterns of alignment could produce rapid and dramatic alterations in the balance of power and in which the tending of existing alliances was a significant strategic imperative that shaped much external behavior. Today, again in stark contrast, there may be only one truly great power, the United States—but for the foreseeable future China stands alone as a rising potential rival. It is not a part of a great power coalition and it has uneasy relations with the two large Eurasian powers, Russia and India, with which it might ally. To be sure, the United States has a web of alliances in Asia, but the relationship with China is essentially bilateral—and perhaps eventually, when China is more equal, bipolar. This is a much simpler game to manage than a multipolar system, with its worries about adverse shifts in alignment and about the reliability of allies. In the crunch, Washington and Beijing can deal directly with one another, which is very different from the dynamic of 1914 when multiple parties were in play. Kenneth Waltz has famously argued that bipolar systems are stable; certainly the U.S.-China relationship looks easier to manage than the multipolar system that led to 1914.

Moreover, Europe before the war was divided into two roughly equal camps; this allowed both sides to envision that there was a chance of victory. The existence of a balance of power in Europe eroded deterrence and facilitated the coming of war. In contrast, though China's rise has been impressive, it still lags behind the United States in many indices of power, and its military is well behind the United States in global reach and technical sophistication, as Rudd states emphatically in his essay.[8] In addition, Washington's Asian (and European) allies augment U.S. superiority. It is hard to see how war will seem enticing or profitable to Beijing when it faces such an overwhelming superiority in aggregate resources and military capability. Rosecrance argues in these pages that overbalance (meaning clear primacy by one side) is the path to peace because tests of strength are unnecessary and unattractive when the discrepancy in power is clear. Such an overbalance will exist for some time if China's power is measured against that of the United States and its international allies.

Two other considerations distinguish the current era from the international context that existed in 1914. One is the existence of nuclear weapons. As Richards discusses in his chapter, nuclear weapons enormously raise the risk and potential cost of war and introduce the specter of truly disastrous outcomes for all concerned; this should, Richards argues, "curb aggressive instincts" and increase the value of avoiding conflict. This is a source of restraint that did not exist in 1914. The other new factor is the remarkable growth of international institutions in the decades since the end of World War II. Rudd identifies the absence of such institutions as one of the "critical factors" in the failure to prevent war in 1914. No one would claim that the existence of international institutions has solved the problem of war or that they constitute a reliable barrier to war and Rudd himself acknowledges the "thinness" of the institutional architecture in Asia. Still, there exists today a number of institutions that permit communication, consultation, crisis management, and the harmonization of state interests; Rudd invokes the European model in suggesting that institutionalization can reduce the role of force and prevent crises and offers the hope that even less robust institutions can help to "moderate the march to war" when crises do arise.

In sum, the 1914 analogy is far from a perfect fit when applied to U.S.-China relations. Many caution against the simplistic deployment of this analogy, and the contributors to this volume demonstrate why. There are many significant differences in international context, in intellectual outlook, and in political configurations. The reassuring conclusion is that the war-prone environment that led to disaster in 1914 is not replicated in our own time: much is missing; much is different.

Cautionary Tales

The 1914 analogy is clearly an imperfect framework for assessing U.S.-China relations, but nevertheless war between Washington and Beijing remains possible. Full recreation of the environment of 1914 is not a prerequisite for war. Further, some lessons from the outbreak of World War I do seem at least potentially relevant today and identify sources of worry and grounds for vigilance.

As the years leading up to 1914 demonstrate, adapting to shifts in the balance of power is difficult and can lead to a pattern of repeated crises as challengers seek to upend the status quo and claim a larger role in international politics while the dominant powers act to protect their place in the international hierarchy. Managing relations between rising and declining powers is particularly fraught with risk and danger. As Allison observes, far more often than not in history the collision between rising and declining powers has resulted in war. No one in this volume would argue that war between the United States and China is inevitable. Nevertheless it does seem sensible to note that the situation in which Washington and Beijing find themselves—predominant power and rapidly rising challenger—is generally perilous and has frequently led to conflict. Moreover, there is abundant evidence that China's rise provokes concern and sometimes harsh reaction in Washington. Even twenty years ago, with the Cold War barely over and China's explosive growth still in its early stages, Aaron Friedberg cautioned that "in the long run it is Asia that seems far more likely to be the cockpit of great power conflict."[9] Today Friedberg, reflecting a current of thought in the U.S. foreign policy debate about China, warns that the United States is performing ineffectually in "the struggle for mastery in Asia."[10] Alarm about the rise of China's military power is now commonplace. "No longer does the U.S. Navy rule the western Pacific as though it were an American lake," laments Robert Kaplan, commenting on "China's seemingly inexorable military expansion."[11] It is not hard to see how U.S.-China relations could go badly wrong; the potential for much more intense hostility and military competition clearly exists. These considerations imply that particular care should be taken in tending this relationship and that every effort should be made to avoid the mistakes and pitfalls of the past.

Furthermore, one of the most troublesome aspects of the international order in 1914 is partially reproduced today. If there is one warning that particularly leaps out from the pages of this volume, it is the danger of entrapping alliances. As noted above, alliance dynamics are singled out as one of the most toxic elements in the picture in 1914. China does not have an extensive network of allies, but its one link in East Asia, North Korea, clearly has the potential to drag China into trouble. The United States' network of bilateral alliances in Asia connect Washington to the interests of a number of states in the region, including some that have long had bad relations with China and some that have ongoing disputes with China. There is the potential for the United States to be drawn into disputes with China in support of it allies. This is, of course, what U.S. allies would want and expect, and failure to support allies can undermine U.S. credibility. The risk, as Rudd cautions in his chapter, is that local conflicts can escalate into great power war. Hence Cooper's warning: beware third countries. The most likely route to war with China is via a dispute involving one or more of the United States' Asian allies.

This is not a purely hypothetical danger. Asia's many territorial disputes, on both land and sea, are potential flash points. Japan and China are feuding over disputed North Pacific islands. Taiwan and China remain stalemated. Rudd describes the welter of maritime boundary disputes in Southeast Asia as constituting a "maritime Balkans."[12] Confrontations and crises have already happened and more are likely. There could well emerge a pattern of recurrent crises, as was true in the decade before 1914. If crises are handled without escalation, complacency could set in. But such crises could gradually grow more malignant, more difficult to handle; mistakes could be made; and complacency could turn out to be a glide path to war. As Rudd vividly puts it, "One of the profound lessons of 1914 is the rapidity with which circumstances can change from utterly benign to utterly catastrophic within the space of months." [13]

Overall, then, many of the factors that are thought to have contributed to the outbreak of war in 1914 do not exist today. In particular, many of the intellectual and internal pathologies that made war more likely and made the crisis difficult to resolve peacefully are absent from the current environment. On the international level, however, we see a different story. The stage is clearly set for rivalry. If U.S.-China relations turn significantly more hostile and competitive, there is a clear potential for arms racing, for destructive diplomatic maneuvering, for Cold War, and for conflict. In a more toxic environment, one of Asia's many potential flash points could ignite a war; the United States' alliances make it likely that Washington will be involved. To make their way to war, leaders in Washington and Beijing do not have to echo the beliefs and reproduce the realities and mistakes of 1914. They can invent their own flawed beliefs and make their own mistakes.

Conclusion

In the introduction to his comprehensive reconstruction of the origins of World War I, Christopher Clark raises the arresting proposition that "far from being inevitable, this war was 'improbable.'"[14] Similarly, drawing on her deep inquiry into the outbreak of the war, historian Margaret MacMillan observes that in 1914 "there were strong arguments for peace" and says that the July crisis "could have gone either way, towards peace or towards war."[15] In his meticulous account of the slide to war in the summer of 1914, T.G. Otte comments that Europe seemed calmer and more quiescent in early 1914 than in previous years and suggests that "it should have been an unremarkable year."[16] Many of the factors that seem in retrospect to have facilitated war in 1914 had been present for years or decades without producing war, so the war that came was in some sense a surprise, was in some sense unexpected.

In a similar manner, war with China seems unlikely. There are strong arguments (economic and otherwise) for preserving the peace. The relationship between Washington and Beijing has its ups and downs, but overall relations are not that bad and contain some reassuring elements of consultation and cooperation. There are occasional crises in Asia (involving sovereignty over island and maritime boundary disputes, for example), but these are handled without recourse to war. As was true in the first half of 1914, one could justify the conclusion that we should expect some "unremarkable years" ahead. But corrosive factors lurk in the background: the perilous dynamic between the predominant and the challenger, the arms race pressures, the web of alliances that connects the United States to potential conflicts in Asia and to allies who want to harness U.S. power to advance their claims in the region, the flash points across Asia that could, in the manner of a remote assassination in the Balkans, ignite a wider war. If war were to come, no doubt many would look back and say it was inevitable, it was predicted, the signs were there, the pressures were understood, there were so many war-promoting factors that it was impossible to preserve the peace. The argument against complacency is strong, and it will matter enormously whether U.S.-China relations are managed wisely or poorly. There are many in the U.S. debate who favor a primarily competitive response to the rise of China, seeking to preserve and maximize U.S. primacy while encircling and containing China. In this volume we find instead—in the analyses of Alexandroff, Rosecrance, and Rudd, for example—the argument that the wise course involves bringing China closer, drawing it into shared institutions, making it a partner in the provision of international public goods, building strategic trust, and preserving and strengthening lines of communication between the two potential antagonists. But even if one accepts that this is the wise course—and clearly many will not—surely one of the lessons of 1914 is that wisdom does not always prevail.

Power Balances, Alliance Ties, and Diplomacy

1

Before the War

Three Styles of Diplomacy

Alan Alexandroff

E VEN BEFORE THE guns of World War I were silenced, many politicians and experts had concluded that Europe's "Old Diplomacy" was responsible for its outbreak. This verdict remained attractive to observers following the end of "the war to end all wars." It explained the carnage and satisfactorily addressed responsibility for the war's costs. As James Joll and Gordon Martel argue in *The Origins of the First World War*, "Many people in the 1920s blamed the international system, the existence of rival alliances, the armaments race, and the evil influence of the 'old diplomacy,' and this indeed set the scene within which the crisis developed."[1]

It was U. S. President Woodrow Wilson, however, who most pointedly and publicly condemned the Old Diplomacy and demanded its replacement with a "New Diplomacy." As early as 1916, President Wilson had begun expressing his understanding of how a New Diplomacy might facilitate global governance and lessen the dangers of war. Over the next two years, he refined these mechanisms and brought them to the Paris Peace Conference in 1918. Wilson's principles included (1) the self-determination of peoples; (2) the end to secret diplomacy and the start of open diplomacy; and (3) the establishment of some form of league of nations to assure peace.[2] As Wilson put it in his speech to the first assembly of the League to Enforce Peace on May 27, 1916, "[What is needed is a] universal association of the nations to maintain the inviolate security of the highway of the seas for the common and unhindered use of all the nations of the world, and to prevent any war begun either contrary to treaty covenants or without warning and full submission of the causes to the opinion of the world—a virtual guarantee of territorial integrity and political independence."[3]

Well before Wilson, however, German Chancellor Otto von Bismarck had developed a "Concert" system based on multilateral diplomacy that had proved highly effective. This system was all but forgotten by the interpreters of World War I.

Building the New Diplomacy

Wilson began to discuss his notion of the New Diplomacy even before the United States had entered the war. Joll and Martel note that Wilson "was much influenced by the British radical tradition which, throughout the nineteenth century, had criticized secret diplomacy and called for a foreign policy based on morality rather than expediency, on general ethical principles rather than on practical calculations about the balance of power."[4]

By January 1918, Wilson had come to identify the "practical" elements that he believed an enduring peace would require. To help him develop his ideas for peace and a comprehensive peace settlement, he appointed a committee of experts. The committee comprised 150 academics, directed by Wilson's close adviser, Col. Edward House, and supervised by the philosopher Sidney Mezes, then president of the College of the City of New York. Wilson referred to the committee's recommendations in a speech before a joint session of Congress on January 8, 1918. In it, he delivered what became known as his Fourteen Points. He stressed that the new processes of peace would see the end of "secret covenants entered into in the interest of particular governments."[5] He declared:

> The program of the world's peace, therefore, is our program; and that program, the only possible program, as we see it, is this:
>
> I. Open covenants of peace, openly arrived at, after which there shall be no private international understandings of any kind but diplomacy shall proceed always frankly and in the public view.
> ...
> XIV. A general association of nations must be formed under specific covenants for the purpose of affording mutual guarantees of political independence and territorial integrity to great and small states alike. In regard to these essential rectifications of wrong and assertions of right we feel ourselves to be intimate partners of all the governments and peoples associated together against the Imperialists. We cannot be separated in interest or divided in purpose. We stand together until the end.[6]

In addition to banishing secret diplomacy and the Old Diplomacy's balance of power system, Wilson argued that a new institution—the League of Nations—was necessary to maintain international peace and stability. Further, Article 10 of the Covenant of the League of Nations states, "The Members of the League undertake to respect and preserve as against external aggression the territorial integrity and existing political independence of all Members of the League. In case of any such aggression or in case of any threat or danger of such aggression the Council shall advise upon the means by which this obligation shall be fulfilled."[7]

Although a major development in the evolution of global summitry, the League institutions remained highly imperfect. Leave aside the fact that the U.S. Senate failed to ratify the Treaty of Versailles and that the United States did not join the League of Nations. Without such a great power member, the League was mortally damaged. In addition, the apparatus of collective security was quite weak. In part as a result of U.S. sovereignty concerns, the League conducted itself principally on the basis of public opinion. As Wilson himself put it, the League would "operate as the organizing moral force of men throughout the world," throwing a "searching light of conscience" on wrongdoing around the world. "Just a little exposure will settle most questions."[8] Even at the outset, this collective security system was built on persuasion, not on great power commitment. As John Ikenberry writes, "The Wilsonian version of liberal internationalism was built not just around a 'thin' set of institutional commitments, but also on the assumption that a 'thick' set of norms and pressures—public opinion and the moral rectitude of statesmen—would activate sanctions and enforce the territorial peace....The sovereignty of states—sovereignty as it related to both legal independence and equality—would not be compromised or transformed. States would be expected just to act better, which for Wilson meant they would become socialized into a 'community of power.'"[9]

Thus the New Diplomacy relied too heavily on broad public opprobrium and too little on the collective obligations and actions of the great powers to sanction aggression.

The Intricacies of Bismarck's Older Diplomacy

The fulsome condemnation by experts and politicians alike of the Old Diplomacy directed attention to the diplomatic practices that emerged in Europe after 1890. These critics failed to consider, however, the international relations structure and diplomacy put in place by Bismarck earlier in the century. Although the period from 1870 to the start of the Great War has been described generally as a classic "balance of power" era, it was in fact divided into two periods. From 1871 to 1890, a concert structure was created and then maintained by Bismarck until he left office. The distinction between what was described by many as a "balance of power" but what others recognized as a "concert apparatus" is vital. As Richard Rosecrance describes the Bismarckian concert, "Bismarck's coalitions…(although…not universal) at least linked four major powers together: Russia, Britain, Germany, and Austria. Only France, the defeated power in the Franco-Prussian War of 1870–71, was left out….The Bismarckian Concert, however, was different from the prior Concert of Europe. Ideology had linked the previous authors of the Vienna settlement. The Bismarckian concert sought only peace, but it could not use ideology to promote it….Thus, the barriers to war were practical, not ideological or military."[10]

How then could such a concert be generated without the earlier ideological identity that marked the first, and better known, Concert of Europe formed after the Napoleonic Wars? The genius of Bismarck was his ability to yoke apparent rivals together and keep them harnessed to one another. The starting point of the Concert was the classic German-Austro-Hungarian accord formed in 1879. The alliance was formed following the Congress of Berlin in 1878, which Russian nationalists argued had led to a humiliating outcome for the Russian Empire. Bismarck apparently believed that the alliance with Austria-Hungary would help to deter Russia from action against Germany and that it would ultimately encourage Russia to improve relations with the German Empire. Also, he regarded the alliance in defensive terms, considering it a significant constraint on Austria-Hungary. The alliance would enable Bismarck to stop Austria from engaging in adventures that might draw Germany into a conflict with Russia in the Balkans. As Joll and Martel suggest, "The alliance, in Bismarck's mind, was an element of stability in Europe since it would both alarm the Russians sufficiently to make them want better relations with Germany and also provide Germany with the power to control Austrian policy towards its Slav neighbours."[11]

Thus for Bismarck alliances had a double-edged quality: they could deter possible aggressors or rivals and then potentially convince them to consider closer relations. At the same time, alliances could constrain partners and help to control their behavior.

In 1882 Bismarck's Concert added Italy and became known as the Triple Alliance. The most crucial element of the Concert, however, was the Reinsurance Treaty between Germany and Russia, concluded in 1887. This treaty was designed to deter Russia or Germany from seeking war with another continental power, here read largely as Austria-Hungary. It was also intended to insulate Germany from war or continuing tensions between Russia and Austria-Hungary.

In addition, Bismarck maintained close relations with Great Britain, in part by making a conscious effort not to challenge it. He began by eschewing an imperial policy, abjuring territory and Asian markets. In fact, Bismarck left it to Russia to constrain British imperial expansion, particularly in Asia. Also, as part of his "benign" defensive alliance strategy, the German chancellor never took steps to challenge Britain over its navy. The kaiser's later naval challenge did much to raise tensions and sour relations between Britain and Germany. As Rosecrance concludes, "Had he continued in power, Bismarck would never have made Kaiser Wilhelm II's blunders after 1890."[12]

The obvious strategic aim of Bismarck's concert diplomacy was to crosscut alliances in an effort to avoid what emerged after his departure: the creation of two alliance blocs—the Triple Alliance and the Triple Entente. Bismarck's successors abandoned his strategy of restraint, seeking instead to create a balance of power system that President Wilson and others were quick to condemn as the Old Diplomacy. The Bismarckian Concert, however, operated with great subtlety and maintained European stability for several decades. Bismarck did not become chancellor until 1862, but his diplomatic efforts harked back to the successes of the Concert of Europe from 1815 to 1848.

The Concert first appeared at the Congress of Vienna in 1814 and was described by Keith Hamilton and Richard Langhorne as a kind of "mobile summit conference."[13] Meeting at Aix la Chapelle in 1818, Troppau in 1820, Laibach in 1821, and Verona in 1822, members of the Concert carried into peacetime the practice of convening conferences that in the past had been devoted to ending a particular war. Presided over by Austria's Klemens Wenzel von Metternich, it sought to allocate territory and political control to conservative regimes or at least those that supported the Concert system. Ultimately, it drove away more liberal states such as Britain and France. Nevertheless, the Concert system continued to operate, though in diminished form. Ambassadorial conferences replaced leading ministerial gatherings. Conferences were held, for example, in 1852 and 1864 in London over Schleswig-Holstein, and in 1876 in Constantinople over the Balkans, and again in 1912–13. Between 1822 and 1914, twenty-six such conferences were held.

Ministerial conferences were not altogether abandoned in the late nineteenth century, though they were infrequent. There were two gatherings that included senior statesmen from most of the great powers: one in Paris in 1856 following the Crimean War and one in Berlin in 1878 after the Russo-Turkish conflict. Although the primary focus of these meetings was the termination of local wars, both acknowledged the diplomatic practice of great power governance and the importance of a stable, peaceful international system. Other proposed calls for conferences, however, such as France's on the eve of the 1866 Austro-Prussian conflict, went unheeded.

Over time, then, the architecture of the Concert system—its "constitution and its constitutional watchdog," as described by Gordon Craig and Alexander George—had faded away.[14] Its ability to change national incentives and constrain state behavior had eroded. In *The War That Ended Peace*, Margaret MacMillan observes that, in the weeks before the outbreak of World War I, the Triple Entente hoped "that somehow the moribund Concert of Europe might come to life again and settle yet another European crisis."[15] Britain's foreign secretary, Sir Edward Grey, favored an ambassadorial conference to be convened in London that would allow the key players, Austria and Serbia, to meet and resolve the crisis. And there were other failed efforts. Germany, for example, rejected a four-power mediation attempt just before the outbreak of war. The practice of calling on the Concert of Europe to maintain peace and international stability was by 1914 ineffective in the face of rising diplomatic and military tensions.

The Assertive Foreign Policy of Wilhelmine Germany

The turn away from Bismarckian diplomacy by Kaiser Wilhelm II and his ministers was gradual but marked. It began with the decision by Chancellor Leo von Caprivi not to renew the Reinsurance Treaty—that critical relationship that tied Germany to Russia—notwithstanding the Triple Alliance of Germany, Italy, and Austria-Hungary. This abandonment of Bismarck's "lifeline" to Russia provided the opening for Russia and France to establish the Franco-Russian alliance, enabling France to escape the isolation that Bismarck had imposed on it following the Franco-Prussian War. The new Franco-Russian alliance was designed, as suggested by Christopher Clark "to meet and balance the threat from a competing coalition. In this sense, the Alliance marked a turning point in the prelude to the Great War."[16]

In Germany, Kaiser Wilhelm assumed a more aggressive posture after Bismarck's departure that raised tensions with Great Britain. Berlin embraced *Weltpolitik* or "world policy." *Weltpolitik* ran counter to earlier Bismarckian policy by placing the German Empire squarely in the imperialist game. As Secretary of State for Foreign Relations Bernhard von Bülow declared in 1897, "We don't want to put anyone in the shadow, but we too demand our place in the sun."[17] This desire for expansion was meant to redress Germany's late arrival on the imperial stage and to allow Germany to catch up with France, Britain, and

Russia. It was a direct rebuff of Bismarckian restraint. Additionally, the kaiser and Adm. Alfred von Tirpitz decided to "challenge" the British navy. Although Tirpitz could not produce Dreadnought battleships at the same rate as Britain, his efforts served to sour relations between the two countries. *Weltpolitik* was viewed with growing distaste by British officials and the British public. As Sir Eyre Crowe, chief clerk of the Western Department of the Foreign Ministry wrote:

> For there is one road which, if past experience is any guide to the future, will most certainly not lead to any permanent improvement of relations with any Power, least of all Germany, and which must therefore be abandoned: that is the road paved with graceful British concessions—concessions made without any conviction either of their justice or of their being set off by equivalent counter-services. The vain hopes that in this manner Germany can be "conciliated" and made more friendly must be definitely given up. It may be that such hopes are still honestly cherished by irresponsible people, ignorant, perhaps necessarily ignorant, of the history of Anglo-German relations during the last twenty years, which cannot be better described than as the history of a systematic policy of gratuitous concessions, a policy which has led to the highly disappointing result disclosed by the almost perpetual state of tension existing between the two countries.[18]

Lessons from History

Notwithstanding the enormous historical inquiry, historians and international relations specialists have failed to achieve any consensus over the origins of World War I, let alone which great power was responsible for its outbreak. Yet President Wilson had no difficulty in concluding what he believed had led to this catastrophic war. He even designed a new international relations system and new diplomatic practices to maintain peace and international stability. The New Diplomacy would reject the balance of power system, secret covenants and other arrangements among the great powers, and the lack of transparency and public involvement in the conduct of diplomacy. Wilson argued that a permanent institution—the League of Nations—would act to maintain international peace and stability where the balance of power system had not. The president believed that if a conference had been called on the eve of war in 1914, the conflict could not have taken place. The parties could not have explained their devious and punitive motives to an observant world, nor would they have mobilized so quickly in the face of popular opinion. But who would enforce the sanctions against a future aggressor nation? Neither Article 10 nor Article 16 of the Covenant of the League provided the necessary enforcement powers. Instead, it would be left up to individual nations.

The tragedy of Wilson's assessment was to view the diplomatic practices of the nineteenth century as all of a piece. He ignored the Concert system and the Bismarckian Concert that had prevailed from the 1870s through 1890.[19] That system might have been useful in 1914. If crosscutting alliances had existed at that time, Europe might not have been divided into the Triple Entente and the Triple Alliance and thus might have averted the face-off of August 1914. The yoking of rivals—holding one's allies close and one's rivals equally close—in a structure of diplomacy would have eliminated the emergence of the two camps. Eliminating Germany's new imperial adventures and its naval challenge to Great Britain would have ameliorated the growing rivalries. It might also have toned down, or made less influential, the voices of anti-German officials in the British Foreign Office.

Conclusion

The state of the global economy, advances in technology, and crosscutting cleavages are just some of the elements that need to be understood in managing great power relations. A number of experts, including Margaret MacMillan, have warned against history's casual use.[20] In regards to U.S.-China relations, she writes, "It is tempting—and sobering—to compare today's relationship between China and America to that between Germany and England a century ago."[21] She notes that increased Chinese military spending, including the buildup of naval capacity, suggests to U.S. strategists that "China intends to challenge the United States as a Pacific power, and we are now seeing an arms race between the countries in that region."[22] Relations between the United States and Japan are terribly important in this context and the rise of China and Chinese assertiveness refocuses attention on the mutual defense obligations between these two allies. In particular, the growing political and military tensions over the Senkakus, as the Japanese call these islands in the East China Sea, or Diaoyutai for China, have become a possible flash point for a Japanese-Chinese conflict that could drag in the United States.

What lessons might be drawn from the Older Diplomacy? Bismarck would certainly be aware of the constraints on allies that alliance relations create. The United States has emphasized publicly that it wants China and

Japan to resolve any international disputes peacefully. Additionally, it may be useful for U.S. officials to caution Japan at least privately against potentially reckless behavior and to suggest limits to U.S. actions to support Japan if a military encounter were to occur in the East China Sea. Bismarck would likely view such a double-edged approach quite favorably.

Going beyond the perils of alliances, Bismarck would seek to find ways of not only deterring China but also of attracting it to join a larger complex of great powers. Even with France, Bismarck sought to draw Paris into colonial ventures (particularly in Tunisia) where its ambitions could be fulfilled without action on the Rhine. Russia was included in his coalition, but Bismarck's idea was for Britain and Austria to play primary roles in limiting Russia, not Germany. In a more recent expression of statecraft, Henry Kissinger endeavored to use China to draw Russia closer to the United States, not to humiliate it. The main challenge today is not to deter China or to form a balance against it, but to attract it to join the most powerful economic combine in the world.

2

Respites or Resolutions?

Recurring Crises and the Origins of War

Arthur A. Stein

A MONG MAJOR WARS, World War I holds pride of place. The war was immediately recognized and has continued to be seen as a cataclysmic event. Within a year of its outbreak, it had already been dubbed "the Great War" and was soon thereafter called "the war to end all wars." Although the latter characterization lasted barely a generation, World War I has continued to be a relevant touchstone for subsequent analysts.[1]

The inherent scholarly interest in the causes of war has been conjoined in this case with the political and historical importance of assigning responsibility for the outbreak of hostilities and the tensions underlying them. Indeed, as Ross Collins notes, "The debate over who started World War I began only weeks after the war declarations."[2] That debate has continued virtually unabated.[3]

Over the years since World War I, scholars have argued about its causes versus its origins. Those who look at causes focus on the specific trigger that began the hostilities and the period between the assassination of Austria's Archduke Franz Ferdinand and the many declarations of war. In contrast, those interested in origins emphasize longer-term structural features, such as the system of European alliances or the long-running arms race.

There has also been disagreement over the decades as to whether World War I was a "war of miscalculation" or a "war by design." Those who see it as the outcome of miscalculation consider World War I a prototypical war that occurred by accident, as interlocking military mobilizations generated an outcome not fully foreseen or desired by any of the warring powers. Those who have feared that a "war by miscalculation" could occur in their own times have stressed the perspective that puts World War I into that category and high-lighted other similarities between that era and the ones in which they write. In contrast are those who hold that Germany wanted war. This was the immediate position at the time of the 1918 Paris Peace Conference, and those who make this argument today believe that fear of another "war by design" is unnecessary, because no country is as aggressive as was pre–World War I Germany.[4]

Much scholarship focuses on the immediate causes of hostilities, on the transition from a state of peace, or nonwar, to a state of war. The current consensus holds that war is a costly form of conflict, and rational leaders want to avoid those costs.[5] Indeed, if a war's outcome were known with certainty beforehand, the participants would be better off simply moving to that postwar state without paying the intervening costs of war. In this sense, wars are like strikes.[6] The bargaining theory of war posits reasons, discussed below, why states cannot arrive at negotiated deals to avoid the costs of war.

This chapter develops an alternative argument about both the origins of war, in general, and those of World War I, in particular. It argues that the origins of many wars, most especially World War I, have lain in recurrent crises. The delineation of the argument below is followed by its application to World War I and a discussion of its implications for international relations theory and contemporary international politics.

War and Strategies in Sequential Crises

The argument developed here rests on a simple premise: that many wars, especially major power wars, do not occur suddenly and without warning. In most cases, that is, war does not occur the first time two states have a serious dispute. Rather, most wars reflect long-standing conflicts of interests and are preceded by crises that are at least temporarily resolved.[7] Yet the underlying conflict between the nations is not truly settled. In other words, the ends of crises do not constitute resolutions, but respites. Great power conflicts experience militarized crises and remissions.[8]

After a pattern of recurrent crises, wars break out when a new standoff between the same powers cannot be resolved as others had been earlier. That is, the strategies that states adopted previously and that were the basis for respites and remissions are not repeated. Consequently, countries adopt a modified Win-Stay Lose-Shift strategy.[9] Strategies that are seen as resulting in a triumph are repeated, whereas those deemed to have resulted in a loss or defeat at another's hands are not.[10]

The history of interactions that ultimately result in war constitutes a critical backdrop providing the tinder for the lit match of the final triggering event. Three brief examples illustrate this argument. Imagine a Prisoners' Dilemma game played once, one that does not result in mutual defection. One state decides to cooperate in the expectation of reciprocity, but the other defects. The next time the two interact in a Prisoners' Dilemma game, the state that defected does so again, but the one that initially cooperated shifts strategies and defects as well.[11]

Alternatively, imagine a game of Chicken, one also treated as a model of international interactions. Both actors in Chicken want to defect while the other cooperates. The game has two equilibriums—those outcomes in which one of the actors defects and the other cooperates. The actors' preferences generate competition in risk taking and brinksmanship, behaviors that have become the hallmark of the game. Imagine a game of Chicken in which one actor has defected and the other cooperates, thus avoiding the outcome of mutual defection. Now imagine a second iteration. The actor that defected the first time has every expectation that the other will again capitulate and that it will again emerge triumphant. At a minimum, that actor has no reason not to defect. The actor whose previous capitulation prevented conflict, however, does not want to be so accommodating and instead stands firm while the first actor expects a repeat of the previous capitulation.[12] Although the choices of rational actors should still not result in mutual defection, this outcome can occur when actors misread each other, something more likely to occur when the game is repeated against the backdrop of previous play in which mutual defection has been averted.[13]

A comparable situation arises when states bargain repeatedly. Even if states have mutual interests, there is usually a bargaining range (the Pareto surface) along which they have a conflict of interest, because each wants to secure more from the ultimate outcome; that increment will come at the other's expense.[14] Now imagine situations of repeated bargaining in which one side gets the lion's share of the spoils. At some point, the party that has accepted the smaller payoff will likely reject such a division and demand more. At the very least, it will not accept a negotiated resolution that provides it less. Repeated distributional conflicts can preclude a bargain even when a mutually beneficial outcome exists.

These examples all assume repetition of the same game, but repeated interaction can also change the game itself to the point where the actors' assessments of the payoffs, not just of the probabilities, change. Again, take the case of two actors playing a game of Chicken. War is the least desirable outcome, and the game ends with one actor cooperating and the other defecting. The actor who cooperated may then reassess the game itself and, in a future crisis, feel that the experience of humiliation and what it wrought was worse than having gone to war would have been. That shift in the assessment of the payoffs changes the game from Chicken to one of "called bluff," in which the actor who no longer finds war the least desired outcome has a dominant strategy of defection.[15] The other actor, who has a contingent strategy and whose preferences have not changed should then shift to cooperation upon realizing that the other actor's preferences have changed. The failure to recognize the other's shift, however, would lead to war.[16]

In each of these cases, a nonconflictual resolution in an initial situation makes a peaceful resolution more difficult to achieve in subsequent interactions. This is the core problem of international politics. States, especially great powers with wide-ranging geopolitical interests and concerns, interact with one another repeatedly. This means that they face repeated crises, some of which entail the risk of war. Successfully averting war once or twice is no guarantee that they will avoid it again. Indeed, the most critical factor in a subsequent round becomes the terms under which conflict was previously averted, whether earlier crises were resolved or went into remission.

World War I constitutes a prime example of this phenomenon. It was preceded by full-blown major power crises that served as precursors to overt hostilities when the two rising powers of Europe, Germany and Russia, each asserted its interests. The other great powers thwarted their ambitions, however, and the game then changed.

The First Moroccan Crisis, 1905–06

The "Moroccan problem was the political barometer of Europe," observes Eugene Anderson, and the 1905–06 Moroccan crisis was the first of those presaging World War I. As Anderson notes, "It contained all those elements that were present at the other crises on the road to the great war."[17] The nations of Europe had long recognized Morocco as an independent country. Conflicting European interests in the nineteenth century had typically been settled by international conferences. And in 1880, at a conference at Madrid, the European powers agreed on a status quo that would not change without all of their agreement.

In the Anglo-French Entente of 1904, an arrangement that settled many of those two nations' long-standing disputes around the world, Britain consented to a free French hand in Morocco in exchange for its own freedom of action in Egypt.[18] Having also concluded agreements with Spain and Italy regarding Morocco, the French in January 1905 pressed the sultan of the Ottoman Empire to accept reforms that would effectively make Morocco a French protectorate. In response, Germany's Kaiser Wilhelm II traveled to Morocco to publicly offer German support for Moroccan independence.

Germany wanted to reaffirm its long-standing interests in Morocco and to end the new British-French cooperation that isolated the Germans. Its strategy failed when great power jockeying solidified the English-French relationship. Sir Edward Grey, who would serve as Britain's foreign secretary until 1916, first assumed that post with the new government that came to power in London in December 1905. One of his first acts was to inform Germany that Britain would not likely remain neutral in a war between France and Germany.

After much maneuvering among the powers, a conference was held in Algeciras, Spain, in 1906 with representatives from Austria, France, Germany, Great Britain, Italy, Russia, Spain, and the United States. Despite extensive efforts to obtain the support of others, Germany found only Austria, its ally, backing its proposal for an independent Morocco rather than de facto French control. In the end, Germany had to accept an outcome that it had earlier deemed unacceptable. German assertiveness had ended up strengthening the twelve-year-old Franco-Russian alliance and the new Anglo-French Entente, with the British and French entering military dialogue in 1905. Most important, the alliance generated a German perception of encirclement and isolation, a view that the Anglo-Russian Entente of 1907 strengthened.

The resolution of the first Moroccan crisis was a disaster for Germany, "the reverse of that intended." Its policy had unraveled, and "the constellation which faced it in 1907 had seemed unimaginable" only a few years before.[19] The crisis "gave a first hint of things to come and foreshadowed the world war." It was a "true 'crisis,' a turning-point in European history" in which "war between France and Germany was seriously, though remotely, contemplated for the first time since 1875."[20] In its history "are mirrored almost all the movements of the Powers with reference to one another."[21]

The Bosnian Crisis, 1908–09

Following the 1905–06 Moroccan crisis came another in the Balkans, one that more closely resembled the crisis that actually precipitated World War I. Its origins lay in the collapse of the Ottoman Empire and the contest between Austria-Hungary and Russia over the Balkans. The Ottoman Empire, which had once controlled much of southeastern Europe, had begun to fray. As one historian puts it, "The origins of the tensions in the Balkans which became the immediate cause of the First World War lie...in Ottoman senescence."[22]

The combination of weakening Ottoman rule and rising nationalist sentiment in southeastern Europe had given birth to movements for autonomy and independence within the Balkans while the great powers jockeyed to control the area. Russia had fought a series of wars with Turkey in the nineteenth century and had become the champion of the Balkan Slavs. In 1877 war with Turkey erupted over uprisings by Slavic subjects of the Ottomans, and Russia's victory liberated most of southeastern Europe from Ottoman rule. The following year Russia dictated the terms of the Treaty of San Stefano, which included independence for Serbia and autonomy for Bulgaria, which was expected to be dominated by Russia. The other European powers met within months, and at the Congress of Berlin an isolated Russia found the terms of the treaty altered. Greater Bulgaria was divided in three, and Austria was allowed to occupy and administer Bosnia and Herzegovina, provinces inhabited primarily by Serbs and Croats. Prince Gorchakov, chancellor of the Russian Empire, called the Berlin conference "the darkest page of [his] life."[23] British Foreign Secretary Lord Salisbury described the resolution of 1878 as "a mere respite."[24]

Two decades later, a crisis erupted in 1908 when Austria-Hungary annexed the provinces of Bosnia and Herzegovina. Russia was prepared to accept this formalization of Austria's position in exchange for Austria agreeing to an amendment to the standing international agreement and reopening the Turkish Straits to Russian warships. Austria reneged, however. And when the independent Kingdom of Serbia objected to Bosnia's annexation and mobilized its army, it received Russian support. A flurry of discussions and negotiations resulted in Russia's diplomatic humiliation. The great powers affirmed Austria's annexation and made no amendments regarding Russian passage through the straits.

The Second Moroccan Crisis, 1911

"The Moroccan problem," writes Anderson, "left behind plenty of raw material from which future conflicts could arise." One of those conflicts again pitted France against Germany in a contest over control of Morocco, where disorder spread to the capital (then at Fez) in March 1911.[25] At that point, the French decided to send an expeditionary force to protect lives and property. They came to this decision even though it represented a breach of the Algeciras settlement of 1906 and disregarded a German warning not to take military action. The Germans' initial response was to signal that this constituted an abrogation of the Algeciras settlement and to demand compensation should the French seek to establish an outright protectorate. Germany also sent a gunboat, the *Panther*, to the Moroccan harbor of Agadir, an action that it justified as necessary to protect German citizens, even though none were there. Franco-German discussions about acceptable compensation proceeded but foundered over German demands for all of French Congo.

Ironically, German efforts to keep Britain uninvolved backfired. The British had not initially fully supported the French, but excessive German assertiveness resulted in Britain signaling that it would back France's position on compensation. During the summer and into the fall of 1911, there were war scares and military preparations, including military staff talks between Britain and France. Finally, in November 1911, France and Germany signed an agreement in which Germany obtained minor concessions in Africa while recognizing French control of Morocco.

Thus France had advanced its geopolitical position and obtained the support of Britain and Russia. Although no formal alliance resulted between Britain and France, their strategies had become more closely aligned. Once again, Germany's assertiveness had led to its humiliating retreat; Germany failed to achieve its stated interests and further antagonized Britain and Russia. It also engendered military as well as diplomatic cooperation between Britain and France.[26]

The July 1914 Crisis

The next European crisis came in July 1914 and was not resolved short of war. Again, a Balkan crisis pitted Russia against Austria. As it had in the past, Germany supported Austria and its decision to present Serbia with an ultimatum after the assassination of Austrian Archduke Franz Ferdinand, an act in which members of the Serbian military were implicated. When Austria attacked Serbia, Russia undertook a partial military mobilization in support of the Serbs rather than accept Austria's action. Moreover, Germany this time rejected a British call, which others had accepted, for an international conference to resolve the dispute between Austria-Hungary and Serbia. More than once, Kaiser Wilhelm told a close friend, "This time I shall not give in."[27]

The possibility of a European war had been both widely feared and widely dismissed in the years before one finally began in 1914. David Starr Jordan, Stanford University's first president and the president of the World Peace Foundation, concluded from his trip to Europe that "no considerable body of rational men in either France or Germany desires war or would look upon it otherwise than as a dire calamity."[28] One reason for thinking war unlikely was that 1914 Europe had weathered multiple crises in which war seemed possible but without belligerencies breaking out. The European publics had little expectation of, or desire for, war.[29]

Some did worry about the prospects of war, however, and saw the respites between crises as themselves being a problem. As French socialist Jean Jaurès put it in April 1913, "Europe has been afflicted by so many crises for so many years, it has been put dangerously to the test so many times without war breaking out that it has almost ceased to believe in the threat."[30] Historian Paul Schroeder puts the point starkly: "Europe's frequent escapes from crises before 1914 do not indicate the possibility that she could have continued to avoid war indefinitely; they rather indicate a general systemic crisis, an approaching breakdown."[31]

The point made here, however, is that the crises were not necessarily a sign of either an approaching systemic breakdown or systemic strength. Rather, the ways in which they were resolved, or more accurately not resolved, sowed the seeds of future problems. Ends of crises that result in clear winners and thus generate a response from the losers of "not next time" or "never again" pose dangers for systemic stability and dim the prospect for war to be avoided in a subsequent crisis.

Implications for International Relations Theory

This theory of the origins of war has implications for the arguments scholars make and the ways they assess them. These arguments and assessments are relevant for policy.

The Limits of Studying the Immediate Causes of War

Wars are the product of ongoing and strategic interactions and of repeated interactions. Wars are the end point of a host of actions and reactions that extend back in time beyond the period immediately preceding the opening of armed hostilities. Prewar crises and the inferences that states draw from them for their subsequent interactions are crucial to understanding the emergence of war.

This argument implies an inadequacy in two prevalent approaches to the study of the outbreak of war. On the one hand are the many studies of war, in general, and World War I, in particular, that examine nations' specific decisions to go to war. In the case of World War I, such studies lead to a focus on July 1914, because two earlier Balkan wars and a long series of quarrels between Austria and Serbia had not resulted in war. The argument becomes one that claims, whether implicitly or explicitly, that because only the specific features of 1914 resulted in belligerencies, only they deserve attention.[32] Such an approach is inadequate, however, because it decontextualizes a sequence of interactions.

On the other hand are structural approaches to the origins of war that focus on long-range dynamics such as the distribution of power and technological change. These are indeed important, but they need to be complemented by an analysis of the repeated crises that lead to war. Further, both approaches need to address why war was avoided in earlier crises, but was not in the one that eventually resulted in war. They need to be able to say what changed.

The Assumption of the Independence of Events

Many studies of international politics, especially quantitative ones, treat events as independent of one another. This is standard practice in studies using large databases of events and disputes. Most analyses of militarized interstate disputes (MIDs) treat such disputes as independent events and correlate measures of purported causal variables with the occurrence of MIDs.[33] They do so because it simplifies statistical inference. Yet such parameter estimates would be suspect if MIDs were not independent events. This chapter does not address whether MIDs are independent events, but it does suggest that state strategies in recurring MIDs are not independent. Hence, attributing war or even the escalation of MIDs to a set of exogenous features rather than endogenous strategic learning is inappropriate.[34]

The Bargaining Theory of War

Scholars of international relations generally share an understanding of war that is built on a simple and singular logic: that wars are costly and states therefore want to avoid them. The failure to achieve a bargain to avoid belligerencies implies information asymmetries (where only conflict can reveal the intensities of preferences), or an inability to divide issues, or an inability to undertake the credible commitments needed to avoid war. This argument points to the difficulties that preclude the kinds of bargains necessary for avoiding costly conflicts.

Yet states that have experienced recurrent crises and remissions have found ways to avoid costly conflicts, despite the existence of informational asymmetries and commitment problems. Thus something must have changed for a crisis to end in war. If bargains to avoid war were possible at one point but not subsequently, informational asymmetries and commitment problems must have arisen between the occurrence of a crisis that successfully avoided war and the crisis that led to one.

The emphasis on informational asymmetry suggests that nations alone know their own resolve and are unable to signal it. Yet this disparity should be at its greatest when an interstate crisis first arises, not after a series of them. Similarly, if war begins because of one state's inability to credibly commit to exercising its expected power, there is no good reason why that would not be so when a rising and a declining power have their first crisis.[35]

In short, any formal model of conflict that looks only at one strategic interaction is incomplete and problematic. It is not the extant features of the final crisis but the repeated play preceding it that precludes a new agreement. War results when states replay crises and change strategies instead of finding a new bargain. The information asymmetry arises because of a state's unwillingness to again accept diplomatic defeat.[36]

Reputation and International Politics

There is a lively debate among scholars of international relations about the role of reputation. Some argue that nations' track records clearly matter, that states assess one another's past histories and adopt strategies based on their understandings of others' past behavior. As a result, states also worry about their reputations. At times, therefore, they act not in accordance with their immediate interests but with an eye to their long-term reputation. In contrast, others argue, there is little empirical evidence that states assess one another's reputations. Instead, they focus on the features of the particular event at hand.[37] Yet the entire debate about reputation in international politics is miscast as one about whether a state's actions affect its credibility— for example, whether a nation choosing to back down is a function of its character or the particular features of a specific crisis.[38]

The argument here does not address whether states worry about their reputations or monitor those of others. It simply argues that states maintain or change strategies as a function of experience. That they continue on a particular course, however, can be seen as evidence of their wanting to maintain a reputation, but it is merely their continuation of a strategy deemed to have been successful in the past. That they change course after experiencing diplomatic defeat derives not from a concern about their reputation but from their wanting to avoid a repetition of the last outcome, which left them dissatisfied or aggrieved. In short, "current calculus theory" entails past experience theory.[39]

Modeling Rivalries and Recurrence

Conflicts and rivalries between pairs of countries occur over extended periods. For this reason, scholars need to address questions about their origins, courses, and outcomes. Yet the small literature devoted to international rivalries is one in which scholars dispute what constitutes a rivalry and the appropriate focus for scholarship. Some even see a focus on rivalries as replacing a "traditional causes-of-war approach."[40] Moreover, the quantitative studies of these interactions provide no logic for when and why conflicts and rivalries result in war. The argument in this chapter provides a logic for when and why crises become more difficult to resolve peacefully.

Conclusion

World War I has remained a specter for a century. During the Cold War, many scholars and policymakers feared the possibility of war by miscalculation and wondered if World War I provided an analogue for the prospect of a war growing out of a crisis between the superpowers.[41] The end of the Cold War brought a fear of the prospect of returning to the structural conditions preceding World War I.[42]

In the early twenty-first century, concern has grown about interstate relations in the western Pacific and the fear that they mirror those in Europe prior to World War I. Kevin Rudd, the former foreign minister and prime minister of Australia, notes that "the region increasingly resembles a 21st-century maritime redux of the Balkans a century ago—a tinderbox on water."[43] Historian Margaret MacMillan, the author of a book on World War I, notes the equivalence as well: "It is tempting—and sobering—to compare today's relationship between China and the U.S. with that between Germany and England a century ago."[44] Historian Christopher Clark arrives at the same conclusion after also writing a book on World War I: "I must say I was struck by the…insight…that…our world is getting more like 1914, not less like it."[45]

They are not alone. It has become commonplace for scholars, policy-makers, and journalists to compare the current conflicts in East Asia to the period preceding World War I. Today, as then, there is the prospect of a power transition in which a rising power faces a declining one. Also in evidence are territorial disputes, trade and investment rivalries, concerns with national honor, and alliances cemented by common geopolitical concerns. But today, as then, there is substantial economic interdependence between the relevant great powers, growing wealth, massive reductions in poverty, growth in education and science, and the arrival of industrialization and modernity. Today, as then, the sense that war would be irrationally ruinous and so readily avoidable coexists with the view that the conflicts that could lead to war are both present and worsening. The international community has already witnessed small-scale crises concluding with respites rather than resolutions. The crises seem manageable. If they come to leave clear winners and clear losers, however, the danger of war will emerge with a subsequent crisis in which one side attempts to reproduce its triumph and the other vows "never again."

3

Better Now Than Later

The Paradox of 1914 as Everyone's Favored Year for War

Jack Snyder

ONE REASON WHY Europe went to war in 1914 is that all of the continental great powers judged it a favorable moment for a fight, and all were pessimistic about postponing the fight until later. On its face, this explanation constitutes a paradox. Still, each power had a superficially plausible reason for thinking this was true.

Germany wanted to fight to forestall the planned future growth of Russian military might. France wanted to fight because the Balkan *casus belli* would bring Russia into the war, guaranteeing that France would not be left to face the German army alone. Austria wanted to fight because Germany had given it a blank check to help solve its endemic, existential security problems in the Balkans. Russia wanted to fight because, unlike in some previous Balkan crises, its army was reasonably prepared and France was already committed to fight.

All of these reasons, however, especially Russia's, prompt crucial questions in ways that merely deepen the paradox. The basic facts about the military and economic capabilities of the powers, their likely war plans, and their domestic political constraints were more or less common knowledge. What would happen in the event of war was fraught with great uncertainty, but this largely shared unknown did not include huge asymmetries of private knowledge. Moreover, key statesmen in each of the powers considered defeat and social upheaval to lie within the scope of possibility. In a dark moment, German Chief of the General Staff Helmuth von Moltke said that he expected "a war which will annihilate the civilization of almost the whole of Europe for decades to come" and bring pressures for revolution.[1] German Chancellor Theobald von Bethmann Hollweg decided not to replant trees on his East Prussia estate because the Russian army would soon be overrunning it.[2] Yet each country decided that 1914 would be a favorable year for war despite having roughly similar information and fearing a chance of disaster.

This kind of paradox is not only an interesting puzzle in its own right, but it has long been seen as a central cause of this war and of wars in general. Decades ago Geoffrey Blainey wrote that wars happen when the sides disagree about their relative power, and each thinks it can win, expecting to do better by fighting than bargaining.[3] William Wohlforth documented this puzzle for 1914, explaining how Blainey's argument figured into calculations that impelled Europe to war.[4] James Fearon later extended and formalized Blainey's insights, using examples from 1914 to illustrate the conditions under which rational states would fight costly wars rather than find a cheaper bargain that could avoid the fight, namely, private information, commitment problems, and indivisibility of stakes.[5]

This hugely and justly influential literature leaves unanswered crucial questions about the timing paradox and its role in causing the war. I argue that none of Fearon's three rationalist mechanisms, articulated in their strictest form, can explain the paradox of the universal, simultaneous view of 1914 as a favorable year for war. Two mechanisms that play a marginal role in his analysis, however—bounded rationality in multidimensional power assessments and attempts to mitigate power shifts through coercive diplomacy—help to explain how Europe's powers became trapped in a choice between war now and war later. These mechanisms were set in motion by background strategic assumptions rooted in the culture of militarism and nationalism that perversely structured the options facing Europe's statesmen in 1914. Whereas Fearon's rationalist theory assumes that states are paying equal attention to all relevant information, in 1914 each power's strategic calculations were disproportionately shaped by self-absorption in its own domestic concerns and alliance anxieties, and this explains the paradox.

The Timing Paradox in Theory

How has the bargaining theory of war understood the puzzle of simultaneous optimism of rivals about their prospects in war? Blainey is concerned mainly with the consequences of disagreements about relative power and less with their causes. He notes that uncertainty about likely outcomes allows both sides to be optimistic, and that information learned in fighting the war reduces disagreements about relative power and leads to peace.[6] What he does not emphasize, however, is that uncertainty should produce mutual pessimism about victory, and thus peace, just as often as it produces mutual optimism and war. Uncertainty per se helps to explain how random variations in expectations might sometimes cause war, but not why universal optimism and war will occur at any particular time.

Blainey also notes that emotions triggered by nationalism might make all sides irrationally optimistic. Adding widespread nationalism to the causal mix, however, does not necessarily lead to universal over-optimism. Europe's powers were not optimistic about everything in 1914. On the contrary, they were all pessimistic about their future prospects if they backed away from a fight in that year; that pessimism is what caused the war. Blainey identified an interesting mechanism, but he left loose ends.

Wohlforth, like Blainey, focuses more on the effects of perceived power, especially Russia's rising might, than on its causes. Wohlforth, drawing mainly on a largely descriptive book by Risto Ropponen, notes that France and Britain evaluated Russia's current military power more highly than did Germany and Austria, but Ropponen does not explain why.[7] One of Wohlforth's conclusions is that Germany was probably wrong to expect that Russia would soon outstrip its power; thus preventive war to stop Russian growth was unnecessary.[8] Indeed, Germany's impending insufficiency of ground forces was arguably caused mainly by Gen. Alfred von Schlieffen's unnecessarily demanding plan to start the two-front war with a go-for-broke offensive against France before turning toward Russia. Schlieffen himself admitted that "this is an enterprise for which we are too weak."[9]

Wohlforth's strongest argument about the causes of universal short-term optimism emphasizes a merely permissive condition: the near parity in power between the two alliances created the possibility that both sides might imagine the possibility of winning.[10] This possibility was magnified by the widespread belief in the efficacy of offensive military operations, which turned small, perceived advantages in military power into temptations to engage in aggressive behavior and made moderate adverse shifts in power seem dire.[11] Still, Wohlforth's argument does not explain the paradox that all sides were more optimistic about war in 1914 than about war later.

Fearon broadens Blainey's argument to include not just disagreements about relative power but also differing estimates of the sides' "willingness to fight."[12] In this framework, Fearon offers three reasons why rational parties might decide to fight rather than come to an agreement that avoids the costs of war: (1) the sides have private information about their strength that they cannot credibly reveal, creating the Blainey problem of simultaneous optimism; (2) the sides cannot credibly commit to honor an agreement if their relative power shifts in the future; and (3) the sides see the stakes of the fight as indivisible in key respects. Subsequent scholarship has debated which of these three mechanisms best explains not only the origins of wars but also the timing and manner of their termination.[13]

The Timing Paradox in 1914

The year 1914 provides a redoubled version of the Blainey problem: not only did the major continental states somewhat overvalue the current relative power of their own alliance, but more important, they undervalued the likely relative power of their alliance in the future. This expectation that conditions could become much less favorable facilitated the conclusion that it would be better to fight sooner than later, even in the face of ambivalence and uncertainty about the outcome of the conflict.

Historian David Herrmann notes that impending changes in the military equilibrium "made the future appear ominous to both sides for different reasons. The situation was paradoxical, but the fears none the less vivid."[14] For the Central Powers, Germany's army expansion was peaking in 1914, and Austria seemed to be reaching the limits of the power potential of its ramshackle state. For the Triple Entente, in contrast, the Russian Duma had just passed a bill that would increase the army's size 40 percent by 1917, and France had just increased its length of military service from two years to three, which would produce a corresponding increase in the size of the standing army once the new cohorts were trained.[15] Notwithstanding these seemingly rosy military trends, the Entente's nightmare was that its alliance would break up if the July crisis, which was engendered by the assassination of Austrian Archduke Franz Ferdinand on June 28, 1914, did not end favorably. Russia, weakened by the 1905 revolution and defeat in the 1904–05 Russo-Japanese War, had failed to back France in its showdowns with Germany over Morocco in 1905 and 1911. Meanwhile France had failed to support Russia against Austria and Germany in the Bosnia annexation crisis of 1908–09. One more such failure, especially given that the improving military balance removed the excuse of incapacity, might prove fatal to the allies' mutual trust and confidence. "If given the choice," says Herrmann, "the Entente leaders would have preferred to wait and fight a war later if necessary, but the crisis over Serbia forced them to decide at once. Both sides were therefore gambling over military eclipse in 1914."[16]

As a result, as they approached July 1914, both sides were in the mood to risk war now rather than face it in adverse conditions later, notwithstanding some hedging by key statesmen. German Foreign Minister Gottlieb von Jagow and his deputy, Arthur Zimmerman, both considered the moment particularly favorable.[17] "I do not desire a preventive war," said Jagow, "but if we are called upon to fight, we must not funk it."[18] A few weeks before the archduke's assassination in Sarajevo, Chief of the German General Staff von Moltke told

Jagow that he should conduct his foreign policy "with the aim of provoking a war in the near future." He was cagier with Austrian Chief of the General Staff Franz Conrad von Hötzendorf, admitting there was a chance that Germany might not defeat France quickly. "I will do what I can. We are not superior to the French."[19] Some argue that Moltke's preventive war talk, just as he was leaving for a spa vacation, was a ploy to scare the civilians into granting a new army bill.[20] But once back in Berlin, Moltke said again on July 29, "We shall never hit it again so well as we do now with France's and Russia's expansion of their armies incomplete."[21]

Ironically, across the border many French officers held the same view. The very next day a prominent French general wrote his son that "a better occasion would never be found" for war. French military attachés in St. Petersburg and Berlin echoed this sentiment.[22] In the spring of 1913 the future French commander, Marshal Ferdinand Foch, had told his future British counterpart, Henry Wilson, that war should not be long delayed. Foch argued that under current circumstances, the war would arise over a Balkan squabble, so Russia would surely be a full participant, whereas Russia might stay aloof from a purely Franco-German contingency.[23] In April 1914 the Russian attaché in Paris wrote the chief of Russia's General Staff, Nikolai Ianushkevich, that French power was peaking relative to Germany's for demographic reasons.[24]

Adding further irony to the paradox was the fact that 1914 was not a good time to initiate war for any of the continental powers, let alone all of them. Every offensive with which any of the continental powers began the war failed to achieve its tactical, strategic, or political objectives. Contrary to the teachings of the militarist cult of the offensive, prevailing technologies of firepower and mobility favored the side that fought on the defensive on thickly populated fronts. As a result, all of Europe's powers would have had good prospects for maintaining their security if they had prepared to stay on the defensive and postponed the war, notwithstanding their different appraisals of relative power balances and trends in power.[25] The perverse bargaining assumptions that crippled diplomacy in 1914 need to be understood in terms of biases in the underlying conceptual strategic framework that helped to cause the crisis in the first place and structured the evaluation of options within it.

Private Information

The simplest potential explanation for the simultaneous view of 1914 as a favorable year for war would be private favorable information that could not be safely or credibly shared with opponents. Such an argument, however, would not be convincing, because so much basic strategic information and many of the participants' assumptions were common knowledge across Europe's strategic elites. Still, a few possible lines of argument are worth considering.

Most key parameters of Europe's strategic situation were well known to Europe's militaries. France, Russia, and Britain knew the general outlines of the German war plan, though the French seem not to have understood Germany's decision to buttress the enveloping right wing with reservists.[26] French newspapers reported that the St. Cyr military academy had used a Schlieffen-type scenario for the cadets' 1913 final exam. In turn, the Germans knew that Russia had created a new army formation around Warsaw, poised for a quick attack toward Germany, in response to the Germans' abandonment of their eastward attack variant.[27] The Russians understood the Germans' motive and preparations for preventive war, having direct intelligence on this.[28] In fact, Russian War Minister Vladimir Sukhomlinov told the French attaché in February 1913 that "Germany is in a very critical position...encircled by enemy forces...and it fears them....I can understand its worry, and as a result the measures it is taking seem natural to me."[29]

This consensus was based on fairly good intelligence and common knowledge about military doctrinal assumptions. Historian Holger Herwig's well-documented study of German intelligence, for example, concludes that Germany based its estimate of military balance trends on detailed, accurate information. "The German sense of peril in 1914 is clearly not ascribable to defects in the system of collecting or analyzing intelligence," he observes. "To explain it, one has to look instead at the perceptual framework into which Germany's leaders set the information which reached them," such as the cult of the offensive, short-war dogma, and the tradition of preventive war thinking.[30]

Other powers' prewar intelligence did not get everything right, but these errors did not matter much for the urge to preventive action, and they were not the result of private information. For example, Russian war planners assessing worst-case scenarios somewhat overestimated the size of the forces that Germany would leave in East Prussia. This misestimate, however, should have made Russia slightly less eager to go to war in 1914 rather than later, when it would have had more troops to mount an attack. In the event, Russia did attack East Prussia and lost the major battle that ensued.[31]

On a broader plane, a large historiographical debate assesses whether Germany expected Britain to stay out of the fight, and whether any misestimate in this regard might have affected Germany's decision to seek a preventive war against Russia. Even if this was Germany's expectation, it is difficult to chalk it up to private information, given that the British leadership did not know themselves what they were going to do until the final minute.[32]

Stephen Van Evera has advanced the strongest theoretical argument linking private information to preemptive attack and preventive war in 1914.[33] Arguing more narrowly than Fearon, he notes that offensive plans can be especially reliant on surprise for success, placing a premium on secrecy— in other words, on private information. In particular, Van Evera argues that the Germans' extreme secrecy about their short-fuse plan to seize the Belgian bottleneck city of Liège left the Russians in the dark about the extremely tight connection between Russia's mobilization measures and general war. Although some recent historical scholarship holds that the Russians, goaded by the French, launched their mobilization knowing that it would lead to war, Van Evera's point remains worth debating historically and is strong theoretically.[34] It demonstrates yet another way in which underlying strategic assumptions about the cult of the offensive may have contributed to the 1914 paradox.

Commitment Problems

Even if Russia had wanted to, it might have been unable to credibly commit itself not to impose an intolerable bargain on Germany and Austria after the expected shift in power in its favor. This situation pushed the Central Powers toward preventive war and largely explains why they considered 1914 a good year for a showdown. This narrative can be accepted only with two major qualifications, however.

First, it does not explain why Germany retained the Schlieffen Plan framework that made Germany so vulnerable to Russian military improvements. Foreign Minister Jagow wanted to resurrect the old eastward mobilization plans of Helmuth von Moltke the Elder, a military genius whose plans for the 1880s envisioned holding the short, fortified Franco-German frontier with a defensive or counteroffensive deployment, carrying out pincer attacks around Russian-held Warsaw, and then negotiating.[35] This plan would probably have worked militarily and eased Jagow's and Bethmann's diplomatic problems, given that Germany would not have violated Belgian neutrality and brought Britain into the war. Moreover, without the British blockade, there would have been no unrestricted submarine warfare and no U.S. intervention to further tip the balance against Germany. Thus the notional Russian commitment problem could have caused World War I only in the perverse situation created by the Schlieffen Plan. In that sense, it demands a further theory to explain Germany's cult of the offensive.

Second, Russia's rising power does not explain why Russia and France accepted 1914 as the showdown year.[36] Indeed, as late as July 18, 1914, Jagow told Germany's ambassador in London that he expected the Russians to stay out of a localized skirmish between Austria and Serbia, because Russia and France would be better off delaying the big confrontation.[37] But not only did they accept the challenge in the seemingly disadvantageous year of 1914, they were eager to have it, because they were focused on a different commitment problem: their commitments to each other.

If the risk that the Franco-Russian alliance would fall apart was crucial to the timing calculations of France and Russia, why was it not just as critical to Germany? Once Germany saw that France would support Russia in July 1914, why did it not pull back in the hope that a future crisis on a different issue might offer an opportunity to divide them? The answer lies not in information or in the inherent structure of the commitment problem, but in the conceptual framework that German strategy imposed on the problem. The military's Schlieffen Plan proceeded from the assumption that France and Russia would fight together and that any war that involved one of them would inevitably involve both. This frame largely ignored the fact that France and Russia had not supported each other in several crises from 1905 to 1911. Admittedly, this lack of mutual support resulted mainly from Russia's temporary military weakness. Once Russian power had rebounded, though, and France and Russia could begin to contemplate fighting, the Schlieffen Plan served as a self-fulfilling prophecy. The German deployment scheme would ensure that France and Russia would be cobelligerents in any Balkan contingency that embroiled Russia. This tendency of German strategy to drive France and Russia together was exacerbated by the tactical practices of some German diplomats, who erroneously believed that threatening Russia or France would strain their alliance to the breaking point.[38]

These points are difficult to fit into Fearon's strictly rationalist version of the commitment problem. Two secondary points in his argument, however, can help to solve this puzzle: bounded rationality and the accumulation of power by territorial conquest.

Bounded Rationality and Bayesian Updating

Fearon notes that one possible explanation for "conflicting expectations of the likely outcome of military conflict" is that "the world is a very complex place, and for this reason military analysts in different states could reach different conclusions about the likely impact of different technologies, doctrines, and tactics on the expected course of battle."[39] If one adds to that the complexity of comparing the hypothetical outcomes of war now versus war four years hence, taking into account not only military factors but also the solidity of alliance commitments, it is hardly surprising that German, French, and Russian statesmen and strategists weighed uncertain factors differently and arrived at seemingly contradictory conclusions. Fearon accepts complexity as a plausible argument, but he sets it aside because it is a "bounded rationality" explanation. It is not one based on strict rationality, which accepts different actors producing systematically different estimates only if they have different information.[40]

What happens, however, if the concept of Bayesian rationality is introduced?[41] All of Europe's strategists engaged in updating their prior expectations about power balances and those balances' implications for commitment problems. This updating proceeded from some baseline expectations that Europe's militaries shared, such as a belief in the advantages of the offensive, but also some assumptions that diverged, especially as Germany and France were focused on completely different commitment problems.

In part, differences in national military culture and doctrinal training shaped the different prior assumptions that served as the baseline for updating. Preventive war thinking had a long, glorious tradition in the Prussian military, going back through Moltke the Elder to Frederick the Great.[42] It is not surprising that German General Staff officers placed considerable weight on this form of rationality when thinking about how to incorporate new information about growing Russian military power. The content and weight of Bayesian priors in different countries may also have been influenced by whose opinion counted most, the soldiers' or the civilians'. New research on France's decision for war in 1914 places heavy emphasis on civilians, especially the militantly nationalist President Raymond Poincaré. His focus was not on trying to determine when Russian military power would peak, but on making sure that Russia fought on France's side. Beginning in 1912, he worked toward making France's diplomatic commitment to support Russia in the Balkans virtually unconditional.[43]

This version of a Bayesian approach introduces all manner of cultural, organizational, and ideological biases in shaping baseline beliefs, which focus attention and frame questions differently as strategists integrate new information into their analyses. Thus Europe's strategists were updating their expectations from different baselines formed through processes of bounded rationality. This is no longer Fearon's strictly rational bargaining model, so he is right to exclude it from his theory. Still, it is important in explaining why the European powers thought so differently about their commitment problems in 1914.

Forestalling the Power Shift

The other reason why Russia and France accepted Germany's challenge to a showdown in 1914 is that Germany and Austria might have been able to forestall the expected power shift through limited conquests in the Balkans and the creation of a sphere of influence around the Black Sea, if Russia and France did not act. In a digression on commitment, strategic territory, and appeasement, Fearon notes that "the objects over which states bargain frequently are themselves sources of military power."[44] Dan Reiter carries this thought to its logical conclusion: during the course of a war, the currently stronger but potentially weaker side may be able to conquer territory that serves as a power resource to diminish or neutralize the anticipated power shift.[45]

Indeed, if the currently stronger power is strong enough, it might be able extort such resources without fighting.[46] This is exactly what Jagow hoped to do in the event Russia abandoned its Serbian ally in 1914, an outcome that he said he preferred to preventive war. Following Reiter's argument, the question was whether the initially stronger power, Germany, could seize sufficient strategic assets to solve its problem of impending relative decline without having to embark on an all-out preventive war. In this sense, coercive diplomacy and limited war might have been a substitute for preventive war.[47]

This is exactly how the Austrians and Germans analyzed the power competition in the Balkans. The Austrians in particular worried, for example, that Serbia's victories in the Balkan wars of 1912–13 had created a marginal but important power shift as a result of which "our forces will no longer be sufficient for both [Russia and Serbia] in the future."[48] Scheming to counteract these adverse trends, they calculated that Romania's sixteen and a half divisions, plus ten new Romanian reserve divisions to be added by 1916, would be a significant positive increment if allied to the Central Powers and kept out of alliance with the Entente. Germany's move in early 1914 to convince the Turks to install German Gen. Otto Liman von Sanders as the commander of Turkish troops in the Straits of Bosphorus was part of this same strategy to contain rising Russian power. If Germany and Austria could neuter Serbia, induce Romania to jump on their bandwagon, and make Turkey a client, Russia might be checked without resorting to a risky, all-out preventive war.[49] The Central Powers, however, had waited too long to push the showdown and the Entente had become stronger. Consequently they found out in August 1914 that permanently redressing the balance without a major war was no longer an option.

The Risk of Continental or World War

As Europe became divided into two more or less equally matched blocs, strategists and political leaders realized that their struggle for power and security
carried the risk of a devastating war, the kind of costly war that Fearon notes
states should be highly motivated to avoid through bargaining. Indeed, they
were. But instead of leading toward compromise, the impetus to bargain led
toward a competition in risk taking. Just as Thomas Schelling later argued
that a nuclear stalemate could foster risky behavior in places such as Berlin
to gain diplomatic leverage from a shared risk of escalation, so too Bethmann
Hollweg's private secretary, Kurt Riezler, published a book in 1914 explaining
that a great European war had become so potentially costly that no one would
fight it, but that this very risk could be a source of diplomatic leverage in a crisis
showdown.[50] Similarly, Adm. Alfred von Tirpitz justified building Germany's
"risk fleet" not on the assumption that it would actually be used to defeat the
British navy in open battle, but that it would deter Britain from taking the risk
of mounting an effective close-in blockade of German ports, giving Germany
a free hand to dominate France and Russia on the continent.[51]

As 1914 approached, all of the powers tried to ratchet up the risks in the
game of coercive diplomacy. New historical writing sees the Russian "trial
mobilization" during the Balkan crisis in the fall of 1912 as an attempt at
coercive diplomacy to deter Austria from intervening against Russia's Balkan
allies and to neutralize any Austrian attempt to intimidate them.[52] Some argue
that the Austrians learned from this crisis the importance of going to the
brink while holding cards, such as the German blank check, that would allow
them to call Russia's bluff.[53]

Meanwhile the Russians became increasingly enamored of coercive
diplomacy as a way to prevail without fighting. In the final year or two before
the outbreak of the war, the tsar's cabinet faced mounting criticism from
the many nationalist voices in the Duma who were demanding an end to
Russia's weak diplomacy. The most powerful, dynamic figure in the cabinet,
Agriculture Minister Alexander Krivoshein, argued for a firm policy of
military deterrence as a way to reconcile the Russian government's inclination
to avoid a premature war with these growing public demands.[54] In response,
Russia's ambassador in London, Count Alexander von Benckendorff, warned
that this policy of deterrent threats, backed by the encirclement of the Central
Powers in the Entente's ever-tightening web, could cause German preventive
aggression rather than deter it.[55] More commonly, notes Herwig, statesmen
and soldiers in every European capital "perceived their own alternatives

always as restricted by necessity or 'fate,'" whereas their opponents were seen as "being embarrassed by a plethora of open choices."[56]

Structural features of the European strategic situation in 1914 set the stage for this decreasing suppleness of crisis diplomacy, but psychological, organizational, and domestic political factors added crucial complications. The thorny issue of the Turkish Straits, where the stakes came closest to being indivisible, illustrates this interplay of international structural and internal decisional factors.

Indivisibility of the Stakes

Of his three core mechanisms of bargaining failure, Fearon places the least stock in the indivisibility of the stakes. He points out that virtually any stakes can be made divisible by side payments or offsetting strategic compensation. He agrees with subsequent empirical work that indivisibility, when it occurs, is more a social construction than a strategic fact.[57]

Nonetheless, Russia did seem to face one of those rare dilemmas where a vital strategic asset really is hard to divide through a credible compromise. The Turkish Straits were a strategic position that was maddeningly difficult to divide, and this complicated bargaining in 1914. Three-fourths of Russia's grain exports were shipped through these straits. When they were closed to commercial shipping during the Italo-Turkish War in 1911, Russia suffered a 40 percent decline in its overall exports. Moreover, Russia was understandably concerned about the passage of foreign naval ships into the Black Sea. Indeed, reflagged German battleships nominally handed over to the Turks in August 1914 wreaked havoc on Russian Black Sea shipping. Conversely, Russia would have liked access to the Mediterranean for its own Black Sea fleet to project power and to protect its commerce. Although some Russians pointed out that holding the straits would make little difference unless the British fleet were allied to Russia and dominated the Mediterranean,[58] Russia still had compelling reasons to want to do so. Divided control, such as giving Russia control over the Bosphorus entrance to the Black Sea while giving another power control over the Dardanelles entrance to the Mediterranean, would not have solved Russia's main problem. Unless Turkey were friendly to Russia or a credible, favorable international straits regime were in place, Russia arguably faced an enormous incentive to seize the straits to prevent a strong, hostile power from doing so first.

This indivisibility created a security dilemma between the Russians and the Turks, and potentially between Russia and whoever else would seek to control the straits. Because the Turks did not want Russia to occupy this core position in their country, they sought to shore up their ability to defend the straits, contracting to purchase Dreadnought battleships abroad and inviting German Gen. Liman von Sanders to command their shore garrison. This situation constituted a security dilemma in the sense that anything that Turkey did to increase its security necessarily decreased the security of Russia, and vice versa.

Mirroring incentives for preventive action in Europe more generally, impending power shifts threatened to trigger offensive action to resolve the security dilemma in the straits. Russia saw its window of opportunity to seize the straits potentially closing as a result of rising German influence there and impending Turkish battleship purchases, which Russia could not match because of the ban on foreign naval ships transiting the straits.[59] Russia was trying to build battleships on a round-the-clock construction schedule in its Crimean naval yards, but these would not be ready for a few years. As a result, the Russians itched to grab the straits preventively unless they could block the battleship purchases.

Ultimately, none of the issues above acted as a trigger to Russia's mobilization in 1914, because its naval staff realized by then that Russia lacked the ability to seize the straits before Turkey could bolster its own Black Sea fleet. The naval staff concluded that "what Russia desires in the next few years is a postponement of the final settlement of the Eastern Question and the strict maintenance of the status quo."[60] Once the war started, Britain blocked Turkey's battleship purchases, but Turkey accomplished the same goal through the reflagging of the German battleships that showed up in the Eastern Mediterranean.

Perceptual Bias in Assessing the Military Balance

Although the structural problem of the indivisibility of the Turkish Straits did not cause the war, the episode described above is nonetheless interesting as an example of the way power balances and shifts could be misperceived and misunderstood by European statesmen.

Russia's allies, to say nothing of its enemies, were loath to appreciate, let alone accommodate, the security dilemma that Russia faced in the straits. Most assumed that Russia's partial mobilization during the Balkan war in October–November 1912 was aimed at Austria, but it was also intended to deter or preempt a Bulgarian occupation of Constantinople. (The self-styled Bulgarian "tsar," Ferdinand, had a full-dress Ottoman emperor's regalia in his closet, made to order from a theatrical costume supplier, just in case his army occupied Constantinople and with it the straits.)[61] Russia's allies were also reluctant to back its protests against the installation of Liman von Sanders as commanding officer in the straits. Further, diplomatic correspondence suggests that Britain may not have grasped that the sale of British-built Dreadnoughts would give Turkey superiority over Russia's Black Sea fleet. First Lord of the Admiralty Winston Churchill may have been clueless, or perhaps just devious, when he told the Russians not to worry about a Turkish purchase, because the ships would not affect the balance between Greece and Turkey, as if that were Russia's concern.[62] Despite the long history of the straits being centrally tied to the general equilibrium of Europe, as war approached in 1914 this issue was discussed as if it were something of a sideshow, comparable, say, to Morocco for the French—a luxury item rather than a necessity.

Europe's powers appear to have had access to roughly similar information about the strategic contest over the straits. If they assessed its strategic significance differently, the cause was most likely a difference in perspective stemming from their different situations, not their information per se. Because Fearon was engaged in a theory-building exercise rather than trying to explain any one particular case, he made a sensible decision to restrict his analysis to rational hypotheses at the national level of analysis. But because my purpose is to understand the dynamic of 1914 in the light of this theory, it is necessary to consider other kinds of hypotheses as alternatives or supplements when rationalist accounts seem underdetermining.

For example, psychological mechanisms might have contributed to the 1914 timing paradox, whether in regards to the European dynamic as a whole or the straits problem in particular. Preventive war makes more sense when the opponent seems innately disposed toward exploitative behavior and thus seems highly likely to take aggressive advantage of the power shift in the future. The so-called fundamental attribution error in psychology describes a mechanism that could have biased all sides to hold this suspicion simultaneously. Laboratory research documents the common perceptual bias that people tend to explain their own actions in terms of situational causes (I had to do it because of the situational pressures that I faced), whereas they tend to explain others' actions in terms of dispositional causes (he did it because that is the kind of person he is). Although some observers might view this bias as rooted in self-justificatory ego defenses, cognitive psychologists typically contend that the different vantage points of actor and observer make situational accounts more available to the actor and dispositional accounts more salient to the observer.[63]

In a strategically competitive relationship, this is likely to produce a systematically biased causal bookkeeping that could lead over time to an engrained perception of the other as innately disposed to be exploitative and hostile. As Robert Jervis noted in his seminal writings on the security dilemma and on strategic misperceptions, such perceptual biases make it difficult for an actor to understand how others can perceive his defensive acts as threatening and as intended to threaten.[64] These biases can also sustain the assumption that only the other side enjoys the latitude to swerve to avoid a collision. Finally, Jervis also notes the psychological bias to see the other side as more unified than it really is, which possibly helps to explain why the Schlieffen Plan took for granted that Russia and France would cooperate with each other in any war scenario.[65]

Skeptics might point out that European diplomats in the multipolar era were schooled in the skills of imagining the complex motives and calculations of enemies and allies. Still, not everyone could rise to the level of Germany's famed chancellor, Otto von Bismarck, and research has shown how cognitive biases affected diplomatic attributions of motives in this period.[66] It seems possible that systematic biases of this kind might have been a background factor that could help to explain the perceptual focus on different strategic problems, divergent assessments of motives and options, and thus some aspects of the 1914 timing paradox.

Integration of Strategy and Implementation under Uncertainty

The institutional disunity of military policymaking and the organizational incoherence of strategic planning in the great powers sometimes produced different strategic assessments within countries, as well as between them. In all of the continental powers, civilian authorities had at best partial control over and knowledge of military strategy, and civilians and military officials sometimes sent different signals based on different strategic assumptions. Even the Austrians puzzled over who ruled in Berlin, Moltke or Bethmann? Historians today still say there is no simple answer.[67]

Russian civilian and military decisionmakers had particularly diverse views and preferences regarding strategy. There was no single, strong leader who had the knowledge, authority, political influence, or coherent vision to integrate all of the diplomatic and military considerations that pulled in different directions. As a result, Russian policy lacked coherence in its changes over time and in its different components at any given time. Russia adopted a rearward, defense-minded concentration plan in 1910, and then proceeded to graft onto it an incompatible, overcommitted plan for multi-pronged offensives in every direction: toward Turkey, Austria, East Prussia, and Berlin itself. These grafts resulted in part from changes in the strategic balance and intelligence on Germany's strategy, but they also reflected bureaucratic compromises in which different military commands each got the offensives that they wanted.[68]

More generally, the weakly led collectivity of civilian ministers and military dignitaries who made Russian strategy could not deliberate coherently to produce consistent strategic priorities, including when would be the favorable moment for war. Governmental decisionmaking over partial mobilization in 1912 and over the military and diplomatic response to the Liman von Sanders crisis was highly factionalized. Clarity of a sort emerged only in February 1914 when a geriatric nonentity, Ivan Goremykin, replaced the leader of the less bellicose faction, Vladimir Kokovtsov, as chairman of the council of ministers. Under this new arrangement, advocates of urgent military preparation, led informally by Agriculture Minister Krivoshein, forged a consensus in favor of firm deterrence of any further Austro-German moves.[69] As in the logroll among Russia's military factions, the compromise among civilian leadership factions resolved internal disputes through the fiction that a synthesis of different factional viewpoints would solve Russia's strategic problems. Thus one reason why Europe's states worked from contradictory strategic assumptions is that they were focused as much on their own internal political realities as on strategic assessments.

Another institutional mechanism that affected the feeling of readiness for war in 1914 was each military organization's inclination to reduce operational uncertainty through preparations to carry out its own plan at the outset of the conflict.[70] When a military organization makes strategic calculations, a highly salient marker seems to be whether the military feels that it is coherently organized to implement its basic plan from an administrative, logistical point of view, and whether its basic force structure is in place for the plan. This sets an absolute rather than a relative milestone. It is about whether the state is ready, not whether it is more ready than the opponent or more ready than it will be in the future.

All of the European militaries felt operationally "ready" in this sense in 1914, whereas one or more had felt egregiously unready in earlier showdowns. In 1914, Russian staff officers were, for good reason, somewhat nervous about the logistics of the East Prussia operations once the troops got off the trains, but as recently as the fall of 1912, the worries were more basic: Were there enough bullets, would the trains run on time, and so on?[71] Herrmann states flatly that Russian mobilization was "impossible" in the 1908–09 Bosnia crisis; in 1914 it was not.[72] Further, Dominic Lieven has argued that Russia was "not radically less prepared for war in 1914…than [it would be] in the next few years."[73] Thus, looking at the balance comparatively and prospectively, Russian War Minister Sukhomlinov could conclude that Russia would remain inferior to the combination of Germany and Austria until 1917 or 1918. At about the same time, assessing preparedness on an immediate, can-we-do-our-job basis, he could declare in 1914 that the Russian army was ready for the big war.[74] This self-referential preparedness illusion may have had both institutional and psychological sources, such as the greater salience of firsthand impressions.[75]

Domestic and International Public Relations

Another factor that heightened the self-absorption of calculations of the best moment for war was each power's need to create the appearance of being the aggrieved party, especially in the eyes of its own public.

Germany and France, in particular, were each concerned about appearing to be the wronged party in the eyes of its domestic public audience. Because of the Schlieffen Plan, France could always count on this, though a seemingly gratuitous German attack on France arising from a Balkan contingency was probably seen as a bonus, and thus a good occasion for war. For Germany, looking like the aggrieved party could hardly be taken for granted, given the blank check to Austria. Once the Russians moved to mobilize first, however, this problem was miraculously solved in a way that might not recur in hypothetical future showdowns. As Dale Copeland shows in detail, many of Bethmann Hollweg's delays and maneuvers in the final days of the July 1914 crisis can be understood at least in part as attempts to win the blame game in the eyes of peace-minded German Social Democrats.[76]

Understandably, each power was more focused on its own domestic justification problem than that of its neighbor. Looking blameless in the eyes of one's own public seemed advantageous even if the opponent's regime also looked blameless in the eyes of its public. Not all statesmen are self-absorbed in this way, however. In 1870, for example, Bismarck was able to view this problem from all parties' perspective in devising his strategy for making France appear to be the aggressor. Few leaders are as deft as Bismarck, however. The mean reverts toward self-referential perception and thus may help to explain the paradox of multiple, simultaneous optimism about war now relative to war later.

Conclusion

James Fearon's rational bargaining theory of war is strong as theory, and theory must always simplify to maintain its generalizability. The simple explanations drawn directly from the theory, however, do not in themselves yield adequate explanations for the puzzle of how France, Germany, and Russia could have all been simultaneously convinced that 1914 was a favorable time for war. Private information was only a problem at the margins. The commitment problem caused by shifting power balances was far more important, but it was driven not by an inexorable structural dilemma but by the social construction of vulnerability as a result of the cult of the offensive in military doctrine and war planning. Specific issue indivisibilities, notably the Turkish Straits dilemma, did not cause the war, whereas the generic notion of an all-encompassing indivisibility, such as the *Weltpolitik* mantra of world power or decline, was a tenet of ideology rather than a structural fact.[77]

Although the basic hypotheses of rational bargaining theory seem inadequate to explain the puzzle of why Europe went to war in 1914, perceptual, organizational, and domestic political spinoffs of these bargaining problems do seem helpful in pointing toward possible answers. Europe's statesmen and strategists tried to reason about the strategic consequences of the balance of power, its trend, and its relationship to the cohesiveness of alliances. They reasoned differently, however, because of self-absorption in their distinctive strategic problems and domestic audiences, and because of different baseline beliefs that served as frames for updating their calculations in light of new, often shared information.

While several aspects of the strategic and political situation of 1914 contributed to the paradox of simultaneous urgency for war, three are worth highlighting. The first is William Wohlforth's permissive condition of the relatively even balance of power, which made it possible for each power to envision conditions under which it could win or lose. This permissive condition established the potential for both optimism about victory now and pessimism about defeat later.

The second is Stephen Van Evera's arguments about the cult of the offensive leading inexorably to preventive war. The offense cult magnified the consequences of power shifts for commitment problems, exacerbated what would have been minor problems of private information, and fed notions of cumulative conquest that made any division of resources and strategic assets look inherently unstable. The belief in the offensive was not grounded in strategic realities. Instead, it was an outgrowth of the organizational interests of Europe's military organizations at a peak period of their narrow professionalization and organizational autonomy in an era when civilian institutions of military oversight were poorly developed. As Holger Herwig has put it, "To concede that the vaunted Prussian General Staff could no longer conduct short wars of annihilation was to admit that war had ceased to be a viable option for the state."[78] Stig Förster concurs: "The 'demigods' inside the General Staff simply could not afford to accept...that war had ceased to be a viable option of policy. Otherwise, not only they but also the whole army would lose their elevated position in German society."[79] More broadly, the cult of the offensive reflected the widespread nationalism that was endemic to that era of European history, highlighting not only the anarchical competition of nation-states at a time of uneven growth, but also the domestic political strategies of elites who used nationalism to survive in the face of the class conflicts of that phase of social modernization.

This directs attention to a third general factor: the focus of European political elites on their own nation's social divisions, factional complexities, and ramshackle governmental arrangements, and on their own tenuous legitimacy. Bargaining with enemies competed with the need to maintain bargains with domestic coalitions and allies. As a result, grand strategy in this era was a three-level game in which the need to cobble together working coalitions on the domestic and alliance levels often seemed more pressing than even the life-and-death threats posed by foreign competitors. Despite sharing a great deal of common knowledge of strategic matters, enemies could not reach a diplomatic compromise because they were hindered by domestic or intra-alliance bargains that were rationalized by strategic fictions tied to nationalism and the cult of the offensive.

How should these insights from the 1914 timing paradox inform thinking about the future power transition that might result from China's economic and geopolitical rise? An overly simple realist take on this problem might expect the rising power to lie low until it becomes the stronger party, while the relatively declining party decides whether to launch an all-out preventive war before the crossover point is reached. The 1914 example suggests that the dynamics of a power transition are likely to be more complicated. The declining power is likely to try to prevent the transition through territorial containment, alliances with regional states, control over economic and military choke points, and coercive means short of major war. This likelihood might place the onus on the rising power to sustain its rise through brinkmanship, arms racing, and efforts to break out of hostile encirclement through coercive diplomacy.

In this process, secondary windows of opportunity might come to dominate thinking about the best timing for a showdown. These might include calculations of alliance solidarity (e.g., an opportunity for the United States created by a moment when Japan and South Korea are cooperating or, conversely, an opportunity for China to exploit an episodic rift between the United States and Taiwan); the need to forestall impending nuclear weapons proliferation (by Japan, South Korea, or Taiwan), which could give both China and the United States a simultaneous incentive to hasten a showdown; an impending Taiwanese declaration of national sovereignty; or the inter- action of a perceived first-strike advantage with a security dilemma on the Korean Peninsula resulting from the collapse of the North Korean regime. Such secondary windows of opportunity could spur China to act "too soon" in the trajectory of its rise.

In such situations, bargaining failures could lead to a costly war not only through simple problems of private information, commitment dilemmas, and indivisibility. Strategic and bargaining calculations are likely to diverge also because of the various states' distinctive strategic cultures, their inordinate focus on their own alliance dilemmas, their self-absorbed military organi- zational habits and concerns, the pressing domestic political implications of their international stances, and systematic differences in causal attributions by actors and observers of action. Although today's world differs in many ways from 1914, any of these general mechanisms might still trigger the para- doxical conclusion that fighting a war now seems better for all parties than waiting for war to come later. It is the task of students of strategic theory and history to be prepared to challenge the kind of assumptions that lock strate- gists into that mind-set.

4

Allies, Overbalance, and War

Richard N. Rosecrance

A T THE START of World War I in 1914 countries fought with one another
knowing that a balance of power was essentially in place. They also
generally understood the wartime strategies that their opponents would
employ. As many have argued, the parties would have been much better
off fashioning a solution to the conflict before it started, giving to each side
roughly what the division of economic and military power between them
would have dictated. Millions of people would not have been killed; billions
of francs, pounds, and marks would not have been wasted. But that is not
what happened. Because war was not ruled out by a balance of strength, no
one was deterred and each major nation thought that it could chance an
encounter of arms. Wars in 1866 (between Austria and Prussia) and in 1870
(between France and Prussia) had been quickly decided, and this precedent
had become a misleading article of faith for heads of nations that helped to
lead countries into battle in 1914. Other important reasons included the "cult
of the offensive," which favored immediate and decisive attacks to catch the
enemy off guard and bring defeat.[1] Great powers also participated in a seesaw
of repetitive crises in which the party that once turned back might not swerve
the next time. Politically, the regimes in 1914 were somewhat insecure, even
sitting monarchs. They had few gains with which to reassure their populations that the future was benign. Germany did not think that it had enough
important colonies. Britain thought the German navy was designed not only
to gain advantage in general, but also to challenge Britain's position abroad
and at home. Trade had come to depend more on empire (where each imperial
leader kept tariffs low for his state's own goods) than on European markets,
which (except for Britain's) had been progressively closed by higher tariffs.[2]
No country felt at ease militarily, politically, or economically. It was time for a
good quick war, especially because most believed that it would come sooner
or later anyway.

The war did not occur, however, because countries were confident of winning. Germany would have been more likely to win if it had struck France in 1887, when Paris had no allies, and not in 1914 when it had two strong supporters, Russia and Great Britain. Germany in fact attacked when it was relatively weaker than key opponents. But as many have seen, a country in trouble or decline may opt to fight even if the outcome of the contest is potentially unfavorable. The value attached to peace and the status quo by one party may lessen even when the balance of force between two opponents remains the same.[3] As seen by a particular state, the value of the status quo can go up and down irrespective of the military balance.

One important element in that valuation is the existence and status of a country's allies. Allies are useful not only as added strength in war, but also as tangible embodiments of the influence of the primary member in garnering international support. For years Austria-Hungary was successful in diplomacy because it was a continual participant in three-nation coalitions in a five-nation great power world. Austria acted to *fait à trois* (make three), as the French saying goes. When Italy hinted that it might move to neutrality in a conflict arising in the Balkans, Vienna felt less assured about its future. From an opposite position, isolated France needed to acquire an ally to balance Germany and made every sacrifice to attract the Russians. Having been dropped by Germany in 1890, the Russians felt the same. Paris and St. Petersburg would go to great lengths to maintain their alliance, and not only because of the mutual service rendered in military terms; neither wanted to be left alone.[4] Somewhat similar motives brought an end to Lord Salisbury's "splendid isolation," as London moved to agreements with Japan (1902), France (1904), and Russia (1907).

Thus in 1914, great powers had at least two motivations: not to lose a war and to maintain their alliances. Obviously the second aim could conflict with the first if, by supporting an ally, a great power got into a conflict it could not win. This is the essential dilemma in what follows: allies frequently were so important that assisting and retaining them became a priority almost equal to avoiding or winning a war. This phenomenon was as true of World War II as World War I.

In international relations, there is much disputation about the relevance and effect of the balance of power.[5] Do balances operate, and if so, what impact do they have? Some scholars assert that balances tend to occur and are stabilizing, that is, they help to prevent war.[6] Others claim that balances take place, but that they lead to conflict between the conflicting (balancing) parties.[7] A third group of scholars asserts that balances infrequently take place largely because of the public goods costs that nations must pay in trying to implement them.[8] Confronting an imbalance, countries usually pass the buck to others rather than join the weaker side where they would have to fight stronger states.[9] Finally, imbalances or over-balances of power occur periodically and may have hegemonic effects.[10]

Each of these views has a long and actively debated history, but the important point for 1914 is twofold. First, the balance of 1914 did by no means prevent war: the commitment of one or two powers led to others being involved in the conflict until it became a world war. It was a chain-ganging phenomenon.[11] Second, if (counterfactually) an overbalance had existed with the United States already allied to the Triple Entente in 1914, Germany and Austria would have hesitated to act.[12]

Balance or Overbalance?

Allies are critical to maintain a balance of power.[13] An overbalance of power can form when a great coalition (e.g., the Concert of Europe after 1815) emerges by negotiated consent. The Concert comprised all major powers including France, the late hegemonic but subsequently more quiescent nation-state. The Concert was a resilient but not unbreakable institution. Its existence depended on countries agreeing to maintain conservative regimes in power and also on self-restraint by the great powers. No one wanted another period of French-style revolutionary warfare that would tip the social scales in Europe and unseat the aristocrats. As social change came to the fore, however, led in part by France's rejection of the autocratic Charles X, international relations became more tentative. In response, in 1830 Belgium sought independence from Holland, and for a time during the revolutionary fervor, France hoped to annex Belgium. England did not want France to control rivers—especially the mouth of the Scheldt, just opposite Dover—and persuaded France to relent on its demands. After agreement on Belgian independence in 1832, however, Britain and France worked increasingly together as the liberal two in a concert that also included the conservative three (Russia, Prussia, and Austria). But because no power wished to repeat the antagonisms of the Napoleonic period, self-restraint held back Russia in its attempts to undermine Turkey, and France in its equally unsuccessful efforts to put an Egyptian prince on the throne of Damascus. (Turkish and British fleets also stood in the way.)

The revolutions of 1848 undermined the Concert agreement. Liberals came to temporary authority in the Frankfurt parliament. Yet they could not stay in power after Russia had intervened to put down the Hungarian revolution in 1849. As one writer commented, "The success of the revolution discredited conservative ideas; the failure of the revolution discredited liberal ideas."[14]

Thereafter both sides sought to buttress their own domestic positions. France moved to seek liberal empire under Napoleon III, and the British embraced liberal ideas, trying to move Austria out of northern Italy. In 1854 France and Britain took out their ire against conservative Russia in the Crimean War, in which diplomacy was occasionally interrupted by battles. In 1856 the Russians surrendered, but did not concede to liberalism.

Successful foreign policy remained the method of staying in power; nationalism would become the savior of conservative regimes resisting liberalism. All countries sought foreign policy successes. France and Austria warred over Italy in 1859, and Austria's failure meant greater success for Sardinia in the effort to unite Italy. Thereafter, however, Prussia (under Chancellor Otto von Bismarck from 1862 on) moved to reinsure conservative rule by successively defeating Denmark, Austria, and France. The conservatives gained a new lease on life as German unification (with the omission of Austria) took place.

The Concert of Europe had no effect on these struggles and only briefly convened in Paris in 1856 to deal with their consequences; it did not act until Bismarck reinstituted a partial concert after 1871. German alliances between 1871 and 1890 brought all countries but France together. Bismarck gingerly and slowly reconstituted an overbalance of power in Europe. First, he resuscitated Austria after its defeat in 1866 and allied with it in the League of the Three Emperors in 1873. When Russia withdrew from this alignment after the Russo-Turkish War, Austria entered into the Dual Alliance with Berlin in 1879. But Germany (i.e., Bismarck) was determined to re-ensnare St. Petersburg, and offered the Reinsurance Treaty in 1887 as a gesture of reconciliation. Meanwhile, to keep Russia in line, Bismarck brought Britain into the Mediterranean agreements of that same year, making it unnecessary for Germany to restrain Russia in the Near East. By 1890 all countries but France (the victim of territorial loss to Germany in 1871) were tied up in the German alliance system. By combining Austria and Russia in the same pacts, Bismarck could restrict each by threatening closer ties with the other. This inconsistency was actually the great strength of German diplomacy, for it left Bismarck with freedom to choose.

After 1890, however, Kaiser Wilhelm II and Count Leo von Caprivi undermined Bismarck's intricate system of alliances and its strong overbalance of power. They dropped Russia and the Reinsurance Treaty in 1890, which meant that St. Petersburg became the potential ally of France. For a while it appeared that the Germans would exchange Russia for Britain, but after Prime Minister William Gladstone took office, Lord Rosebery, the new foreign secretary, could not sustain Lord Salisbury's closeness with

Berlin. Had he succeeded, a British-German coalition would have more than substituted for the Russo-German connection because Britain got on famously with Austria. But the failure to draw in London (also a colonial enemy of France) meant that the European world moved from overbalance to a mere balance of power, as France and Russia allied in 1894. The Triple Alliance was now opposed by a nearly equal Franco-Russian alliance. Under Joseph Chamberlain's influence, the British renewed overtures to Berlin in 1899–1901, but they were rebuffed by Chancellor Bernhard von Bülow who was animated by the doctrine of "the free hand." The free hand meant that Germany did not have to ally with England to prevent its union with France and Russia, because France would always differ with Britain over colonial policy. France and Britain had nearly gone to war over Fashoda in the Sudan and control of the headwaters of the Nile in 1898.

Having failed with Germany, Britain now turned to Japan, the only other power that could restrain Russian expansion in the Far East, and the Anglo-Japanese alliance was concluded in 1902. This put France in a quandary: Since Japan and Russia were rivals in the Far East, would France's alliance with Russia cause a conflict with Britain? France needed a rapprochement with Britain to avoid such an outcome, and the Anglo-French Entente was negotiated in 1904. Thus gradually, almost imperceptibly, what had been an overbalance of power in favor of Germany now became a balance of power as France, Russia, and Britain became progressively closer.[15]

A Western Overbalance

A half-century later, the United States' postwar coalitions gradually became dominant against opponents and acquired broadened influence. The Brussels pact brought Germany's continental foes (Britain, France, Italy, and Benelux) together in 1948. In 1949 the United States and Canada joined, and in 1955 Western Germany was admitted. Thus began the process that gradually led to the unification of the West and the great preponderance of Western economic power. West Germany's economy grew by 10 percent annually during the 1950s, while France and Britain regained their prewar strength. The alliance expanded east, with Greece and Turkey joining. The United States regained economic growth in the 1960s, and the process was matched by the gradual lessening of Soviet development rates, which had been at 5 percent per year in the late 1950s and early 1960s, but declined to 2 percent by the mid-1970s (and were reduced to 1 percent in the 1980s). Equally important, Western technology grew dynamically during the 1960s and culminated in the successful moon landing in 1969. Computers entered Western inventories by 1974, with Apple and IBM vying for ascendancy in desktops as Intel fashioned a near monopoly in microprocessors. This Western gain was buttressed by success in military technology, as greater accuracies and new types of warheads stemmed Soviet success in strategic weapons. New battlefield control by airborne warning and control systems (AWACs) countered Soviet strength in conventional weapons. By the mid-1980s, the Soviet thrust for European dominance was over, and Soviet leaders, especially Mikhail Gorbachev and Eduard Shevardnadze, came to see agreement with the West as the best future strategy.

The U.S.-Russian Cold War came to an end because Western states led by the United States finally achieved a decisive level of superiority over the Soviet bloc in both economic and military terms. At that point, the Soviets decided to try to join the West, but Russia did not qualify for membership because of its lack of political freedom and respect for the rule of law. Its relative industrial decline did not help it in the scales of world power. Since then, Moscow has achieved greater oil and natural gas production, but it also has remained a more or less isolated entity in world politics, taking some risks with its aggressive stance in Ukraine. It has had difficulty attracting other states peacefully to join its side.

Allies and War

World War I occurred because allies had to be bailed out. In this instance, major power support of minor allies (Russia assisting Serbia and Germany aiding Austria) served to bring on rather than deter the war. In 1914 there was no strong disincentive against aiding beleaguered allies. Each side could calculate that it might win if it acted quickly and decisively.[16] As shown, however, if Britain had been able to bring the United States into the Triple Entente before 1914 (instead of its de facto entry in April 1917), that juxtaposition would have created an overbalance that might have deterred Germany and Austria and prevented the war.

In sum, minor allies throughout history posed the following difficulty: they committed a great power to take a strong stand against an opponent without giving it the superior strength to do so. They added to the incentives to make war, rather than increasing the disincentives that might have prevented it.

The great difficulty in maintaining an appropriate relationship between allies and potential opponents is further illustrated by attempts to prevent World War II. By 1939 Britain needed to stop Germany; in terms of domestic politics alone, the British government could not tolerate further losses to Adolf

Hitler. Zara Steiner writes, "Britain and France took up Hitler's challenge. They were Great Powers and were not prepared to relinquish their positions without a battle."[17] But determining how to stop Germany presented intractable problems for London. Ideally, Britain should have recruited a powerful ally to overawe Germany and force it to back down. There were only two candidates for this role: the Soviet Union and the United States. The United States was the preferred choice, but in 1938–40 it was not yet ready to make a commitment to Britain. Congress would not permit President Franklin Roosevelt to amend the neutrality laws. In fact, this could happen only if the German threat became much greater to both Britain and the United States. In this respect, Britain had to lose further ground to persuade the United States to intervene.

Russia was the other possible savior, but Hitler tied up Russia in the infamous Nonaggression Pact of August 23, 1939. Thus, when Britain clinched the alliance with Poland on August 26, 1939, it added little to the balance against Germany and failed to prevent war on September 3. Fighting over Poland would get Britain involved in eastern Europe, where it could not possibly prevail against Germany. Not surprisingly, Hitler did not believe that Neville Chamberlain would declare war.[18] Britain could not win alone, and aside from France, it had no powerful allies. Further, it had no access to Poland geographically, so it could not practically assist Warsaw. It was also dependent on exports of machinery, which came from the same machine-tools industries that would be needed for armaments production. As the British treasury pointed out, given Britain's shortage of financial resources, the country would have to limit rearmament and shift back to exporting capital goods in two or three years' time.[19] How then could it declare war? In purely rational terms, Hitler had good reason to believe that London could not act against him.[20]

Creating an Overbalance of Power

Smaller states can get their major allies into war without necessarily contributing to victory, though sometimes a powerful ally does make the difference between victory and defeat. An overbalance of power that might obviate a war altogether is difficult but not impossible to create.

For an overbalance to work, the tendency toward structural balance has to be overcome. Polarization is an independent cause of conflict. Consistency in structural (social) balance in which all enemies are on one side and all friends on the other is likely to provoke conflict between them. According to the Arab proverbs: an enemy of an enemy is a friend; a friend of a friend is a friend; an enemy of a friend is an enemy; and a friend of an enemy is an enemy.[21]

A complete structural balance occurs when all of the proverbs are fulfilled. Carrying out the terms of full structural balance (and polarization), however, will create difficulties. Under a strict balance, a great power has to decide whether to endorse an ally or the friend it may oppose. If so, an absence of structural balance is more likely to bring and hold the world together than a rigid social balance of diametrically opposed parties.[22] As a policy program, this means maintaining the ally and an opposing great power in separate compartments of friendly relations. It is important to retain the ally, but not jettison the great power friend. One must find a way to accommodate whatever inconsistency may be involved in maintaining a mutually favorable connection with countries that are antagonists.

Bismarck squared this circle, retaining strong ties with both Russia and its Austrian rival in 1887.[23] But by 1914, Bismarck's successors had concluded that they had to support Austria (against Serbia) even when this would be to act directly against Russia (and potentially Britain). Thus allies may move up and down in the scales of priority. In 1956 the United States remained an ally of Britain and France, but acted against them in the Suez crisis.[24]

For a major power, the ideal is to remain on good terms with the ally and the alternative great power, refusing to make a final choice between them, just as Bismarck refused to choose between Russia and Austria in the Three Emperors' Alliance of 1873 and again after 1881. Henry Kissinger did the same in the period 1971–74, moving the United States toward China, but not so close as to sacrifice the possibility of détente with the Soviet Union. The link with China was designed to discipline, not ostracize, the Soviet leader. In response, President Leonid Brezhnev became so committed to the U.S. link that he supported Richard Nixon to the last in the Watergate crisis. Kissinger entertained the possibility of a stronger tie with Moscow even before Mikhail Gorbachev's reforms of the late 1980s.

The problem in 1914, however, was not only that of selecting a priority ally, but also the order in which allies were sought—that is, "sequencing."[25] In the early stages of a conflict, a state makes preliminary choices that may (if fully adhered to) determine later decisions to bring in other powers. Agglomeration (bringing all parties together) is the appropriate remedy, but as James Sebenius shows, a state may have to reassure one power before bringing in another.[26] In 1879 Bismarck chose Austria, but he leavened this choice by concluding the Reinsurance Treaty with Russia eight years later.

As applied to China and the United States, Washington may have to choose Japan first, but it may later want to draw in Beijing. Kissinger first selected China not to isolate Russia but to bring it to his way of thinking over time. A generation later, President George H.W. Bush succeeded in persuading the Soviet Union to compromise its claims against the West. He reached agreement to end the Cold War, thereby implementing elements of the Kissinger strategy.

Power factors are important to the choice. A direct attempt to create a condominium between two contending great powers (leading to duopoly) is unlikely to occur and may not last if tried. President Barack Obama did not succeed in preliminary efforts with either Chinese President Hu Jintao or Xi Jinping. But one side can begin to draw together what in time could become a preponderant coalition; at a certain point, this agglomeration might grow strong enough to attract the other great power as well.

In a more recent example, France and Germany did not have enough strength or diplomatic clout to bring Britain into the Common Market in 1957, but they could do so in the early 1970s, when many other states had already joined what was to become the European Union and a kind of joining momentum had been established. The key, as Sebenius shows, is to recruit an important friend of the recalcitrant great power whose engagement could pave the way for the latter's accession.[27] In the U.S. effort to influence China, it could start by bringing Japan, then India, then Russia into the accord. This could ultimately attract a China that would have nowhere else to go.

The United States and China?

Power balances can lead to war; overbalances can attract the potential adversary to join. What is the implication of this relationship for the United States and China in the future? Power relationships are changing as China rises. If China were to accumulate (with allies) equal power with the West (the United States, the European Union, and perhaps Japan), it might achieve a balance of power, but it would not thereby prevent war.

Nor should analysts remain sanguine that a generally peaceful relationship between China and key Western powers will solve all problems in the future. Sean Lynn-Jones and Charles Maier both observe the relative equanimity of early twentieth-century relations between Britain and Germany (a cordiality that helped to settle major Balkan issues in which both Russia and Austria were involved in 1912 and 1913).[28] Yet despite the possibility that Anglo-German friendship would smooth matters in 1914, it did not. Could China's friendship with the United States also be misleading, now or in 2030? The problem is that allies as well as power relationships frequently get in the way.

This can happen even when cooperation between great power parties has been growing steadily over a period of years. Even in an ostensibly peaceful context, potential antagonists sometimes cannot afford to absorb any more (real or imagined) affronts to their diplomatic and international position and decide to take a tough stand. Russia did this in 1914.[29] Past friendships may then count for little. Despite its comfort with Germany and the "Willy-Nicky" correspondence between the two emperors, Russia under Sergey Sazonov and Vladimir Sukhomlinov would make no further obeisance to Berlin and stood firm against the Austro-German demands on Serbia in 1914. Instead, Russia would act to help its de facto ally, Serbia. In response, Germany sided strongly with Austria.

Would the United States act to support its Far Eastern allies against China? As China's naval power develops, Beijing might be tempted to conclude that the United States will back away from confrontation in East Asia. Observers are aware, however, that the United States has not only nominal but also crucial allies in the region. The United States could not tolerate a loss of Japan any more than it could accept a loss of Europe. Thus the dilemma posed by allies may be a continuing problem besetting U.S.-Chinese relations.[30]

Conclusion

This chapter argues that the great power participants in 1914 faced the worst of all possible worlds: They committed their support to a particular ally (Serbia or Austria) whose role in the war would be less than decisive.[31] It would involve the great power in war without winning. In 1939 the issue was even clearer. Poland could not win the war for Great Britain—it could only involve London in war. It was a liability rather than an asset. But Britain could not tolerate any more losses: its "value of peace" had radically declined as it entered a zone of loss. Serbia added nothing to Russian power in 1914, but St. Petersburg could not yield again and still maintain its international standing relative to Germany and Austria.

Usually, hegemonic great powers have the greatest number of allied responsibilities and the most extensive periphery of interests. It is hardest for them to back down. The United States may well fall into that overextended category in the years ahead. But will it be able or willing to jettison needed allies? That is far from certain.

By 2030 the China issue will be paramount in world politics. Beijing will be tempted to expand against U.S. allies in East Asia, particularly Japan and possibly Vietnam and the Philippines. The United States will certainly view Japan as a crucial ally and will not be willing to yield to China's challenges.

In diplomatic terms, this means that both Washington and Beijing will need to craft strategy to create a greater rapprochement before this challenge occurs. These reflections underscore the point that "winning a war" is not the only desideratum in international politics, and allies are critical to a state's estimate of its international position. The United States and China would do better to create steadily an overbalance of power by forming a large great power grouping in world politics.

The United States is establishing this core grouping by reinsuring its connections, both political and economic. Uniting the two halves of the Western alliance creates a bloc of more than $33 trillion in gross domestic product. If Japan is added, the sum approaches $40 trillion, becoming the most attractive and technologically advanced network in world politics. At some point, China will seek and will likely be offered membership in this over-balancing coalition as its internal economic and political reform proceeds.

In his Farewell Address in 1796, President George Washington warned Americans of the danger of "entangling alliances." Permanent alliances with one party, he averred, tended to "infuse into one the enmities of the other." Intrigues with France might get the United States into war with England, as it did later, with 40 percent greater losses for the former colonies than Britain suffered in the War of 1812.

Although President Washington did not use these terms, he strongly implied that allies of great powers may cause war by entangling major states in relatively minor conflicts. Once drawn into a dispute, great powers may find themselves in a major war. In this chapter, I have sought to show that the centrality of crucial and even nonessential allies is a powerful factor in provoking conflict between principals on both sides. This factor is not likely to be changed in the next few years and will continue to cause conflict between China and the United States in East Asia.

5

Economic Interdependence and War

Richard N. Cooper

D OES A HIGH degree of economic interdependence between countries reduce the probability of war between them? The issue has salience for this volume because the outbreak of the Great War in August 1914 followed four decades of rapidly growing economic interaction among the countries of western Europe, as well as between them and the far corners of the world. The period 1870–1913 has sometimes been called the "first globalization," which was followed a hundred years later by a second great period of globalization.

The outbreak of war in 1914 is frequently adduced as evidence that high economic interdependence does not ensure that war will not take place between the relevant countries—and so it was. Often cited in this connection is Norman Angell, to the effect that high economic interdependence and the resulting common economic interests should make war inconceivable.[1] Similar arguments are made today with respect to the modern world, particular regarding the relationship between the United States and China.

Growth of Economic Interdependence

Technological developments followed by capital investment greatly reduced both the cost and the uncertainties associated with long-distance communication and transportation in the late nineteenth century. These developments included, most notably, the telegraph and the use of steam power for locomotion both on land and at sea. The modern era can plausibly be dated from the 1860s, which saw the laying of the first successful transatlantic cable in 1866; for the first time, a message could travel much faster than a person (and the diseases the messenger might carry). London had been linked to Paris in this way fifteen years earlier. The transcontinental railway in the United States and the Suez Canal were both opened for operation in 1869, signifi-

Table 1. Merchandise Exports (percentage of gross domestic product)

	1870	1913	1973	1998
United Kingdom	12.2	17.5	14.0	25.0
France	4.9	7.8	15.2	28.7
Germany	9.5	16.1	23.8	38.9
Spain	3.8	8.1	5.0	23.5
Russia	n/a	2.9	3.8	10.6
United States	2.5	3.7	4.9	10.1
India	2.6	4.6	2.0	2.4
China	0.7	1.7	1.5	4.9
Japan	0.2	2.4	7.7	13.4
World	4.6	7.9	10.5	17.2

Source: Ronald Findlay and Kevin H. O'Rourke, "Commodity Market Integration, 1500–2000," in Michael D. Bordo, Alan M. Taylor, and Jeffrey G. Williamson, eds., *Globalization in Historical Perspective* (Chicago: University of Chicago Press, 2003), p. 41.

cantly easing transportation between Europe and Asia and between Asia and the populated east coast of the United States. The steamship greatly reduced travel times and their variability compared to sailing vessels; the travel time from Britain to New York shrank from five to seven weeks in the 1830s to a reliable two weeks in the 1870s. These developments, and soon thereafter the invention of refrigeration, resulted in a veritable explosion of trade and movements of financial capital, people, and ideas. Also, many European countries, led by Britain, reduced their duties on imports.

Table 1 presents the ratio of merchandise exports to estimated gross domestic product (GDP, a measure of the total economic output of a country for a given year) for 1870, 1913, 1973, and 1998 for nine leading countries and for the world. The table shows that trade in 1870 was more important for Britain, the world's leading trading nation, than for other countries. By 1913 the importance of trade for Britain had grown by nearly 50 percent (to more than 17 percent) and by proportionately even more for the other listed countries. Germany also showed a relatively heavy dependence on exports (as did most smaller European countries such as Belgium, the Netherlands, and Switzerland, not shown here). That dependence was notably less for France, and still less for Russia and the United States, both of which had high protective tariffs against imports (84 percent on manufactures in 1913 in

Table 2. Foreign Assets (percentage of gross domestic product)

	1914	2005
United Kingdom	92	244
France	67	174
Germany	26	99
United States	8	90
Japan	neg.	50

Sources: The percentages for 1914 are calculated from Angus Maddison, *The World Economy: A Millennial Perspective* (Paris: Organization for Economic Cooperation and Development, 2001), p. 260. The percentages for 2005 are calculated from Richard N. Cooper, "Global Imbalances: Globalization, Demography, and Sustainability," *Journal of Economic Perspectives*, Vol. 22, No. 3 (Summer 2008), pp. 93–112.

Russia, compared with 44 percent in the United States, 20 percent in France, and 0 percent in Britain). According to well-established economic analysis, such tariffs will eventually also hurt exports.[2]

The period between 1913 and 1973 witnessed two world wars and the Great Depression of the 1930s, all of which discouraged trade—partly through disruption and lower incomes, partly through the sharp increase in trade-restrictive policies, which gradually began to ease starting in the late 1940s. The importance of exports for Britain actually fell between 1913 and 1973, as it did for China, India, and Spain, all of which had introduced strong trade-restricting policies. But for the other countries listed in table 1, exports were more important economically than they had been even in 1913. This relative importance had greatly increased by the end of the century, during the next period of globalization. The only exception was India.

Table 2 offers a different measure of interdependence: the importance (again relative to GDP) of ownership of assets abroad for five leading capital-exporting countries in 1914 and in 2005. (These are gross assets, not netted against liabilities to foreigners, which also grew substantially, because much British investment, for example, was in the United States and vice versa.) By 1914 the foreign assets of Britain—by far the largest investor abroad—were already approaching GDP in magnitude. France's foreign assets, though considerably lower than Britain's, were also quite significant; much lower were those of Germany and the United States, the other largest economies. Much of this foreign investment was lost or sold during the world wars. In the second half of the twentieth century, however, foreign investment resumed on an even larger scale. By 2005 it reached more than twice GDP for Britain and nearly twice for France. It was not far short of GDP for Germany and the United States (the world's largest foreign investor in dollar value). In 2005 foreign investment represented half of the GDP of Japan, the world's second largest economy after the United States.

In addition to goods and financial capital, people began to move on a large scale in the late nineteenth century, facilitated by the greater ease and lower cost of long-distance travel, mainly from Europe to North and South America, but also within the British Empire, especially from India to many other British possessions, and from China. Gross annual emigration from Europe rose from less than 300,000 before 1865 to 700,000 in the 1880s to more than 1.2 million in the first decade of the twentieth century.[3]

Moreover, ideas—especially those involving technology—were rapidly being disseminated. The demand for railroads and steam locomotives, first developed in Britain, spread to other parts of the world. Construction was often facilitated by British investment. British and other European and increasingly American machinery involved not only facilitated trade in goods, but also introduced new techniques of production. As a consequence, national economies became increasingly tied together through multiple channels.

Rehabilitating Norman Angell

Against this background, Norman Angell wrote *The Great Illusion*. Angell was disturbed by the naval race taking place between Britain and Germany during the first decade of the twentieth century, especially the construction by both sides of huge Dreadnought-class battleships. This enterprise was vastly expensive in budgetary terms, and Angell could not see how it could possibly be useful, because war or even the threat of war could not produce greater prosperity. The book's main message was not that a high degree of economic interdependence between these two large economies would make war between them inconceivable, but rather that it would make such a war stupid (my term, not Angell's). Concretely, even the "winner" in a war between Britain and Germany would be worse off after the victory than before. In Angell's view, such an outcome would stand in sharp contrast with those of many previous wars, where the winner could plausibly expect to gain in booty or in territory. Modern economies were built on money and credit, both requiring trust and benign conditions that would be destroyed or badly damaged by war under modern conditions. In this, he was completely correct. Victorious Britain was worse off after the war, having inter alia depleted its overseas investments to pay for the war, not to mention having lost or suffered the maiming of thousands of young men. The same was true for France. Although he couched many of his arguments in general terms, Angell was specifically addressing Britain and especially Germany (as Niall Ferguson has noted), not all countries or even all European countries.[4]

Origins of the Great War

Why then did such a stupid war ever take place? Here is not the place to recount in detail the sequence of events leading to the German invasion of Belgium on August 3, 1914, or the extensive imputation of motivations, or the "domino" logic of the relationships among events. These have been examined many times, and interpretations continue to differ a century later.[5] Nonetheless, it is useful to briefly review the main events, given that over previous decades international tensions had also occasionally run high. In some cases, the result was limited war, but in the end the conflicts were "managed" diplomatically. In general, compared with earlier periods in Europe, the nineteenth century was one of peace after the defeat of Napoleon in 1815, having been managed by the Concert of Europe. To be sure, there were several wars involving the major powers: the Crimean War of 1853–54, pitting Britain, France, and Turkey against Russia; the Austrian-Prussian War of 1866; the Franco-Prussian War of 1870–71; and the Russo-Turkish War of 1877–78. All of these wars, however, were relatively brief, limited in their military engagements, and settled through negotiations. In 1879 Germany and Austria formed a five-year alliance, renewing it regularly until 1918. A newly created Italy joined in 1882, forming the Triple Alliance. In partial response, France and Russia formed an alliance in 1894. Britain maintained its distance from such formal alliances, although from time to time it was wooed by both groups. In 1912 joint British-French military planning started, creating French expectations of British support under some circumstances, without (as the British government occasionally reminded France) representing a formal commitment.

By 1900 Britain had established itself as the dominant power, a position never definitively accepted by France, which was still smarting from its defeat in 1871 and the loss of Alsace-Lorraine, as well as its rebuff at Fashoda in 1898. Britain and France viewed Germany as a rising power that posed some threat to each. In economic terms, however, the United States, safely on the other side of the Atlantic and with a tradition of self-absorption, was by 1880 larger than any of the three western European economies. But from a German and Austrian perspective (as well as among some French who viewed the development more positively as a counterweight to Germany), Russia was the rising power. Both Germany and Austria perceived Russia as a potential threat to their interests in eastern and southeastern Europe and in the Near East. Italy, Japan, and the United States were aspiring powers, joining the scramble for overseas colonies late in the century. Spain and Portugal had passed their prime. The Ottoman Empire, based in Istanbul, was considered the "sick man of Europe" and probably on the verge of collapse; and the Austro-Hungarian dual monarchy was also viewed as very fragile.

There were far fewer centers of policymaking in 1913 than there are now, roughly fifty as opposed to more than two hundred today. All of Africa, except Ethiopia, was under the effective, usually determining, influence of one or another European country. This was also true of Asia, except for Japan, China, Siam (Thailand), Persia, and Afghanistan. Even in those countries, European influence and rivalries were strong. Most of the Western Hemisphere had separated from European control, although British influence remained strong in some places. Independent countries were concentrated in Europe and the Western Hemisphere.

In the decades before 1914, European countries engaged in a variety of tense situations and conflicts. An incomplete list includes the British-German naval race; Fashoda in 1898; the Boer War in 1899–02; Morocco in 1905–06 and again in 1911; the Austrian annexation of Bosnia-Herzegovina in 1908, which represented a particular affront to Russia; Tripoli, Libya, in 1911; and two Balkan wars in 1912–13, involving Serbia, Bulgaria, Greece, Montenegro, and the Ottoman Empire. Each was brief and brought to an end by intercession of the great powers through a combination of threats and negotiation. These experiences created a climate of expectation that the European powers could manage matters well enough to keep them from spiraling out of control. Some of the powers, however, were not so sure. Germany passed an army law in July 1913 to raise the size of its peacetime army by 136,000 to 890,000 men. France followed a month later with its controversial Three Year Law, extending the term of conscripts and raising the French army to 700,000 men. And in October, Russia adopted its Great Program to raise its winter peacetime army by 800,000 men by 1917.[6]

July 1914

On June 28, 1914, Archduke Franz Ferdinand, nephew of Habsburg Emperor Franz Josef and heir to his throne, was assassinated in Sarajevo by a Bosnian Serb. The assassin was suspected of being encouraged and supported by elements of the Serbian government. In Austria a vigorous debate arose about how to respond to this provocation. Vienna received the infamous "blank check" from Berlin to deal with the affront as it thought appropriate. Hungarian Prime Minister István Tisza objected to the threat of war—a war urged by, among others, German Chief of Army Staff Franz Conrad von Hötzendorf. Eventually Tisza relented on the condition that no Serbian territory be absorbed into Austria.

From July 20 to July 23, a summit meeting was held in St. Petersburg with French President Raymond Poincaré, joined by newly installed Prime Minister and Foreign Minister René Viviani and Russian Tsar Nicholas II, accompanied by several senior officials. To avoid Franco-Russian coordination of their responses, Austria did not want to act until Poincaré was on his way by warship back to France. Germany had hoped for quick and decisive action by Austria, whatever it chose to do, but the resulting forty-eight-hour ultimatum to Serbia with hard conditions was not made until July 23 (with Poincaré and Viviani at sea), nearly four weeks after the assassination. Perhaps surprisingly, Serbia gave a generally responsive albeit ambiguous reply, clearly rejecting only one of the conditions. Austria, however, wanted to punish Serbia once and for all for its impudence and anti-Austrian behavior over the preceding five years. Immediately after receiving Serbia's reply, Austria began to mobilize its forces, declaring war on Serbia on July 28. Soon thereafter it bombarded Belgrade (which was within reach from Hungarian territory), although it was not prepared to invade until August 12.

It was understood in Russia and elsewhere that Russian mobilization of its army would be more time consuming than mobilization in Germany, Austria, or France. Russian officials ordered in succession a premobilization, a partial mobilization, and a full mobilization. The tsar canceled the full mobilization order on July 29 and then reinstated it a day later. On July 31, Austria responded with a general mobilization, and Germany declared a "state of threatening danger of war," followed by a full mobilization on August 1, when France also mobilized. Germany, influenced by Chancellor Theobald von Bethmann Hollweg's sense of legal rectitude, declared war on Russia. Germany's war plan (the Schlieffen Plan going back to 1908) entailed first hitting France hard, westward through Belgium away from the heavily fortified French-German border. Germany hoped that this swift action would force France to sue for peace early, thus permitting the German troops to move eastward to face the slowly responding Russians. In a preemptive move, Germany invaded Luxembourg on August 2, and requested Belgium to allow its troops to pass through Liège to the French border. When the Belgians (predictably) denied the request, Germany invaded on August 3 and declared war on France. This invasion tipped the balance within the neutral-leaning British cabinet toward declaring war on Germany, as Britain had been a guarantor of Belgium's neutrality and integrity since its creation in 1830. Strategically, Britain did not want Germany lodged on the banks of the Scheldt River directly opposite it. Foreign Minister Sir Edward Grey argued that without strong reaction to this German provocation, Britain's credibility (to use a contemporary term) would be questioned around the world. Germany's chief of the General Staff, Helmuth von Moltke, had insisted on the invasion of France through Belgium for technical military reasons. Moltke was driven partly by strategy but even more by the details of logistical planning—"war by timetable," as A.J.P. Taylor later called it.[7] In the words of Sean McMeekin, Moltke's action was "a political, diplomatic, strategic, and moral blunder of the first magnitude."[8]

Who then was responsible for starting the European-wide war among the major powers? Austria wanted war, but only with Serbia. Austria assumed that unambiguous German backing would keep Russia at bay. France and particularly Britain were not especially concerned—the archduke's assassination and Austria's reaction were just another set of events in the troublesome Balkans, to be managed (as in the past) with skillful diplomacy. It is also true that in July 1914 the British government was again preoccupied with the question of home rule for Ireland. Meanwhile France was preoccupied with the sensational trial of Madame Henriette Caillaux, who had been charged with killing an editor for his attacks on her husband, Joseph Caillaux, leader of the Radical Party and prospective prime minister. Caillaux had called for a less aggressive foreign policy, causing Poincaré to fear that he would reduce the size of the French army.

The Russians knew that their mobilization would provoke a German mobilization and probably lead to a major war. President Poincaré, Russia's strong ally, was conspicuously anti-German. He probably did not seek war, and he certainly wanted to avoid starting one that would alienate Britain, whose support he sought and expected. At the same time, Poincaré probably welcomed war if it started elsewhere and if he could count on Russian support, to rectify past wrongs and eliminate future threats by Germany. Thus the earliest decision for a European war was made by Russia.

Russia

In 1914 Russia was formally an absolute monarchy under Tsar Nicholas II, a weak personality but the ultimate decisionmaker on matters of foreign policy and war and peace. Russia had greatly expanded eastward in the eighteenth and nineteenth centuries, and still harbored territorial aspirations in China and Korea (challenged by Japan) and in Persia and Afghanistan (challenged by Britain). It also wanted more secure borders in Europe. It had its eye on the Carpathian Mountains, west of Austria's East Galicia, after having already absorbed Finland and much of Poland. Above all, it sought control of access to the Mediterranean and wider oceans from the Black Sea through the Bosphorus and Dardanelles. In practice, this meant controlling Istanbul. Spiritual and religious reasons lay behind this objective, not to mention economic and geopolitical ones. Russia saw itself as the "third Rome," the seat and protector of Orthodox Christianity since the fall in 1453 of Constantinople and the Byzantine Empire. Many Orthodox Christians lived under Ottoman rule and arguably were treated as second-class citizens.

Russia's experience with major domestic disturbances, including pressures for relief from absolute rule, led in 1906 to the creation of an elected legislature (Duma). Although the Duma gained some legislative powers, the tsar retained ultimate authority. Russia had also suffered a crushing defeat, both on land and at sea, by Japan in 1904–05, over which country would be dominant in Manchuria and Korea. Compared with the increasingly industrialized western Europe and North America, Russia was a relatively backward country. Its leaders, however, wanted to catch up, more to obtain power and status than to bring prosperity to their people. In the pre-1914 period, Russia was showing some success: its GDP grew at 2.4 percent a year in the period 1870–1913, slower than Germany but faster than Britain, and by an impressive 6 percent a year in 1908–13.[9] Industrialization was beginning to take hold, largely with strong government initiative and support, including high import tariffs, even higher than those in the United States at the time.[10] Russia's economy, however, was still largely self-contained and localized. A large country with poor internal transportation, it was exporting grain from Odessa primarily through the Bosphorus and importing modern equipment from western European countries through the Baltic to St. Petersburg. (An indicator of internal transportation difficulties is that it was also importing grain from high-cost Germany into northwestern Russia.) By 1913, Russian officials were feeling confident again, although some were still greatly worried about further internal disturbances.

Russians saw the main obstacles to their territorial ambitions in the west as the Austrian and Ottoman Empires, and their most serious potential adversary as Germany. Russia was mainly concerned not only about Germany's alliance but also about its strong commercial interests in the Ottoman Empire, reflected, for example, in the prospective Berlin to Baghdad railway. It relied on its alliance with France, strongly reaffirmed in the July 1914 summit, to distract and preoccupy the German army in the event of war. The Russians played skillfully on the strong residual resentment at the reparations and loss of Alsace and Lorraine in 1871, still in living memory for most French leaders.

If war occurred, Russia planned an amphibious invasion of European Turkey, near Istanbul, as well as from the Caucasus in eastern Anatolia. It also planned to invade eastern Galicia. Meanwhile the French would tie up the main German forces in the west. In sharp contrast, the French wanted Russia to attack Germany in East Prussia as soon as possible to draw significant German forces away from the western front. France made large loans to Russia in 1906 on the condition that Russia reach an armistice with Japan, permitting its troops to move west, and again in 1913 on the condition that Russia improve its railway network. The objective was to bring Russian forces into action more quickly. Indeed, capital outflows from both France and Germany (as reflected in table 2) during the pre-1914 period were often politically motivated, encouraged, and approved.[11]

Russian prospects in 1914 seemed formidable, at least to German and French leaders. Russia had a large and growing population; it was industrializing successfully; and it had plans to raise the size of its standing winter army (including conscripts) to 2 million by 1917, an army that would be better trained and better equipped than it was in 1913 and would surpass the German army in size. Above all, as Patrick McDonald has emphasized, Russia had a much stronger fiscal position than either France or Germany, thanks in part to profits from state monopolies such as the railroad and production of vodka.[12] From Germany's perspective, Russia was the rising power. At the same time, Poincaré worried that in time Russia would become less dependent on France, both strategically and financially. Thus time was not on France's side.

Russia had a more immediate concern: an amphibious invasion of Turkey would require naval predominance in the Black Sea, which Russia had in 1913. The Ottomans, however, had ordered four new Dreadnought-class battleships from abroad, including two from Britain that were scheduled for delivery in late 1914 or 1915. Under the Straits Convention of 1841, modified only slightly in the Berlin Treaty of 1878, no country, including Russia, could move warships through the Turkish Straits in peacetime. Russia therefore had to build its own warships in the Black Sea, but battleships of such quality would not be ready until 1917. Delivery of the Dreadnought warships would provide Turkish naval dominance in the Black Sea in the near future, thus foiling any sea-based attack.

Russia's interest in a European war was thus very different from that of other countries. If all went well, Russia could expect to gain economically, as well as in stature, territory, and population, from a successful war. As shown in table 1, Russia's economic engagement with other countries was much lower than that of the western European countries. Controlling the straits would increase Russian influence in the eastern Mediterranean (possibly threatening the Suez Canal, Britain's key route to India) and make foreign trade from southern Russia more secure. (The Ottomans had briefly closed the Turkish Straits to Russian commercial trade during the Balkan wars, but reopened them after international protest.) Russian incentives were thus very different from those of Britain or Germany, about which Angell was writing. (According to Nicholas Lambert, the Dardanelles campaign of 1915 was meant not only to provide strategic diversion from the western front, but even more to permit export of Russian grain, badly needed in Britain, and the transfer of British arms into Russia.)[13]

Unfortunately for Russia, not all went well. To be sure, First Lord of the Admiralty Winston Churchill diverted the two Ottoman battleships to the British navy, thus preventing their delivery to Istanbul. Early in the war, however, two German warships trying to escape British pursuit in the Mediterranean were granted refuge in Ottoman waters. The larger of the two, the *Goeben*, though not a Dreadnought, outclassed all of the Russian warships in the Black Sea. This of course compromised Ottoman neutrality in the war. In response, the Germans "sold" the two ships to Turkey, along with their German crews and commanders, who were commissioned in the Ottoman navy (with permission from Berlin). This unexpected development effectively made a Russian amphibious attack prohibitive.

Russia's main military thrust was in East Galicia, where its armies initially gained the advantage (Austria had moved many troops south to invade Serbia, wrongly guessing that Russia would not attack). But to support its French allies, Russia also invaded East Prussia with two army corps. Together they outnumbered the defending Germans. But as a result of poor communication and coordination between the Russian armies (and some antagonism between the two Russian generals), the Germans defeated both corps in the battle of Tannenberg—another event unanticipated by the Germans, who had been prepared to retreat to a more defensible line, and by the Russians.

Personalities and Public Opinion

In standard discourse, a tendency exists to personify nations and governments. But people, not countries, make decisions. Foreign and military policy in all the great powers in 1913 was made by relatively few people, albeit influenced by press commentary in all countries, even in Russia. Meanwhile the press often reflected the views of organized pressure groups and of public sentiment more generally. In Russia Tsar Nicholas II was the ultimate decisionmaker on these issues, but he was strongly influenced by Foreign Affairs Minister Sergey Sazonov and Minister of War Gen. Vladimir Sukhomlinov, as well as by other members of the cabinet. In France Poincaré was the dominant figure, even though as president he had few formal powers. Prime Minister Viviani, a mere placeholder until the trial of Madame Caillaux concluded, was inexperienced in foreign affairs. Joseph Joffre commanded the army. In Germany the erratic Kaiser Wilhelm II, often belligerent in words but shrinking from actual combat, was the highest authority, with Bethmann Hollweg as chancellor and Moltke as chief of the General Staff. In Austria Franz Josef was emperor, advised by Count Leopold von Berchtold on foreign policy with Conrad as army chief of staff. H.H. Asquith was prime minister of Britain and Grey its influential foreign minister. The cabinet participated in most key decisions.

The top military figures in Russia, Austria, and Germany had direct access to their monarchs, without necessarily going through the civilian ministers. In all three cases, not only did they have responsibility for preparing for war, but in each case, they advocated on behalf of it: Conrad with respect to Serbia, Moltke with respect to Russia (thereby taking on France), and Sukhomlinov with respect to Vienna and Istanbul. Prime ministers and foreign ministers, though generally more cautious, were gradually brought around, whether by external events or internal argument.

There were serious antiwar voices in all countries and in all governments. These voices were eventually sidelined (e.g., Prime Minister Vladimir Kokovstov in Russia) or overwhelmed by events (e.g., the assassination of Archduke Franz Ferdinand or Germany's attack on Belgium in the case of Britain).

Press commentary in 1913 was widely divergent, from chauvinistic and even xenophobic to cautionary and internationalist. Publics, however, were easily worked up by the actions of potentially hostile foreigners. Once the war started, the press and public opinion, with rare exceptions, became nationalistic and hostile to the enemy. Partial exceptions were polyglot Austria and relatively uneducated Russia, where conscription was universal but unpopular.

The consequences of the war are well known. It was much longer and much more costly in lives and resources than anyone had imagined in 1914. Four empires disappeared, and the two leading European democracies were greatly weakened. Russia experienced a revolution (with German help in transporting Vladimir Lenin from Switzerland to Finland) that introduced a communist dictatorship for the next seven decades. If leaders had forecast the actual costs, they (and even the generals) undoubtedly would have worked much harder to avoid war. Every government, however, thought not only that its approach had a chance of working in the country's perceived interests, but that it would work. Moltke was perhaps the most pessimistic, but he was also pessimistic about the alternatives and, on balance, opted for preventive war.

Conclusion

It is doubtful whether one can learn lessons from history. But if there are any to be learned, they may be the wrong ones. Consider Germany's belief in 1914 that it could drive France quickly to plead for an armistice, as it did in 1871, or that winners of wars can gain in material terms, as they often had in the past. Nevertheless, history can stimulate the imagination. It is possible, as Angell warned in 1910, and as occurred in 1914–18, that even the victor may end up much worse off than it was before the war. Russia, however, was the least interdependent of the great powers.

For most countries, including China and the United States, economic interdependence is much greater in 2014 than it was in 1914. Beyond the direct budgetary costs, war would be extremely costly for both countries. That it would be more costly to China than to the United States, because of the likely quicker recovery of the United States from the 2008–09 Great Recession, is small consolation. The governments of both countries recognize this reality.

The lesson of this chapter is to beware of third countries. Do not focus on the leading protagonists alone. Every society has vulnerabilities that skillful outside parties can exploit to engender conflicts that are objectively irrational in material terms. Who might those third countries be in the contemporary context? North Korea, Taiwan, and Iran come immediately to mind. Yet, it is also worthwhile to keep a watchful eye on others, including perhaps Japan and, yes, even Russia, which might calculate that a serious conflict between China and the United States would enhance its status in the world—something that some Russians always seem to be seeking without having to earn.

Debating the Thucydides Trap

6

The Thucydides Trap

Graham Allison

HOW SHOULD POLICYMAKERS and analysts think about relations between the United States and China in the decade ahead? Common frames include two twenty-first-century nations; two twenty-first-century great powers; an already established power and a developing one; two members of an emerging international rule-based order; a status quo power and a revisionist power; and a Group of Two or potential Group of Two. Each frame captures facets of a much more complex reality. Of the many challenges that U.S. and Chinese leaders will face over the coming decade, however, none is more illuminating than two countries' need to escape the "Thucydides Trap."

The analogy to Thucydides is a reminder of the dangers that can emerge when a rising power challenges a ruling power—as Athens did Sparta in Ancient Greece and as Germany did Britain a century ago. Most of these dangerous challenges have ended badly, often for both sides. In eleven of fifteen cases in the past five hundred years, the result was war. In cases where the parties escaped war, huge, painful adjustments in the attitudes and actions of both the challenger and the challenged were required.

Most observers believe that the chances of the United States and China finding themselves in a war that would leave both countries devastated is as unlikely as it would be unwise. The centenary of the start of World War I, however, offers a bracing reminder of humans' capacity for folly. The statement that war is "inconceivable" reflects not what is possible, but what human minds are able to conceive. In 1914 very few imagined the slaughter to come, and on such a scale that it demanded a new category: "world war." By 1918 Europe lay in ruins: the kaiser was gone; the Austro-Hungarian Empire had dissolved; the Bolsheviks had overthrown the Russian tsar; France would continue bleeding for a generation; and Great Britain was shorn of the flower of its youth and treasure. A millennium in which Europe had been the creative center of the world came to a crashing end.

To explore whether there are relevant parallels for the United States and China today, this chapter considers, among other things, what one of the key players, Chinese President Xi Jinping, has to say about the Thucydides Trap.

Xi Jinping on the Thucydides Trap

In one of the brashest statements in recent memory about China's national aspirations for the coming decade, President Xi Jinping presented his thinking to a group of international leaders at a November 2013 conference, "Understanding China," hosted by the Berggruen Institute on Governance. In the presentation, Xi remarked that "we all need to work together to avoid the Thucydides Trap—destructive tensions between an emerging power and an established power, or between established powers themselves."[1] His proposed "new form of great power relations" is meant as a direct response to that challenge.

Earlier in the same presentation, Xi addressed the question, "What are the primary goals for China?" He said, "We summarize them as two centenary goals: first, we aim to double the 2010 level of GDP [gross domestic product] per capita income and build a moderately prosperous society by 2021 when the Communist Party of China marks its one hundredth anniversary. The second goal is to turn China into an all-around modern and socially advanced country by the middle of the century when the People's Republic marks its centenary." Achievement of these goals will fulfill the "China dream" for "renewal and rejuvenation of the Chinese nation and civilization."[2] Thus, unlike most political leaders, who often take great pains to avoid being specific, Xi unambiguously laid out his aspirations for China.

China's leaders have studied the historical record of rising states and are aware of the many risks confronting them. A decade ago Xi's predecessor, Hu Jintao, addressed this topic in a study session in which the entire Politburo participated. The session, "A Historical Investigation of the Development of the World's Main Powers since the Fifteenth Century," included scholars who would later produce a Communist Party–sponsored television documentary miniseries, *The Rise of Great Powers.* Their goal was to help shape the discussion of China's rise among Chinese elites and the public. The series highlighted mistakes made by Germany, Japan, and other states as they rose to great power status and began challenging the existing order. Chinese slogans such as "hide your strength, bide your time," and "peaceful rise" reflect an awareness that achievement of China's objectives will inescapably upend the international order created by the United States.

Lee Kuan Yew on the Rise of China

In thinking about the rise of China, most policymakers and analysts approach the subject with caution—fearful of giving offense or of just being wrong.

Will China's economic growth rate continue at two or three times that of the United States, making it the largest economy in the world sometime in the next decade or two? Are China's current leaders serious about their country displacing the United States as the number one power in Asia in the foreseeable future? Will China follow in the footsteps of Germany and Japan and take its place in the international order established by the United States in the aftermath of World War II? How will China's behavior toward other countries change if China becomes the dominant power in Asia? Will China challenge the United States militarily in the next decade or two?

The best answer to all of these questions is that no one knows. Nonetheless, political leaders, investors, and members of the business community thinking about whether to go to China must, of necessity, place their bets.

So even though no one knows all of the answers to the questions above, the person who plausibly knows the most is the world's premier China watcher, Lee Kuan Yew. As Ezra Vogel's 2011 biography of Deng Xiaoping notes, the individual outside China who had the greatest impact on Deng and on China's march to the market was Lee.[3] Deng called Lee his "mentor," and every Chinese leader since Deng has consulted Lee when making critical decisions. In Xi Jinping's words, Lee is "our senior who has our respect."[4] While Lee is a great admirer of China, his first commitment is to the survival and well-being of Singapore. He has therefore watched events in China with an intense need to know. Lee has never been reluctant to express direct, even provocative views. Having recently celebrated his ninetieth birthday, he was prepared to offer especially candid answers to some tough questions.

In *Lee Kuan Yew: The Grand Master's Insights on China, the United States, and the World*, Robert Blackwill and I recorded Lee's succinct responses to the following key questions.[5]

Will China overtake the United States and become the largest economy in the world in the foreseeable future? His answer is yes. "The chances of it going wrong in China…are about one in five. I would not say zero, because their problems are weighty ones: system change, business culture change, reducing corruption, and forming new mindsets."[6] Nevertheless, his answer is a firm yes.

"Are China's leaders serious about displacing the United States as the number 1 power in Asia?" Lee replies, "Of course. Why not? They have transformed a poor society by an economic miracle to become now the second-largest economy in the world....Theirs is a culture 4,000 years old with 1.3 billion people, many of talent....How could they not aspire to be number 1 in Asia, and in time, the world?"[7]

How will China behave toward other countries as it becomes the dominant Asian power? In Lee's words: "At the core of their mindset is their world before colonization and the exploitation and humiliation that brought. In Chinese, China means 'Middle Kingdom'—recalling a world in which they were dominant in the region, other states related to them as supplicants to a superior, and vassals came to Beijing bearing tribute."[8]

Lee notes that Singapore already has to live with a dominant China. And in that world, "they expect Singaporeans to be more respectful of China as it grows more influential. They tell us that countries big or small are equal: we are not a hegemon. But when we do something they do not like, they say you have made 1.3 billion people unhappy....So please know your place."[9]

In Lee's view, China's rise will inevitably change the balance of power in Asia and the world. In contrast to Japan and Germany, however, China will not take its place within an international order led—and dominated—by the United States. As he says, "Unlike other emergent countries, China wants to be China, and accepted as such, not as an honorary member of the West."[10]

Lee notes that Americans will find this adjustment uncomfortable. But in his view, "The U.S. cannot stop China's rise. It just has to live with a bigger China, which will be completely novel for the U.S., as no country has ever been big enough to challenge its position. China will be able to do so in 20–30 years." For the world, "The size of China's displacement of the world balance is such that the world must find a new balance in 30–40 years. It is not possible to pretend that this is just another big player. This is the biggest player in the history of the world."[11]

Yet Lee does not expect China to directly challenge the United States in the foreseeable future. He notes that "in the security arena, the Chinese understand that the U.S....has built up such an advantage that direct challenges would be futile. Not until China has overtaken the U.S. in the development and application of technology can they envisage confronting the U.S. militarily." In the meantime, "its strategy is to grow within this framework, biding its time until it becomes strong enough to successfully redefine this political and economic order."[12]

Lee's judgments and forecasts may be right or they may be wrong. At a minimum, they are bracing and almost certainly closer to the mark than the judgments and forecasts of others.

Thucydides: Rise, Fear, and Entangling Alliances

In *History of the Peloponnesian War*, Thucydides wrote, "What made war inevitable was the growth of Athenian power and the fear which this caused in Sparta."[13] While others focused on an array of contributing causes, Thucydides identified the core problem: the inexorable, structural stress caused by a rapid shift in the balance of power between two rivals. Thucydides highlighted the two key drivers that, in general, create this structural dynamic: the rising power's understandable pride, sense of entitlement, and demand for greater say and sway, on the one hand, and the fear, doubt, and insecurity these stir up in the established power, on the other.

Over a half century, Athens emerged as a pinnacle of civilization. Philosophy, history, drama, architecture, and democracy all burst on the scene beyond anything previously seen. This stunning rise—and the Athenians' attendant naval power—understandably shocked Sparta as the established land power on the Peloponnese. For a rising Athens, increasing confidence, pride, and expectations that it should command greater respect were, Thucydides explained, no surprise. As Athens' power grew, so too did its awareness of past injustices, its sensitivity to instances of disrespect, and its determination to revise the hierarchy of Greek city-states to reflect new power realities. How could Athenians not be prouder, believe that their interests deserved more weight, and expect that they should have greater influence in resolving differences? At the same time, as Thucydides explained, it was natural for the Spartans to see Athenians as unreasonable, even ungrateful, given that the existing order had provided the very security in which Athens was able to flourish.

In sum, the Thucydides Trap refers to the inevitable unease that accompanies a sharp shift in the relative power of potential competitors. Under such conditions, unexpected, and what would otherwise be insignificant actions by third parties can provide a spark that leads to results that neither major competitor would have chosen. Thucydides knew of course that this was more complicated. Having identified the primary driver, he explains how this predictably leads both the established power and its rival to strengthen alliances with others. One of the oldest principles of international politics holds that the enemy of my enemy is my friend. For Sparta and Athens, this meant "thickening" links with their allies. But while tighter ties to smaller powers can add weight to an alliance, they can also produce the potential for dangerous entanglements. (It was for this reason that George Washington famously cautioned America to "beware entangling alliances.") As Thucydides explains, when Corcyra attacked Corinth, Sparta felt it necessary to come to Corinth's defense, leaving Athens little choice but to support a member of its league. Subsequently, one blunder after another produced the Peloponnesian War. After thirty years of fighting, both states were laid waste, leaving Greece vulnerable to foreign domination by Persia.

Conclusion

The reason for framing the challenge between China and the United States in Thucydidean terms is not to argue that war between them is inevitable. Rather, it is to recognize that a business-as-usual approach could lead to conflict. Preventing war will require extraordinary efforts by leaders of both countries.

For the United States, accustomed to its position as number one in the international order, China's inevitable demand to revise the status quo raises major concerns. The *Pax Pacifica*, established and enforced by the United States for seven decades since World War II, has provided an economic and security blanket to the nations of Asia—including China. It has allowed them to enjoy unprecedented peace and prosperity. Demands for change, especially through unilateral actions, not only seem ungrateful but raise alarms. Historically, when rising assertiveness becomes hubristic and fear turns to paranoia, mutual exaggeration can feed misperceptions and miscalculations. This in turn can spur unintended consequences.

In 1914 the Austro-Hungarian emperor took the assassination of Austria's Archduke Franz Ferdinand as an opportunity to reestablish his authority in Serbia. Russia felt obliged to come to the rescue of its Orthodox cousins in the Balkans. Germany supported its Austro-Hungarian ally in the hope that success in the Balkans would make it a more valuable counterbalance to the Russian-French threat. The rest is history. As Christopher Clark explains in *The Sleepwalkers*, his recent book on the origins of World War I, European leaders proceeded "watchful but unseeing, haunted by dreams, yet blind to the reality of the horror they were about to bring into the world."[14]

Mark Twain observed that history never repeats itself, but it does sometimes rhyme. True, 2014 is not 1914. Nevertheless, consider that the U.S. government has told the Chinese and Japanese governments that Article 5 of the U.S.-Japan Mutual Defense Assistance Agreement applies to the Senkaku Islands. So when an out-of-control Chinese or Japanese pilot or captain is showing off and downs a plane or sinks a ship, then what? As sinologist and former Australian Prime Minister Kevin Rudd has noted, Northeast Asia is more fractious and dangerous now than at any time since the fall of Saigon.

Is it possible to sketch a scenario in which the major players sleepwalk into war? Fortunately, not with any ease. There could of course be a situation in or over the South or East China Seas in which U.S. and Chinese warships or aircraft collide. Recall the 2001 incident in which a hot-rodding Chinese pilot collided with a U.S. spy plane, forcing it to make an emergency landing on Hainan Island. Tense moments ensued, but both governments contained themselves and the crisis was resolved. Recently a Chinese ship in the South China Sea cut one hundred yards in front of a U.S. cruiser. Had the U.S. ship not stopped, the two would have collided. Although playing Chicken with military ships and aircraft is foolish, both the United States and China have examined these possibilities so thoroughly in war games that it is reasonable to expect cool heads to prevail before matters take a dangerous turn.

Another scenario that could spark a war in the coming years resembles China's recent unilateral declaration of an "air identification zone" over disputed islands in the East China Sea. Imagine a similar move triggering an escalatory response from Japan, leading to the downing of a plane or sinking of a ship with scores of casualties. A process of retaliatory risk taking could eventually result in a small conflict between Japan and China at sea in which dozens of ships and planes are destroyed. Expecting the U.S. Navy and Air Force to stand with it, Japan could adopt a tit-for-tat strategy with the expectation that China would ultimately back down, certain that with assistance from the U.S. military Japan would have a decisive advantage.

Could such a scenario play out in the future? If Thucydides were alive today, he would note a certain symmetry with flash points in the past. My bet, however, is that such a scenario will almost certainly not materialize. Still, a note of caution is warranted. The awareness of President Barack Obama and President Xi Jinping that war would be folly for both the United States and China is relevant but not dispositive. None of the leaders in Europe of 1914 would have chosen the war they got and that, in the end, they all lost. Indeed, knowledge of their century-old mistakes offers a vivid reminder of the perils of complacency today.

To avoid this fate, American and Chinese leaders will have to open their minds to appreciate in grander historical terms the magnitude of the challenge before them. Both the U.S. and Chinese governments must think creatively in deciding how to deal with the other. Even tougher, both will have to lead their societies in making substantial, painful adjustments of attitudes and actions if they are to capitalize on what has the potential to be a hugely beneficial relationship.

7

Thucydides Dethroned

Historical Differences That Weaken the Peloponnesian Analogy

David K. Richards

THE THUCYDIDES TRAP is a concept derived from the assertion of the Greek historian Thucydides that the rise of Athens and the fear it created among Spartans made the Peloponnesian War inevitable. The idea of a "trap" leading inevitably to war has been applied to the rise of Germany, prior to the outbreak of World War I in 1914, which posed a threat to the existing hegemon, Great Britain. It is a useful frame for thought and discussion. Both the rise of Athens and the rise of Germany were followed by devastating wars lasting longer than most expected. These wars were preceded by the ascension of a new power and the relative decline of the established power. One hundred years after the start of World War I, a reexamination of the historical record is certainly warranted, if only to illuminate the differences between then and now that may be overlooked.

The Calculus for War in the Twenty-First Century

Scholars and other analysts have used the concept of the Thucydides Trap to frame discussions about the prospects of maintaining peace between the United States and China in the years ahead, as China inexorably gains economic power and influence. At the 2014 Davos World Economic Forum, Japan's prime minister, Shinzo Abe, told the audience that recent tensions between Japan and China were similar to those that characterized the competition between Britain and Germany prior to World War I. He went on to say that although Britain and Germany enjoyed good trade relations, as do China and Japan today, this was not enough to overcome their strategic rivalry. His rhetoric, which echoed the concept of the Thucydides Trap, engendered an angry response from Beijing. Although spokesmen for both Japan and China vowed that their countries did not want war, anxieties about a potential conflict have escalated among many business, financial, and political observers.

A comparison of the current economic and military rivalries between China and the United States—or between China and Japan, an important U.S. ally—with those that prevailed in ancient Greece and pre-1914 Europe reveals several important differences that weaken the force of the Thucydidean analogy. First is the existence of nuclear deterrence; second is the West's open world trading system. The first eliminates any prospect of profitable gain from war, which existed in the minds of the leaders of ancient Greece and late nineteenth-century Europe; the second removes the competitive trade tensions that were a dominant characteristic of both earlier periods. A third difference is that civilians make up the current leadership in the United States, Japan, and China, having reached their positions by demonstrated experience and ability. In addition, political power is dispersed among cabinet committees, parliaments, and courts. In both ancient Greece and pre-1914 Europe, power was concentrated in the hands of a class of aristocratic landowners committed to honoring a long-standing military tradition. In ancient Greece, leaders gained their positions of influence and power primarily through a combination of demonstrated ability and military success. In contrast, the monarchs of Austria, Russia, and Germany were hereditary, autocratic military commanders in chief who lacked successful leadership experience in war.

In the twenty-first century, the rules of the international relations game differ tremendously from those of ancient Greece, or even those of pre-1914 Europe. For example, today nuclear weapons influence the calculus of war by curbing aggressive instincts and belligerent rhetoric. The awesome destructive power of atomic weapons has already been demonstrated, and it is obvious to all of the world's political leaders that there can be no winners or "profits" in a nuclear war, only losers trying to cope in an irradiated world. The task of leaders is to prevent nuclear war, to avoid mistakes, to monitor control over the weapons, and to settle all disputes peacefully. The growth of China's economic power, regardless of how the size of the Chinese economy may compare with that of the United States, or how large China's defense budget is, will not change this equation.

The strategic uncertainties arising from advances in new forms of nonnuclear weaponry, misleadingly termed "unconventional," will not change this twenty-first-century calculus. Unlike the ancient Greek world or pre-1914 Europe, the advance of military technology is difficult to monitor and impossible to confidently predict. For example, it was much easier for spies to follow the construction of Dreadnought-class battleships than it is for analysts to monitor advances in cyberwarfare. Increases in military budget levels are not clear indicators of the rapidity of technological advance or of increasing military capabilities. Neither China nor the United States can be certain of the other side's capabilities to compromise its command and control functions. Nor can they assume that the capabilities of ships, missiles, planes, and other military assets will remain uncompromised by cyberwarfare under combat conditions. The strategic uncertainties of rapid technological change may even be an added deterrent to nonnuclear conflict between the United States and China.

Another significant difference is that the opportunity for great powers to gain control, at little cost, of potentially profitable territory, such as Kuwaiti or Iraqi oil fields, is over. The era of opportunity peaked in the three or four decades of empire building prior to 1914. Success depended on a large technological advantage in weaponry over the local population or dominant, well-disciplined conscript armies, or both. The end was made clear by the stalemate war of 1914–18, and demonstrated once again in World War II and Vietnam. Although territorial domination might seem possible today, the recent experience of the United States in Iraq and Afghanistan has shown the difficulties of such an endeavor. Through appeals to the Russian population, however, President Vladimir Putin was able annex Crimea.

Furthermore, there is little point in wars of conquest in a world where trading systems are open for nearly all basic commodities and most goods and services, except for military goods, some agricultural products, and the movement of labor. Since World War II, the United States has opened its home markets to Germany, Japan, numerous developing countries, and finally China, even at notable cost to U.S. producers and their employees. The benefits have been garnered by American consumers; global living standards have risen; and no wars have occurred between large countries. When the advocates of protectionism can be held at bay, the world is a much safer place. Trade protectionism was endemic in ancient Greece, and it was reintroduced in the late nineteenth century in all countries, including the United States. The one exception was Britain, and even Britain introduced Imperial Preferences with its colonies and with Canada and South Africa.

In sum, the twenty-first-century calculus of war, though not perfect, is much more stable than it was in ancient Greece or pre-1914 Europe.

The Inevitability of War: Athens, Sparta, and Persia

In fourth-century B.C.E. Greece, war was, if not continual, almost an annual occurrence. The political and economic dynamics of ancient Greece were fundamentally unstable and considered as such by those then living. Thucydides' idea that war was inevitable was not terribly profound. The risk-reward calculus supported the logic of nearly continuous war. On the plus side, there was obvious profit in wars of conquest and control of territory—additional colonies, farmland, natural resources, slaves, taxes, and tribute. On the other hand, to be conquered meant almost certain loss of property, power, and life—or possible enslavement. With each generation, aggressive and ambitious new leaders emerged in Athens, Sparta, and Persia, as well in many smaller communities, who were fearful of the catastrophic prospect of enslavement but saw opportunity in war; they were willing to incur the obvious risks of combat to win the outsized gains of victory—political power, material riches, even heroic renown.

The rhetoric of Greek leaders supported this logic of war. Pericles proclaimed in a speech at the start of the second Peloponnesian War, "All who have taken it upon themselves to rule over others have incurred hatred and unpopularity for a time; but if one has a great aim to pursue, this burden of envy must be accepted, and it is wise to accept it. Hatred does not last for long, but the brilliance of the present is the glory of the future stored up for ever in the memory of man."[1]

In 500 B.C.E., Persia was by far the largest military power; it controlled the Mediterranean coastline from Egypt to Macedonia. The Greeks fought repeatedly with the Persians for control of the islands and coasts of the Aegean Sea and the eastern Mediterranean. In 498 B.C.E., the Athenians sent several triremes in support of a rebellion against the Persians by the Ionian Greeks; they attacked and burned the provincial Persian capital of Sardis. The Persians struck back with three unsuccessful invasions of Greece, which included the famous Greek army victory at Marathon in 490 B.C.E. and naval victory of 480 B.C.E. at Salamis.

After these victories, the Athenians formed the Delian League, and the Spartans established a similar league of allied cities and colonies to defend against the likelihood of subsequent Persian invasions and make raids on Persian-controlled areas. In addition to being defense networks, these leagues were closed trading networks and their members mutually antagonistic; there was pressure to expand each network of loyal colonies to maximize the trading gains as well as the military strength of a large network. Members of the Delian League were required to pay tribute to Athens in the form of men, triremes, or cash. Those who refused to pay or preferred to remain neutral toward both leagues were punished by blockade, invasion, and conquest.

Conflict began between the Athenian- and Spartan-led leagues, even while hostilities continued with the Persians. The first Peloponnesian War lasted thirteen years, ended by a thirty-year peace that in fact held for only thirteen years. War may not have been constant, but it was not difficult to forecast that any period of peace was likely to be short-lived. Because of the fundamentally unstable nature of the system of trade and defense, Thucydides' prediction that war was "inevitable" was not a difficult call.

World War I: Weak Monarchs and Changing Times

Debates about the causes of World War I have been ongoing for a century. Several extensive, well-researched accounts of the years leading up to 1914 have recently been published, and the most common conclusion is that Germany was not solely to blame, as was once widely believed. That earlier consensus of political opinion—that Germany was at fault—resulted in the misguided demand for German reparations at the 1919 Paris Peace Conference, which John Maynard Keynes brilliantly illuminated in *The Economic Consequences of the Peace*. Adolf Hitler's speeches repeatedly justified war as the rightful means of rectifying the humiliating wrong done to the German people by the Treaty of Versailles.

The task here is not to counter this consensus, but to delineate some of the details of pre-1914 Europe that created the instability that led to war five weeks after Habsburg Archduke Franz Ferdinand was assassinated in Sarajevo, a provincial capital in the Balkans. The first factor is that the economic power, prestige, and leadership abilities of the hereditary monarchies were weak. The wealth of landed aristocrats and the autocratic rulers of Austria, Russia, and even Germany was under severe economic pressure from the sharp decline in grain prices that started in the 1870s. The long-standing foundations of their military prestige and power—land, horses, and wagons—were becoming obsolete, both economically and strategically, replaced by two new industrial capabilities: cheap ocean transport by steamship and rapid troop transport by rail. The legitimacy of the monarch's power was also being undermined by agitation for greater democratic freedom and ethnic independence. The multilinguistic Habsburg Empire lived in fear of possible dismemberment. Tsar Nicholas II of Russia had put down a revolution in 1905 but remained, despite some token adjustments, an atavistic autocrat in the opinion of most Russians (and most Europeans). Monarchs, including in Germany where the parliament had no control over the military budget, turned to their military leaders for policy advice on how to best govern in the new conditions; they received traditional military solutions, including wars of conquest, usually outside Europe.

Russia, upon completion of the trans-Siberian railroad, attempted to carve out a piece of Manchuria, but was confronted and defeated by Japan in 1904–05. Germany challenged France with gunboat diplomacy in Morocco in 1906, but its attempts to isolate Britain from France at the Algeciras Conference failed; in 1907, the Entente Cordiale united Britain, France, and Russia in a defense pact against the Central Powers. The French wished to be positioned to possibly reverse the 1871 loss of Alsace and Lorraine; the Russians wanted to carve up the Austro-Hungarian Empire; the British wanted land support to help counter the German naval buildup. The German public was enraged by this "encirclement"; Kaiser Wilhelm II and Adm. Alfred von Tirpitz turned naval strategy away from building surface ships toward submarines and torpedoes. In 1908 Austria formally annexed Bosnia, which it had administered since 1878, after the Ottomans were driven out; Austria's action irritated the Balkan Slavs and touched off a crisis with Russia that was averted by a German threat to back Austria.

A common query runs through many of the attempts to explain the start of World War I: Why did political leaders decide to wage war in 1914, even while they seemed reluctant and hoped that war could be avoided? The Austrians delayed their attack to "put Serbia in its place" for several weeks after the assassination of the archduke; the German and Russian sovereigns, who were cousins, exchanged telegrams in a last-minute attempt to avoid war. There was a sense that the European leaders were somehow trapped into acting against their will, pressured by the beliefs and expectations of those around them.

Hesitation came from the monarchs, however, not their military advisers. It was the inability of the hereditary monarchs of Austria, Russia, and Germany to say no to war, to stand down their war planners, that is most striking in the five weeks after the June 28 assassination that preceded the start of the war on August 1. Nominally the monarchs were in control, but they lacked the conviction and courage to do anything other than follow the traditional military playbook of how great powers were supposed to behave.[2]

Each country considered itself—and was told by others that indeed it was—a great power. Each acted in accordance with what great powers were traditionally expected to do, which was to resolve conflicts by threatening military confrontation or by going to war. To back up its threats, to bolster its security, and to underpin its status as a great power, each European power (except Britain, which relied on naval supremacy) maintained a standing conscription army of at least one million men, backed up with large reserves, readied for attack. It was universally accepted military doctrine that decisive advantage went to the first to mobilize and send troops quickly by train to the frontier to go on the offensive.[3] Delay risked loss of territory, at a minimum, and possible quick defeat, in a few weeks, as France had suffered in 1870.

In July 1914, even though many thought war was likely—some even thought inevitable—few believed war, particularly a long war, was imminent. A British battle fleet paid a friendly visit to Kiel that July, and Kaiser Wilhelm cruised around the Norwegian fjords. *The Sleepwalkers,* the title of one recent book on the period, seems very apt.[4]

> The sense of security more often springs from habit than from conviction, and for this reason it often subsists after such a change in the conditions as might have been expected to suggest alarm. The lapse of time during which a given event has not happened is, in this logic of habit constantly alleged as the reason why the event should never happen, even when the lapse of time is precisely the added condition which makes the event iminent.
> —George Eliot, *Silas Marner*

No war between the great powers of Europe had occurred since the Franco-Prussian War of 1870–71, and no long war had occurred since the time of Napoleon. Yet new circumstances, particularly the extensive growth of rail networks, made the habitual military strategy of brinkmanship very dangerous. Railroads allowed large troop movements to the frontiers in a matter of days rather than weeks, as had been the case with horse and wagon. Rapid railway troop movement obliterated time that in the past might have been used to try to diffuse the crisis with a diplomatic pause. Railway wagons, unlike horse-drawn wagons, did not need to stop to catch their breath. Once mobilization had been ordered, there was no longer time for a diplomatic pause, a conference, to try to diffuse a crisis.

Railroads, if scheduled with precision, could move vast numbers of troops and munitions to the frontier where they could go on the offensive with overwhelming strength—unless the other country had also mobilized quickly and had moved sufficient forces to counter the offensive. The logic of this strategy of offensive attack with overwhelming strength implied that the rapid troop movements could not be stopped without risking quick defeat—if the other side, meanwhile, had moved its own troops to the frontier and gone on the offensive. In other words, mobilization meant that war was inevitable. At the same time, any offensive into enemy territory could easily get bogged down ten or twenty miles beyond the reach of its own rail logistical support. Meanwhile the defense could quickly reinforce, with its own rail network, against any chosen point of attack. Unless overwhelming force gained decisive victory, stalemate and a long war was likely. Thus the urgency of the military leadership of each of the great powers and the logic of German Chancellor Helmuth von Moltke's argument to the kaiser: if Russia mobilized, then its ally France would mobilize; therefore France must be attacked, and attacked in strength. To not follow the train schedules in the Schlieffen Plan meant defeat.

In 1914 Austria, the weakest of the atavistic monarchies of Europe, chose war on Serbia as a way to quash Serbian nationalists, as well as to punish Serbia for the assassination of the archduke. Germany gave a "blank check" of support to Austria because their monarchical interests seemed threatened by the assassination in Sarajevo. Russia, particularly the Russian military, its status still tarnished after its defeat by Japan, chose to mobilize to back the Orthodox Slavs of Serbia; it was a matter of Slavic unity and honor, as well as a necessity to restore Russia's military standing. When Russia mobilized, France and Germany were compelled to mobilize as a defensive measure. Each sovereign made these decisions at the urging of their top generals. Each leader was reluctant to take the fateful step, but each did. They had allowed the military planners to take control.

Leaders are not free to make decisions on their own. They are hemmed in by the influence of constituents, by prevailing public opinion, by the demands and expectations of others. This power of prevailing opinions and expectations was recognized in the time of Thucydides and guided the leadership of ancient Greece. As Pericles told the Athenians: "A spirit of reverence pervades our public acts; we are prevented from doing wrong by respect for the authorities and for the laws, having a particular regard to those which are ordained for the protection of the injured as well as those unwritten laws which bring upon the transgressor of them the reprobation of the general sentiment."[5]

Old, habitual ways and the aristocratic codes of conduct appropriate for those leading great powers ruled the monarchical war ministries of Europe. The legitimacy of this status-conscious, isolated, close-knit, often family-related group of leaders was threatened by demands for democracy and ethnic nationalism. Meanwhile landed agricultural wealth had suffered a dramatic fall in the years after 1873, when railroads and steamships enabled wheat from the American Midwest to drive down European wheat prices by 50 percent. Faced with these new, uncertain conditions, the monarchs turned to the traditional playbook of military brinkmanship, a playbook, it could be argued, that had resulted in relatively short wars that had won territory for Prussia from Denmark in 1864, Austria in 1866, and France in 1870 and had averted, via diplomacy, several crises in the two decades prior to 1914. Because railroads had been incorporated into military strategy, however, the playbook had become very dangerous. There was no longer time for a diplomatic pause, just as there is no time today if one launches a nuclear attack.

It was not simply the rise of Germany and the fear of Great Britain that made World War I inevitable, as the Thucydides Trap argument implies. What was inevitable was that autocratic governance in Russia, Austria, and Germany would have to adjust to changing conditions—industrial growth, demands for democracy, and ethnic nationalism—or be swept aside. Stronger leadership could have adjusted to the new conditions; stronger sovereigns might have said no to the generals when they urged mobilization. But the hereditary monarchs of pre-1914 Europe—who also were military commanders in chief—lacked experience in war and deferred to their generals in matters of strategy. World War I was not just Germany's fault. Europe had a faulty atavistic system of hereditary governance bound for failure.

Conclusion

Contemporary governance is much more stable than in the past. Leaders have gained power through demonstrated ability and judgment, not hereditary right. All recognize that nuclear war must be avoided, that tensions must be dampened and disputes settled peacefully. The greatest danger is the possibility that the leaders of future generations may not embody the abilities, judgment, and attitudes of the leaders of today. Nuclear weapons, the restrictions of the world economy, and intelligent democratic leadership all suggest a progressive movement beyond the confines of the Thucydides Trap.

8

Thucydides, Alliance Politics, and Great Power Conflict

Charles S. Maier

U NFORTUNATELY, GOOD HISTORY does not yield simple lessons. Still, there are analogies from the past that policymakers and students of international relations might derive as they contemplate contemporary Chinese-U.S. relations. The purpose, of course, is to avoid Chinese-American conflict, above all military conflict. The centenary of World War I is a reminder that disastrous confrontations can arise even if no party wants one. Indeed, there is a compelling fascination with great wars that seem "inevitable," whether from the ancient world or the recent past.

To a degree, "inevitability" is an optical illusion, because history is written about the wars that did take place and less about those that were avoided. The history of the Cold War occupies a middle ground: a long ideological and strategic struggle between global systems that seemed close to full-scale war many times, but in which participants avoided the worst. Most observers hope that scholars and others will be able to write the history of the great war that did not place; even better would be a history of great power relations that never yielded the same degree of tension that the Cold War did. The Cold War is a story of crossing a large lake on very thin ice. It would be wise not to test the ice in a similar way in the decades to come. One never knows in advance, however, whether it may be just too thin—as it was in 1914.

Some wars occur because of outright aggression. It eventually became clear that Adolf Hitler's demands in eastern Europe would lead to war (if not infinite appeasement); so, too, Japan's invasion of China in 1937 (if not the takeover of Manchuria in 1931). Even more interesting, however, is why wars arise when neither side seems to want control of additional territory. The puzzling cases are those in which one side or the others feels so insecure that it initiates an escalation or attacks preemptively because it fears the consequences of inaction.

Two explanatory models are relevant to this narrative; they do not preclude each other, but come into relevance at different levels of abstraction. At a high level of abstraction is the "Thucydides Trap," as laid out by Graham Allison.[1] Here, strong states are resisted by their neighbors. A second model is grounded in the logic of alliances. In a historical reconstruction, the analyst must dig deep to understand the intractable move toward war. The remote view elegantly summarizes the reasons for conflict, but provides insufficient insight into the process of escalation. And while this view suggests tragic inevitability, it is the closer view that reveals the choices that existed and how they were sequentially foreclosed.

The Thucydidean Model

Thucydides wrote, "But the real reason for war is, in my opinion, most likely to be disguised by such an argument. What made the war inevitable was the growth of Athenian power and the fear which this caused in Sparta."[2] This is the situation that Robert Gilpin refers to as a "hegemonic war": a terrible conflict that often attends the transition of great power hegemony, as one power feels it is waning and another is rising.[3] Examples are numerous: Rome and Carthage in the third century B.C.E., Persia and the Ottomans in the sixteenth century; Habsburg Catholics and Protestant princes from the Reformation through the Thirty Years' War; the Catholic Habsburgs and Catholic French in the later seventeenth century and eighteenth century; and Britain and France from 1756 through 1815.

A modern example of the Thucydides Trap that comes most readily to mind is the Anglo-German antagonism at the end of the nineteenth century, as Great Britain—hitherto secure as the organizer of a maritime empire and unaligned among the continental states—felt threatened by the rising power of Germany, which was not only becoming its equal or superior in industrial terms, but setting out to build a battle fleet that seemed to have no purpose other than to challenge Britain's. In response, Britain abandoned its "splendid isolation" and committed itself to a series of agreements, which even if not formal alliances limited its freedom of action in any crisis. Moreover, these commitments—the Anglo-Japanese alliance of 1902, the Entente Cordiale of 1904, and the Anglo-Russian understanding of 1907— aligned Britain with countries, in the case of France and certainly Russia, that had often been seen as its earlier rivals.

The poignancy of this situation arises from the circumstance that there was no way to allay British suspicions or, conversely, to remove the conviction among many in German ruling-class circles that Britain was seeking to block the German rise to parity, that indeed London was "encircling" Germany with alliances. Each power's response only aggravated the perception of its counterpart that the other state wanted to undermine its own security and global position. Accompanying this perception had to be the belief that the vulnerability of each power would only increase, that any change in the balance of forces and alignments must weaken it—therefore that there was an argument for preemption or at least facing up to war in any particular crisis rather than waiting for a future clash when it would be weaker.

Still, the perceptions of the two sides were not identical. British policy circles might well have believed that Britain was doomed to second-rate status if Germany continued its naval expansion. Germany, however, did not see Britain as an existential threat until war was under way. Rather, German policymakers feared an escalatory trend that would ultimately undermine Germany's continental security, namely, the growing combined strength of France and Russia. The French increased their manpower through a three-year service law. And by 1910, the Russians were recovering from their defeat in the Russo-Japanese War of 1904–05, continuing to industrialize, and enhancing their logistical agility by building railroads (thus undermining German plans for coping with a two-front attack). British forces were thought to be largely irrelevant for that decisive clash on land.

Thus World War I was not the culminating episode of Anglo-German antagonism, as British historiography would suggest. Rather, the war between Britain and Germany was a consequence of Germany and Russia going to war and France being immediately pulled in. The direct sources of friction between London and Berlin were being resolved. The Germans had largely accepted that they could not wrest hegemony or even parity in surface ships from the British. The problem that the German General Staff and many among the civilian leaders thought truly dangerous was the growth of Russian power. If Germany was Britain's naval nightmare, Russia was Germany's army nightmare—largely because the modernization of Russian railroads upset the calculus of relative Russian immobility on which the German two-front strategy (defensive or preemptive) had depended. Ultimately it was the German fear of Russian continental power and the possibility that Balkan instability might drag Russia into war against Berlin's Habsburg ally that made the situation so dangerous. In effect, Germany and Britain had different nightmares of decline, but Germany's led more directly to the war that resulted. The conflict between Britain and

Germany and the ultimate intervention of the United States decided the second half of the war, when naval power and blockade and a fresh infusion of troops for the fighting of 1918 became important. It was crucial for the outcome of the war, not to its origins.

Similarly, two and a half millennia earlier, Athens did not fear Spartan power directly. Still, both Athens and Britain had alliance commitments or (were goaded into such arrangements) that led them to wager on force to avoid their allies' defeat. War resulted because each decided it had to protect a lesser power. To be sure, the implications of this analysis are pessimistic. First, the "true" intentions of either Germany or Britain, or Sparta or Athens, were irrelevant. Implicitly, any change in the balance of power or the "corollary of forces" must have appeared threatening to both sides.

Second, it is unhelpful to talk about "misperceptions" as a cause of conflict. The perceptions that arose were not unilateral conclusions that were panicky or depended on analyzing the other side's intentions; they arose from the geometry of the overall situation. This observation does not mean that either the Peloponnesian War or World War I was inevitable. But to avert escalation, one or both sides would have had to signal that it was prepared to accept a compromise, a step made far more difficult when allies are involved.

Third, military modernization presents particular difficulties. What one side sees as a necessary upgrading of forces (even if not an expansion) must appear to the other as a significant danger. It often raises the threat of a decisive defeat at the opening of a war, thus serving as an added goad to preemption.

Fourth, it is therefore difficult to describe or to accept any equilibrium of forces as stable. Most seem momentary and elusive and likely to become disadvantageous from the perspective of each side.

This combination of factors made up the case for the arms races, on land and at sea, that preceded 1914. It was also the situation at decisive moments in the nuclear arms race, such as the crisis over medium-range missiles at the beginning of the 1980s. It takes courageous leadership to persuade any country's hawks that military equilibrium is possible.

None of the analyses above implies that the wars that were unleashed arose from the pessimistic logic that seemed to prevail. Even World War I might have been avoided, if the wisdom to do so had been at hand. The Serbian circles that supplied the Black Hand could not have cared less about the systemic consequences of their assistance to assassins. The French had long goaded the Russians to firmness. The Austrian chief of the General Staff was prey to fatalism about the Russian danger. The Germans did not think about the consequences of encouraging the Austrians, and their generals were fearful of the Russians. The British did not feel they were in a position to make clear the consequences of German war in the west, and so on. Still, the Balkans crises of 1912–13 had been overcome.

These facts do not mean that the Thucydides Trap was irrelevant: it describes a framework for potential conflict that was highly threatening for peace—and awareness of its logic probably contributed to its potential for emerging. Another logic, however, was also at stake, as Thucydides' own detailed account makes clear.

"Entangling Alliances"

When Thucydides referred to Sparta's fear of Athens as the real cause of the Peloponnesian War, he used the concept of cause differently from when describing the lead-up to war. Historians like to fall back on expressions such as "underlying causes," "ultimate causes," or, in Pierre Renouvin's famous phrase, *causes profondes*. These expressions, however, do not describe the incremental wagers on escalation that lead to the brink of war and beyond. They suggest a foundational trend—whether military and diplomatic, or economic, or intellectual and cultural—that, in retrospect, seems to frame the larger interval of time. The terms amount to saying that from a remote perspective certain characteristics of the situation came to prevail: "real cause" or "underlying cause" is another way of saying "persisting variable." It describes encompassing a temporal perspective more than the sequential triggering of responses.

Thus, when Thucydides explains the coming of war, he dwells on the fateful role of multiple actors (even within a bipolar framework). His war arose out of entangling alliances brought into play by the conflict of Corcyra and Corinth. Thucydides describes that background in considerable detail in the first book of his history. Even more generally, the buildup to the war, which occurred over a generation, was marked by incidents of allied compellence— preventing or punishing defections, sometimes with the most brutal methods. Thucydides might well have concluded that the real cause of the war was less mutual fear of Athens and Sparta than each hegemon's belief that discipline among its allies was the overriding test of its viability. Further, such discipline in the Hellenic world meant the preservation of a reliable domestic regime— oligarchic in the case of Sparta, democratic in the case of Athens. Security required not just hegemony but imperium, the right to command and the right to have politically friendly forces in power. (This, too, was the situation in the Cold War from 1948 until 1989.)

Immediately following his preface, Thucydides launches into a discussion of "entangling alliances," which formed the substance of his story of the origins of the war. The debates at Corinth, Athens, Sparta, and elsewhere reveal all of the policy dilemmas confronting great powers: the Epidamnians appeal to their mother city, Corinth, when they are attacked by the Corcyreans; the Corcyreans enlist the aid of Athens, allegedly for defense only against the Corinthians. The Corinthians lose a naval battle and find the buffer city of Potidea besieged (think Belgium) and appeal to Sparta, chiding the Spartans for their long inaction in the face of the rising Athenian empire:

> ...It was you who in the first place allowed the Athenians to fortify their city and build the Long Walls after the Persian War. Since then and up to the present day you have withheld freedom not only from those who have been enslaved by Athens but even from your own allies. When one is deprived of one's liberty one is right in blaming not so much the man who puts the fetters on as the one who had the power to prevent him, but did not use it—especially when such a one rejoices in the glorious reputation of having been the liberator of Hellas.
>
> ...As for the Athenians, we know their methods and how they gradually encroach upon their neighbors. Now they are proceeding slowly because they think that your insensitiveness to the situation enables them to go on their way unnoticed; you will find that they will develop their full strength once they realize that you do see what is happening and are still doing nothing to prevent it.
>
> You Spartans are the only people in Hellas who wait calmly on events, relying for your defence not on action but on making people think that you will act. You alone do nothing in the early stages to prevent an enemy's expansion; you wait until your enemy has doubled his strength. Certainly, you used to have the reputation of being safe and sure enough: now one wonders whether this reputation was deserved....[4]

Thucydides further exposed the ruthless difficulties of alliance politics in the speeches that Athenians and Melians deliver in their famous dialogue. To allow defections from an alliance would be to encourage other defections. To apply a politics of terror, as Athens increasingly resorted to, would be to risk an even wider collapse of associates.[5]

Alliance politics were also crucial in 1914. The German Crown Council decided on July 6 that it must show support for Austria, not envisaging that the Austrians would use their blank check, which Kaiser Wilhelm II gave to the Austrians on July 5 to force a war against Serbia. By the time the consequences of this recklessness had become clear in the last days of July, Berlin would have to tell its ally that it would be on its own if the Russians intervened. Yet, it was not prepared to take this step, especially because its leaders by this point were convinced that a conflict with Russia was inevitable at some point and the odds would become increasingly adverse. Britain faced the same dilemma vis-à-vis France. If London did not rush to assist Paris at the end of July, then all of the agreements concluded during the past decade would be undone. So, too, if Paris did not support St. Petersburg, the Russians might give way as they had in 1909, when Berlin insisted they accept the Habsburg annexation of Bosnia.

The same pressures are endemic in many alliances. Consider the relationship of Britain and France in the 1920s, and especially between 1936 and 1939, as Arnold Wolfers starkly explained many years ago.[6] By accepting the occupation of the Rhineland in 1936, France had suggested to its eastern allies that its system of alliances had no teeth. The 1938 Munich agreement only aggravated that signal—a conclusion Moscow drew a year later when it agreed to a nonaggression pact with Germany. Faced in March 1939 with Hitler's annexation of Bohemia-Moravia and the dismemberment of Czechoslovakia, Britain and France extended far more ironclad guarantees to Romania and Poland. Thus, no matter the hegemonic reach of adversarial powers, they face excruciating choices because of alliance politics. They must always decide whether danger is greater by supporting an ally (especially a weaker ally), even when it behaves irresponsibly—as Austria-Hungary did in 1914—or by abandoning it.

None of this means that stronger powers cannot escape being held hostage by their lesser partners. In the autumn of 1938, Edvard Beneš could probably have forced France into a war with Germany by refusing to accept Hitler's demands for cession of the Sudentenland. But France feared loss of its ally in the West, Great Britain, and together the two powers pressured Beneš into accepting the deal. It hardly brought "peace in our time," but it did avoid general war for a year—whether wisely or not is not the issue here. More recently, the United States has been unwilling to let Israel block negotiations with Iran on the nuclear issue.

World War I appeared virtually inevitable in retrospect, and indeed it would have been difficult to avert after so many preceding crises—Morocco in 1905; Bosnia in 1908–09; Morocco again in 1911; and the Ottoman collapses of 1911, 1912, and 1913. Nonetheless, had Russia contented itself with a general threat against Austria's war against Serbia instead of partial mobilization, had France earlier cautioned Russia, had Germany been willing to threaten Vienna with a withdrawal of support, had Britain been willing and able to acknowledge its entanglement with France, then war might have been avoided. Here is the excruciating dilemma: alliances are effective deterrents only when there is no hint of defection, but if they no longer deter, defection is required to avoid a conflict. The costs of war may be acceptable or not—something knowable only in retrospect.

Conclusion

Today the role of alliance links seems most applicable in the Middle East and the western Pacific. Their huge relevance to current Chinese-American relations needs no belaboring. The United States supports a whole structure of formal and less formal commitments to the security of the states in the western Pacific. Their proximity to China means that Beijing perceives an asymmetry of claims. After all, China has no equivalent set of commitments in the Caribbean or Western Europe. That each side will perceive an excessive ambition on the part of the other is inevitable: it is not a misperception, but an inevitable conclusion. The United States is the power with the more anguishing security commitments—if its allies have an assertive policy, then its policy must be both to support and to restrain them. Think of the U.S. commitment to Israel in the Middle East and the security pacts with South Korea and Japan. Such a joint thrust is very difficult to manage, above all in an era when the media play so large a role in the public presentation of international issues. Ambiguity is not their strong suit. On the other hand, the large power that confronts an alliance structure might be thought to have a natural interest in not exposing that structure—no matter how potentially adversarial it might seem—to the harsh testing of its cohesion. The closer one comes to such existential tests, the more likely events can escape control and restraint can be trumped by domestic politics or simple miscalculation.

In the western Pacific, the contestation of small islands makes problems perhaps needlessly difficult. In the 1950s, the policy of President Dwight Eisenhower and Secretary of State John Foster Dulles was to assert U.S. defense of Quemoy and Matsu, islands directly off the Chinese Coast. At the time, many Americans deplored this tenacity, but it had a logic: assert an interest in even the smallest of rocks far from American shores and next door to the Chinese coast to demonstrate the strength of the United States' commitment to Taiwan. Now the rocky islands—Senkakus/Diaoyutai—are farther from China's coast, and it is Japan and not Taiwan that sees its security as primarily threatened. This time, too, the islands are embedded in a margin of ocean control that is as contested an issue as sovereignty over the rocks themselves. And this time, too, the credibility of U.S. alliance politics is being tested by a major allied country (Japan) that inevitably will have its own debates over security and could choose a policy more assertive than Washington would prefer.

I am not a student of this region or of these debates. This chapter is designed merely to show (1) that an objective definition of what constitutes aggressive or ambitious behavior and what constitutes defensive and restrained behavior is elusive if not impossible; (2) that any foreign policy dependent on alliance commitments can raise excruciating problems for the larger power as well as the smaller one; and (3) that opinions will always divide in a common-wealth between those who see wisdom in supporting allies no matter what their policies may be and those who would threaten possible lack of support. Thus the causes of escalation emerge from the dynamic within an alliance as well as between rivals.

Such dilemmas can attend ordinary powers without global ambitions. When hegemons are involved, the dilemmas are even more acute, because the ordinary restraints of distant geographies (versus those nearby) do not apply. Distance from the metropole matters less for global powers—there is, in effect, no faraway place. The United States has played a great power role in the western Pacific since at least 1898. Indeed, its unwillingness to cede to the Japanese exclusive control over the region (particularly over China) helped to preserve the Chinese polity in the early 1940s. Now these ambitions appear inappropriate to many Chinese. There are no obvious resolutions to many of these problems, and inventing "doctrines" can have only limited success. The only safe conclusion is that it is worth remembering that great wars always seem to arise out of triggering events, perhaps inconsequential in their own right, but bringing to bear all of the accumulated tensions within states and within alliances as well as between great powers.

The Inside Story:
Domestic Factors and the
Roots of War, Then and Now

9

War, Revolution, and the Uncertain Primacy of Domestic Politics

T.G. Otte

F EW SUBJECTS HAVE attracted the attention of historians and political
scientists more than the origins of World War I. It is the "long debate."[1]
In it, the school of thought arguing the case for a primacy of domestic politics,
originally advanced by Eckart Kehr, has gradually extruded the older Rankean
notion of the *Primat der Aussenpolitik* (primacy of foreign policy).[2]

If Kehr's argument fell initially on stony ground, from the late 1960s
onward a younger generation of historians proved more receptive. By then there
was a growing sense that the older paradigms yielded increasingly diminishing
returns. To the "Young Turks," especially in West German and U.S. academic
circles, Kehr's attempt at a reversal of primacies appeared forward looking. The
Primat der Innenpolitik (primacy of domestic politics), powerfully articulated by
a host of neo-Kehrites in the 1970s, suggested a more penetrating understanding
of pre-1914 foreign policy, in general, and arms races and imperial competition,
in particular. In the more extreme versions, foreign policy atrophied into little
more than a function of fundamental socioeconomic and political crises of
Europe's old regimes. External crisis and, *in extremis*, war, as Arno Mayer has
argued, were a means of avoiding revolutions at home: "The decision for war
and the design of warfare were forged in what was a crisis in the politics and
policy of Europe's ruling and governing classes." External conflict, according to
Mayer, had mutated into an instrument of domestic politics. The concomitant
preference of Europe's embattled elites for diversionary strategies "predisposed
them to fan smouldering fires of confrontation instead of exerting themselves
to dampen or extinguish them." Because of this pervasive "predilection for
war," Europe was gripped with a sense of imminent catastrophe.[3]

The twists and turns of the evolution of this school of thought are outside
the confines of this chapter.[4] Suffice it to say that the wheel has begun to turn

again, as a new generation of scholars is in the process of rediscovering the older Rankean precepts, with their emphasis on the separate nature of foreign policy and the inherent logic of the great power system.[5] Although a welcome development, there is nevertheless the risk of losing some of the insights offered by Kehr and his later disciples.

What follows is an attempt neither to bury nor to resurrect a defunct paradigm. Rather it is to test some of its assumptions and explanations against the extant evidence for their continued utility. It also seeks to broaden the discussion by examining developments across Europe so as to free the discussion from some of its Anglo-German distortions with its implicit teleology of an inevitable war. The focus here is also explicitly on the shorter-term political, and often constitutional, crises that engulfed most of the powers during the last few years before 1914. This choice is informed by the understanding that it is easier to assert the significance of *les forces profondes* than it is to demonstrate any causal nexus between them and specific policy decisions. Here as elsewhere, the long run is a misleading guide to understanding political decisionmaking.

Finally, this examination of the domestic aspects of great power politics at the end of the long nineteenth century is inspired by Leopold von Ranke in at least one respect. Just as the founder of history as an academic pursuit sought to reconstruct the history of the Reformation in Central Europe on the basis of Venetian legation reports, so contemporary diplomatic reporting informs the following discussion of the social and political crisis of Europe before 1914. In many respects, they are the first drafts of many histories.

Domestic Disruptions and Paralysis of the German State

Until World War I, and often well beyond, in all of the major powers, the framing and executing of foreign policy was the preserve of a professional elite that was exclusive in its social background, education, and recruitment practices.[6] Although often distinct from their own societies, these elites were nevertheless not hermetically sealed off from their surroundings; members shared a strong sense of political and social crisis in the years before 1914. As one British official observed, "There is a dangerous spirit of general unrest observable in all European countries."[7]

The most prominent manifestation of domestic fragility was the growing paralysis of the existing systems of governance. Political deadlock affected most of the countries of Europe. As Eyre Crowe observed, "There seems to be an epidemic of constitutional difficulties everywhere."[8] But if such difficulties were widespread, they were particularly prominent in the three eastern military monarchies, where the existing constitutional arrangements were on the brink of succumbing to political sclerosis.

In many respects, Germany was the most advanced of the three eastern powers. The constitution of 1871 had been tailored by Prince Otto von Bismarck to suit his personal inclinations. While he had skillfully coordinated and manipulated German policy, following his fall in March 1890, no one was in a position to exercise a balancing influence on the competing interests in Berlin. Bismarck's authority and charisma, as his successor-but-one evocatively put it at the time, had "shrunk and compressed" the personalities of all around him. Following his dismissal, "they are all expanding like sponges one has put in water. This has its advantages, but also its dangers. The unifying will is absent."[9] In subsequent years, leaders with swelled heads competed for influence, but neither Bismarck's successors nor the Reichstag was able to fill the power vacuum in Berlin. Behind the imposing façade of an authoritarian monarchy, buttressed by an advanced industrial economy and a powerful military, the Wilhelmine state was engulfed in a "permanent crisis of state." In the chaos of competing power centers, with ill-defined and often overlapping departmental mandates and mostly dependent on the favor of Kaiser Wilhelm II, a fluctuating constellation of forces determined German domestic and foreign policy.[10]

Wilhelm II's "personal regime," an attempt to gather popular support (*Sammlung*) around the illusion of a Caesarian leadership model, was a political experiment. It ended in failure. Neither of the last two German chancellors before World War I was capable of offering strategic guidance. Prince Bernhard von Bülow, the emperor's favorite and the public face of the personal regime, was a silky courtier and canny tactician with a penchant for beautifully turned phrases and brilliant, if somewhat grandiloquent, *Weltpolitik* (world politics) rhetoric. Yet neither his speech-making nor his flamboyant political gestures could hide the essential emptiness of the personal regime or the conspicuous absence of a grand strategy for Germany. His frequent shifts, moreover, undermined the parliamentary combination of National Liberals, conservative Agrarians, and the conservative-leaning Catholic Center party that composed the Bülow bloc.[11] Following the merger of three hitherto separate liberal groupings into a single, progressive left-liberal party, and given the seemingly inexorable rise of the massed and well-organized ranks of the Social Democratic Party (SPD), there was now a significant political force in German politics pressing for substantive parliamentary reform so as to make the imperial government responsible to the Reichstag as opposed to the kaiser.[12]

Nor was Bülow's successor, Theobald von Bethmann Hollweg, in a position to stabilize the imperial regime. If Bülow had been a somewhat unscrupulous but vacuous political operator, Wilhelmine Germany's last peacetime chancellor was the opposite. Having risen through the ranks of the domestic civil service, he was the prototype of a Prussian bureaucrat: educated, industrious, and straight-dealing: "His instinct is to face and grapple with difficulties rather than to go round them....He acts with apparent decision, but having decided on his line of policy he is apt to worry himself and his subordinates with doubts as to whether, after all, his decision was right."[13] Bethmann's shortcomings were not merely of a personal kind. His character traits and the systemic flaws in German politics reinforced each other. His "policy of the diagonal"—an effort to cobble together shifting majorities by reaching out to his vociferous critics on the conservative right and to the left, without offering anything substantive in return—was little more than an attempt to administer political problems by technocratic means.[14] If anything, it threw into sharper relief the failings of the existing political regime. Whatever the chancellor's character flaws, Germany's disorganized constitutional arrangements made it well nigh impossible for Bethmann to provide sustained leadership.

Germany's ambitious naval construction program further underlined the lack of coherence in its politics. At the root of German naval ambitions was an amalgam of strategic calculations—the ambition to increase Germany's international influence among the established naval and imperial powers—and considerations of domestic politics. As for the latter, these were shaped by assumptions about the navy as a powerful symbol of national unity, around which the nation, otherwise riven with class and other divisions, could gather, a process aided by a government-orchestrated navalist propaganda campaign. To an extent, an ambitious naval program, with full order books for the industrialists and steady employment for the industrial working classes as its corollary, was seen as a panacea against both the further growth of the socialist movement and any stirrings of ambitions for greater political partici-pation on the part of the industrial middle classes. There were also personal, bureaucratic empire-building ambitions at work. For the kaiser, the navy was one of only two institutions directly subject to his control, the other being the imperial postal service; and an admiral's uniform was a more fitting attire for a kaiser, especially when pursuing the experiment of the personal regime, than a postman's outfit. Similar ambitions of departmental empire building were also behind the machinations of Adm. Alfred von Tirpitz, whose brain-child was the German High Seas Fleet.[15]

Yet here, too, behind the glittering appearance of the swelling lines of battleships, lay the reality of an absent strategic coherence, indecisiveness, and inability of the institutions of the state to coordinate policy. It was not lost on contemporaries that Tirpitz was "afraid of Krupp [the arms manufacturer] and the Navy League."[16] This mattered more especially in view of the growing demands that the military and naval armaments programs—the biggest expenditure items of the Reich government—placed on the imperial treasury. Its financial commitments exceeded its revenues by far, and the resulting deficit was financed through loans or increases in indirect taxation. Even so, by 1906–07 Reich finances were in urgent need of wholesale reform. An attempt to introduce a form of inheritance tax remained abortive, but contributed to the collapse of the Bülow bloc. Subsequent efforts in that direction were equally ineffective. In 1913 a defense supplement was voted through by the Reichstag to finance the army bill of that year, but it remained an ad hoc measure. The imperial government continued to be caught between the conservative right, ready to torpedo any reform measures that diminished the privileges of the aristocratic elites, and the left, which demanded far-reaching reform measures, the SPD having supported the supplement in the expectation that it would lead to a progressive national income tax. On the eve of the war, Reich finances had hit a fiscal ceiling, but the necessary reforms were beyond the reach of the government.[17]

The demands for the introduction of a national income tax threatened to bring about a constitutional crisis. Certainly, as one British diplomat noted, the extensive armaments programs on land and at sea had been "an expensive amusement," which had curtailed Reich finances: "There seems good reason to hope that time will not be far distant when public opinion in the [German] Empire generally will force the Junkers in Berlin to abstain from a demand for further sacrifices....We shall be within measurable distance of saner conditions." There was now an "incipient movement towards democracy" in Germany.[18] German officials took much the same view. Already in the 1912 Reichstag elections, the SPD had won around one-third of the votes cast, and its 110 deputies (out of 397) formed the largest group in the German parliament; the trend of recent events suggested a strong possibility of an SPD-liberal majority in the 1917 elections, and with it the prospect of the conservative forces being condemned to a permanent minority.[19]

On the eve of the assassination of Austria's Archduke Franz Ferdinand in Sarajevo, the Wilhelmine state was thus paralyzed, incapable of change and of coherent strategic decisionmaking in equal measure, and without the ability to open up to new political forces, let alone absorb them. This did not, however, make the Wilhelmstrasse susceptible to viewing war as a solution to domestic problems. Far from it: in fact, senior officials appreciated the desta-bilizing effects of foreign complications. Gottlieb von Jagow, the state secretary at the Foreign Office, was fearful that any crisis might bring about the fall of Bethmann Hollweg and thus be "another step towards a parliamentary regime."[20] The chancellor, too, was driven by the prospect of "the worrisome descent into parliamentarianism, which threatened to occur."[21] In sharp contrast to his critics among the extreme conservatives, Bethmann did not think that a war would lead to "a healing of the internal situation in Germany, and in a conservative sense. He—the chancellor—thinks on the contrary that a world war, because of its incalculable consequences, would immensely increase the power of Social Democracy...and bring many a throne crashing down."[22] Ironically, this was also the view of the Social Democratic leadership: "Instead of a general strike we wage war for [general] Prussian franchise."[23]

Pace the advocates of a more extreme version of a primacy of domestic politics, then, the prospect of domestic disruptions acted as a restraint on the German leadership on the eve of World War I. At the same time, the paralysis of the Wilhelmine state also explains the tendency of the Wilhelmstrasse to let other powers determine German foreign policy, principally Germany's Austro-Hungarian ally but also Russia.[24]

The Habsburg Empire—External Crises and Internal Strife

Paralysis of a different kind affected the Habsburg Empire in the years before 1914. Recent scholarship has rightly queried older assumptions about Austria-Hungary as a doomed empire, destined to break apart over the contending ambitions of its many nationalities.[25] Even so, in the years before 1914, there could be no doubt that this ancient entity faced fundamental structural problems. To a large extent, these were rooted in the cumbersome arrangements of 1867, which had reconstituted the Habsburg Empire as a dual monarchy with practically autonomous governments in the Austrian and Hungarian halves, held together by the ruling dynasty; three common ministers (foreign affairs, war, and finance); and the delegations, two quasi-parliamentary assemblies to whom the common ministers had to render an account of their activities at certain intervals.[26]

The 1867 dualist *Ausgleich* (compromise) was a "marvellous machinery which through a multitude of wheels and levers made one of the smallest nations in Europe [Hungary] into a Great Power."[27] The Austro-German and Magyar authorities had to move in unison, or the empire would not move at all.

Power had thus shifted from Vienna to Budapest, and the latter's veto powers had the potential of triggering serious constitutional crises of the kind that had shaken the Habsburg Empire in the 1860s. Already the tardy renewal of the so-called economic *Ausgleich* in 1897, a tariff and trade agreement combined with a complex financial formula to settle common expenditure, had conjured up the specter of a major constitutional stand-off between the two governments and, worse, Magyar separatism. Leaders of both halves of the empire raised their heads again in 1903, this time over an army bill. Although the aged Emperor Franz Joseph and the Magyar prime minister, Baron Géza Fejérváry de Komlós-Keresztes, succeeded in breaking the opposition's back, the prospect of further disruptive constitutional disputes had not been dissipated.[28]

The potential of language quarrels to spark serious political dispute was never far from the surface in the sprawling Habsburg dominions. This affected not only relations between Vienna and Budapest but also the politics of each of the two halves of the monarchy, the Cisleithanian (or Austrian) and the Transleithanian (or Magyar). Although most of the language quarrels were local or at most provincial in character, their combined effect was to weaken the internal cohesion of the empire, undermining the confidence of the Habsburg leadership in foreign affairs. As Count Kasimir Badeni, the Austrian premier between 1895 and 1897, observed, "A state of nationalities cannot wage war without danger to itself."[29] Badeni had been appointed as "an Austrian Bismarck" to settle the festering language dispute in Bohemia, where the once dominant German landowners were confronted with a growing and increasingly assertive Czech group. All of Badeni's attempts at conciliation failed, however. Both parties felt "utterly ignored" by him; it was, as one of the conservative leaders noted, "a fight of autonomous parties against centralism."[30] Neither Badeni's modest electoral reform project nor his *Sprachenverordnung*, an attempt to regulate the use of the German and Czech languages in internal administration, were successful. Far from being able to forge a stable *Reichsrat* (upper house) majority from the moderate groupings of all Cisleithanian nationalities, Badeni had to witness the parties dividing along ethnic lines. Even the German conservatives organized themselves in different parties in Bohemia and the Alpine provinces. Badeni's attempt at a language compromise, meanwhile, led to brawls in the *Reichsrat* and street riots in Prague and the German-speaking parts of Bohemia as well as in Vienna and Graz.[31] In the end, Badeni had to go. But his fall shook the confidence of the Habsburg elites in the ability to reform the empire, and this was to be one of the psychological preconditions for the decisions of July 1914.[32]

Indeed, a decade and a half after Badeni's fall, matters looked worse. Political stalemate in the Bohemian Diet conjured up the specter of a fiscal catastrophe in the kingdom. Neither the dissolution of the Diet by imperial patent nor the appointment of a technocratic administration could overcome deadlock, and the Austrian premier, Count Karl Stürgkh, had to govern with the aid of emergency powers. By 1913 the German-Czech dispute in Bohemia was "going from bad to worse."[33] "I consider the *Ausgleich* [in Bohemia] to have failed for a long time to come," admitted the viceroy in early 1914: "Politics are a disgusting business."[34] Across the empire, one British official noted, "The situation not only in Bohemia and Galicia, but also in Hungary and Croatia can be summed up in one word 'deadlock.'"[35]

The Magyar half of the empire, indeed, was similarly paralyzed. Successive governments in Budapest pursued a vigorous Magyarization policy among the Slav populations of Transleithania, especially under the premiership of Count Károly Khuen-Héderváry de Hédervár between 1910 and 1912. On the eve of the war, under the more astute guidance of Count István Tisza de Borosjenö et Szeged, Budapest showed itself more accommodating to Croatian demands for greater autonomy. Tisza, however, was a determined defender of Magyar supremacy, and the "starting point of... [his] policy was that a solution of the crisis must be sought within the limits of the Ausgleich and of the political unity of the possessions of the Crown of St. Stephen [i.e., Hungary]."[36]

Although the efforts of Tisza and his predecessor, László Lukács de Erzsébetváros, to win over some of the principal Croatian leaders bore some fruit, the situation in that kingdom was far from stable. Since June 1912, the newly appointed *ban* (or viceroy), Baron Eduard Cuvaj von Ivanska, had ruled with an iron fist, making ample use of emergency powers granted to him by Vienna.[37] His quasi-absolutist regime provoked a violent backlash. Cuvaj himself was the target of two unsuccessful assassination attempts in June 1912 and August 1913.[38] So was his successor as *ban*, Baron Iván Skerlecz de Lomnicza, in May 1914, the governor of Galicia, Count Andrzej Potocki, having been shot dead by a Ukranian nationalist student in 1908. Cuvaj's Croatian commissariat had a destabilizing effect on neighboring Bosnia-Herzegovina, where Gen. Oskar Potiorek, the provincial governor, was forced to establish an emergency regime as well. A partial state of siege was declared over the provincial capital, Sarajevo, though the measures taken "only add[ed] strength to the smouldering fire of Serbian hatred of Austro-Hungarian rule."[39]

Thus the confluence of external crises, such as the Bosnian annexation crisis of 1908–09 and the two Balkan wars, as well as internal strife created a febrile atmosphere in the affairs of the Habsburg Empire, whose outward manifestations were treason trials (such as the so-called Agram or Friedjung trial), press censorship, politically motivated assassinations, parcel bombs, and emergency rule.[40]

The variegated nationalities questions aside, the imperial authorities were also confronted with the political problems arising from the general mobilization of the masses. In the capital, the Christian Social movement, under the anti-Semitic demagogue Karl Lueger, whose charisma was exceeded only by his opportunism, had established for itself a permanent dominance that lasted intact until Lueger's death in 1910. Elsewhere, the Social Democratic Party gained in strength, though it too was in practice more a loose, tactical federation of organizationally largely autonomous national parties.[41] For all their differences, the Lueger movement, which fed on the anxieties of the petit bourgeoisie of the capital, and the Social Democrats, were each capable of mobilizing large numbers among the urban population, and so challenged the essentially premodern structures of the Habsburg Empire.[42]

In the Austrian half of the empire, the authorities ruled through emergency measures. The year 1912 was "a year of stagnation." Parliament had failed to ratify the budget, and Cisleithania "entered into an *ex lex* [sic] state of affairs."[43] Nor did matters much improve. There was stalemate in Bohemia, where German conservatives and Czech nationalists sabotaged the latest language compromise.[44] In the Magyar half of the empire, meanwhile, the rise of the Hungarian Social Democratic Party caused some concern. Although small, it was disciplined "like a regiment."[45] Its threat of a general strike turned out to be a feeble weapon, but electoral reform remained a divisive issue in Hungarian politics. Tisza's attempts, in early 1914, to gerrymander constituency boundaries through a redistribution bill led to scenes of violence in the Hungarian parliament, and only the outbreak of the war in July arrested the crisis.[46]

If all these developments constrained the authorities in Vienna and Budapest as well as the imperial government, a further complication arose from the tensions between the aged emperor and his designated successor, Archduke Franz Ferdinand. While Franz Joseph and his entourage at the Schönbrunn court were content to preserve the status quo as best they could by administrative means, the Habsburg heir had assembled around him a younger generation of men willing to reform the empire by breaking the dualist monopoly on power. The tensions between the two groups should not be exaggerated. For the most part, the emperor kept Franz Ferdinand away from the levers of power. Even so, the incipient Schönbrunn-Belvedere dualism complicated matters. His reform ideas notwithstanding, the archduke was a gifted but decidedly authoritarian future ruler, and his reform schemes were

in essence clerical-conservative. Above all, he appreciated that radical constitutional reforms might be the harbinger of civil war and foreign intervention.[47]
The specter of internal disruptions also made him wary of external complications. Domestic consolidation meant "peace abroad. That is my *credo*."[48]
Indeed, during the Balkan wars of 1912 and 1913 the archduke exercised a
restraining influence on Habsburg decisionmaking, and so helped to keep in
check those who argued for a preventive war against Serbia. Such an "idea is
madness....We shall have war with Russia. Should the kaiser of Austria and the
tsar knock each other off their thrones and clear the way for revolution?"[49]

The archduke's restraining influence in foreign affairs mattered in two
respects. First, the two Austrian prime ministers before 1914, Baron Richard
von Bienerth-Schmerling and then Count Karl von Stürgkh, were nonen-
tities, content to leave foreign policy in the hands of stronger men, until
1912 to Foreign Minister Count Aloys Aehrenthal, and from 1913 to Tisza.
To their minds, Balkan affairs and the Southern Slav question were of vital
importance to the survival of the Habsburg Empire, with the difference being
that Aehrenthal advocated a policy of firmness in dealing with the smaller
Balkan nations whereas Tisza was more cautious. Second, the younger
generation of Habsburg officials, many of whom had gathered around the
archduke at the Belvedere, conceived of political questions in terms of
willpower and brute force. With Franz Ferdinand's removal from the scene
by an assassin's bullet on June 28, 1914, these elements were now unchecked.
For them the murder of the archducal couple at Sarajevo presented "the
first advantageous opportunity for a destructive strike against the kingdom
[Serbia]." Such a move was necessary now "to secure the monarchy a few
decades of tranquil internal development and to preserve undiminished the
crown of the empire."[50]

In the case of Austria-Hungary, concerns about the sprawling empire's
internal stability unquestionably played a significant role in foreign policy
decisionmaking. In essence, Habsburg domestic statecraft focused on maintaining the carefully calibrated system of mutual dissatisfaction by means of
minimal concessions, largely in response to attempts at political blackmail by
sectional interests, usually camouflaged by demagoguery. Regarding foreign
policy, fear of domestic disruption for the most part acted as a restraint—the
volatile state of affairs in the provinces, the dualist constitutional *Ausgleich*
structures, and the incipient Schönbrunn-Belvedere dualism largely para-
lyzing policymaking. It is thus one of the profound ironies of World War I that
the assassination of the Habsburg heir brought movement into the sclerotic
decisionmaking structures in Vienna, and so cleared the way for war.

Russian Economic Prosperity and Political and Social Instability

Russia was affected by paralysis of a different kind on the eve of World War I. In many respects, the country was in a much better position than the other two eastern empires. The Russian economy had recovered from the two shocks of global economic turbulence around 1900 and from domestic turmoil in the aftermath of the 1905 revolution.

Russia's economic revival impressed foreign observers. The consolidation of state finances had produced a *"situation financière et économique tout à fait extraordinaire,"* a French banker commented at the end of 1913.[51] Far from being backward, the Russian economy in the years before 1914 grew on average by 3.25 percent per year. By 1913, the country's national income exceeded that of France by a hefty 171.5 percent and was just short of that of Great Britain (97.1 percent). Some pockets of real backwardness remained, but in 1914, Russia's economy was the fourth largest in the world.[52]

Economic prosperity, combined with the effective repression of radical opposition under the conservative-liberal prime minister Pyotr Arkadevich Stolypin, suggested that a semblance of order had been restored. Indeed, if the political concessions granted in the aftermath of the 1905 revolution inaugurated nothing but a form of "pseudo-constitutionalism," in the last years before the war the tsar and his ministers had recouped significant powers and competences, and now largely governed with the aid of emergency and other administrative decrees. As so often before, the monarchy appeared to have "outwit[ted] its opponents by making concessions when in trouble and withdrawing them as soon as its position solidified."[53]

There could be no doubt that the imperial regime had regained its composure after the dual trauma of external defeat and internal revolution in 1905. If there was an appearance of calm, there nevertheless was a worm in the rosebud of tsarism. Stolypin, whose cautious reform program and ruthless suppression of radical opposition had done so much to stabilize the regime, was killed by a revolutionary in 1911. His death furnished the very forces the slain prime minister had sought to preserve with an opportunity to dismantle his legacy, and encouraged Tsar Nicholas II to reassert his authority over the policymaking process. Whereas Stolypin had held the chairmanship of the council of ministers in conjunction with the ministry of the interior, the tsar now distributed these offices to different officials. In January 1914, he also reversed the previous arrangement of the chairman of the council of ministers holding that office jointly with another ministerial position. It was a surreptitious coup d'état, intended to enhance the tsar's authority among his ministers. This was underlined by his appointment as premier of Ivan Loginovich Goremykin—"old, lazy, reactionary," "an elderly gentleman devoted to quietism," and scarcely capable or willing to intervene authoritatively in ministerial decisionmaking. Indeed, the tsar never wished Goremykin to do anything of the kind. He was intended to be nothing but a superannuated figurehead, chosen to preside over ministers whose standing and influence were so balanced that not one of them could establish himself as the dominant force. Making Goremykin chairman of the council of ministers was meant to destroy the authority and power of that office.[54]

The tsar's coup, however, had unintended consequences. In setting out to undermine the position of the prime minister, he ushered in a period of incessant intrigues among the ministers; the two most unscrupulous of them had, in fact, urged Nicholas to embark on this experiment. This scheming duo— Aleksander Krivoshein, who held the important agriculture portfolio, and Nikolai Maklakov, the minister of the interior—were at the center of political intrigue. In practice, for much of the first half of 1914, the Russian government was in a state of permanent confusion. Already shortly before Kokovtsov was ousted, "the disorganisation among them [the ministers] is so great," Bernard Pares, then a young scholar visiting Russia, observed in a sharp-eyed memo- randum. Maklakov and his clique strove "to make an atmosphere of the glorification of power and contempt of everything else." The ministers were "all at sixes and sevens, but they have all been at work...with their intrigues for many months past." Russia was a country "where everything is in transition, and the Government is at once so disorganised and unrepresentative."[55]

If the upper echelons of the Russian state were in disarray, the rightward shift of opinion in the Duma, as evidenced in the outcome of the elections to the Fourth Duma, presented a further complication. The parties of the moderate right, moreover, had begun to stagnate, a tendency to split having paralyzed both the once dominant Octobrists and the Kadets. On the eve of the war, as Pares noted, "there is hardly a party that has not splits in it, and that includes even the extreme Rights."[56] The forces of the right, however, were in a stronger position; and they were certainly more vociferous. Maklakov and other senior officials left unchecked, indeed aided, their anti-Semitism, for instance, in the notorious "Beilis affair" in 1911–13. Its toxic mix of conspiracy theories and ritual murder fantasies derived its potency from the deeply rooted hostility toward the *inorodtsi'i* (aliens) in Russian society.[57] The affair itself certainly "tended to increase the animosity of the Russian peasants towards the Jews"—a convenient safety valve for belea- guered ministers in St. Petersburg.[58]

The nationalist forces were also largely critical of the government's seemingly timid foreign policy. They were less inclined to respond to appeals to pan-Slav solidarity—the preserve of the moderate and liberal groups in the Duma after 1907. Pan-Slavism, after all, was ill suited to dealing with Polish demands for greater autonomy within the Russian Empire. The right's approach to foreign affairs might have been inchoate, itself the product of intellectual confusion, but the foreign minister, Sergey Sazonov, was reluctant to offend his critics. A brother-in-law of Stolypin, the assassinated former premier, Sazonov was mindful of the need to retain his monarch's confidence and the support of the conservatives in the Duma—for instance, during the various Balkan crises in 1912–13.[59] Although the noisy protestations of the pan-Slavs and extreme chauvinists scarcely constituted a viable alternative foreign policy agenda, they vented a deeply entrenched sense of frustration at Russia's ineffectual diplomacy since 1905;[60] and Sazonov was not the man to defuse that situation.

Although there were no clear indications of profound prerevolutionary instability in Russia in 1914, there was no doubting the growth of the labor movement. Russian society, the British ambassador reflected in early 1914, was "deeply permeated by revolutionary sentiments." Nevertheless, "Beyond a large number of semi-political, semi-economic strikes, accompanied occasionally by hurried processions through the streets, quickly dispersed by the police, and by brief displays of the red flag, there have been no overt manifestations...that could be traced to revolutionary propaganda."[61] The ambassador's assessment was shrewd enough, but it captured only part of the wider picture. Although still dwarfed by the sheer numbers of the peasantry, the ranks of the industrial workforce had swelled by about a third in the four years before the war, and many of the newly hired workers were attracted to the straightforward radicalism of anarchists or Bolsheviks. It was their "restlessness and sense of estrangement" that contributed to the rise in industrial strife during the first half of 1914, most notably in St. Petersburg itself.[62] Overall, Russian society and politics were unstable: "No one here can have any doubts that, even if the current calm may last for years, one has to reckon with the possibility of a new revolution breaking out."[63]

This sense of estrangement was by no means confined to the urban working classes. The government's by now habitual postponement of constitutional reforms, "and the severity of the administrative régime, which has seemed to be accentuated rather than mitigated under...[Maklakov], has resulted in a growth of discontent among the law-abiding elements of different classes, which has expressed itself with ever increasing plainness and emphasis."[64] As the German consul-general observed during the festivities surrounding the Borodino centenary, these had "brought about no rapprochement between the tsar and the nation, but...they show anew the broad and deep chasm that exists in Russia between Court, government, military, and the clergy on the one hand and the economically and intellectually productive forces of the nation on the other, and which threaten to widen and deepen further under the pressure of the current reaction."[65] The discontent among moderates and conservatives was exacerbated by the perceived rise of labor. Extreme nationalists argued that a test of the national will would heal social divisions, whereas the moderates "saw the 'paralysis' of the regime as the real reason for Russia's defeats in the Balkans and were gradually recruited to the nationalist cause."[66] For their part, the tsar's ministers had come to view pan-Slavism as a "palliative against revolutionary propaganda."[67]

The deep divisions in Russian society and politics mattered. What was most striking about the situation in Russia on the eve of the war was "the prevalence and intensity of hatred: ideological, ethnic, social."[68] Yet elements of the country's political elite had developed a sophisticated understanding of the interaction between external complications and internal developments. The moneyed classes and other "influential circles" in the Russian capital were against war: "They fear major internal complications as a consequence of a war; their interest in the Balkans was not so great that they would want to run such an immeasurable risk."[69] In his now famous memorandum of February 1914, Pyotr Durnovo, a former police chief and minister of the interior, warned that a future European war was likely to be protracted; that the Russian army, economy, and society would disintegrate under the strain of such a conflict; that the masses would rise; and that anarchy and a wholesale revolution would be the consequence.[70]

By July 1914, Russian politics had reached a dead-end. Whatever greater authority tsarism had acquired by weakening other institutions had been purchased at the price of political disarray in the upper echelons of the Russian state. In so doing, Nicholas II and his ministers hollowed out the Russian government's authority and weakened the forces of moderation. To an extent, therefore, the lack of strategic rationality and the sheer incompetence displayed by Russian ministers and senior military officers in July 1914 were symptomatic of a deeper malaise of the Russian state before World War I.

Stalemate in France and Britain

The domestic situation in the two western powers was different. France and Britain were not affected by a deeper political or social malaise, but here too politics had reached a stalemate. The reasons for this situation were varied and reflected the different political cultures and recent experiences of the two countries. France presented a paradoxical picture. It is one of the peculiarities of Europe on the eve of World War I that few regimes were as stable and solid as the French Republic. Threatened many times since 1871, it had not only survived but its domestic enemies—the Bonapartists, clericals, Bourbon loyalists, and assorted other anti-republicans—had long been in retreat. If none of them had entirely faded away, nor their anti-parliamentary attitudes completely evaporated, their popular support certainly had contracted and the countryside, so long the redoubt of conservative anti-republicanism, had fallen.[71] Indeed, the advocates of either Bourbon or Bonaparte restoration no longer presented identifiable and independent formations, having become indistinguishable from mainstream conservatives who had made their peace with the republic. In the general election of 1910, only seventy deputies stood on an anti-republican platform; in the elections in June 1914, their number had dwindled even further. But if the republic was secure and its foundations were solid, the same could not be said of French party politics.[72]

The Dreyfus Affair and the subsequent judicial and parliamentary struggle against the inequities perpetrated on the officer at the center of the scandal, Capt. Alfred Dreyfus, had enforced a degree of unity among the nonconservative parties, but it did not long survive that campaign. With its end began a period of confusion, which threw party politics into disarray, from which they emerged only with the formation of Georges Clemenceau's coalition government in 1917.[73] On the eve of World War I, party politics remained volatile, subject to various currents and countervailing tendencies. The three-year army law of July 1913 had polarized French domestic politics. The parliamentary elections of April–May 1914 had produced a left-wing majority in the chamber, the subtleties of the second ballot aiding the radicals, but the formation of a new government proved a difficult and protracted undertaking.[74] The balance of parliamentary forces, however, was complicated by the idiosyncrasies of the existing political parties. The Radical-Socialist majority was not as strong and cohesive as it appeared. Of the 238 radicals, for instance, some 100 regarded themselves as "nonradical"; and among the Socialists there were some 30 "nonsocialists." The prime minister since June 14, 1914, René Viviani, whose political career had begun in close association with the Socialist Party, now considered himself an "independent socialist." Like so many governments of the Third Republic, his administration was not built on solid foundations, and its survival was by no means certain. It was ostensibly more to the left than any of the recent governments. But the anticlerical, republican-socialist Viviani was forced into an uneasy partnership with the "Man of Lorraine," right-wing President Raymond Poincaré. Ideological differences aside, the two men had little regard for each other. To the president's mind, Viviani, who held the positions of prime and foreign minister in conjunction, was utterly ignorant of international politics. On reading telegrams from Vienna, Poincaré recorded maliciously in his diary, Viviani was wont to refer to the Habsburg foreign ministry at the Ballhausplatz as "the Boliplatz or the Baloplatz."[75]

These personal animosities tended to accentuate the two men's different views on foreign policy. Viviani was skeptical of what he considered the pessimistic outlook of senior diplomats, and their undue deference to the alliance with Russia. Somewhat suspicious of the motives behind Russia's Balkan entanglements, he preferred a cautious and moderate approach to foreign affairs.[76] Yet, he had to confront the predicament that all French foreign ministers had faced since 1894. While reluctant to encourage Russia to interfere in any Austro-Serbian dispute, he was anxious to do nothing that would strain France's vital relations with St. Petersburg. For that reason, for instance, he went out of his way to assure Russia of the new government's desire to maintain France's armed strength.[77]

Poincaré, meanwhile, thought the premier not only ignorant of foreign affairs but also "hesitant and pusillanimous." The president therefore sought to assume tighter control of foreign policy during the July crisis.[78] His struggle with Viviani for political control reflected his determination to ensure that French policy continued to cleave to the Russian alliance, come what may. France's security was founded upon the rock of that alliance. To his mind, it was "the supreme guarantee of the European order."[79] The principal task of French foreign policy was to cultivate France's existing ties with Britain and Russia, ideally to turn them into a new triple alliance. In parallel, France's military striking power was to be enhanced further. The policy was later called "Poincaristic," but it aligned with French military thinking in the aftermath of the Franco-German Agadir crisis of 1911 and its emphasis on offensive warfighting doctrines.[80] For Poincaré, French national security and the stability of Europe rested on the balance of power based on a clear and strict separation of two alliance blocs, without any softening along their edges, let alone interpenetration of any kind.[81] If the tensions between Poincaré and Viviani complicated matters, then at least in one respect French foreign policy was adrift, literally so when the two men returned from a state visit to St. Petersburg on July 27, 1914, cooped up on board the warship *France* and only intermittently in receipt of the latest telegrams.[82]

Finally, in July 1914, French domestic concerns also mattered, because much of the country's political elite was distracted by the murder trial of Henriette Caillaux, wife of former Premier Joseph Caillaux. Caillaux was a luminary on the left and perhaps the only man capable of leading such disparate political forces. The proceedings commenced on July 20, culminating in the defendant's triumphant acquittal eleven days later. The salacious tittle-tattle surrounding the forthcoming trial, however, kept the French public and political elite enthralled, not least because it threatened to reveal embarrassing details about the financial dealings of various politicians and events during the Agadir crisis. Indeed, until the end of July, the French newspapers gave greater prominence to the trial than to the events in a faraway corner of the Balkans.[83]

The domestic situation in Britain on the eve of the war bore superficial similarities to that in France. Here, as in France, the beleaguered government of the day could not presume its continued existence. And as in France, tensions between the different strands of opinion that formed the ruling party had the potential of tearing the government apart. But there were also significant differences. Perhaps the most difficult challenge for the student of Edwardian Britain lies "in overcoming the certainty, unknown and implausible to contemporaries, that the period constitutes a terminus."[84] It was only from the perspective of the events after midnight on August 4 that British liberalism appeared destined to suffer a "strange death," or that the Conservatives, more crisis-prone than the Liberals before 1914, were bound to revive to dominate much of the twentieth century, or that Labour was set to emerge as the other big party and usher in a period of "class politics."[85]

This caveat aside, Edwardian politics were nevertheless engulfed in a multitude of crises. Britain's external relations appeared placid in the first half of 1914. As one British official commented, "I have not seen such calm waters [since 1910]."[86] But domestic politics were in a deplorable condition; and this circumstance acted as a constraint on Sir Edward Grey during the July crisis. The Liberal government under Herbert Henry Asquith was in office, but seemed scarcely to be in power. Without a functioning parliamentary majority after the two indecisive general elections of 1910, ministers were dependent on a motley crew of Irish nationalists, Labour, and their own truculent and capricious Radical wing.

The 1910 elections had dealt a blow to the morale of Liberals and Unionists. But if neither side could draw much comfort from the two contests, their effect was felt more especially on the Liberal side. Four years earlier, some

399 members of Parliament had to squeeze themselves behind the government's front bench in the House of Commons. In January 1910, the Liberals lost no fewer than 127 seats to the Unionist opposition, leaving the two parties in a stalemate, a circumstance that the second election at the end of the year did not alter. Indeed, the Liberals were now two seats behind. Although this parliament would continue to sit until 1918, the government increasingly gave an impression of intellectual and physical exhaustion. Spurts of intense activity could not hide the absence of an overarching theme to government policy; that the government, in fact, was buffeted by gusts of wind blowing from different political directions. A loyal Liberal member was struck at the end of 1911 "by the way in which the majority of Ministers during the last few years have aged. Bald and grey; grey and bald—and most of them young men in the prime of their life....No previous Ministry in history has undergone such a continuous and heavy strain."[87]

The simmering constitutional crisis over the powers of the House of Lords, triggered by the peers' refusal to pass David Lloyd George's quasi-Labour "People's Budget" in 1909, was eventually settled in 1911 following hitherto unprecedented royal intervention.[88] To an extent, the arrangements to come were of a temporary kind. In a fluid political situation, British politics operated under an "interim constitution."[89] No sooner had the matter been settled than another, even graver crisis erupted, one that raised the specter of civil war in Britain for the first time in three hundred years. With the absolute veto powers of the Lords removed, the Irish Nationalists asserted their negative power by demanding a Home Rule bill, which Asquith introduced in 1912, alongside a bill for the disestablishment of the Anglican Church in Wales. Both Irish and Welsh nationalism challenged the political status quo of post-1867 Britain, the latter in a more muted manner, the former more violently.[90] Far from appeasing Irish nationalism, the proposed Home Rule scheme for devolving certain powers to an Irish parliament but within the framework of the British imperial state threatened to deepen the fissures that rent British politics. While under the leadership of Sir Edward Carson, Ulster Protestants threatened to organize themselves in paramilitary volunteer forces, Asquith equivocated. The six counties of Ulster were included in the Home Rule bill, but the prime minister did not turn against the Carsonite movement.

In March 1914, the "Curragh mutiny" laid bare the government's imperfect control of the Army in Ulster, when senior officers refused to obey London's orders to disarm the Unionist volunteers, who had acquired a monopoly on weapons. In June, Asquith introduced an amending bill that allowed Ulster to opt out of Home Rule for six years. Nothing, however, could reconcile Ulster leaders to devolution. With Nationalists and Unionists locked in a suicidal embrace, Ireland was drifting toward civil war. Ministers in London were resigned to the fact that, whenever the bill reached the statute book, "the Carsonite leaders would find it very difficult...to postpone doing something"; they would be "compelled to raise the flag somehow or other in Belfast."[91] All the while, a significant section of the Conservatives condoned the actions of mutinous army officers and encouraged rebellious Ulstermen.[92] Indeed, it was not until July 24, 1914, the day after the Austro-Hungarian ultimatum to Serbia, that the Cabinet took note of the Balkan crisis, "the gravest of many years past in European politics."[93]

There were other problems that competed for the attention of British ministers. As in Germany, the rise of organized Labour presented a challenge. As in Germany, British politicians sought to contain it. In sharp contrast to Germany, however, they could draw on a long-established tradition of piecemeal reforms and cooperation across class boundaries so as to co-opt the new movement. Given the transformation of British politics as a result of World War I, attempts to assess the true strength of the Labour Party will always contain an element of speculation. For the purposes of this chapter, it is suffi-cient to note that, in the last few years before 1914, support for Labour had stagnated, if not indeed receded.[94] The party itself was in a weaker position now than in 1906. The loss of the trade unions' political levy to finance the parlia-mentary Labour Party following the court of appeal judgment in the "Osborne Case" forced Labour to cooperate with the Liberals to secure passage of the Parliament's Salaries Act in 1911 and the 1913 Trade Union Act, which allowed the unions to establish political funds. As one of the Labour leaders predicted already before 1910, "When a government is kept in, or put out, by Labour votes, the Labour Party is hampered by its responsibilities as the other party is tormented by its weakness."[95]

On the eve of the war, the progressive Lib-Lab alliance of 1906 had lost much of its luster. While the parliamentary Labour party was weaker, the wider Labour movement had become more militant. Waves of strikes had crippled the mining, metal, and transport industries since 1911: "The country is witnessing the outbreak of a very violent industrial civil war. In London, Liverpool, Birmingham, Manchester, Sheffield, Bristol, and Glasgow...ordinary life...has been upset and the wheels of commerce have gone off the accustomed lines."[96]

Lloyd George was a capable mediator between competing political interests and a shrewd deal-maker with Labour leaders. His national insurance legislation and his land reform campaign in 1913–14 were, to an extent, a ploy to contain the Labour movement, to win back working-class support for the Liberals—"the artisan class which is wavering between Liberalism and socialism"—and to reenergize his own flagging party.[97] But these were controversial policies; their popularity disputed—the Lloyd George acolyte C.F.G. Masterman suffered the indignity of several by-election defeats on account of the insurance question; and on the right wing of the party, resistance stirred against this surfeit of radicalism and in defense of property.[98]

Another source of instability in Edwardian politics was the vociferous and increasingly militant female suffrage movement. For all the windows broken in its course, the campaign of systematic disruption of Liberal events and intimidation of Liberal politicians did not pose a threat to the Edwardian political system as such—but it created tensions. A Conciliation Bill in favor of female suffrage failed to pass in 1910; an attempt by the government to introduce votes for women on the back of a bill to abolish plural votes was ruled out of order by the speaker in 1913. If the noisy demonstrations, hunger strikes, and a martyr's death beneath the hoofs of the king's Derby horse had something of a tragicomedy about them, they nevertheless added to the stresses within the ruling party: "The outrages of the Militants are scandalous beyond expression," noted an otherwise mild-mannered member of Parliament in the spring of 1914.[99]

In the early summer of 1914, senior ministers were "jumpy, irritable, overworked, and unhappy"; they were "disturbed at the unpopularity of Insurance, at the failure of the Land Campaign…now at the failure of his [Lloyd George's] Budget to command any measure of enthusiasm."[100] The governing party's flagging fortunes, the crisis over Ireland, and industrial strife—the so-called Triple Alliance of railway, mine, and transport workers' unions threatened a general strike for the autumn—consumed much of the government's political energy in the spring and summer of 1914. For any Liberal administration, this was a toxic combination, one that threatened to dissolve the broad coalition that was the Edwardian Liberal Party. If mass industrial disputes coincided with civil unrest over Ulster, warned Lloyd George, "the situation will be the gravest with which any Government in this country has had to deal for centuries."[101] For once the mercurial Lloyd George did not exaggerate. With the government's stock devalued and still slumping further, "The Liberal Party in the House…is at present engaged in trying to save its own skin," observed a sympathetic parliamentary correspondent toward the end of July. The trend of recent by-elections, indeed, pointed to a Unionist election victory in 1915.[102]

Finally, some consideration needs to be given to the internal dynamics within the ruling party. Grey and the Foreign Office were not ignorant of the disruptive potential of Balkan crises. But if another spat in that region escalated, remarked one British official, "I should not like to attempt any forecast in regard to this."[103] The immensity of the choice aside, equally problematic was the corrosive effect of foreign policy on Liberal unity; and Grey's policy was not without fierce critics, especially so among the nonconformist and radical wing of the party. During the foreign secretary's speech to the Commons on November 28, 1911, defending his handling of recent great power crises, for instance, he "was cheered *heartily* by the Tories. The Liberals listened for the most part in silence."[104] To many right-thinking Liberals, the notion of a European war was quite inconceivable: "There is no more reason why the Germans should cross the North Sea and invade England than why the good people of Norwich should march forth to seize and plunder the shops of the good people of Ipswich," opined one backbencher.[105] Throughout the July crisis of 1914, until the violation of Belgian neutrality robbed the last radicals of their illusions, there was among them the "very strong feeling that whatever happens amongst the other European powers England must keep herself out of the quarrel."[106]

The outbreak of World War I arrested the various Edwardian crises and restored a species of British *Burgfrieden* (truce) on the basis of the status quo. On the eve of the continental conflict, however, the combination of these conflicting pressures helped to reinforce Britain's relative aloofness from Europe's final crisis. Whatever Grey's handling of the events of July 1914 in general, short-term calculations of parliamentary arithmetic and party political tendencies played a role. It would have been impossible for Grey to issue a more emphatic and earlier warning to Germany, as has so often been argued, ever since Lloyd George gave the idea his imprimatur. As Grey's parliamentary private secretary, Arthur Murray, explained years later: "It is not open to doubt…that if Grey had insisted on sending an ultimatum of this character to Germany, Lloyd George would have led a revolt in the Cabinet; the Cabinet would have dissolved; and the country would have been split from top to bottom."[107] Grey was entirely justified in his attempt to avoid this. Divided countries, after all, count for nothing in international politics.

Conclusion

On the eve of World War I, domestic crises engulfed the great powers, but they took different forms in different countries. In the three eastern military monarchies, the premodern political status quo, with its absence of responsible governments, was no longer capable of containing, let alone resolving, the social, political, or ethnic tensions in these societies. Nor were these polities, authoritarian to varying degrees, capable of opening to new social and political forces. In France and Britain, the existing political regimes were more stable and their survival not in doubt, the barely suppressed constitutional crisis in the latter notwithstanding. The effect of this pervasive sense of domestic crisis, however, was the same in all of the major powers in that it hampered the ability of governments to act with confidence. It was a restraint rather than a spur to go to war. Standing close to the crater's edge, and staring down into the abyss of social and political turmoil, if not revolution, it seemed more sensible not to move than to take a possibly fateful step. *Pace* the advocates of a *Primat der Innenpolitik*, Europe's leaders did not pursue diversionary strategies to deflect attention from the deeper malaise of their respective societies. *Pace* the adherents of the Rankean notion of a *Primat der Aussenpolitik*, foreign policy was not framed in a hermetically sealed environment but was subject to domestic influences. The decisions for war in 1914 reflected political paralysis in some countries and a crisis of governance in others. To appreciate this dynamic process of interaction between the external and internal spheres of politics is not to assert the primacy of one or the other. Rather it is to turn the primacy of domestic politics from its head and onto its feet, and to place it in the midst of the messiness of politics.

No single lesson is to be learned from this process. Nor can it be condensed to the single issue of tensions between status quo and revisionist powers. The study of history may yield empirical data, but history is not the source of normative guidelines. Nor does it equip its student with predictive powers. There is no formula to be distilled from past events, but their examination "provide[s] an *exercise for judgment*."[108] If history were nothing but a mechanical repetition of the past, no change would ever occur. Historical parallels are therefore inexact, and those drawn to such exercises should be mindful of the dangers of locking themselves into self-fulfilling prophecies. This has particular relevance for analyses of the geopolitical shifts at the beginning of the twenty-first century, and the rise of China especially. With the 1914 centenary, "Davos Man" in the West but also many Chinese strategic commentators have been tempted by the seemingly apparent parallel with Europe on the eve of World War I. To cast China in the role of the kaiser's empire is problematic, however, with respect to both modern China and Wilhelmine Germany. But similarly, it may well prove illusory to assume that, with growing prosperity, China will have to become a more open and rule-governed polity. To project China's further rise on the basis of its economic development over the past few decades—itself a return to some form of normality in global economic trends[109]—defies economic experience; the assumption of inevitable liberalization projects Western experience on China while ignoring the latter's distinct culture.

It would be rash to venture predictions of any kind. What is beyond doubt, however, is that China's leadership has to tackle fundamental domestic problems as well as navigate the shifts in twenty-first-century geopolitics. The demographic pressures of a rapidly aging population, decreasing productivity rates, and the sharply diverging fortunes of the country's coastal regions and its interior are formidable challenges to the country's political and economic model. Faced with such problems, no leadership in Beijing is likely to plunge China into a global, strategic confrontation. This is perhaps all the more so because power relationships are likely to be decided by China's economic growth, the strength of its education system, fiscal robustness, and infrastructure spending rather than merely by military hardware. Given China's domestic challenges, the experience of pre-1914 Europe is relevant in at least this respect: if history has anything to suggest, it is that domestic paralysis and the inability of governments to offer strategic leadership are as much a threat to international stability as the ambitions of revisionist powers—if not more so.

10

Domestic Coalitions, Internationalization, and War

Then and Now

Etel Solingen

T HE SOURCES OF World War I are numerous and widely studied. Some scholars have argued that they are underdetermining individually but overdetermining collectively. The purpose of this piece is not to fuel the battle among theories claiming complete explanatory power, but rather to examine some lessons for contemporary international relations. Much of the recent commentary on the war's centenary evokes similarities between Germany in 1914 and China in 2014, and between globalization then and now. There are crucial differences on both accounts, however.

I advance an approach that transcends rigid renditions of primacy where domestic politics (*Innenpolitik*) or foreign policy (*Aussenpolitik*) alone explains outcomes. Rather, my approach hinges on domestic coalitions that operate as transmission belts between the two. Coalitions that aggregate state and private actors define the kinds of links to the global economy, and to their strategic (coalitional) cluster, that best serve their political survival. Internationalizing coalitions thrive with increased engagement in the global economy, inward-looking coalitions with decreased engagement. In turn, the global economy and the relevant strategic context—the balance of external threats and opportunities that coalitions face—provide different constraints and inducements for each coalitional type. Resulting (coalitional) balances of power—within and across states—have implications for whether or not coalitions will be more or less averse to the risk of war. Strategic clusters dominated by inward-looking actors will exhibit less aversion to war than internationalizing clusters. The nature of dominant coalitions thus provides a conceptual anchor for understanding the links between internal and external politics in 1914 and 2014. As an analytical category, coalitions draw greater attention to agency in debates that all too often emphasize international structure, impersonal forces, and inevitability. Two interrelated core claims rest on this basic analytical building block.

First, despite apparent similarities in the domestic coalitional models of putative revisionist challengers—Germany and China—important differences defy facile analogies. Real-world coalitions can never match ideal types, which are abstractions by definition. Yet Germany's dominant coalition under Wilhelm II's *Kaiserreich* (1888–1918) was closer to the inward-looking category: it joined protectionism and militarization under a hypernationalist tent; it overwhelmed domestic internationalizing adversaries and sought to freeze reigning agrarian/industrial structures; and it was prone to brinkmanship while projecting aggressive expansionist aims. Although China today may elicit some parallels, its internationalizing leaders have anchored their political survival to the global political economy. While facing intermittent inward-looking challenges, internationalizers within and beyond the Chinese Communist Party (CCP) have dramatically increased their sway in the post–Deng Xiaoping era. Their internationalizing strategy has facilitated a historical transformation of socioeconomic structures. China's leaders rely on nationalism strategically, sometimes unleashing nationalism and at other times restraining it. In addition, they must reconcile nationalism with continued internationalization, which remains the basis of their strategy for regime survival.

Second, some observers may contest the extent to which contrasts between Germany and China overwhelm the similarities between the two. Yet the specific "world-time"—global, regional, political, institutional, economic, and temporal contexts within which coalitions operate—widens the gap between 1914 and 2014 further. With regional coalitional clusters and the global political economy diverging across both periods, so do the links between domestic and external politics. Germany's strategic coalitional cluster—particularly Russia, Austria-Hungary, and Serbia—reflected some of the same inward-looking features as Germany. Hypernationalism, protectionism, and external expansion lowered collective aversion to war. In contrast, China's strategic coalitional cluster within and beyond the region is far more internationalizing than Germany's 1914 counterparts. Furthermore, China's reliance on foreign direct investment (FDI) as the dominant source of external capital puts China firmly in regional and global production chains. Along with other features, globalized production networks—spread over many countries—are the main drivers of contemporary globalization. Globalized production is much less vulnerable than trade was in 1914 and creates unprecedented alternatives to wars of expansion. Most important, the domestic costs of enhancing or decreasing economic openness, attracting or spurning FDI, are far more salient for domestic political survival today than they were in 1914. International institutions favoring internationalizing coalitions have replaced the institutional vacuum reigning in 1914. These and other circumstances discussed below suggest that ahistorical analogies could therefore mislead; invoking them as if history must recur could inadvertently create new realities unfavorable to peace. Imperfect analogies can lead the sides to act on the basis of erroneous interpretations.

The next sections develop the conceptual argument, apply it to pre–World War I Germany, compare Germany in 1914 with China in 2014, and evaluate the contrasting world-time within which each case was/is embedded. The conclusions address implications for international relations theory, noting that notwithstanding major differences between 1914 and 2014, predictions about war (as war itself) are always risky.

Internationalization, Coalitions, and War

Many of the studies that address globalization's presumed failure to prevent World War I rely on quantitative measures of interdependence, primarily trade flows. They rarely dwell on political mechanisms connecting those indicators with domestic politics. The nature of dominant political-economy coalitions, and their implications for war and peace, is one such mechanism. A theoretical tradition along these lines focused on great powers historically, whereas newer variants explain external conflict and cooperation across contemporary states more broadly.[1] The distributional consequences of internationalization provide a useful analytical point of departure. Expanding international markets and institutions affect domestic incomes, prices, employment, and politics. Some groups benefit from international exchange, others do not. The kinds of ties linking politicians, sectors, parties, and institutions to the international context influence their conceptions of interests and their choice of strategies. The effects of internationalization are not restricted to political economy, however; they are also felt by cultural groups and social movements that perceive internationalization and crude market forces as threatening their values or identities. These movements are receptive to appeals for placing communal "organic" values, such as nationalism, ahead of all others.

Politicians understand the mobilizing capacity of economic interests, norms, identity, and historical myths associated with dilemmas of internationalization. They thus organize constituencies across the state-society divide into competing coalitions and craft models of political survival attuned to those coalitional preferences. Two Weberian "ideal-typical" models—one internationalizing and the other inward-looking—capture the essence of those preferences.[2] The two models vie for control over wide-ranging policies affecting the nature and depth of international economic exchange. Politicians who endorse internationalizing models attract actual or potential beneficiaries of economic openness, including internationally competitive sectors and consumers. Politicians advancing inward-looking models logroll across constituencies adversely affected by openness, including proponents of state entrepreneurship, nationalism, "self-sufficiency," and military-industrial complexes. The two models, which differ in the extent to which states replace or enhance markets, also entail different conceptions of grand strategy. Grand strategies define approaches to global and regional economic and political structures, as well as to the internal extraction and allocation of resources.

The grand strategies of the two models involve synergies across their international, regional, and domestic pillars.[3] Internationalizing grand strategies emphasize access to global markets, capital, and technology; regional cooperation and stability; and domestic macroeconomic stability that reduces uncertainty, encourages savings, and enhances investment (including foreign investment). External crises and conflict compromise those synergies, fueling unproductive and inflationary military expenditures, protectionism, and state entrepreneurship under a mantle of "national security." Each of these pillars of internationalizing strategies dampens incentives for war; collectively they weaken them further. Conversely, inward-looking models benefit from grand strategies that enhance the viability of statist, nationalist, protectionist, and military-industrial complexes. External insecurity and competition offer rationales for extracting societal resources, collecting monopoly rents, creating cartels, rewarding protectionist constituencies, and undermining internationalizing competitors. The strategy entails extensive statist ownership; rent seeking via tariffs and multiple exchange rates; and price controls and overvalued currency to raise wages and profits in nontraded goods. Forceful territorial expansion helps to extend the size of protected markets and squeeze out competitors.[4] Hypernationalism, military prowess, arms races, and myths of encirclement divert attention from costs (including opportunity costs) borne largely by consumers and domestic internationalizing rivals. Inward-looking drivers multiply the probability of crises and war, by design or unintentional "slither."[5] Competitive outbidding—for example, when inward-looking factions try to outdo one another in nationalistic credentials—leads to spiraling nationalism and pushes moderates to more extreme positions than they might have preferred.[6]

The relative strength of coalitions vis-à-vis domestic and external competitors determines whether strategies are more pristine or diluted versions of the ideal type. The relative incidence and strength of respective coalitions within a given cluster of states define the strategic (coalitional) context. Comparable internationalizing coalitions converge on mutual incentives to avoid war. Their strategies are thus collectively stable; they create an environment inimical to inward-looking adversaries, undermining the merits of economic closure, militarization, and war. Converging strategies in clusters dominated by similar inward-looking coalitions are also collectively stable, or hardened against mutations toward internationalization. Competing nationalist, protectionist, and militarized coalitions across states feed off one another. This strategic dynamic lowers the barriers against escalating conflict and undercuts internationalizing adversaries throughout the cluster. Such constellations generate greater brinkmanship and structural tendencies toward war even when the latter may not be anyone's highest preference. Coalitions and their associated models of political survival thus filter similar external pressures and inducements differently, adapting them to their grand-strategic requirements.

The argument outlined thus far adds an important component often missing in standard theories of interdependence and peace that ignore political agency. Trade openness (imports plus exports/gross national product) can provide important information—a useful simplification for how global and domestic political economies interact—but a simplification nonetheless. Yet coalitions rise and fall on account of a much more multifaceted political calculus; they must respond to wide-ranging domestic-international interactions, including those stemming from security considerations. Thus, although the relative strength of internationalizers may sometimes dovetail with trade openness levels, it cannot be easily inferred from them. South Korea's trade openness was merely 20 percent in 1963—not too different from inward-looking North Korea's—when President Park Chung-hee adopted an internationalizing model and military restraint vis-à-vis North Korea. Internationalizers from Singapore to Turkey advanced such models under initially incipient rates of trade to gross domestic product (GDP). Rising ratios can expand the beneficiaries of growing trade openness—and sometimes their political power—but they can also buttress inward-looking countermovements.[7] The latter can also thrive under declining trade openness. China's internationalizers faced inward-looking challenges under very low openness in the 1980s but also under much higher levels in the 2010s. The relationship between trade openness and coalitional models is thus not linear. Rather it is affected by domestic contestation, political dynamics, institutional variation, global world-time, and noneconomic forces mobilized under nationalist/internationalist banners.

In sum, coalitions can have independent effects on, and be differently affected by, interdependence. The latter does not exist in a political vacuum; whether or not interdependence dampens incentives for war is contingent on political agents exerting dominance over crucial decisions in particular historical contexts. The character of the global and regional political economy at particular world-times affects the viability of respective models. Whether markets and geography are expanding or contracting; whether international institutions underwrite mutual commitments to free trade and investment or to protectionism; and other dynamics of international exchange weigh heavily on coalitions' wherewithal, as do domestic institutions. Coalitional ideal types, let alone their empirical referents, thus vary over time and space. While adding analytical richness and empirical validity, coalitions are also complex, demanding, dynamic, and contingent categories.[8] More explicit specification of causal mechanisms and political microfoundations may help to resolve apparent inconsistencies regarding the association between global economic exchange and incentives to avoid war.

Three important clarifications are in order before introducing the empirical applications of this general argument. The first reiterates that Weberian ideal types are not historical or "true" realities but conceptual constructs or limiting concepts against which real situations are compared. As ideal types, they need not fit any particular case completely; they provide instead a heuristic, a shortcut for reducing a far more complex reality down to some fundamentals.[9] Second, to minimize *post hoc ergo propter hoc* reasoning, I focus here on processes leading up to the outbreak of World War I rather than its aftermath. The war itself might have provided an easier case for the general argument insofar as war often radicalizes inward-looking coalitions further and weakens their internationalizing adversaries, at least initially. Third, I concentrate on Germany and China because they stand at the center of contemporary comparisons as putative rising challengers. Despite revisionist work on the sources of World War I, and the recognition that there was no single culprit for its eruption, Wilhelm II's *Kaiserreich* remains a crucial part of the war puzzle.[10] Yet this is quite different from arguing that Germany bore exclusive responsibility for launching a calculated world war, or that it did so to escape domestic crisis. Nonetheless, the signals emanating from the *Kaiserreich*'s inward-looking ruling coalition reduced internal and external ambiguity about its intentions. Coalitions act as signaling mechanisms vis-à-vis domestic and foreign audiences. In the absence of complete information (i.e., in the real world), strategic interlocutors make coalitional composition and behavior a crucial basis for inferring each other's intentions. Germany's dominant coalition and its inward-looking counterparts among allies and adversaries thus reinforced the odds of war.

Germany's Ruling Coalition before World War I

Over the several decades preceding World War I, an inward-looking, statist-protectionist, militarized ruling coalition progressively entrenched itself in German politics. The pillars of the coalition were mostly Prussian landowners (Junkers), Ruhr-based heavy industrialists, and the military. In 1879, the year Germany allied itself with Austria-Hungary, this "iron and rye" coalition insti-tuted high tariffs. New agrarian tariffs passed in 1887 were perceived by Russia as an economic declaration of war. The *Kaiserreich* promoted aggressive hyper-nationalism and a military buildup as the glue that would sustain Germany's ruling coalition. This political construct—pivoted on hypernationalism and a military buildup—was expected to curtail demands from a rising middle class; to undermine centrifugal forces including Länder (constituent states), ethnic, class, and other forms of particularism; and defeat socialists, free traders, and other opponents.[11] By the 1890s, Wilhelm's *Weltpolitik* ("world policy" associated with colonial expansion in Europe, the Near East, and Africa) and the battle fleet buildup had exacerbated Anglo-German rivalry. These policies also deepened the military's influence, fostered by Wilhelm, who appointed Adm. Alfred von Tirpitz as state secretary for the navy. *Sammlungspolitik* (the politics of rallying together), developed in 1897, was designed to reaffirm the protectionist social compact and undermine Social Democrats. The latter—rising from 20 to 30 percent of voters (1890s to early 1900s)—opposed agricultural tariffs, *Weltpolitik*, and Prussian militarism. *Sammlungspolitik*, *Weltpolitik*, protectionism, hyper-nationalism, militarization, and expansionism became tightly connected and synergistic. Nationalist pressure groups funded by state and private cartels and the military—Flottenverein, Wehrverein, Kolonialverein, Alldeutscher Verband—agitated on behalf of this agrarian-industrial-military complex (AIMC) to secure raw materials largely via imperial expansion.[12] A strong conservative bureaucracy presided over execution of the AIMC's grand strategy.

Forceful demands for protection from once free-trading Junkers—who now feared global competition and declining prices—increased tensions within the AIMC in the 1890s. Expanding trade, capital, and labor mobility offered some industries incentives to oppose protection. Chancellor Leo von

Caprivi signed trade agreements lowering grain tariffs to gain market access for industrial exports and advance a German-led Mitteleuropa customs union. Junkers formed the Agrarian League (Bund der Landwirte) in 1893 to resist Caprivi and freer trade, fueling the ranks of the "Conservatives" Party. The chambers of commerce and Industrialists League (Bund der Industriellen), created in 1895 by light manufacturing exporters, endorsed Caprivi's project, but a Junkers' onslaught led to his replacement. Finance Minister Johann von Miquel launched *Sammlungspolitik* to restore iron-rye cooperation. The coalition thus became a veto group within the Interior Ministry's Economic Committee, enforcing protection and sponsoring industrial and banking cartels that could resist external and internal competition.

As Germany was becoming more integrated in the global economy by the early 1900s, uncompetitive—particularly agrarian—sectors denounced growing dependence on imported food, raw materials, and industrial unfinished and finished products. Russian and U.S. protectionism, the collapse of the French treaty system that had kept European protectionism relatively low (on which Germany free rode), and statism (the state was the single largest owner of property) nurtured the inward-looking model and a more aggressive Mitteleuropa concept. Kaiser Wilhelm described it as a German-led counter to the United States; Caprivi considered it targeted against Russia. Many others saw it as countering Britain, the United States, and Russia.[13] Navy expansion provided heavy industry with a convenient escape from global competition as well as insurance against economic contraction, cementing AIMC synergies with militarization. Heavy industrialists and shipbuilders besieged the Reichstag and Naval Office to demand an expanded navy. Junkers and industrial and banking cartels populated the Reichstag, enjoying high political access to military, foreign ministry, and other bureaucracies. Chancellor Bernhard von Bülow increased minimal grain tariffs in 1902, further undermining workers and exporters. The tariffs inflicted "a brutal intervention into Russia's economy," but were also made irreversible by treaties.[14] Dissatisfied agrarians threatened to endorse lower industrial tariffs unless industrialists approved higher agrarian ones, which were eventually enacted in 1905.

As Peter Gourevitch argues, it is more accurate to describe opponents of protectionism as supporting freer—rather than free—trade or lower taxes.[15] This opposition was handicapped by lack of government support; great heterogeneity of interests (consumers, producers, manufacturers, and urban and rural constituencies); and deep divisions over property rights, taxes, and much more. Caprivi recognized that further German insertion in the global economy would have served proponents of lower tariffs better.

Yet that was exactly the path not taken, thus weakening incipient internationalizing forces that were progressively overwhelmed by protectionist majorities even in chambers of commerce. The National Liberal Party's right wing, funded by heavy industry, represented belligerent *Weltpolitik* and virulent opposition to social democracy. A center wing, led by Ernst Bassermann and Gustav Stresemann, and initially backed by some banks and exporters, was more moderate but weaker. Once associated with the Industrialists League, this center group merged with the League's erstwhile rival—the heavy industrialists' stronghold, the Central Association of German Manufacturers—in 1906. The center wing eventually yielded to electoral considerations and right-wing pressures on foreign policy, especially after 1912, when Social Democrats became the largest single party in the Reichstag. The Liberals' left wing ("Young Liberals"), friendlier to freer trade and accommodation with Social Democrats, held little influence and compromised with their party's majority. The Hansa League for Commerce, Trade, and Industry, a grouping of internationally oriented traders, industrialists, bankers, and middle-class craftsmen formed in 1909, also opposed extreme protectionism and intolerance of social democracy.[16] Yet under heavy attack from Wilhelm, the chancellor, and iron-rye forces, the Hansa League split and declined politically.

Resistance by Länder and localities, which collected income and property taxes but exempted feudal landowners, offered the *Kaiserreich* few alternatives for relief from growing financial constraints.[17] It had thus depended heavily on agrarian tariffs for about 47 percent of its revenue since the 1890s. Bülow regarded such chronic financial constraints as Germany's Achilles' heel (and main rationale for avoiding war at that time), but Conservatives defeated his 1909 proposed inheritance tax. Under Chancellor Theobald von Bethmann Hollweg, some financial and commercial interests urged more equal taxation and opposed iron-rye demands for higher tariffs upon the expiration of Bülow's treaties. Yet new 1909 taxes on sales and financial transactions spared large landowners, funded the fleet, and undermined popular support for *Sammlungspolitik*. Social Democrats became the largest single party—one-third of the Reichstag in 1912—allowing Bethmann to pass a direct imperial property tax (including inheritance) only in 1913.

The links between the AIMC's domestic and international pillars were thick. The tariff bill and Second Naval Law, passed in 1900, buttressed the iron-rye's logroll, its basic political quid pro quo. Thus industry got the fleet and *Weltpolitik* while Junkers got tariffs, increased income, and continued political dominance.[18] Agrarian tariffs paid for shipbuilding and obviated direct taxation of wealth, further burdening a growing working class. Coal and steel, as well as some shipping and arms industries, became core beneficiaries of naval expansion and imperial designs. Leading weapons manufacturer Alfred Krupp peddled patriotic virtues and economic reasons for war, in line with a ferociously nationalistic media. Coal magnate Emil Kirdorf agitated against yielding Morocco's ore resources in 1911, calling continued access to those resources "a question of life and death," even as some German bankers sought a compromise.[19] Iron-ore industrialists proclaimed the 1871 borders with France unfavorable to Germany. Others urged annexation of a captive, autarchic, *Mitteleuropa* (France included) to free Germany from food dependence, capital scarcity, and saturated domestic markets.[20] Reichstag Junkers claimed that Caprivi's treaty with Russia would cost German agriculture more "than a miserable war."[21] Grain protectionism was a crucial component of *Wehrwirtschaft* (war preparedness); Junkers, nationalists, and the military pressed the need for "food security" to avoid shortages during a looming war. The AIMC thus turned protectionism into "high politics": it radicalized rallying themes (*Sammslungpolitik, Weltpolitik, Machtstaat*); called for military preparedness and protected markets overseas; fueled enmity toward Russia, France, and Britain; and tightened together domestic and external rationales for militarism. Even advocate of *Machtpolitik* (reliance on power politics and physical force) "Young Liberal" Friedrich Naumann warned against the AIMC's strategy of feigning fear to further its interests.[22]

Documented evidence abounds regarding the expected "integrating" benefits of aggressive *Weltpolitik* for strengthening the inward-looking model. The policy was expected to enhance synergies between protectionism and military buildup and between war and the dismantlement of "democracy." Explicit efforts to make Russia appear the aggressor would arguably not only keep Britain out of war but would also bond Social Democrats to the war consensus.[23] Tirpitz connected an offensive fleet with economic gains and subduing Social Democrats. At a 1912 war council meeting, Wilhelm along with most German military advisers strongly endorsed Gen. Helmuth von Moltke's assessment that "war is inevitable, and the sooner the better."[24] Although hardly deciding for war, that meeting is part of a list of extensive records revealing support for war by key actors who, eventually, won over Bethmann and a Reichstag majority.[25] Tirpitz may have wanted a navy as an end in itself, but his and others' warnings of "encirclement" (*Einkreisung*) and external "threats" acquired a life of their own, fostering greater acceptance of military aggression.[26]

Bethmann offered his resignation (cast in terms bound to be rejected), arguing against war in 1912 to salvage negotiations with Britain. He also acknowledged Germany's gamble, including potential unintended costs of war domestically, leading him to seek Social Democratic complicity. Despite occasional cold feet, however, Bethmann accelerated the army's expansion; claimed that public opinion expected a new naval law and a third squadron and that the military must have those; shared the prevailing expansionist bandwagon (Germany is "condemned to spread outward"); agreed that "the people need a war"; encouraged British neutrality to enable Germany's continental conquest; conceded that war with Russia was necessary for *Kaiserreich* "independence"; circumvented restraining influences in July 1914; endorsed Wilhelm's "blank check" to Austro-Hungary encouraging immediate war on Serbia; overruled Wilhelm's belated "Halt-in-Belgrade" effort to delay it; rejected British offers of four-power mediation; and subsequently admitted this was "in a sense" preventive war.[27]

Although war was not inevitable, the signals emanating from Germany's ruling coalition reduced internal and external ambiguity about its intentions. Internationalizers weakened by statist protectionism and cartelization, Social Democrats, Progressives, the Hansa League, and "Young Liberals" were all sapped. Many succumbed to hypernationalism along with significant segments of the middle class. Extremists had devoured "moderate" allies, including Bülow, Bassermann, Stresemann, and many others, even in the Industrialists League.[28] "Moderates" differed in emphasis on submarine, battle fleet, or army expenditures but hardly opposed them despite Germany's chronic financial scarcity, high debt, and poor credit. Bethmann's "policy of the diagonal," seeking to cement AIMC dominance, effectively anchored the policy in the "cult of the offensive."[29] The AIMC, forcefully resisting democracy, had the upper hand, overwhelming internationalizing and democratic alternatives unable to stem the tide of war.

Scholars will continue to debate whether Germany implemented a deliberate war plan or exploited opportunities unleashed by the assassination of Archduke Franz Ferdinand of Austria in Sarajevo in June 1914; whether Germany could wage a cheap, short, triumphal war; whether Bethmann failed to predict British reactions; whether personalities, associations, or Wilhelm acted on principled or other grounds; whether militarism was elite based or populist; whether military or civilian wings of the AIMC were in charge or bore greater responsibility for war; whether this was a conquering domestic coalition or one strong enough to impose its narrow interests on others; and other important questions. Yet overall the aggregation of a hypernationalist, protectionist, and militarist ruling coalition emphasizing armed buildup, economic self-reliance, and territorial expansion made war more possible than it would have been under a different coalition facing identical international configurations.[30] For the AIMC, Germany's "place in the sun" included, at a minimum, a captive Mitteleuropa. Protectionism limited its resources and tightened financial bottlenecks, the latter providing another subterfuge for war advocates to pronounce the utility of war sooner than later. The costs of restraint were far more prohibitive for that particular German coalition than they might have been for others. Revealing how domestic alliances constrain and entrap no less than external ones, extremists pushed moderates—not always kicking and screaming—beyond the latter's comfort zone with war gambles. Foreign failures and responses by France, Russia, and Britain designed to restrain or foil aggressive German actions and ambitions became fodder for coalescing ever-stronger support for the war bandwagon. As noted below, an inward-looking cluster mutually reinforced the odds of war.

In sum, coalitional profiles alone may be insufficient for explaining World War I (claims of sufficiency are rare in social sciences), but one can hardly escape the conclusion that they were necessary in boosting the probability of war, by providing crucial background for understanding why war obtained and complementing historical diplomacy typically tracing how catalytic events unleashed the Great War.

China's Ruling Coalition: Similarities and Contrasts with Germany's *Kaiserreich*

The political models underlying the *Kaiserreich* and today's China contain some commonalities. The disjointedness between rapid socioeconomic change, on the one hand, and stagnant political institutions, on the other, remains a core parallel. At the broadest level, the *Kaiserreich* was a multiparty democracy largely in form but rigged and autocratic in practice. China is an autocratic single-party state where competing factions vie for control and political rights are suppressed. Yet important contrasts are no less significant.

First, the *Kaiserreich* relied on different sources of revenue extraction than has China post-Deng Xiaoping. These differences bore implications for political accountability; for the availability of compensatory resources; for reliance on strategies to freeze versus transform sociopolitical structures; for instrumental uses of nationalism; and for relative costs of war. AIMC pressure and Länder monopoly over income tax locked the *Kaiserreich* into protectionism and dependence on customs for 47 percent of its revenues. This dependence reinforced the *Kaiserreich*'s commitment to freeze existing agrarian/industrial structures. Financial constraints were the price for preserving the AIMC, making direct taxation, lower military expenditures, or further borrowing (in a tight domestic capital market) more difficult. Consumers thus largely underwrote military expenditures; demands for increasing those arguably buttressed calls for war sooner lest one could not be financed later. Such demands reinforced the cult of the offensive.[31] As financial constraints mounted, symbolic content—*Sammlungspolitik*, hypernationalism, the fleet, Mitteleuropa, myths of empire as the primary currency of regime survival—tilted the balance further from *panem* (bread) toward *circenses* (circuses).

By contrast, trade is a leading source of employment creation in China; in 2011 tariffs contributed less than 3 percent of central government revenue, down from 5.5 percent in 2007.[32] China's internationalizing strategy has also enabled greater compensatory resources, unleashed a historical transformation of socioeconomic structures, lifted 600 million people out of poverty, and generated a large middle class. Symbolic content—"reform and opening" (*gaige kaifang*), "peaceful rise" (*heping jueqi*), "peaceful development" (*heping fazhan*), and a "well-off" society (*xiaokang shehui*)—could not but be internationalization friendly. Reminiscent of the *Kaiserreich* in some ways, nationalism remains an intrinsic ingredient of regime survival in China. Nationalism is deployed (and withheld) strategically to soften the rough edges of rapid modernization; to complement social transformation; and to compensate for growing inequality, suppressed household consumption, and democratic deficits.[33] Yet the currency of regime survival remains both *panem et circenses*: nationalism must contend with internationalization as pivotal for delivering prosperity and national power alike. Even sacred cows such as food security and self-sufficiency in grains, erstwhile used by nationalists to protect farmers (as in the *Kaiserreich*), are giving way to global comparative advantage.[34]

Second, whereas Germany's strong inward-looking forces overwhelmed internationalizers, the latter's sway within and beyond the CCP has increased dramatically. On the ashes of Mao Zedong's autarchic model, Deng Xiaoping and his successors have forged an internationalizing strategy that requires dramatically different allies and "brandings" than the *Kaiserreich*'s. Regional and global instability were anathema to luring FDI, technology, imports of natural resources, and broad international acceptability—all key ingredients for domestic stability, economic growth, and continued political control. A "charm offensive"—synergistic with the internationalizing model—allowed deeper cooperative relations within and beyond the region and greater openness to multilateral and regional institutions. An internationalizing strategy and regional stability paved the road to (and paid the bills for) a well-off society and a rapidly growing middle class, particularly in the coastal regions. The strategy had increased trade openness to 68 percent by 2008, more than twice Germany's 33 percent pre–World War I average.[35] China's economy is far more integrated with the world today, and in different ways (explored below) than the *Kaiserreich* was in 1914. Moreover, Germany's trajectory evolved from freer trade in the nineteenth century to protectionism; China's from Maoist autarchy to post-Deng openness and massive trade surpluses and foreign reserves (nearly $4 trillion by 2013).

Inward-looking factions intermittently defy China's internationalization, feeding on unresolved rural reform, urbanization, local-central tensions, unemployment, an aging population, corruption, environmental threats, high FDI dependence for growth, absence of political freedoms, and other challenges. The state sector employs about half of the urban workforce in schools, hospitals, and state-owned enterprises in banking, oil, petrochemicals, telecommunications, steel, electricity, and other sectors. Some agricultural and inland sectors, as well as segments of the People's Liberation Army, propaganda, and security services, also resist internationalization. Inward-looking constituencies, many Maoist holdovers, remain overrepresented in the Central Committee and other party organs, bureaucracies, and large state-owned enterprises.[36] Bo Xilai's effort to logroll those constituencies behind the "Chongqing model" and "sing red songs" movement (despite his earlier promotion of foreign investment as Chongqing Party secretary) contributed— along with his corrupt practices—to his political demise.[37]

China's leaders survive politically by straddling coalitional camps to control them both. Inward-looking challengers, however, hardly approximate Germany's AIMC stranglehold thus far. Indeed, rampant protectionism is regarded as less viable or desirable despite regulations favoring domestic enterprises (e.g., technology transfer). President Xi Jinping, with extensive experience working with the private sector in coastal areas, has secured both a CCP mandate to assign the market a "decisive" economic role and personal control over the military, domestic security, propaganda, and anticorruption machines. Commitments to fair, open, and transparent market rules remain a significant challenge. Yet the third plenum of the 18th Party Congress and the 2014 National People's Congress signaled continued allegiance to market reforms, financial liberalization, trade, FDI, and GDP growth. The private sector already generates most GDP, and more of the post-1980 generation works in private and foreign firms than older generations.[38] Liberalization of finance and key industries remains a major bottleneck. The emphasis on "rebalancing" and domestic consumption is associated with demographic transition, a sluggish global economy, competition from low-wage countries, and other factors. Rebalancing signals efforts to reach a new equilibrium and create less dependence on exports, not necessarily retrenchment from the global economy. Although some of the latter cannot be altogether discounted given the political pressures described above, few see signs of a return to autarkic designs in the foreseeable future.[39]

Third, Germany promoted aggressive nationalism to stem Länder, minority, religious, and class particularism, another pattern eerily close to CCP's on/off reliance on nationalism to deflect internal centrifugal and external challenges. Yet, as argued, China's model has required blending nationalism with peaceful internationalization, the latter a crucial ingredient for enhancing both prosperity and state power. Aggressive militarized imperialism was central to Germany's nationalist brew. China's hostility in the South China Sea in recent years is worrisome but has not yet extended to systematic militarized means for securing overseas resources worldwide. Inward-looking forces encouraging virulent nationalism do creep into maritime disputes and air defense identification zones. Such incursions raise a crucial dilemma for internationalizers: how to modulate nationalism—and control the military—while preventing self-entrapment; or how to prevent shifts from tamer (internationalization friendly) to a more rabid nationalism that could derail or disrupt internationalization.[40] Sometimes provocations reach risky levels, as in the Diaoyu/Senkaku, Spratlys, and Paracel Islands disputes and in economic coercion vis-à-vis Japan (rare earths) and the Philippines. Social media is a major outlet for nationalist agitation, reminiscent of 1914. Yet official calls for imperial expansion like those that animated the *Kaiserreich* remain marginalized, and China's rallying slogans (cited above) could not be more different. Amid violence leading to the killing of Chinese nationals in May 2014 in Vietnam, Xi Jinping urged restraint. In a message directed as much toward domestic as external audiences, he declared that there is no gene for invasion in Chinese people's blood.[41] War could only puncture "China's dream" enabled by peaceful internationalization. As World War I suggests, however, nationalism is not always controllable; it can breed unintended consequences and subvert domestic civil-military balances with ominous implications.

Contrasting World-Time: Internationalization circa 1914 and 2014

Whether or not these and other contrasts between Germany's *Kaiserreich* and China overwhelm similarities—a topic bound to elicit sharp disagreements—does the constellation of international and domestic factors in 1914 versus 2014 introduce additional considerations that weaken the analogy?[42] As argued, coalitional ideal types, let alone their empirical referents, vary over time and space. The changing nature of the global economy, domestic politics, and institutions carries different implications for the viability of distinctive models and their international effects.

First, the contemporary context within which coalitions operate differs substantially from that preceding World War I. Whereas some consider external economic considerations to have been peripheral for decision-makers in 1914, particularly in Germany, today's global context features far more centrally for decisionmakers and publics alike. The costs of enhancing or decreasing economic openness, attracting or spurning FDI, are far more salient for political survival in a world of many more democracies, and even in autocratic contexts. Domestic institutions—central banks, bureaucracies, legislatures, parties, unions, social movements, and the media—absorb or refract the effects of the global economy more than ever before. They also demand stability, employment, rising incomes, lower taxes, welfare benefits, and equitable burdens. The political power of internationalizing constituencies is unprecedented (though not irreversible), strengthened by intra-industry trade and integrated production chains.[43]

Whereas China's regime survival hinges foremost on economic prosperity tightly connected to internationalization, *Kaiserreich* military expenditures undermined prosperity amid dire financial constraints imposed by the *Kaiserreich's* inward-looking model. China's military modernization has not yet overtaken compensatory resources needed to offset autocratic rule, but could do so if unchecked, increasing risks to regime survival. The military absorbed 6–16 percent of China's central expenditures (2007–13), but claimed more than 80 percent of *Kaiserreich* appropriations (1890–1913), accounting for more than 65 percent of its total debt.[44] Cabinet directives dismantled civilian control of the military while AIMC dominance engineered Reichstag approval of military budgets. Whether or not China's army has become more powerful politically or outspoken is highly contested. Internationalization yielded resources to satisfy demands for modernization, but military budgets remain subordinated to CCP control. An unraveling of civilian dominance would not bode well and might narrow the gap with pre–World War I Germany. At present, however, China does not approach the *Kaiserreich's* military autonomy or militarization of state and society. The consolidation of disparate agencies into a unified coast guard seems designed to further tighten Xi Jinping's control.

Second, variations in the nature and comparability of regional clusters create different dynamics of strategic interaction. The *Kaiserreich* faced a far more inward-looking coalitional cluster beyond its borders than China does today. Germany's own nationalist, protectionist, and militarist model was pervasive and contagious; it reinforced other inward-looking models that strengthened it in turn. Germany pioneered alliances and raised tariffs ahead of others; led in dependence on customs relative to total revenue (two to four times higher than most great powers at the time); unleashed an arms race; and projected extreme hypernationalism. Russia reciprocated with tariffs, nationalism, threats, and militarization. Nationalists everywhere nurtured one another; the military enjoyed significant power and autonomy throughout European states; and early twentieth-century statist protectionism suppressed internationalizing private capital politically not only in Germany.[45] Early twenty-first-century East Asia, and the global context within which it is embedded, looks substantially different. Not only have internationalizers (including a record large consumer class) expanded both intra- and extra-regional trade and investment to unprecedented levels—much higher than the 1914 strategic cluster—but they are also better endowed politically to defend their interests.[46]

Free-trading Britain was exceptional in 1914, more reliant on direct and graduated taxes (primarily income and inheritance, which paid for military expenditures). The state owned half as much of the economy as in Germany and Austria-Hungary. Britain also featured a large and politically strong commercial and industrial middle class fostered by internationalization, and a trade openness ratio averaging 47 percent. There were few peasants or militaristic aristocrats logrolling rabid nationalism and Britain's army and arms industry were weaker than Germany's. Its nimbler political institutions were better able to absorb demands for expanding rights than those of Germany, Russia, or Austria-Hungary. British internationalizers enjoyed a unique position, confining German-style inward-looking forces to the fringes. Along with the City of London and other economic/commercial constituencies, British shipbuilders—focused on merchant ships—and exporters were averse to war. Challenging expectations that hegemons drag challengers into war to prevent their own decline, Britain delayed firm alliance commitments and hesitated to declare war until Germany's assault on neutral Belgium overcame internal (including cabinet) opposition to war.[47]

Germany's AIMC weaved its visceral antipathy to democracy, the bourgeoisie, socialism, and republicanism into allegations of encirclement by Britain and France, emblems of advancing democratic industrialism.[48] The external and internal wars were, in some respects, one and the same; from an AIMC vantage point, the British defeat of the Boers was a strike against agrarian feudalism within Europe itself. In contrast, Chinese leaders promoting industrialization via internationalization denounce putative pro-democracy pincer movements by domestic and international adversaries, at least partly for their alleged potential to derail internationalization. Furthermore, internationalizers in China's strategic cluster—stronger than their 1914 counterparts—share converging incentives to tame interactive nationalism, even as Japan's and China's inward-looking factions test the boundaries.[49]

Third, pre–World War I internationalizers faced a radically different global economic, political, and institutional context. Lower transportation costs and other innovations, not free-trade policies, drove trade expansion under rising tariffs.[50] Germany's 1879 tariffs encouraged generalized tariffs elsewhere, as the world-time favored dominant preferences for protection, neomercantilism, statist entrepreneurship, private cartels, and nationalism. No golden age for free traders, a global institutional vacuum bolstered protectionism, which enjoyed a much better reputation than it does today. In contrast, widespread economic liberalization has underpinned extraordinary trade expansion over nearly seven decades now. International institutions (the General Agreement on Tariffs and Trade/World Trade Organization, the International Monetary Fund, the World Bank, the European Union, and bilateral, multilateral, and regional preferential trade agreements) have facilitated collective action in trade liberalization, softening the rough edges of globalization even in the Great Recession's aftermath. Arvind Subramanian and Martin Kessler summarize additional exceptional features of twenty-first-century trade integration: China plays a mega-trader role comparable to pre–World War I Britain (not Germany); historically unprecedented trade in goods and services grew from 11 percent of world GDP (early 1970s) to 33 percent (2012); and trade expansion is faster than ever (hyperglobalization). Additionally, today's trade integration is dematerialized (growing emphasis on services); democratic (embraced widely); crisscrossing (similar goods and investments from South to North and vice versa); nested in preferential trade agreements and networks; and on the cusp of mega-regionalism linking the largest traders with each other.[51]

Finally, FDI among strategic interlocutors was negligible in 1914. Richard Rosecrance notes that trade underpinned Germany's growth before World War I, as it does in China; yet the latter has relied on FDI as the dominant source of external capital, acquiescing to high dependence on dynamic regional and global Western and Japanese production and supply chains and value-added content.[52] The centrality of networked technology and geographical dispersion of production raise the costs of domestic substitution. Multinational corporations' geographically diversified portfolios are deemed an effective and unprecedented substitute for conquest, enabling access to foreign markets, raw materials, and supplies without resorting to war.[53] Globalized production acts as both a more crucial and less vulnerable driver of contemporary globalization than trade was in 1914. Opportunity costs of closure to FDI are politically prohibitive and compel stronger legal and institutional infrastructures for attracting and protecting it. Easier substitutes for unstable production links further lower FDI's vulnerability. Extensive financial globalization raises additional opportunity costs. Actors willing to disrupt those ties to the global economy through militarized conflict face higher political obstacles today than in 1914.

Conclusion

Debates over the sources of World War I will likely endure until the end of history. There is even little agreement on whether any of the powers were itching for war or whether all of them were. Coalitional accounts contribute to that debate by dwelling on deeper, crucial sources of war and peace. Such accounts infuse agency and provide vital information on why some states find themselves self-isolated, vulnerable, encircled, "slithering" into powder kegs such as Sarajevo or, in some cases, choosing war deliberately. Coalitions are signaling mechanisms vis-à-vis domestic and foreign audiences. Strategic interlocutors make coalitional makeup and behavior an essential source for inferring each other's intentions in the absence of complete information. Such signals can sometimes discourage foreign interlocutors from deepening economic exchange with aggressive inward-looking models. The latter may not "cause" wars, but signal maximalist intentions at home and abroad, making war more foreseeable. Inward-looking coalitions may have no monopoly over "accidents," "faits accomplis," or "blunders," but their protocols infuse the strategic context with a higher potential for war. Internationalizers, particularly when equipped with compensatory resources to minimize domestic adjustment costs, are less likely than their inward-looking competitors to "leap into the dark" Bethmann style.[54] These expectations, of course, suggest significant tendencies rather than inevitability.

The coalitional argument also clarifies contradictory findings regarding interdependence and war by providing a mechanism capable of explaining why, when, and how economic exchange with the world may or may not inhibit war. Correlational data cannot affirm causal effects, least of all for an $N = 1$ (World War I), and they entail risks of incorrect inferences. Coalitions cannot be simply derived from interdependence ratios. They are fundamentally political agents enabled and constrained by institutions, acting as transmission belts between external inducements and domestic political power.

Coalitions translate incentives vis-à-vis the global economy into inputs on war and peace; they are thus crucial categories at the very vortex articulating *Innenpolitik* and *Aussenpolitik*. The line between the two *Primats* (primacies) is fluid, making coalitions the stuff of high politics. Growing interdependence may broaden the scope of beneficiaries of internationalization, but such dependency can also strengthen inward-looking resolve to reverse it. Extant interdependence ratios certainly provide important information. Yet they may fail to capture future expectations; risks and opportunities capable of mobilizing political constituencies; and institutional processes and mechanisms that amplify or thwart their power.

While taking the political corollaries of preferences regarding internationalization seriously, this argument differs from reductionist views that the *Kaiserreich* declared war only to escape domestic crisis. Or that it necessarily favored a world or a continental—rather than a "localized"—war. Or that it bore exclusive responsibility for it.[55] The *Kaiserreich*'s strategic coalitional context—imbued with nationalism, militarism, protectionism, and imperialism of its own— did not precisely exude moderation. It thus strengthened German referents vis-à-vis their domestic adversaries. Strategic contexts dominated by inward-looking models marginalize internationalizers internally, raising their costs for opposing war. A strongly internationalizing cluster might have lowered those costs. This argument turns Leninist theory on its head: internationalizers can have incentives to avoid, not promote, war; it is their weakness that contributed to the breakdown of restraints in 1914. Lumping "the bourgeoisie" into a single category thus obscures important—and evolving—domestic distributional consequences from global economic engagement and war.

The 1914 strategic cluster arguably provides a most-likely case for confirming inward-looking tendencies to discount the risk of war or "slither" into one. A scenario of inward-looking models growing dominant in East Asia and unleashing major war would also align with those theoretical expectations.[56] The trends discussed earlier suggest that the prospects for this may be small in 2014, though nontrivial. Internationalizers have turned China into the world's largest mega-trader. Yet the volatility in China's charm index (and Japan's) can be traced, to a significant extent, to protracted domestic coalitional competition. Two other hypothetical scenarios could challenge expectations from the general theoretical framework discussed here. The first would be a major war among strong internationalizing actors. The second assumes an entrenched inward-looking cluster that retreats from the global economy but also retains a strong commitment to preserve Asia's decades-old absence of war. Domestic coalitional balances of power are dynamic and sensitive to both domestic and external trends. This implies an open-ended dynamic, separating this argument from teleological ones that consider internationalization to be linear and unproblematic and interstate wars obsolete.

Predictions about war (as war itself) are always risky. Understanding the conditions that may increase or decrease its odds remains a tall order. A key quandary is whether East Asia's archetypical model is robust enough to sustain the peace. The favorable global and regional circumstances that lubricated the model cannot be taken for granted. Although it survived major crises in 1997 and 2008, the model could be buffeted by external shocks that deepen internal rifts and reverse coalitional balances. Unlike 1914, however, contemporary coalitions do not thrive or decay in a global institutional vacuum. International institutions weigh in on coalitional competition, typically buttressing internationalizers. East Asian nationalism remains an important threat but must also compete with strong countervailing internationalizing forces. Civilian control of the military remains robust. Furthermore, despite serious disputes, explicitly militaristic will-to-war is more politically constrained than in pre–World War I annals. These trends may be more auspicious than the 1914 world-time, but also leave ample room for improvement.

The cult of the offensive played a major role in 1914, as did rigid alliances, a dangerous shortcut to decisionmaking in Sarajevo's aftermath that warns against "blank checks." Calculations favoring war sooner than later were rampant then, revealing the precarious ground on which balance of power calculations sometimes stand.[57] Systemic power structures cannot be ignored, but coalitional balances of power can help to override them. The radicalization of Germany's coalition fueled parallel trends elsewhere, congealing ever more inflexible alliances that hardened Germany's coalition in turn.[58] Democracy is a crucial glue of contemporary U.S. alliances, and the realm of converging internationalizing democracies has proven robust to sustaining the peace among them. Converging internationalizing models, though perhaps less robust for curtailing war in the absence of reciprocal democratic checks, remain significant constraints. China's internationalizers share incentives with the West—and much of the rest—to bolster a stable global economy.

The relationship between rising powers and war is thus not overdetermined but conditioned more on coalitional arrangements in rising and declining powers than on abstract, contested measures of relative international power. Rising hypernationalist, military-controlled, protectionist, and aggression-prone coalitions may be met with greater external resistance than internationalizing ones. The rise of post-1945 Germany has not led to war; only extremist fringes fueled by the Euro crisis equate it with earlier historical incarnations that—under imputations of encirclement—twice led Germany down the path of destruction. Naval expenditures and propaganda harmed its social fabric, pauperized workers, and invigorated self-consuming nationalism. Wars unleashed even more virulent social unrest, crisis, and humiliation. The contrast with present-day Germany could not be starker: a democratic, internationalized, unified economic powerhouse eschewing unilateralism, militarism, and nuclear weapons. It is hard to imagine that China's leaders, who are facing considerable domestic challenges, are not sensitive to this history.

Contemporary world politics is not an independent occurrence, and especially not independent of World War I, World War II, and the Cold War. Surely the tragedy of the twentieth century, and the unintended effects of playing up hypernationalist cards, informs today's powers. Whether that legacy leads to profound transformations in the institution of war hinges on distilling appropriate lessons from the path to the Great War. Arguing that China in 2014 is Germany in 1914 is neither precise nor constructive. Ahistorical analogies between then and now may not only be imperfect, but they can infuse actors with misguided and perilous protocols for international behavior. The choice between presumed atavistic tendencies toward war and peaceful accommodation exists; and coalitions are crucial to that choice. Mark Twain putatively declared, "History never repeats itself but it rhymes." There is plenty that may rhyme with World War I today but even more that does not. All sides must make sure that gap never narrows.

11

European Militaries and the
Origins of World War I

Stephen Van Evera

WORLD WAR I stemmed largely from two military-related causes. First, the professional militaries of prewar Europe used their imposing political power to lobby hard for war. Unlike today, European militaries had massive influence in the halls of government. Also unlike today, these militaries were very hawkish. They relentlessly pushed for war, or for policies that would cause war, in Germany, Austria, and Serbia. In Russia and France, the warmongering was less intense, but both countries pushed decisively for war at crucial moments in the July 1914 crisis. The great power and extreme hawkishness of pre-1914 militaries was a lethal combination and a key cause of the war.

Second, European militaries purveyed war-causing myths that persuaded civilian policymakers and publics to pursue belligerent policies on their own account. The most important myth was the "cult of the offensive"—the false claim that in warfare the attacker had the advantage and that conquest was correspondingly easy while defense was hard. Militaries purveyed other pernicious myths as well. These misperceptions primed Europe for war.

Absent the malign influence of European militaries on civilian decisions and perceptions, World War I would not have occurred. The militaries caused the war.

European Militaries Were War Lobbies

Before 1914 military political and social power was greatest in Germany, but militaries also wielded great power in Austria-Hungary, Russia, and Serbia. Only in Britain and France was military influence kept within reasonable bounds. Everywhere militaries used their power to push for war or for policies that raised the risk of war. Their pressure was often decisive. The makers of war unleashed the dogs of war.

Historians widely agree that the German military exerted a dominant influence on Wilhelmine German policy.[1] Wilhelm Deist notes the "extraordinary predominance of the military over the civilian authorities" in the Wilhelmine era.[2] Adolf Gasser stresses that the military, not the civilian leaders, dominated German public affairs.[3] Friedrich Meinecke notes that Wilhelmine German officers enjoyed vast prestige, writing that the German "lieutenant moved through the world as a young god and the civilian reserve lieutenant as a demi-god."[4] Isabel Hull observes that the Wilhelmine German military had "enormous popular prestige" and "complete independence" from civilian rule, achieving "ascendancy vis-à-vis the civilian leadership" after around 1905–06.[5] Louis Snyder observes that the German Navy League attained far more power in German politics than most German political parties.[6] Gordon Craig writes that the German army became "a state within a state, claiming the right to define what was, or was not, to the national interest and to dispense with those who did not agree."[7]

Kaiser Wilhelm II idolized the German officer corps, filling his entourage with officers and spending most of his time with them.[8] He rarely rejected their advice. Other German civilians deferred obsequiously to German military leaders on policy questions. For example, Baron Friedrich von Holstein, a top German Foreign Office official, accepted without discussion Gen. Alfred von Schlieffen's unwise plan to invade Belgium in the event of war with France, explaining: "If the Chief of the Great General Staff, and particularly a strategic authority like Schlieffen, thought such a measure to be necessary, then it would be the duty of diplomacy to adjust itself to it and prepare for it in every possible way."[9] One can almost see him cringing and shuffling his feet. German Chancellor Theobold von Bethmann Hollweg also lamely agreed to Schlieffen's plan, writing that "political measures had to be shaped in accordance with the needs of the [military] campaign plan."[10] Germany's defeat in World War I was sealed with this blunder—it brought Belgium, Britain, and ultimately the United States into the war against Germany—but German civilians never studied its implications, instead trusting Schlieffen's judgment. Schlieffen had no qualifications to shape foreign policy. Yet in Germany, he ruled supreme on key foreign policy matters.

German cabinet ministers who crossed the military lost their jobs. Between 1871 and 1914, military pressure forced the resignations of two German war ministers, a minister of foreign affairs, a minister of the interior, and two chancellors.[11] The army chief of staff had the right of private personal access to the kaiser.[12] The chief of the military cabinet saw the kaiser privately three times a week.[13]

Militaries were powerful in other states as well. In Austria Army Chief of Staff Gen. Franz Conrad von Hötzendorf and several other generals were major shapers of policy. These generals played a key role in pushing Austria toward war in 1914. In Russia soldiers had large influence over foreign and military policy. During the July crisis, top Russian commanders played a central role in persuading other leaders to approve Russian mobilization measures. In Serbia the military cowed civilians into accepting its belligerent and reckless schemes. The Serbian army had a chilling record of ruthless violence against civilians who crossed them. In 1903, Serbian officers overthrew the pro-Austrian Obrenović monarchy, in the process murdering the king, his wife, her brother, and several cabinet ministers. In 1914 two organizers of the 1903 coup, Col. Dragutin Dimitrijević and Voja Tankosić, were still on the scene, with Dimitrijević now serving as army intelligence chief. Serbian civilians were appropriately unnerved. Fearing another coup, they shrank from curbing the army's recklessly aggressive foreign policy ideas; and, crucially, they turned a blind eye to Dimitrijević's plan to assassinate Austrian Archduke Franz Ferdinand at Sarajevo in June 1914. Better the archduke than themselves.[14]

Across Europe militaries enjoyed immense standing and prestige. Michael Howard summarizes, "The armed forces were regarded...as the embodiment of the Nation."[15] European heads of state postured as military officers in a way that is now unthinkable. For example, they usually wore military uniforms in public settings (except in republican France). Other top officials often did likewise. When he first appeared as chancellor in the German Reichstag, Bethmann Hollweg wore a major's uniform.[16]

The policy advice of European militaries was almost uniformly hawkish in every country. Nearly everywhere top officers called stridently for war in every crisis during the lead-up to 1914. Only in Britain did the military not form an important lobby for war or for policies that would cause war. In Germany top army generals pushed hard and often for war. Their clamoring grew louder over time and built to a crescendo during 1909–14. Their reported calls for war form a long list: Gen. Helmuth von Moltke the Elder in 1875, for war against France;[17] Generals Moltke the Elder, Alfred von Waldersee, and the German General Staff in 1887, for war against Russia;[18] Generals Alfred von Schlieffen, Karl von Einem, Wilhelm Groener, Wilhelm von Dommes, Erich von Ludendorff, Colmar von der Goltz, and the German General Staff in 1905, for war against France; Generals Moltke the Younger,

Moritz von Lyncker, and Wilhelm Dommes in 1909, for an Austrian war on Serbia that risked triggering a general continental war; Generals Moltke, Hans von Plessen, and the German General Staff in 1911, for war against France and Britain; Generals Moltke, Dommes, and Plessen in 1912, for war against Russia, France, and Britain; the kaiser's military entourage in early 1913, for war against Russia and France; General Moltke, several times during May and June 1914, for war against Russia and France; the General Staff in early July 1914 for war against Russia and France; Generals Erich von Falkenhayn, Lyncker, and Plessen, on July 5, 1914, for a hard-line policy toward Serbia that risked a general European war; Generals Moltke and Falkenhayn on July 29, for a general European war; and Generals Moltke, Falkenhayn, and the General Staff on July 30, for a general European war.

These generals were Germany's top army officers. They held the army's most powerful jobs: chief of the General Staff, war minister, chief of the military cabinet, quartermaster general of the General Staff, and commandant of military headquarters. They represented its most prestigious and influential military organizations, the General Staff, and the kaiser's military entourage. Their arguments carried great weight and inevitably had a large impact on German policy. They called for war in every crisis during 1905–14. War was their response to every situation, their solution to every problem.

Moltke the Younger was the single loudest voice for war in the German government. As army chief of staff, he counseled war repeatedly between 1906 and 1914. When crises arose, he appeared like clockwork to push the kaiser and Chancellor Bethmann Hollweg toward war. Historian Annika Mombauer notes Moltke's "consistent and desperate pressurizing for war" during the lead-up to 1914.[19] Isabel Hull writes that "Moltke systematically and continuously pressed for…war, while the [kaiser's] military entourage joined in the chorus."[20] Historian Stig Förster writes that "Moltke is well-known to have been one of the prime warmongers in Imperial Germany."[21]

Moltke based his case for war on preventive logic. He argued regularly that war is inevitable; others are bound to attack us sooner or later; we can win if we strike today, but later we will be too weak. In January 1909, during the Bosnian annexation crisis, Moltke urged Austrian Chief of Staff Conrad to use the crisis as a pretext for an Austrian war on Serbia. In Moltke's mind the time was right: Austria should move against Serbia while Serbia's main ally, Russia, was relatively weak, and could therefore be deterred from entering the conflict or be defeated if it did.[22] The risk of causing a general war was large: despite its weakness, Russia might well have responded by attacking Austria, sparking a continental conflict.

Moltke favored war against France and Britain during the 1911 Moroccan crisis,[23] and he angrily denounced the kaiser's decision to let the crisis pass without war: "If we once again emerge from this affair with our tail between our legs, if we cannot bring ourselves to make energetic demands that we would be ready to force through with the help of the sword, then I despair of the future of the German Reich. In that case I will leave. But before that I will make the request to get rid of the army, and to have us placed under Japan's protectorate."[24]

During the next crisis, a dispute during 1912–13 over the aftermath of the first Balkan war, Moltke remained on the warpath. In the famous "war council" meeting with the kaiser on December 8, 1912, Moltke urged "war the sooner the better" against Britain, France, and Russia.[25]

The year 1913 found Moltke spending more time preparing for war than recommending it. In late 1913, he tried to cow Belgium into agreeing that German troops could invade France through Belgium. Moltke warned the visiting Belgian king at a dinner that a Franco-German war was imminent and that Belgium would suffer "severe" consequences if it failed to cooperate with German military actions.[26] He cautioned, "Nothing will be able to resist the force of *furor teutonicus* once it has been unleashed. The smaller states would be well-advised to side with us, for the consequences of the war will be severe for those who are against us."[27]

While enjoying a cure together at the Carlsbad spa, Moltke and Austrian Chief of Staff Conrad in May 1914 planned an early war against Russia and France. Moltke argued that "any delay [in launching war] would amount to a reduction of our chances."[28] Moltke and Conrad then agreed that Germany and Austria should "not hesitate on a suitable occasion to proceed with vigor and, if necessary, to begin the war."[29]

On May 20 or June 3, Moltke lobbied Germany's top diplomat, Foreign Secretary Gottlieb von Jagow, to instigate an early war against Russia and France. Jagow recorded Moltke's arguments, made during a car ride from Potsdam to Berlin: "The military superiority of our enemies would [in the next two to three years] be so great that he [Moltke] did not know how we could overcome them. Today we would still be a match for them. In his opinion there was no alternative to making preventive war in order to defeat the enemy while we still stand a chance of victory. The Chief of the General Staff therefore proposed that I should conduct a policy with the aim of provoking a war in the near future."[30] On June 1, Moltke was again heard wishing aloud for war: "If only it would finally boil over—we are ready and the sooner the better for us."[31]

On July 29, as the July crisis came to a head, Moltke pushed for mobilization and war. Saxon military attaché Leuckart von Weissdorf reported, "There is no doubt that the Chief of the General Staff is in favor of war, whereas the Chancellor is holding back. General von Moltke is alleged to have said that we shall never find as favorable a moment as now when neither France nor Russia have finished enlarging their army organization."[32]

Perhaps most important, Moltke usurped civilian authority on July 30, when he insisted that Chancellor Bethmann Hollweg end his belated but promising efforts to resolve the July crisis, and that Germany instead mobilize its army and attack Belgium and France. In a scene made for the movies, Moltke appeared uninvited at a crucial meeting between Bethmann, Falkenhayn, and Adm. Alfred von Tirpitz at 1:00 p.m. on July 30. Moltke's precise words are unknown, but within hours Bethmann had crumpled, agreeing to drop his peace effort and instead launch mobilization, and thus war, the next day at noon.[33]

Many other top German officers also called loudly for war during these years. Long-time Army Chief of the General Staff Alfred von Schlieffen (1891–1905), Prussian War Minister Karl von Einem, General Staff railway department head Wilhelm Groener, Gen. Wilhelm von Dommes, Gen. Erich von Ludendorff, Gen. Colmar von der Goltz, and most of the army General Staff all urged war against France during the 1905 Moroccan crisis. They reasoned that France was ripe for attack while its Russian ally was reeling from defeat in the 1904–05 Russo-Japanese War.[34]

In 1909 Chief of the Military Cabinet Gen. Moritz von Lyncker and General Dommes joined Moltke in calling for an Austrian war on Serbia.[35] Lyncker hoped this would trigger general war, because he regarded "war at the present moment as desirable in order to escape from difficulties at home and abroad."[36] In 1911 he advised war again, this time against France during the Moroccan crisis, now joined by Hauptquartier Commandant Hans von Plessen.[37] Ludwig von Gebsattel, the Bavarian military attaché in Berlin, reported that military officers in Berlin broadly favored unleashing a war with France in 1911 over the Moroccan issue: "In military circles, especially here in Berlin…it is emphasized that we should use the [present] situation, which is broadly favorable to us, to strike."[38]

Plessen and Dommes urged war against Russia and France in 1912, Plessen declaring in December: "Now I wish it would come to this! [i.e., to war]. The earlier, the better! The great liquidation must come sometime!"[39]

The General Staff urged war against Russia and France in February 1913, on grounds that "if there is a further postponement of the great decision, both France and Russia would be able to catch up" in modernizing their armies.[40]

In November 1913, a Belgian observer noted the prowar lobbying of army officers toward Kaiser Wilhelm: "The Kaiser is surrounded solely by generals who no doubt have received the order to speak the same language as the Chief of the General Staff [Moltke].... [Their advice] is intended to change H.M. peace loving-attitude and to convince him of the necessity of this war."[41]

In May 1914, General Staff Quartermaster Gen. Georg Graf von Waldersee urged war on grounds that "the chances of achieving a speedy victory in a major European war are *today* still very favorable for Germany and for the Triple Alliance as well. Soon, however, this will no longer be the case."[42]

In early June 1914, an observer in Berlin reported that "many military men were demanding" a preventive war.[43]

In early July 1914, after the Sarajevo assassination, the General Staff favored immediate war against Russia and France. The Saxon military plenipotentiary in Berlin noted, "The Great General Staff...would regard it with favor if war were to come about now. Conditions and prospects would never become better for us."[44] Around the same time, Chancellor Bethmann Hollweg mentioned ongoing lobbying for war by the military, noting in conversation "the preventive war being demanded by the military."[45] Historian Luigi Albertini believes that this lobbying helped to turn Bethmann toward war: "It cannot be doubted...that Bethmann's attitude was influenced...by that of the military."[46]

Generals Falkenhayn, Lyncker, and Plessen supported a hard-line policy at a crucial meeting on July 5, 1914, where the kaiser decided to issue his famous "blank check" to Austria regarding Serbia.[47] This fateful decision put Europe on a track toward war.

Sometime in July 1914, Falkenhayn obliquely expressed agreement that Russia's rising strength called for a German preventive war.[48] Falkenhayn also pushed on July 29 to order the preliminary mobilization of German forces (unsuccessfully);[49] and pushed on July 30 (successfully, together with Moltke) to order preliminary mobilization,[50] with the correct expectation that full mobilization and war would promptly follow.

The General Staff reportedly "rose in protest" on July 30 against Bethmann's late efforts to cool the crisis by restraining Austria from mobilizing.[51] They hoped instead for mobilization and war. German officers at the War Ministry in Berlin were elated on learning that war was erupting on July 31. A visitor at the ministry found a party atmosphere: "Everywhere beaming faces, people shaking hands in the corridors, congratulating one another on having cleared the ditch."[52]

No senior German general recommended restraint at any point during the crises of 1905–14, except for short-term tactical reasons.[53] Top officers always gave the same advice: for war. Overall, German military leaders were remarkably consistent, unanimous, and vociferous voices for war during the lead-up to World War I. Their voices had a crucial impact on German decisionmaking. Albertini summarizes that Bethmann "was completely overwhelmed by the military" on July 30 when he agreed to move to war.[54]

Elsewhere in Europe, top military officers also formed a noisy lobby for war at important moments. In Austria-Hungary a coterie of top commanders, led by army Chief of Staff Franz Conrad, formed a loud chorus for war. Conrad called for war a least thirty times during January 1906–June 1914. He urged a preventive war against Italy—formally an Austrian ally—in 1907 and 1911.[55] He advised war against Serbia in 1906, in 1908–09, on at least twenty-five occasions in 1913, and in May 1914.[56] On one occasion, Austrian Emperor Franz Josef refused his call for war by saying: "Austria had never started a war." Conrad countered, "Unfortunately, your majesty."[57]

Most important, Conrad pushed for an extreme response to the assassination of the Austrian archduke in Sarajevo on June 28, 1914. Austrian Prime Minister Leopold Berchtold initially favored a restrained response that Russia and the other Entente powers could accept. Specifically, Berchtold proposed that Serbia be compelled to destroy the extreme nationalist groups in Serbia and purge Serbia's security forces of extremist collaborators, but that Serbia not be attacked if it complied.[58] Conrad argued instead for promptly smashing Serbia by force—"nothing will have effect but the use of force."[59] After more lobbying by Conrad, the Austrian government chose Conrad's policy over Berchtold's, setting Europe on its path toward war. Berchtold later characterized Conrad's policy in 1914 as "war, war, war."[60] Austrian War Minister Alexander Krobatin and Gen. Oskar Potiorek joined Conrad in agitating for war against Serbia.[61] Potiorek was "a vociferous advocate of military action against Serbia" in 1914.[62]

Senior Russian military leaders advised war repeatedly during the lead-up to World War I. Russian Minister of War Gen. Vladimir Sukhomlinov favored war during the 1912–13 Balkan crisis, arguing in November 1912 that war was inevitable "and it would be more profitable for us to begin it as soon as possible," as a war "would bring [Russia] nothing but good."[63] Russian military leaders played a key role in pushing Russia toward its decision to fully mobilize its army at the end of the July crisis. The American chargé in St. Petersburg reported on July 27 that the Russian army was "clamoring for war."[64] Historian Imanuel Geiss summarizes that Russian Foreign Minister Sergey Sazonov and the Tsar Nicholas II eventually "yielded to pressure from the Russian generals," who pressed hard for full mobilization on July 29 and 30.[65]

French officers, like their German, Austrian, and Russian colleagues, reportedly saw the 1913 Balkan crisis as an opportune moment for war. French civilian leaders were wisely unpersuaded.[66]

During the July crisis, French officers pushed belligerent policies that helped trigger war. Marshal Joseph Joffre, France's top soldier, instigated the launch of French preliminary mobilization measures, which began on July 25. This was a fateful step, as German hawks later cited these French measures as reasons why Germany should mobilize and move to war on July 30.[67] Joffre also successfully insisted on August 1 that France fully mobilize, threatening to resign if his demand was refused. This French mobilization would have triggered German mobilization and war if Germany, unknown to the French, had not already decided on mobilization and war the day before.[68] The French General Staff also reportedly favored war during the July crisis. An observer in Paris reported on July 30 that "the French General Staff is for a war" and was recommending mobilization measures.[69]

Serbian, Italian, and British officers were bellicose. The Serbian army favored a very hard line during the July crisis, demanding the categorical rejection of the Austrian ultimatum, and war.[70] (Cooler heads prevailed, and Serbia conceded to most Austrian demands.) Italian officers breathed the fire of preventive war. In May 1914, Italian Chief of Staff Gen. Alberto Pollio suggested that the Triple Alliance break its (imagined) encirclement by launching a preventive attack against the Triple Entente: "Do we now really wait until the opponents are prepared and ready? Is it not more logical for the Triple Alliance to abandon all pretense of civility and to start a war ourselves which will one day be forced upon us, while there is time?...Why do we not begin the unavoidable war now?"[71] A British officer described the bellicosity of British navy officers: "We prepared for war, talked war, thought war, and hoped for war. For war would be our opportunity."[72]

European military pressure for war before 1914 was both extreme and anomalous. At no other time or place in modern history have militaries called so unanimously and so vociferously for war; nor have militaries been more hawkish than civilians by such a wide margin. What accounts for the ultra-belligerent pressure of pre-1914 militaries? This phenomenon lacks an agreed explanation and bears further study.

The role of European militaries in steering European governments toward World War I has been understated by scholars.[73] For example, in his important study on World War I's origins, Marc Trachtenberg concludes that there was "no 'capitulation' to the generals; the military had in no sense taken control of policy."[74] The evidence offered here, however, indicates that several

European governments faced strong demands from their generals for war and capitulated to these demands. Germany is the clearest case of capitulation, especially in the late crucial hours of the July crisis. Militaries also turned policy decisions toward war in Austria, Russia, France, and Serbia.

Militaries Purveyed Bellicist Ideas That Caused Conflict

Pre-1914 European militaries used their power and prestige to shape national attitudes as well as national policies. They purveyed five myths that primed Europe for war; (1) there existed a cult of the offensive—the false claim that in warfare the offense had the advantage and that conquest was easy; (2) empires are valuable, returning large rewards to their possessors; (3) war is beneficial, cheap, uplifting, noble, fun, a fine thing indeed; (4) states tend to jump on the bandwagon and concede to big-stick diplomacy—intimidation wins friends; and (5) others are hostile; hence war is inevitable; hence war should be instigated if good conditions for it arise.

These myths to helped spark the July 1914 crisis and made it harder to manage. They fueled aggressive, belligerent, and reckless foreign policies. They made policy blunders more likely and harder to undo. The July crisis occurred and spiraled out of control largely because the elites and publics of Europe believed these myths. The cult of the offensive was the most important and pernicious of these ideas, but all five played a major role in setting the world ablaze.

The Cult of the Offensive

In 1914 the defense had a large advantage in warfare. Highly accurate fast-firing rifles, machine guns, and barbed wire made frontal attacks against entrenched defenders nearly impossible. Railroads enabled defenders to move troops to threatened sectors much faster than attackers, who had to walk. Armies grew so large that decisive flanking maneuvers by one army against another became impossible. Instead, defending armies could stalemate attackers by entrenching themselves across entire combat theaters. The superior power of the defense was often and vividly demonstrated in the major wars of the pre-1914 period, including the American Civil War, the Russo-Turkish War of 1877–78, the Boer War of 1899–1902, and the Russo-Japanese War of 1904–05.

Yet throughout Europe, militaries preached that the offense had the advantage and that countries could easily conquer one another. Civilian leaders widely believed these myths and shaped foreign policy accordingly.

The defense dominated in reality, but the offense dominated in the minds of prewar European leaders.

Militaries also adopted highly offensive doctrines. These doctrines grew progressively more offensive until, with France's adoption of the offensive Plan 17 in 1913, every European power had an offensive doctrine.[75]

The German army glorified the offense in strident terms and imbued German society with similar views. General Schlieffen declared that "attack is the best defense,"[76] and that "one cannot defeat the enemy without attacking."[77] Gen. Friedrich von Bernhardi, a best-selling author, proclaimed that "the offensive mode of action is by far superior to the defensive mode," and that "the superiority of offensive warfare under modern conditions is greater than formerly."[78] General Moltke the Younger endorsed "the principle that the offensive is the best defensive."[79] Gen. August von Keim, founder of the German Army League, argued that "Germany ought to be armed for attack," because "the offensive is the only way of insuring victory."[80] A 1902 German General Staff study explained that Germany could defend itself "only when we take the offensive."[81]

Surveying the Wilhelmine German military scene in retrospect, historian Martin Kitchen sees an "obsession in the [Wilhelmine German] army with attack at all costs."[82] This obsession shaped the Schlieffen/Moltke Plan, which mandated rapid decisive attacks on Belgium, Luxembourg, France, and Russia. Specifically, German forces would sweep through Belgium and Luxembourg in a few days, invade France from Belgium, envelop and destroy French forces by the fortieth day of the war, and then move east to attack Russian forces.

The French army became "obsessed with the virtues of the offensive," in the words of B.H. Liddell Hart.[83] Its 1895 infantry regulations declared that "the passive defense is doomed to certain defeat; it is to be rejected absolutely."[84] Marshal Ferdinand Foch preached that "the offensive form [of war] alone...can lead to results, and must therefore always be adopted."[85] In 1913 Army Chief of Staff Joffre declared that the French army "no longer knows any other law than the offensive.... Any other conception ought to be rejected as contrary to the very nature of war."[86] Col. Loyzeaux de Grandmaison taught that almost any offensive plan was better than a defensive plan, and that any who criticized the army's offensive concepts thereby showed their moral weakness and unfitness for high command.[87] Other French officers proclaimed it necessary that "the concept of the offensive penetrate the soul of our nation"; that "defeat is inevitable as soon as the hope of conquering ceases to exist"; and that "there is only one way of defending ourselves—to attack as soon as we are ready."[88]

Faith in the offense spread to French civilians. France's president, Clément Fallières, announced: "The offensive alone is suited to the temperament of French soldiers....We are determined to march straight against the enemy without hesitation."[89] Emile Driant, a member of the French chamber of deputies, expressed the common view: "The first great battle will decide the whole war, and wars will be short. The idea of the offense must penetrate the spirit of our nation."[90]

French officers spoke confidently of what France could achieve in an aggressive war. Joffre's deputy, Gen. Edouard de Castelnau, boasted in 1913: "Give me 700,000 men and I will conquer Europe!"[91]

French military doctrine reflected these offensive biases.[92] In Marshal Foch's words, the French army adopted "a single formula for success, a single combat doctrine, namely, the decisive power of offensive action undertaken with the resolute determination to march on the enemy, reach and destroy him."[93] Accordingly, France adopted a strategy of all-out attack through Alsace-Lorraine in the event of war with Germany. A defensive French plan that met Germany's armies at the Belgian border would have smashed the 1914 German offensive on the Belgian frontier, but French forces began the war by lunging into Alsace-Lorraine, thereby letting the German armies in Belgium plunge deep into France.

Other states caught the same virus. The British military rejected defensive strategies despite its experience in the Boer War, which demonstrated the power of entrenched defenders against exposed attackers. Gen. W.G. Knox wrote: "The defensive is never an acceptable role to the Briton, and he makes little or no study of it," and Gen. R.C.B. Haking argued that the offensive "will win as sure as there is a sun in the heavens."[94] General Sukhomlinov, noted that Russia's enemies were directing their armies "towards guaranteeing the possibility of dealing rapid and decisive blows....We also must follow this example."[95] The Russian army field regulations for 1912 declared, "Offensive actions serve as the best means for attainment of a given objective."[96] Russia accordingly adopted an infeasibly ambitious strategy of attack on both Germany and Austria at the outset of war.[97]

Even in Belgium the offensive found proponents. Belgian forces were vastly inferior to Germany.[98] A Belgian attack on Germany would have been suicidal. Yet, under the influence of French ideas, some Belgian officers favored an offensive strategy, evolving the bizarre argument that "to ensure against our being ignored it was essential that we should attack," and declaring that "we must hit them where it hurts."[99]

A few military officers, mostly planners hidden away in back rooms, doubted the offensive dogma. Their planning forced them to study the defensive realities that most denied. They almost never expressed their doubts to outsiders, however. Hence their doubts had no impact on the making of foreign policy or military strategy in any country. Instead, the premise that the offense was strong widely shaped official thinking and action.[100]

Six dangers of war arise when governments think the offense is strong.[101] First, states adopt more aggressive foreign policies. They do this both to exploit opportunities and to avert dangers. States expand because they can, aggressing because aggression is feasible. States also expand because they must: they are more afraid that others will conquer them, so they aggress to gain assets they need to secure themselves against other aggressors. "Grow or die" logic drives them toward expansion for self-preservation.

Second, states resist others' expansion more fiercely. Any increase in others' power or reduction of their own power is more dangerous to their safety, so they fight harder to protect the status quo. Hence status quo powers collide more violently with states that seek to change the status quo.

Third, windows of opportunity and vulnerability open wider. This raises the risk of preventive war. When the offense is strong, smaller shifts in the ratio of forces between states create bigger shifts in their relative capacity to conquer and defend territory. Attacking when one has a material advantage is more likely to bring victory; being attacked when one has a material disadvantage is more likely to bring defeat. As a result, states have more incentive to attack if they think the material balance will shift against them. The "now or never" case for war is more compelling for declining states.

Fourth, the size of the advantage that accrues to the side mobilizing or striking first increases. This raises the risk of preemptive war. Given that smaller shifts in force ratios have larger effects on relative capacity to conquer and defend territory, states have more incentive to mobilize first or strike first if this will change the force ratio in their favor. Hence they are quicker to mobilize or attack in a crisis. The case for preemptive war—"we must strike first to avoid being struck first"—is more compelling for all states.

Fifth, states adopt more competitive dog-eat-dog foreign policy tactics, especially brinkmanship and faits accomplis. Winning disputes becomes more important, relative to avoiding war, because national survival is more precarious. Gaining or protecting assets that provide security is more urgent, taking priority over avoiding war. Hence states resort to more dangerous political tactics to win disputes.

Sixth, alliances become tighter and unconditional. States' survival depends more on their allies' survival. Hence states must support even allies that provoke conflict with others. As a result, alliances tend to become unconditional, as states pledge to support allies even in wars provoked by the ally. Local wars can then spread to become regional or global wars, as each belligerent drags its allies into the melée.

These dangers appeared and flourished in Europe during the years before 1914 and helped to cause the war.

Expansion and Resistance

Before 1914 Germany pursued wider spheres of influence in eastern and western Europe, Africa, and the Middle East. Austria pursued a wider sphere in the Balkans. Both German and Austrian expansionism was fueled largely by a search for greater security: Germany sought security from Russia, Austria from Serbia. Their neighbors resisted fiercely. World War I stemmed largely from the collision between German/Austrian expansion and others' resistance to it.

Preventive War

Before 1914, German hawks (especially military officers, as shown earlier) argued for preventive war, warning that Russia was on the rise and would attack Germany later. Hence Germany should attack Russia while it still had the upper hand.

Preemptive War

Russia and France launched their fateful preliminary military mobilizations on July 25 to seize a first-mover advantage, or to deny it to Germany, or both. Their mobilizations triggered German mobilization on July 30, and war.

Faits Accomplis

Both Austria and Germany adopted cutthroat fait accompli diplomatic tactics before and during 1914. In July 1914 their strategy amounted to a grand fait accompli, featuring a surprise ultimatum to Serbia with a short deadline. Their decision to adopt a fait accompli tactic left little room to avoid war when the Entente powers chose not to accept it.

Tight Alliances

Both the Triple Alliance and the Triple Entente operated as unconditional alliances in 1914. Germany supported Austria unconditionally. France supported Russia unconditionally. Britain sought to condition its support for Russia, but could not find a way to do this. As a result, the alliances served as a conveyor belt that dragged all of Europe into a local conflict between Austria and Serbia plus Russia.[102]

More Bad Ideas Purveyed by European Militaries

Before 1914, European societies widely embraced four additional misperceptions that poisoned international relations and helped to spark war. The sources of these misperceptions are not entirely clear and need further study. Current evidence suggests, however, that these myths, like the cult of the offensive, emanated mainly from Europe's militaries and their propaganda apparatus.

"Empires Are Valuable."

Before 1914, Europeans widely exaggerated the political and economic benefits that conquests would provide. This misconception was common throughout Europe. Like many other misperceptions, however, it was most pronounced among the armed forces and in Germany.

Military officers often warned that national economic survival depended on acquiring more territory. Germany's Adm. Georg von Müller, for instance, saw Germany locked in a "great battle for economic survival"; without new territories, "the artificial [German] economic edifice would start to crumble and existence therein would become very unpleasant indeed."[103] General Bernhardi declared that "flourishing nations...require a continual expansion of their frontiers, they require new territory for the accommodation of their surplus population." In France Marshal Foch spoke in similar terms.[104]

Such views were widely echoed by civilians, especially in Germany, where many warned that economic and demographic imperatives required German expansion. During the Moroccan crisis, Germans declared that acquiring economic rights in Morocco was "essential" to the German economy, and "a question of life and death" to German industry.[105] Germany required new territories to contain its growing population, which might otherwise starve, or might emigrate, causing the population to lose its sense of German nationality. One author wrote in 1911 that Germany "must expand if she does not want to be suffocated by her surplus population."[106] Another wrote in 1896 that Germans were "forced by our geographical situation, by poor soil...by the amazing increase in our population...to spread and to gain space for us and for our sons."[107] These ideas fed the belief that expansion was imperative for German national development: "We have only one choice: to grow or to waste away."[108]

These arguments reflected voodoo geoeconomics. They were invented from whole cloth and asserted without evidence. They were backed by no studies or research. They were wrong, but they were widely believed.

"Others Are Hostile, War Is Inevitable."

Before 1914, Europeans widely exaggerated the aggressiveness of their neighbors. This misperception was not universal. Some Europeans' perceptions of Germany and Austria were fairly accurate: they saw Germany and Austria as aggressive, and they were. On average, however, Europeans overstated others' aggressiveness.

European militaries led the way in fueling such perceptions. In Germany the generals portrayed their country as surrounded by rapacious enemies who were only waiting for the right moment to pounce. General Schlieffen warned in 1909 that Russia was guided by an "inherited antipathy of Slavs for Germanic peoples," England was an "implacable enemy," and France made "the idea of *revanche*...the pivot of her whole policy."[109] In 1911 Maj.-Gen. Martin Wandel of the Prussian Ministry of War agreed that Germany was "surrounded by enemies," and Bernhardi declared that Germany was "menaced" by "Slavonic waves."[110] These warnings were wildly untrue,[111] but were widely believed in Germany.

Militaries elsewhere also exaggerated the malevolence of other states. Britain's First Lord of the Admiralty recommended a preventive attack on France in 1898 because "the row would have to come, it might just as well come now as later."[112] (The lord fortunately lost the argument; the row did not come; and France and Britain were soon allies.) Russia's Gen. Yuri Danilov drew plans based on the worst-case assumption that Sweden, Romania, Turkey, Japan, and China would all join the Central Powers in a war against Russia. "He left out only the Martians," one postwar critic declared.[113]

Warnings such as these were echoed by academic allies of the military and by nationalist scholars and propagandists. Guided by the German navy's propaganda office, the German "fleet professors" warned that Germany was being surrounded and strangled by an insatiable and malevolent Britain. Hermann Oncken and Otto Hintze falsely asserted that Britain aimed to keep Europe in turmoil so that Britain could conquer the world;[114] and historian Houston Stewart Chamberlain (a zealous naturalized German) warned Germans that his visits to England in 1907 and 1908 had uncovered "a positively terrifying blind hatred for Germany, and impatient longing for a war of annihilation."[115] Wilhelmine German schoolchildren were taught that Britain had always tried to keep Germany as weak, disrupted, and small as possible, and that "Germany is a land entirely surrounded by enemies."[116] The German press conveyed the same message to its readers: "Our enemies have long lain in wait for a suitable moment to attack us"; "Russia is arming for war against Germany"; Germany's neighbors "want to...trample us down from all sides"; and Germany faces "enemies all around—permanent danger of war from all sides."[117]

Such images ultimately gripped the German elites, and to a lesser extent those of other states. In 1901 the kaiser saw his country "surrounded by enemies"; in 1913 he maintained that "the war between east and west was in the long run inevitable."[118] A Russian statesman wrote that "the conflict may be postponed, but that it will come some day we must remember every hour, and every hour we must arm ourselves for it."[119] Some British leaders saw themselves isolated and besieged: Lord Rosebery in 1899 described Britain as only a "little island…so lonely in these northern seas, viewed with so much jealousy, and with such hostility, with such jarred ambitions by the great empires of the world, so friendless among nations." Another Briton, writing of Anglo-German relations in 1898, claimed that "an actual state of war against England began some time ago."[120]

In sum, many Europeans, led by militaries and Germans, imagined a world of states so belligerent that even peaceful states were wise to attack neighbors before the neighbors attacked them.

"War Is Beneficial, Cheap, Uplifting, Noble, Fun, a Fine Thing Indeed."

Before 1914, European militaries widely portrayed war as beneficial for society—a healthy, happy, glorious activity, valuable for its own sake. For example, the *Jungdeutschland Post*, a propaganda organ of the German Army League aimed at teenagers, painted a picture of joyous combat and happy death for fallen warriors in German wars of the future:

> For us as well the great and glorious hour of battle will one day strike.…Yes, that will be a great and happy hour, which we all may secretly look forward to…quiet and deep in German hearts the joy of war and a longing for it must live, for we have had enough of the enemy, and victory will only be given to a people who go to war with joy in their hearts as if to a feast.…Let us laugh as loud as we can at the old women in men's trousers who are afraid of war and therefore complain that it is ghastly or ugly. No, war is beautiful. Its greatness lifts a man's heart high above earthly things, above the daily round. Such an hour awaits us. We must wait for it with the manly knowledge that when it has struck it will be more beautiful and wonderful to live forever among the heroes on a war memorial in a church than to die an empty death in bed, nameless.…Let that be heaven for young Germany. Thus we wish to knock at our God's door.[121]

In the same spirit, General Bernhardi admonished his many readers to recognize war as a "powerful promoter of civilization" and "a political necessity...fought in the interest of biological, social, and moral progress."[122] War promoted civilization by weeding out the unfit. It was "a biological necessity of the first importance, a regulative element in the life of mankind which cannot be dispensed with....Without war, inferior or decaying races would easily choke the growth of healthy, budding elements, and a universal decadence would follow."[123]

Academics, the press, and other publicists also painted a glorified image of war. German newspapers told their readers that "we Teutons in particular must no longer look upon war as our destroyer....At last we must see it once more as the savior, the physician"; that "it has been established beyond doubt that regular war is not only the broadest and noblest solution imaginable, but also the periodically indispensable solution to the preservation of State and society"; and that war promised the "renewal and purification of the German people."[124] One German newspaper told its readers on Christmas Eve that war was "part of a divine world order" that ensured the preservation of "all that is good, beautiful, great and noble in nature and in true civilization."[125]

Elsewhere in Europe a similar image of war took hold, although less strongly. In Britain Hilaire Belloc declared, "How I long for the Great War! It will sweep Europe like a broom, it will make kings jump like coffee beans on the roaster,"[126] and historian J.A. Cramb felt that war could purify and challenge growing nations, and "universal peace appears less as a dream than as a nightmare."[127] In France one general argued in 1912 that "it is manifest that war has its role in the economy of societies and that it responds to a moral law."[128]

Members of the European political and economic elite believed that foreign wars would strengthen their domestic political position against democrats and socialists. In their view, foreign threats would unify the nation, and successful war would enhance the prestige and standing of incumbent regimes and elites. Thus, while war might bleed the country, it would benefit those who ruled. Again, these "social imperial" ideas were most popular in Germany, where one German newspaper outlined the benefits of a confrontational and expansionist policy: "We shall never improve matters at home until we have got into severe foreign complications—perhaps even into war—and have been compelled by such convulsions to bring ourselves together." Another newspaper wrote that a war would ensure "the restoration to health of many political and social institutions."[129] German soldiers and statesmen often echoed this theory.[130]

These opinions were reflected in the ecstasy with which many Europeans greeted the outbreak of the war in 1914. Thomas Mann exclaimed, "Thank God, the soldiers had come to put an end to the rotten old world, with which we were fed up!"[131] The English poet Edmund Gosse saw a "beautiful result" in the "union of hearts" produced by the war, and the Russian composer Igor Stravinsky welcomed the conflict as "necessary for human progress."[132] Friedrich Meinecke, the liberal German historian, later remembered August 1914 as "one of the great moments of my life which suddenly filled my soul with the deepest confidence in our peoples and the profoundest joy."[133]

States "Bandwagon"; Intimidation Wins Friends

Before 1914, Europeans widely assumed that states usually chose allies by bandwagoning with the stronger side rather than balancing against it. They also assumed that intimidation was more effective than conciliation at persuading other states to cooperate.[134] States sometimes do bandwagon, and intimidation can succeed, but Europeans exaggerated the frequency of both kinds of behavior. This error caused Europeans to exaggerate the feasibility of expansion both for themselves and for their adversaries. Consequently, they exaggerated both the practicality and the necessity of expansionist policies. The army also encouraged counterproductive bellicose diplomatic tactics that fed spirals of hostility that intensified as big-stick tactics were applied in a futile attempt to address hostility produced by the last application of the big stick.

The German military was the main purveyor of bandwagon and wave-the-big-stick thinking. It often used bandwagon notions to justify the expansion of the German fleet and the development of offensive German army war plans. Admiral Tirpitz sold his grand fleet with a "risk theory" that claimed that a large German fleet could frighten Britain into accepting German continental expansion. General Schlieffen held that the German army could discourage Britain from even trying to defend France by defeating France in the first battle of a war.[135]

Faith in intimidation also colored German civilian thought, illustrated by Max Weber's aphorism: "Let them hate us, as long as they fear us."[136] Such ideas fed hopes that Germany could expand by intimidating its neighbors. They also led Germans to exaggerate the political benefit that Germany would enjoy if it enhanced its power through expansion. Pan-German leaders argued that a policy of peaceful expansion-by-intimidation could succeed once Germany showed its "mailed fist"; there would be "no one on the Continent (and probably not even Britain) who would not give in."[137] Likewise—evidently influenced by Admiral Tirpitz's risk theory—German Foreign Secretary

Jagow believed that, despite British warnings to the contrary, Germany could cow Britain into neutrality in a future conflict.[138]

Germans adopted bellicose tactics in the crises of 1905, 1911, and 1914 partly in hopes that they could split the opposing alliance by intimidating or humiliating its member states.[139] Bandwagon ideas also led Germans to inflate the value of the empire they sought to acquire, by suggesting that a larger, stronger Germany could cow others into friendship. One German newspaper foresaw that "through a world war...the German people will acquire a position in Mitteleuropa which will make a repetition of such a general war against us impossible."[140] Another German writer foresaw that if Germany could conquer France and Austria, "the natural pressure of this new German Empire will be so great that...the surrounding little Germanic States will have to attach themselves to it under conditions which we set."[141] Conversely, some Germans expressed fear that other states could eliminate Germany's sphere of influence through intimidation, unless Germany proved more intimidating or was able to control these states directly.[142] Bandwagon assumptions thus contributed to both the hopes and fears that underlay German expansionism.

What led European militaries to purvey these myths and misperceptions? The false ideas outlined here served the organizational interests of European militaries. Militaries can claim larger budgets and enjoy more prestige, hence more autonomy, when their countries are insecure; when national problems can be solved by attacking/invading others; when the empires that militaries might conquer seem valuable; when neighbors are poised to attack; when military power can be used to intimidate others into alliance or cooperation; and when war is healthy or beneficial. Under these conditions, militaries become master problem-solvers for the nation. Their military power becomes a miracle tonic that cures all ills, with few negative effects. Militaries can then lay strong claim to big budgets, status, respect, and autonomy—things all organizations covet.

These organizational goals are a constant, however, whereas the malignant conduct of European militaries before 1914 was extreme and anomalous. What was different about the pre-1914 era? Why did the European militaries' pursuit of standard organizational goals translate into unusually malignant behavior?

Before 1914, military officers in much of Europe (especially in Germany) came heavily from the aristocratic class. Also, they lived apart from society, cocooned in splendid self-isolation on military bases. The officers' sense of aristocratic superiority, combined with their social isolation, led to cult-like customs and attitudes; to bizarre beliefs and values that flourished and intensified in a social echo chamber, protected from outside criticism; to an overweening sense of their own entitlement to power and authority; and to a contempt for the societies they served.[143] The officers' contempt was expressed in their confident belief that officers had little to learn from civilians, and little obligation to serve civilians or treat them respectfully. Civilians were social inferiors. They were unfit to engage in dialogue with officers. They had no ideas worth hearing. They were sheep, to be led by deception. They were cannon fodder. Officers widely believed they should decide national security policy for the nation. They possessed the superior judgment of the well-born and well-bred. Others should defer accordingly. In their view, war should be chosen and pursued with scant regard for the misery that it inflicts on society. War is necessary; it brings a butcher's bill; the bill must be paid; none should complain. Reflecting these attitudes, top officers showed little empathy for the hardships of the troops who bled and died under their command during World War I. They were cold as ice toward the suffering of those under them.

These attitudes may help to explain how European militaries could shamelessly propagandize their own societies with self-serving distortions. They may also explain how these militaries could recommend war so often and so cavalierly, with few pangs of conscience or regret.

World War I: An Inadvertent War

World War I was "inadvertent" in the sense that it was unintended. Specifically, it stemmed from actions that were not intended or expected to produce war.[144] Judging whether a war is advertent or inadvertent requires an assessment of the match or mismatch between policymakers' preferences and the results of their policies. If policymakers preferred no war over the war that occurred, and could have chosen no war, the war is inadvertent. If so, World War I was inadvertent in several ways.

First, the war was inadvertent from the perspective of the German leaders who instigated the July 1914 crisis. German leaders triggered and sustained the July crisis by encouraging Austria to make severe demands on Serbia on July 5–6, and then by supporting those Austrian demands during July 23–29. These actions did not cause the outcome the Germans intended. Quite the opposite: they caused an outcome the Germans badly sought to avoid.

Five outcomes were possible in July 1914: world war (WW)—Britain, France, Russia, and Serbia fight Germany and Austria; continental war (CW—France, Russia, and Serbia fight Germany and Austria; Austria destroys Serbia (ADS)—Austria conquers Serbia and partitions it among Serbia's neighbors; Serbia destroys Black Hand (SDBH)—Austria compels Serbia to destroy the Black Hand assassin group and other extremists by occupying Belgrade until

Serbia complies, but otherwise leaves Serbia intact and sovereign; and status quo ante bellum (SQAB)—the conditions of June 28, 1914 continue unchanged, with Serbia remaining a regional base for Serbian nationalist extremism.[145]

Chancellor Bethmann Hollweg, the key German civilian leader, probably preferred continental war over other crisis outcomes. This is indicated by, among other things, Bethmann's failure to pursue a Serbia destroys Black Hand settlement even after he had learned of Russian preliminary mobilization on July 27. Russian preliminary mobilization put the crisis on a clear trajectory toward continental war, because Germany would eventually have to mobilize in response, and Germany would attack when it mobilized. News of Russian preliminary mobilization therefore warned Bethmann that the crisis would end in continental war unless Germany accepted an SDBH settlement. He faced a choice between CW and SDBH at that point, and he chose CW. A belligerent choice.[146] Bethmann, however, also was averse to world war. He probably ranked WW as his least favorite option, probably because it involved a large risk of German military defeat. His aversion to WW is indicated by his effort early on July 30 to restrain Austria and end the crisis, moving things toward an SDBH outcome, after he learned beyond doubt overnight on July 29–30 that any war would be a world war, not a continental war. Bethmann's full preference order was probably as follows: CW > ADS > SDBH > SQAB > WW. He preferred continental war to Austria destroys Serbia, which he preferred to Serbia destroys Black Hand, which he preferred to the status quo ante bellum, which he preferred to world war.

Kaiser Wilhelm, like Bethmann, put world war at the bottom of his wish list, fearing, like Bethmann, that Germany might lose a world war.[147] If true, the result that German civilian rulers caused was not intended. Indeed, it was the result they least desired. They were bellicose, but not so bellicose that a world war had appeal. If during the crisis they had seen where things were headed, they would have instead accepted an SDBH outcome (which Russia and Britain also probably would have accepted). And if before the crisis they had known where things were headed, they never would have started trouble. Instead, they would have sought agreement by all the great powers that Austria could impose an SDBH solution on Serbia, or perhaps even let the moment pass and accepted a SQAB outcome.

General Moltke assumed prime control over German policy on July 30. His preference ordering was more aggressive than that of Bethmann and the kaiser, probably running CW > WW > ADS > SDBH > SQAB. In other words, world war was not his first choice, but it was a high choice. Thus the results of the July crisis were much less inadvertent for him. Even though the July crisis led to world war, which was not his first choice, he still would have opted to instigate the crisis on July 5–6 and to continue it during July 23–30 had he known where it was going.[148]

Thus World War I was inadvertent for the German civilians who launched and managed the crisis during July 5–30. It was not inadvertent for the general who pushed the crisis over the edge on July 30, but he was able to instigate war only because the civilians set the table for his action. Their actions were key. If so, the war was essentially inadvertent.

Second, World War I was inadvertent from the perspective of the Russian leaders who ordered Russian preliminary military mobilization during July 24/25. Records of Russian decisionmaking indicate that Russian leaders did not intend or expect that Russian premobilization would cause war. Rather, they hoped it would deter it.[149] Minister of Agriculture Alexander Krivoshein, Russia's most influential minister, stated at the July 24 meeting that Russia should seek peace, and the best road to peace was a firm policy toward Germany: "Our policy should aim at reducing the possibility of a European war [but] if we remained passive we will not obtain our objective....The most judicious policy Russia could follow in present circumstances was a return to a firmer and more energetic attitude toward the claims of the Central-European powers."[150] There is no sign that Krivoshein thought that premobilization made war more likely. The same is true of Foreign Minister Sazonov. Although he feared that war was likely—exclaiming *"C'est la guerre européenne!"* on learning of the Austrian ultimatum on July 24—he clearly wished to avoid war,[151] and showed no signs of believing that premobilization would bring it about.

Russian leaders were unaware at that point that mobilization meant war for Germany. They had no knowledge of the planned German attack on Liège. Hence they were unaware of the mechanism that guaranteed that mobilization meant war for Germany. Hence they were unaware that mobilization inexorably meant war. Hence they were unaware that if their premobilization triggered German mobilization, war was certain. Hence they wrongly believed that failing to premobilize would be more dangerous than premobilizing. Albertini summarizes that when Sazonov approved preliminary mobilization, "he does not seem to have had any conception of what would be the consequences." Sazonov thought he could start mobilization measures "without any danger to the peace which he was so genuinely seeking to safeguard."[152]

As the situation developed, on July 30 Moltke, Falkenhayn, and the General Staff used the Russian premobilization as a major excuse to insist that German peace efforts end and German mobilization begin. A telegram drafted for Bethmann on July 30 explained German moves toward war: "General Staff just tells me that military preparations of our neighbors, especially on the east, compel speedy decision if we do not wish to expose ourselves to surprises."[153] Thus Russian premobilization was a key trigger for German mobilization and war, but Russian leaders neither expected nor desired this result.

Less is known about the thinking of French decisionmakers who authorized premobilization measures during July 25–30. Nevertheless, what seems true of Russia also seems true of France. There is no reason to believe that French leaders were aware of the planned German attack on Liège. Hence, like the Russians, they were likely unaware of the mechanism that caused mobilization to make war certain. They were therefore unaware that their preliminary mobilization made war inevitable. Clearly, they did not want war. If this is true, the war-causing effect of their preliminary mobilization was not expected or desired.

Hence World War I was inadvertent for Russian and French policymakers. They launched their premobilizations without expecting or desiring to cause war. These mobilizations had an important war-causing effect, however: Moltke and Falkenhayn exploited them to persuade German civilians to launch German mobilization and war on July 30. Russian and French premobilizations thus give World War I a second inadvertent dimension.

The cult of the offensive primed Europe for these mistakes. When the offense is strong, circumstances are less forgiving. Blunders provoke quick reactions that make them irreversible. As a result, there is a greater risk of inadvertent conflict.

Conclusion

What caused World War I? Simply put, the militaries of Europe went rogue. They unwisely pressured their governments for war until they got their way. They purveyed myths and illusions that primed their governments to choose war of their own accord. Absent these actions, no war would have occurred. Military professionals sworn to protect their countries instead pushed foolish policies and false ideas that caused immense harm to their countries.

Could this happen again? A rogue military scenario is very unlikely in today's top two powers, China and the United States.

Civil-military relations in China are benign.[154] The Chinese People's Liberation Army (PLA) is highly civilianized. The Chinese Communist Party (CCP) has found ways to inhibit the PLA officer corps from developing a strong independent corporate identity, separate from its identity as an element of the Communist Party. Hence PLA officers do not see themselves as having major parochial organizational interests that are distinct from the

CCP's interests; hence they are not driven to protect such interests, and they rarely push for ideas or policies that would advance such interests against the interest of the CCP or the wider society. In a sense, there are no civil-military relations in China. There are only relations between the military and nonmilitary elements of the CCP. Both elements see themselves as Party members above other identities.

The U.S. military has strong traditions of subordination to civilian authority. It has sometimes worked to influence U.S. public opinion on foreign policy and national security matters,[155] but never to the extent seen in Europe before 1914. In recent years, U.S. officers have often counseled restraint when offering advice on foreign policy. A rogue military scenario for the United States is implausible.

The rogue military danger, however, is very alive in a dangerous place: Pakistan. Parallels between Pakistan and Wilhelmine Germany are striking. The Pakistani military wields great power in Pakistani society. Since Pakistani independence in 1947, it has made and broken many governments. Today it dominates public discourse and shapes politics from behind the scenes. Like the pre-1914 German army, the Pakistani army draws the bulk of its officers from Pakistan's economic elite. Its officers live cloistered lives apart from civilians. They widely view Pakistani civilian society with contempt: as sheep to be milked of resources and led by manipulation. As an emblem of this contempt, in 1971 the Pakistani military murdered hundreds of thousands of its fellow citizens in what was then East Pakistan (now Bangladesh), in one of the greatest mass murders of modern times.[156] With this massacre, Pakistani officers showed that they arrogate to themselves the right to murder law-abiding Pakistani citizens whose politics they disagree with.

The Pakistani military believes and purveys organizationally self-serving myths and bellicist notions that raise the risk of war in South Asia. These myths parallel myths from of 1914.

The first myth—empires are valuable—is embodied in Pakistan's counterproductive efforts to control neighboring Afghanistan by proxy through the Taliban and to acquire Kashmir through violence. Toward these goals, the Pakistani military has sent thousands of its young people on death-ride missions into Kashmir and plunged Afghanistan into a nightmare of Taliban extremism, brutality, and civil war. Pakistan's imperial projects are a cruel folly, justified by military mythmaking.

With the second myth—that others are hostile—the Pakistani military purveys a false-victim narrative that vastly exaggerates past mistreatment of Pakistan by the United States. (In fact, the United States has supported and subsidized Pakistan for most of its history.) It also exaggerates mistreatment of Pakistan by its neighbors, and mistreatment of Islam by the non-Muslim world. Overall, the narrative is a web of slanderous fabrications.

The third myth—intimidation wins friends, others bandwagon—finds expression in Pakistan's support for spectacular terrorist tactics against India, exemplified by attacks on the Indian parliament in New Delhi in 2001 and on Mumbai in 2008, as well as its support for the Taliban's brutal intimidation tactics in Afghanistan. The spectacular terror attacks on India brought India and Pakistan close to war. Pakistan's support for the Afghan Taliban has fostered a Frankenstein monster in the form of the Pakistani Taliban, which has brought mayhem back home to Pakistan.

The extreme belligerence of pre-1914 European militaries finds echoes in Pakistan's recent reckless uses of violence. Pakistan's belligerence is manifest in its provocation of the 1965 and 1999 wars with India, as well as in incidents recounted above—its support for the Afghan Taliban, its proxy war in Kashmir, its instigation of spectacular terrorist acts in India, and its support for violent global jihadism. The Pakistani army has long engaged in hidden but close cooperation with al-Qaida—a relationship that endangers the very existence of Pakistan should al-Qaida ever use weapons of mass destruction against the West.[157] The army supports the Afghan Taliban in killing U.S. troops, even while it receives U.S. foreign aid. It murders domestic opponents and critics with impunity—for example, prominent Pakistani journalist Syed Saleem Shahzad in 2010.[158]

Pakistan's rogue military is turning Pakistan toward becoming a rogue state. Drawing the Pakistani military into a more constructive relationship with its society and its neighbors should be an important U.S. foreign policy goal. The most important lesson from World War I for the present, however, is the danger of seeking military solutions for political problems. China and the United States have not resolved this problem.

A Century after Sarajevo: Taking Stock and Looking Forward

12

Inevitability and War

Joseph S. Nye Jr.

WORLD WAR I killed some 20 million people. In one battle, the Somme, 1.3 million were killed and wounded, compared with only 36,000 casualties when Germany defeated Austria half a century earlier. World War I was a horrifying war of trenches, barbed wire, machine guns, and artillery that ground up a generation of Europe's youth. It not only destroyed people; it destroyed four European empires: German, Austro-Hungarian, Ottoman, and Russian. Until World War I, the global balance of power was centered in Europe. After World War I, Europe still mattered, but the United States and Japan emerged as great powers. World War I also ushered in the Russian Revolution of 1917, prepared the way for fascism, and accelerated the ideological battles that wracked the twentieth century.

How could such a catastrophic event happen? Bernhard von Bülow, the German chancellor from 1900 to 1909, met with his successor, Theobald von Bethmann Hollweg, in the chancellor's palace in Berlin shortly after the war broke out. "I said to him, 'Well, tell me, at least, how it all happened.' He raised his long, thin arms to heaven and answered in a dull, exhausted voice: 'Oh, if I only knew!' In many later polemics on war guilt I have often wished it had been possible to produce a snapshot of Bethmann Hollweg standing there at the moment he said those words. Such a photograph would have been the best proof that this wretched man had never wanted war."[1] Perhaps in self-exoneration, Bethmann came to regard the war as inevitable. The British foreign secretary, Sir Edward Grey, agreed. In April 1918, he said he had "come to think that no human individual could have prevented it."[2]

Are there lessons from this war applicable to contemporary U.S.-China relations? The British journalist Martin Wolf writes that "history, alas, also teaches us that friction between status quo and revisionist powers may well lead to conflict, however ruinous the consequences. Indeed Thucydides, the great ancient historian, argued that the calamitous Peloponnesian war was due to the alarm that the growing power of Athens inspired in Sparta."[3] Historian Margaret MacMillan adds that "it is tempting—and sobering—to compare today's relationship between China and America to that between Germany and Britain a century ago."[4] After drawing a similar comparison, the *Economist* concluded that "the most troubling similarity between 1914 and now is complacency."[5] Some political scientists, such as John Mearsheimer, have stated that "to put it bluntly, China cannot rise peacefully."[6]

Citing Thucydides in regard to the rise of China is not new. I plead guilty to having published such a comparison more than fifteen years ago.[7] But as Richard Neustadt and Ernest May warned, historical metaphors and analogies can be misleading when differences in context are not made explicit.[8] To some extent, World War I was caused by the rise of German power and the fear it created in Great Britain, but the war was also caused by the rise of Russian power and the fear it created in Germany, the rise of Slavic nationalism and the fear it created in Austria-Hungary, and myriad other factors that differed from those of ancient Greece. Today there is a greater difference in the overall power of the United States and China than there was between Germany and Britain in the last century. Metaphors can be useful as general precautions, but they become dangerous when they convey a sense of historical inevitability. There are structural similarities about the three situations—ancient Greece, World War I, and U.S.-China relations—but also important differences in context that allow opportunities for human agency to matter. In fact, even in the paradigm case of the Peloponnesian War, there was more room for human agency than some of today's commentators realize. Citing Thucydides can become a trap.[9]

Misreading the Peloponnesian War

In the middle of the fifth century B.C.E., Athens and Sparta had a truce that Corcyra ultimately convinced Athens to break with the following argument: "There are three considerable naval powers in Hellas: Athens, Corcyra, and Corinth. If Corinth gets control of us first, and you allow our navy to be united with hers, you will have to fight against the combined fleets of Corcyra and the Peloponnese. But if you receive us into your alliance, you will enter upon the war with our ships as well as your own."[10] The Athenians decided to break the treaty, because, in Thucydides' words, "the general belief was that whatever happened, war with the Peloponnese was bound to come."[11] Ironically, the belief that war was inevitable played a major role in causing it. Athens felt that if war was going to come, it was better to have two-to-one naval superiority than one-to-two naval inferiority.

Cooperation is difficult to develop when playing a Prisoners' Dilemma game once, or when one thinks that the last move in an iterative game is approaching. Game theorists such as Robert Axelrod have shown that after many games, the best results on average were obtained by learning to cooperate. Axelrod warns, however, that cooperation in tit-for-tat reciprocity is an optimal strategy only when one has a chance to continue the game for a long period, when there is a long "shadow of the future."[12] That is why the belief that war is inevitable is so corrosive in international politics. When a state believes that war is inevitable, it is very close to the last move. If the state suspects that its opponent will cheat, risking defection is better than cooperating. That is what Athens did, and one sees a similar dynamic as European states debated whether to delay mobilization in July 1914.

The classical Greek case is not as straightforward as Thucydides asserts, however. Thucydides concluded that the cause of the war was the growth of Athenian power and the fear it caused in Sparta. Donald Kagan has shown, however, that Athenian power was not growing. Before the war broke out in 431 B.C.E., the balance of power had begun to stabilize. And though the Spartans worried about the rise of Athenian power, Kagan contends they had an even greater fear of a slave revolt.

Thus the immediate or precipitating causes of the war were more important than Thucydides' theory of inevitability admits. Corinth, for example, thought that Athens would not fight; it misjudged the Athenian response, partly because it was so angry at Corcyra. Pericles overreacted; he made mistakes in giving an ultimatum to Potidaea and in punishing Megara by cutting off its trade. Those policy mistakes made the Spartans think that war might be worth the risk after all. Kagan argues that the growth of Athenian power caused the first Peloponnesian War earlier in the century, but that the Thirty-Year's Truce doused that flame. So to start the second Peloponnesian War, "the spark of the Epidamnian trouble needed to land on one of the rare bits of flammable stuff that had not been thoroughly drenched. Thereafter it needed to be continually and vigorously fanned by the Corinthians, soon assisted by the Megarians, Potidaeans, Aeginetans, and the Spartan War Party. Even then the spark might have been extinguished had not the Athenians provided some additional fuel at the crucial moment."[13] In other words, the war was caused not by impersonal forces but by bad decisions in difficult circumstances.

Although there are no absolute answers in debates over structure and agency in human events, very little is ever truly inevitable in history. Human behavior is voluntary, although there are always external constraints. As Karl Marx famously observed, men make history, but not in conditions of their choosing. The ancient Greeks made flawed choices when they were caught in the situation well described by Thucydides and by Prisoners' Dilemma games. The security dilemma made war highly probable, but highly probable is not the same as inevitable. The thirty-year unlimited war that devastated Athens was not inevitable. Human decisions mattered.

The Multiple Causes of World War I

Generations of historians have examined the origins of World War I. It is impossible to isolate one cause, though Woody Allen tried to in his movie *Zelig*: "England owned the world and Germany wanted it." More seriously, parts of the answer lie at each of three levels of analysis: international, domestic, and individual.[14]

At the level of the international system structure, there were two key elements: the rise of German power and the increased rigidity in the alliance systems. The rise of German power was truly impressive. German heavy industry surpassed that of Great Britain in the 1890s. By 1914 Britain's share of the world's industrial production had shrunk to 10 percent, while Germany's share had risen to 15 percent. Germany transformed some of its industrial strength into military capability, including a massive naval armaments program.[15] A strategic aim of Germany's Tirpitz Plan was to build the second largest navy in the world, thereby advancing Germany as a world power. This expansion alarmed Britain, which began to feel isolated and worried about how it would defend its far-flung empire. In 1907 Sir Eyre Crowe of the British Foreign Office wrote his famous memorandum in which he concluded that although German policy might be vague and confused, Britain could not allow one country to dominate the continent of Europe. Crowe argued that the British response was nearly a law of nature.

Britain's response to Germany's rising power contributed to the second structural cause of the war: the increasing rigidity in the alliance systems in Europe. In 1904, parting from its geographically semi-isolated position as a balancer off the coast of Europe, Britain moved toward an alliance with France, and in 1907 the Anglo-French partnership broadened to include Russia. Germany, seeing itself encircled, tightened its relations with Austria-Hungary. As the alliances became more rigid, diplomatic flexibility was lost. The balance of power no longer featured shifting alignments that characterized the era of German Chancellor Otto von Bismarck. Instead, the major powers wrapped themselves around two poles that accentuated the security dilemma emphasized by defensive realists. As Christopher Clark observes,

"The bifurcation into two alliance blocs did not cause the war....Yet without the two blocs, the war could not have broken out in the way it did."[16]

There were also changes that altered the process of the system that had once been called the "Concert of Europe." One was the continuing rise of nationalism. In eastern Europe, pan-Slavism threatened both the Ottoman and Austro-Hungarian Empires, which each had large Slavic populations. German authors wrote about the inevitability of the Teutonic-Slavic battles, and schoolbooks inflamed nationalist passions. Nationalism proved stronger than socialism when it came to bonding working classes together, and stronger than the capitalism that bound bankers together. Indeed, it proved stronger than family ties among the monarchs. Germany's Kaiser Wilhelm II once hoped that because war was impending over the assassination of a fellow royal, Russian Tsar Nicholas II would see things the same way he did. By then, however, nationalism had overcome any sense of aristocratic or monarchical solidarity.

A second cause for the loss of moderation in the early twentieth-century balance of power process was a rise in complacency about peace. The great powers had not been involved in a war in Europe for forty years. There had been crises—in Morocco in 1905–06, in Bosnia in 1908–09, in Morocco again in 1911, and the Balkan wars in 1912–13—but they had all been manageable.[17] The diplomatic compromises that resolved these conflicts caused frustration, however. Afterward, there was a tendency to ask, "Why didn't we make the other side give up more?" Additionally, there was growing acceptance of social Darwinism. If the strong should prevail, why worry about peace? Long wars seemed unlikely, and many leaders believed that short decisive wars won by the strong would be a welcome change.

A third factor contributing to the loss of flexibility in the early twentieth-century balance of power process was German policy. As Eyre Crowe said, it was vague and confusing. There was a terrible clumsiness about the kaiser's policy of seeking greater power. The Germans were no different from other colonial powers in having "world ambitions," but they managed to press them forward in a way that antagonized everybody at the same time—just the opposite of the way Bismarck played the system in the 1870s and 1880s. The Germans antagonized the British by starting a naval arms race. They antagonized the Russians over issues in Turkey and the Balkans. They antagonized the French over a protectorate in Morocco.

The second level of analysis examines what was happening in domestic society, politics, and government prior to World War I.[18] Observers can safely reject Vladimir Lenin's argument that the war was simply the final stage of capitalist imperialism. It did not arise out of imperialist conflicts on the colonial peripheries as Lenin had expected. In 1898 Britain and France confronted each other at Fashoda, however, and if war had occurred then, it might have fit Lenin's explanation. The war broke out sixteen years later in Europe, and even then bankers and businessmen strongly resisted it. Grey felt that Britain had to prevent Germany from gaining mastery of the European balance of power. At the same time, he worried about convincing the London bankers to go along with declaring war, and his Liberal Party was split on the issue.

Two other domestic causes need to be taken more seriously: first, the internal crises of the declining Austro-Hungarian and Ottoman Empires; and second, the domestic political situation in Germany. Both Austria-Hungary and Ottoman Turkey were multinational empires threatened by the rise of nationalism. In addition, the Ottoman government was very weak, very corrupt, and an easy target for nationalist groups in the Balkans that wanted to free themselves from centuries of Turkish rule. The Balkan wars of 1912–13 pushed the Turks out, but in the next year the Balkan states fell to war among themselves while dividing the spoils. These conflicts whetted the appetite of some Balkan states to fight Austria. If the Turks could be pushed out, then why not the Austrians too?

Serbia took the lead among the Balkan states. Austrian elites feared disintegration and worried about the widespread predictions of decline. In the end, Austria went to war against Serbia not because a Serb assassinated Austrian Archduke Franz Ferdinand, but because Austria wanted to weaken Serbia and prevent it from becoming a magnet for nationalism among the Balkan Slavs. Gen. Franz Conrad von Hötzendorf, the Austrian chief of staff, stated his motives clearly: "For this reason, and not as vengeance for the assassination, Austria-Hungary must draw the sword against Serbia.... The monarchy had been seized by the throat and had to choose between allowing itself to be strangled, and making a last effort to prevent its destruction."[19] Disintegration of an empire because of nationalism was the more profound cause of the war, not the slaying of an archduke.

Another important domestic-level explanation of World War I lay in the domestic politics of Germany.[20] Many historians now believe that Fritz Fischer and his followers overstated Germany's social problems as a key cause of the war. For example, Russia's internal divisions also deserve attention. According to Fischer, Germany's efforts toward world hegemony were an attempt by German elites to distract attention from the poor domestic integration of an industrializing German society. He notes that Germany was ruled by a domestic coalition of landed aristocrats and some very large industrial capitalists, the Coalition of Rye and Iron. This ruling coalition used expansionist policies to support foreign adventures instead of domestic reform—circuses in place of bread. They viewed expansionism as an alternative to social democracy. Internal economic and social tensions in Germany are not sufficient to explain World War I, but they do help to explain one source of the pressure that Germany put on the international system after 1890.

A final domestic-level explanation appeals to the crisis instability of the situation in the summer of 1914. Military leaders in all countries shared a "cult of the offensive," favoring rapid mobilization and deployment, dramatic strategies involving sudden flanking movements of armies or dramatic break-through assaults, and freewheeling tactics of maneuver.[21] In fact, as military planners discovered the hard way, the prevailing military technology of the day did not favor the offense, but European leaders believed that it did. With the July crisis, leaders felt enormous pressure to get in the first blow. Of course, this particular explanation does not facilitate an understanding of why Europe sat on a powder keg. It does help in understanding why the spark in the Balkans traveled so quickly along the fuse.

What about the first level of analysis, the role of individuals? What distinguished the leadership on the eve of World War I was its mediocrity. The Austro-Hungarian emperor, Franz Joseph (1830–1916), was a tired old man who was putty in the hands of General Conrad and Count Leopold von Berchtold. Ironically, had he not been assassinated, Franz Ferdinand would have been a restraining force. In Russia, Tsar Nicholas was an isolated autocrat who spent most of his time resisting change at home. He was served by incompetent foreign and defense ministers. As MacMillan writes, "It was Russia's misfortune, and the world's, that its leadership was so inadequate as it was about to head into a major international storm."[22] In Germany Kaiser Wilhelm suffered from a great sense of inferiority. He was a blusterer, a weak and extremely emotional man. Although he did not control policy, his position at the apex of the system gave him influence that encouraged Germany to pursue a risky policy without skill or consistency. Personality did make a difference. There was something about the leaders, the kaiser in particular, that made them significant contributory causes of the war.

Was War Inevitable?

If World War I was overdetermined, does that mean it was inevitable? The answer is no; war was not inevitable until it actually broke out in August 1914. Even then, it was not inevitable that four years of carnage had to follow.

Three types of causes are distinguishable as regards their proximity in time to an event. The most remote are deep causes, then come intermediate causes, and those immediately before the event are precipitating causes. An analogy is building a fire: the logs are the deep cause, the kindling and paper are the intermediate cause, and the actual striking of the match is the precipitating cause.

In World War I, the deep causes were changes in the structure of the balance of power and certain aspects of the domestic political systems of the participants. Especially important reasons were the rise of German strength, the development of a bipolar alliance system, the rise of nationalism and the resultant destruction of two declining empires, and German politics. The intermediate causes were German policy, the rise in complacency about peace, and the personal idiosyncrasies of the leaders. The precipitating cause was the assassination of Franz Ferdinand in Sarajevo by a Serbian terrorist and Austria-Hungary's subsequent ultimatum to Serbia.

In retrospect, things always look inevitable. Indeed, some structuralists might say that if the assassination had not occurred, some other incident would have caused the war, because precipitating events are like buses—they come along every ten minutes. Thus the specific event at Sarajevo was not all that important; some incident would probably have occurred sooner or later.

This type of argument can be tested by counterfactual history. What if there had been no assassination in Sarajevo? The deep and intermediate causes suggested a high probability of war, but a high probability is not the same as inevitability. Using the metaphor of the fire again, logs and kindling may sit for a long time and never be lit. Indeed, if it rains before somebody comes along with a match, they may never catch fire.

Suppose there had been no assassination in Sarajevo in 1914, and no crisis occurred until 1916; what might have happened? One possibility is that the growth in Russian strength might have deterred Germany from recklessly backing Austria. In 1914 Gen. Helmuth von Moltke and Foreign Secretary Gottlieb von Jagow, two of the German leaders who were influential in precipitating the war, believed that war with Russia was inevitable. They knew Germany would have a problem fighting a war on two fronts and would have to knock out one side before fighting the other. Russia, although larger, had a poor transportation system, so it could be put off for the second strike. After victory over France, Germany could turn east and take its time to defeat the Russians. That was the Schlieffen Plan.

This strategy might have become obsolete by 1916, however, because Russia was using French money to build railroads. In the 1890s, it would have taken the Russians two or three months before they could have transported all of their troops to the German front, giving Germany ample time to fight France first. By 1910 that time had shrunk to eighteen days, and the German planners knew they no longer had a large margin of safety. By 1916 the margin would have been gone, and Germany might have had to drop its two-front strategy. Consequently, some German leaders thought that a war in 1914 was better than a war later.

If no assassination and no crisis had occurred in 1914, and the world had made it to 1916 without a war, it is possible that the Germans might have felt deterred, unable to risk a two-front war. They might have been more careful before giving Austria a blank check, as they did in 1914. Or they might have dropped the Schlieffen Plan and concentrated on a war in the east only. Or they might have come to terms with Great Britain or changed their view that the offense had the advantage in warfare. Britain was already having some second thoughts about its alliance with Russia because of Russian actions in Persia and Afghanistan. In sum, in another two years a variety of changes related to Russian strength might have prevented the war. Without war, German industrial strength would have continued to grow, and Germany might have become so strong that France and Britain would have been deterred.

One can also raise counterfactuals about what might have happened in Britain's internal affairs if two more years had passed without war. The Liberal Party was committed to withdrawing British troops from Ireland while the Conservatives, particularly in Northern Ireland, were bitterly opposed. There was a prospect of mutiny in the British army. If the Ulster Revolt of 1913 had developed further, it is quite plausible that Britain would have been so internally preoccupied that it would not have been able to join the coalition with France and Russia. Certainly many historically significant changes could have occurred in two more years of peace. Returning to the fire metaphor, there was a high probability of rain.

What Kind of War?

Another set of counterfactuals raises questions about what kind of war would have occurred rather than whether a war would have occurred. It is true that Germany's policies frightened its neighbors and that Germany in turn was afraid of being encircled by the Triple Entente, so it is reasonable to argue that war was more likely than not. But what kind of war? The war did not have to be what is now remembered as World War I. Counterfactually, four other wars were possible.

One counterfactual was a simple local war—"the third Balkan war." Initially, German leaders expected a replay of the Bosnian crisis of 1908–09 when the Germans backed the Austrians, and Austria was therefore able to make Russia stand down in the Balkans. On July 5, 1914, when the kaiser promised full support to Austria-Hungary, the expectation was for a local war. The kaiser and other officials continued their vacation plans so as to avoid alarming the other powers. Contrary to some assertions, they were not planning a preventive war.[23] When they realized their miscalculation, the kaiser made efforts to keep the war from escalating—hence the famous last-minute Willy-Nicky telegrams between the kaiser and the tsar. If such efforts had been successful, one might today recall not World War I, but merely a relatively minor Austro-Serbian war of August 1914.

A second counterfactual possibility was a one-front war. When the Russians mobilized their troops, the Germans also mobilized. The kaiser asked General von Moltke whether he could limit the preparations to just the eastern front. Moltke replied that it was impossible, because any change in the timetables for assembling the troops and supplies would create a logistical nightmare. The general told the kaiser that if he tried to change the plans, he would have a disorganized mass instead of an army. There were more possibilities, however. And had the Germans acted earlier to reassure the French, or had the kaiser insisted, there might have been a one-front war.[24]

A third counterfactual is to imagine a two-front war without Britain: Germany and Austria versus France and Russia. If the British Expeditionary Force had not been there to make the difference, Germany might well have won. It is possible that Britain might not have joined if Germany had not invaded Belgium, although Belgium was not the main cause of Britain entering the war. For some people, such as Sir Edward Grey and members of the Foreign Office, the main reason for entering the war was the danger of German control of the Continent. Britain, however, was a democracy, and the cabinet was split. The left Liberals opposed war, but when Germany swept through Belgium and violated Belgian neutrality, it allowed the pro-war Liberals to overcome the reluctance of the antiwar Liberals and to repair the split in the British government.

A fourth counterfactual is a war without the United States. Shaking his fist at an American visitor during his postwar exile, the kaiser complained that "you are responsible for my being here."[25] By early 1918, Germany might have won the war if the United States had not tipped the military balance with its entry in 1917. In 1916 President Woodrow Wilson won re-election on a platform of staying out of the war. One of the reasons the United States became involved was the weakening of Bethmann Hollweg and the decision of the German military to recommence an unrestricted submarine campaign against Allied and American shipping. There was also some German diplomatic clumsiness, as when Germany sent the Zimmermann telegram in February 1917 instructing its embassy in Mexico to approach the Mexican government regarding an alliance against the United States—a message that Britain decoded and passed to the United States. Washington regarded these intercepted instructions as a hostile act. These factors led the United States to enter the war, but even then, it is worth noting that one of the options Wilson considered was "armed neutrality."[26]

This counterfactual analysis first suggests ways in which the war might not have occurred in 1914 and, second, ways in which the war that occurred did not have to become four years of carnage, which destroyed Europe as the heart of the global balance of power. It suggests that World War I was probable, but not inevitable. Human choices mattered.

The Funnel of Choices

History is path dependent. Events close in over time, degrees of freedom are lost, and the probability of war increases. The funnel of choices available to leaders, however, might open up again, and degrees of freedom could be regained. If one starts in 1898 and asks what war was most likely in Europe, the answer would have been a war between France and Britain, which were eyeball to eyeball in a colonial dispute in Africa. But after the British and French formed the Entente in 1904, a Franco-British war looked less likely. The first Moroccan crisis in 1905 and the Bosnian crisis in 1908–09 made war with Germany look more likely, but some interesting events occurred in 1910. Bethmann Hollweg sought détente with Britain. Britain implied that it would remain neutral in any European war if Germany would limit its navy. At that same time, it looked as if renewed colonial friction between Britain and Russia in Asia threatened a collapse or erosion of the Triple Entente. In other words, in 1910 the funnel of choices started to widen again.

The funnel closed once more, however, with the second Moroccan crisis in 1911. When France sent troops to help the sultan of Morocco, Germany demanded compensation in the French Congo and sent a gunboat to Agadir on the Moroccan coast. Britain prepared its fleet. French and German bankers lobbied against war, and the kaiser pulled back. Nevertheless, these events deeply affected public opinion and raised fears about German intentions.

Although the Balkan wars in 1912 and 1913 and the increased pressure on Austria set the scene for 1914, there was also a renewed effort at détente in 1912. Britain sent Lord Haldane, a prominent Liberal politician, to Berlin, and the British and Germans resolved a number of outstanding issues. Also, by this time it was clear that Britain had won the naval arms race. Perhaps the funnel would open up again.

In June 1914, the feeling that British-German relations were improving was strong enough for Britain to send four of its Dreadnought battleships to Kiel for a state visit. If Britain had thought war was about to occur, the last thing it would have done was put four of its prime battleships in an enemy harbor. Clearly, the British were not thinking about war at that point. In fact, on June 28, British and German sailors were walking together along the quay in Kiel when they heard the news that a Serbian terrorist had shot an Austrian archduke in a faraway place called Sarajevo. History has its surprises, and once again, probable is not the same as inevitable.

Conclusion

Accidents, personalities, and choices make a difference even if they work within limits set by the larger structure, the situation of insecurity that resembles the Prisoner's Dilemma. That was true of both the Peloponnesian War and of World War I. As Christopher Clark has summarized, once catastrophes occur, "they impose on us (or seem to do so) a sense of their necessity. This is a process that unfolds at many levels....The quest for the causes of the war, which for nearly a century has dominated the literature on this conflict, reinforces that tendency: causes trawled from the length and breadth of Europe's prewar decades are piled like weights on the scale until it tilts from probability to inevitability. Contingency, choice, and agency are squeezed out of the field of vision." Clark concludes, however, that in 1914 "the future was still open—just. For all the hardening of the fronts in both of Europe's armed camps, there were signs that the moment for a major confrontation might be passing."[27]

Is it possible to draw contemporary lessons from this history? Scholars and policymakers must be careful, because analogies can mislead and many myths have been created about World War I. For example, some observers say that World War I was a preventive war by Germany. Although some Germans such as von Moltke held that view, the evidence shows that key elites did not. Others portray World War I as an accidental war, but it was not purely accidental. Austria went to war deliberately. And if there was to be a war, some in Germany preferred a war in 1914 to a war later. There were miscalculations over the length and depth of the war, but that is not the same as an accidental war. It is also said that the war was caused by an uncontrolled arms race in Europe. But by 1912, the naval arms race was over, and Britain had won. Although there was concern in Europe about the growing strength of its armies, the view that the war was precipitated directly by the arms race is too simple.

On the other hand, scholars and policymakers can draw some lessons from the long slide into World War I. One lesson is to pay attention to the process of a balance of power system as well as to its structure or distribution of power. Moderation evolves from the process. Stability is not assured by the distribution of power alone. Another useful lesson is to beware of complacency about peace or believing that the next crisis is going to fit the same pattern as the last crisis: the July crisis of 1914 was supposed to be a repeat of the Bosnian crisis of 1908, though clearly it was not. World War I was supposed to be a repeat of the 1870–71 Franco-Prussian War. In addition, the experience of World War I suggests that it is important to have military forces that are stable in a crisis, without any feeling that one must use them or lose them. The railway timetables were not the major determinants of World War I, but they did make it more difficult for political leaders to buy time for diplomacy.

Today's world is different from the world of 1914 in several important respects: one is that nuclear weapons have given political leaders the equivalent of a crystal ball that shows what their world would look like after escalation. Perhaps if the emperor, the kaiser, and the tsar had had a crystal ball showing their empires destroyed and their thrones lost in 1918, they would have been more prudent in 1914. Certainly, the crystal ball effect had a strong influence on U.S. and Soviet leaders during the 1962 Cuban missile crisis, and it would likely have a similar influence on U.S. and Chinese leaders today.

Another change in context, as John Mueller has noted, is that the ideology of war is much weaker in many major societies.[28] In 1914 war was thought to be inevitable, a fatalistic view compounded by the social Darwinist argument that war should be welcome because it would clear the air like a good summer storm. Although Winston Churchill was not typical of all of his compatriots and there are some myths about the degree of eagerness for war in August 1914, Churchill's *The World Crisis* describes this feeling: "There was a strange temper in the air. Unsatisfied by material prosperity, the nations turned restlessly towards strife internal or external. National passions, unduly exalted in the decline of religion, burned beneath the surface of nearly every land with fierce, if shrouded, fires. Almost one might think the world wished to suffer. Certainly men were everywhere eager to dare."[29] Margaret MacMillan argues that "they accepted the coming of war with resignation and a sense of obligation, persuaded that their nations were the innocent parties...and the soldiers did indeed tell their families that they would be home for Christmas.[30]

Although nationalism is growing in China today, and the United States entered two wars after the terrorist attacks of September 11, 2001, it is inaccurate to describe the prevailing climate in either country as bellicose or complacent about a limited war. China aspires to play a larger role in its region, and the United States has allies to whose defense it is committed. Miscalculations are always possible, but they can be managed with the right policy choices. The legitimacy of the Chinese government depends on a high rate of economic growth, and the top leaders in Beijing realize that China will need many decades before it approaches the sophistication of the American economy. Where Germany was snapping at Britain's heels (and passed it in industrial strength), the United States remains decades ahead of China in overall military, economic, and soft power resources.[31] Moreover, China cannot afford a policy like that of the kaiser's Germany. Too adventuresome a policy risks its gains at home and abroad. Finally, China and the United States face a number of issues such as energy, climate, and financial stability where they have strong incentives to cooperate.

In other words, the United States has more time to manage it relations with a rising power than Britain did a century ago, and China has incentives for restraint. Too much fear can be self-fulfilling. Whether the United States and China will manage their relationship well is another question. Human error and miscalculation are always possible. That will be a matter of human agency and choice, however. Among the lessons that scholars and policymakers should take away from this history of a century ago is to beware of Greeks, Europeans, or analysts bearing analogical gifts, particularly if they have a whiff of inevitability.

13

Lessons from Europe 1914 for Asia 2014

Reflections on the Centenary of the Outbreak of World War I

The Honorable Kevin Rudd

A S A CHILD, I grew up on a farm just outside a small town called Eumundi in Queensland in northeastern Australia. Back then, Queensland was to Australia what perhaps Bavaria was to Germany: rural, religious, and generally conservative. Eumundi's total population then was 162, although several hundred more could be added if one included the surrounding farming districts. I would frequently go to play with my cousins in town in the park outside their home, often playing soldiers, as most young boys from most cultures do, fighting imaginary battles against imaginary enemies. But our battles were made easier in the hot Australian summer sun because of the shade of the enormous Moreton Bay fig trees that covered the park.

One day I noticed that each of these giant trees had a tiny plaque at its foot with the faded names of Australian soldiers from the Great War (1914–18). In all, in this tiny community, which back in 1918 was even tinier, a total of twenty local lads had been killed out of a district of only a few hundred people. Of course, this was but one small part of the global carnage that became "the war to end all wars." Like local communities in Germany, Russia, France, Belgium, and Britain, these towns were never the same again, as their social fabric was literally ripped apart. Globally, we became members of what Drew Faust, in her great social history of the American Civil War, has called "The Republic of Suffering," as for the first time in human history we perfected slaughter on a truly industrial scale.[1]

In Australia no single community across our vast continent was without loss, resulting in thousands of similar memorials being built across our country. Of a total population of 4.8 million at the time, 416,000 put on the uniform, 332,000 went into the field, 60,000 were killed, and 152,000 were wounded, with a staggering casualty rate of 64 percent—the worst of all of the combatant states. What is remarkable in the Australian reflection on this, the centenary of World War I, is that this contribution to the carnage came from a country 6,000 miles away from Sarajevo, which no Australian had ever heard of until the cabled newspaper reports of the assassination of Austrian Archduke Franz Ferdinand on June 28, 1914. This was just one small part of the total carnage, which saw three-quarters of a million British, 1.3 million French, 1.7 million Russians, and 2 million Germans killed in a war that in January 1914 nobody thought possible.

On January 1, 1914, Germany's chancellor, Theobald von Bethmann Hollweg, stated: "The policies of the other countries [in Europe] are in harmony with the Government's and no troubles are now anticipated."[2] David Lloyd George reciprocated from London on January 3. When asked whether it was time to start overhauling British arms expenditure, he said: "I think that it is the most favourable moment that has presented itself during the last twenty years....Our relations with Germany are infinitely more friendly now than they have been for years...and the revolt against armaments has spread throughout Christendom."[3] In the United States, the *New York Times* in its New Year's Eve editorial reflected the general sentiment when looking ahead to 1914; it wrote glowingly of "the growing rapprochement between Germany, France, and England."[4] With the benefit of 20/20 hindsight, it is possible today to conclude that the warning signs had been there for all to see for at least the previous seven years, when in 1907 Russia finally entered into its own "entente" with Britain. This agreement completed the structure of competing alliances that would eventually take the world to war. Before 1914, however, a degree of strategic calm, even complacency, had set in. After all, a balance of power had now been constructed and a string of crises, including two Balkan wars, had been successfully navigated. The thought of a general European war had come to be regarded in most capitals as virtually impossible.

One hundred years later, many scholars and policymakers are still dumbfounded by World War I, as they struggle to understand what Joseph Nye elegantly describes elsewhere in this volume as its deep, its immediate, and its precipitating causes, and to reflect on what lessons, if any, they might have for the future.[5] As German Foreign Minister Frank-Walter Steinmeier stated in February 2014, World War I is the key to understanding the history of the twentieth century.[6] To which should be added that the study of the war is equally relevant to the current century as well. Taking Christopher Clark's cautionary tale to heart in his recent monumental account of the deliberations in capitals in the decade before the crisis of the summer of 1914, it is critical that policymakers today do not become "the sleepwalkers" of our current age, drifting imperceptibly from strategic complacency, to a form of "learned helplessness," into the perceived inevitability of conflict, be it in Europe or Asia today. In 2014, as in 1914, what Clark refers to as the multiple "mental maps" are as relevant today in the digital age as they were back then in the early days of the telegraph.[7] The attitudes of policy advisers and decisionmakers on how their own states should behave in a given set of strategic circumstances, on how other states are likely to behave, as well as the domestic political contexts in which critical decisions are made are key determinants of behavior.

Does History Repeat Itself?

Australians do not have a particularly unique perspective on the causes, effects, and lessons of the Great War. Nonetheless, we are all shaped, to greater or lesser degrees, by our respective historical narratives, whether we are conscious of them or not. In Australia's case, our historiography on the causes and content of the war to end all wars was shaped by a cocktail of unquestioning loyalty to the idea and the reality of the British Empire; a sense of national vulnerability to our isolated strategic circumstances in Asia, and therefore a commitment to the principle of collective imperial defense—all combined with a growing contempt for the incompetence of British generalship during the actual conduct of the military campaign as the war ground on. On the impacts of the war, particularly in Asia, and on the lessons it may hold for Asia's security challenges for the future, we bring a different historical lens to bear. At their best, Australians see themselves as the West in the East, but also as part of the East. With the rise of Asia, Australians lie increasingly at the crossroads of both history and the future. They are deeply conscious of their western civilizational origins but also the deep need, dictated by their immediate geographical circumstances, to understand the diversity, complexity, and differences of their own region as well.

Buried deep within the question about European history repeating itself in Asia is the more fundamental question of whether history repeats itself at all, and if it does, whether it does so with sufficient specificity to be useful for policymakers. This question in turn leads to the profound philosophical debates between necessity and agency, between structure and agency, or between a determinist view of history and one where humankind chooses to determine its own history. There is already a vast literature on this, which cannot be reviewed here. As a relatively recent policymaker, however, my conclusion, and therefore the assumption that I bring to bear in this analysis, is that a determinist view of history is unempirical, irrational, and above all unhelpful. Unempirical because diplomatic history teaches us that nothing is ever neatly replicable. Irrational because it denies the potency of human agency, instead believing we are all slaves to deep mystical, magnetic forces from which we can never ultimately escape. Unhelpful because it potentially instills in the official class a sense of learned helplessness, passivity, and inertia. This in turn renders history, diplomatic or otherwise, a curiosity for the academy but utterly pointless for the policy community.

The reverse assumption is that politics, diplomacy, and leadership all matter; that individuals shape history, sometimes incrementally, other times decisively; and therefore that alternate futures are always possible. Within this framework, diplomatic history offers us patterns of cause and response in common circumstances. But because circumstances are never precisely replicable, absolute predictability is equally impossible and the opportunities for individual agency are therefore considerable.

Located at another extreme end of the theoretical debate are those who argue that the phenomenon of unprecedented globalization has fundamentally changed the behavior of states forever. Thus diplomatic history has been rendered redundant as any sort of useful guide for the future.

Effective foreign policy analysis needs to occupy the middle ground in this complex conceptual terrain: at once mindful of the deep, proximate, and more immediate causalities at work within international politics, but at the same time capable of imagining alternative futures, for Asia, Europe, and the global order, where political and diplomatic leadership becomes the decisive variable.

Europe in 1914

Before examining any historical applications from "old Europe" to "modern Asia," it is important to identify historical principles emerging from World War I that might be generically applicable to other circumstances. On this question itself, there is wide divergence among historians. Yet, there are also remarkable commonalties on the list of possible principles, while recognizing deep disagreements on the degree of potential application elsewhere. These commonalities should be of interest not only to the academy but also to the deliberations of the policy community.

First, there is the long-standing realist view of international relations that holds that the only reliable basis on which to obtain peace, security, and stability is through a balance of power. This view goes to the heart of international relations theory and the perennial paradigm debates among realism, liberal internationalism, structuralism, constructivism, cosmopolitanism, and their various derivatives—all concerned with the animating forces ultimately shaping the international behavior of states and nonstate actors. It also goes to the theory and application of the so-called Thucydides Trap, whereby conflict becomes inevitable between a rising power and an established power, with its often-cited historical examples of Athens and Sparta; Britain and Germany in World War I (and possibly Germany and Russia as well); and today China and the United States. Graham Allison, author of the defining analysis of the decisionmaking processes behind the 1962 Cuban missile crisis and now the leading contemporary authority on the Thucydides Trap, has recently noted fifteen cases in which rising powers have rivaled established powers over the last five hundred years; the result in eleven of these cases was war.[8]

Whatever one's conclusions about international relations theory and the Thucydides Trap, it is safe to assume that the so-called balance of power between the Triple Entente and the Central Alliance in 1914—in both substance and perception—failed spectacularly to preserve the peace. Deterrence failed comprehensively. Furthermore, this failure occurred despite the awareness on the part of all of the military leaderships of all of the antagonists of the capacity of new, modern military technologies to totally revolutionize the face of modern warfare, as demonstrated by both the rapid and unprecedented destruction wrought in both the American Civil War half a century before and the Franco-Prussian War soon after. The advent of nuclear weapons at the end of World War II, and later the doctrine of mutually assured destruction, has provided for some a renewed legitimacy for the central organizing principle of a balance of power or, more precisely, the deterrent power of a balance of nuclear terror. Proponents argue that this doctrine has succeeded in preserving the peace for more than two-thirds of a century. Skeptics argue that there have been far too many near misses for comfort.

Since the end of the Cold War, or what may in time come to be referred to as the end of the "First Cold War," the question arises as to whether the international community has entered a new phase where various state actors are now prepared to take greater risks than before, less concerned, and therefore less constrained, by the risks of nuclear contagion or conflagration. As Clark noted in 2013, before recent developments in Ukraine, "It seems to me that our world is getting more like 1914, not less like it.... We are just starting to come to terms with the fact that we are no longer in a world that is disciplined by the standoff between two nuclear hyper-powers. And what we are drifting back to is a polycentric world with many sources of conflict. So in some ways, our world is drifting back towards 1914, even if the ocean of time between us and the First World War gets larger and larger."[9]

A second principle arising from the debate on causalities concerns the classical view that a primary factor driving international conflict arises from competing national interests over political sovereignty and territorial integrity. Yet the truth about World War I is that it was not fundamentally driven by conflicting territorial disputes in Europe itself, although both in Paris and in Berlin the question of who owned Alsace-Lorraine was never far from the surface. Nor was it driven primarily by competing colonial aspirations around the world. What was at stake were conflicting claims of political sovereignty between pan-Slav nationalism, on the one hand, and the continued claims of the Austro-Hungarian Empire, on the other. If, however, one were to look at the effects and not just the causes of the Great War—in particular, the imposition on Germany of the punitive clauses, on both reparations and territory, in the 1919 Treaty of Versailles—these became the most potent political catchwords that aided the rise of German fascism, ultimately leading to another world war.

Third, there is the principle of the escalation of local conflicts into global conflicts, exacerbated by the complex world of alliances, treaties, and that curious nineteenth-century ambiguous term of diplomacy—"understandings." The rapidly evolving series of events during the summer of 1914, from the assassination of Archduke Franz Ferdinand in Sarajevo in June until the guns of August, was exacerbated by the problem presented by the dynamics and demands of military mobilization, and by what has been described as the "cult of the offensive," so prevalent among much of the European military leadership of the time. This in turn was exacerbated by the driving diplomatic dynamic created by a complex web of interstate and alliance obligations, both real and perceived, stated and unstated. Combined with the military "preparedness" dynamic described above, the overall "force of events" pointed in a single direction—namely, war— and therefore required a massive counter-dynamic at the most senior political levels across Europe to arrest this built-in momentum of the system. Standing against the dominant dynamic, even as rationality increasingly demanded it, became more difficult with each passing day. Within the internal politics of each system, the politically easier course was to embark on the path of least resistance. The domestic political price for dissent was high, even among the monarchies, particularly given the nationalist political mood in all capitals. Escalation therefore became increasingly irresistible, with the result that options for de-escalation were progressively closed off. As Otto von Bismarck remarked, it would be "some damned foolish thing in the Balkans" that would ignite the war.[10] As with many other observations made during his long political career, the Iron Chancellor once again would be proven right.

This local escalation leads to a fourth principle, namely, the failure of diplomacy to either manage the crisis, or better still prevent it, or at least ameliorate it. This failure raises detailed questions concerning the professional competence, personal motivations, and ideational convictions of individual players. It also brings into focus the physical processes and the established culture and protocols of diplomatic communication that would be drawn on during the long month of July 1914—just as it probes the structural capacity of diplomats (i.e., those supposedly trained to understand the mind-set of the foreign party) to materially influence the final decisions of their principals. As German Foreign Minister Steinmeier has again noted in early 2014, the core mission of diplomacy was not to allow the parties to dispute to find themselves "at a dead-end," but instead constantly to be in the business of constructing the political space for a possible way out.[11] Regrettably this did not happen. Through a combination of diplomatic exhaustion, political capitulation to the prevailing public "mood," and a growing sense of inevitability, the military option was ultimately chosen.

Fifth, not only was there a failure of diplomacy; there was also a more fundamental failure of politics. If politics is about leadership rather than just "followership," then its mission is not simply to act as an echo chamber for the politics of the lowest common denominator, but instead to explain, to advocate, and to persuade the public that there are other ways through a crisis. Among the most disturbing images from World War I are the photographs of scenes of wild jubilation of the crowds gathering in the central squares of Berlin, London, Vienna, Paris, Sydney, Auckland, and Toronto when war was declared. Politics had done little to constrain their publics' appetites for nationalist excess or to prepare them for the slaughter that was to come. As noted above, politics had become captive to Clark's multiple "mental maps" about how great powers should behave, and how the alliance system should work, rather than how to creatively resolve a deep systemic crisis that threatened the future of the entire system. Furthermore, Clark argues against the view that the European political class was powerless to act against the accretion of events, creating what he describes as "the illusion of a steadily building causal pressure" rendering politicians impotent.[12] Intervention became more difficult, but it was always possible.

A sixth and, I believe, critical factor in the analysis of the outbreak of World War I was the absence of effective regional or international institutions to moderate, tame, or even prevent the march to war. The Hague Conventions of 1899 and 1907 on the conduct of warfare and on the peaceful arbitration of international disputes had begun to create a thin tissue of global governance. The Permanent Court of Arbitration had been established in 1900, moving into the Hague Peace Palace in 1913. Its principal benefactor,

Andrew Carnegie, proclaimed to the leaders of the world, "International Peace is to prevail through the Great Powers agreeing to settle their disputes by international law, the pen thus proving mightier than the sword."[13] The truth, however, was that this nascent international institution was incapable of creating a culture of political cooperation and peaceful dispute resolution that could soothe the sharp edges around the crisis of 1914. Europe would have to wait another full generation, the failure of the League of Nations, another world war, and the birth of the United Nations before the founders of the European project, now called the European Union, were finally able to prevail. Although beyond Europe, notwithstanding the advent of the United Nations, whose charter accords it the status of the supreme global institution to safeguard global peace and security, the international system remains brittle in the face of international crises that still threaten the peace today.

One final principle on which to reflect from this war to end all wars was the failure of economic globalization to prevent it. Economic historians have come to classify the half century before 1914 as the "first great globalization." The era witnessed unprecedented trade, investment, and capital flows across European and global borders. But despite the financial and economic lunacy of going to war, neither the financial nor the corporate leaderships across the various capitals of the time were able to arrest the atavistic forces of political nationalism that swept away all that lay in its path. A parallel debate about the "second great globalization" (1991–) and whether it is now finally creating a new transnational political reality that in the future will be able to sweep away the historical logic governing the international behavior of states continues to this day.[14] Certainly the quantum, the dimensions, and the immediacy of interconnectedness between national economies and polities are of a different caliber today than they were a hundred years ago. Globalization is "thicker" than before, driven by the radical contraction in the time and space of global transactions made possible by new technologies and the parallel intensity of the global movement of peoples. The idea that this has now tamed the beast of primordial nationalisms remains heroic, however. In postmodern Europe perhaps, but even there the rise of anti-globalist parties that now routinely command around 20 percent of the vote underlines the limitations of the European project. Beyond Europe the challenge is far greater, whatever the economic data may suggest.

Contemporary Asia

So what is one to make of modern Asia a century after the cataclysmic events that destroyed the old European order in 1918, one that had governed the

European continent since the defeat of Napoleon and before? To begin with, no one in Europe can forget that European colonialism has left a profound mark on most of Asia, much of it profoundly humiliating. Nobody in Asia has forgotten that fact, together with the sense of white superiority and the episodic claims of social Darwinist rationalization for the European imperialist binge that went along with it. With the exception of Japan, parts of China, and Siam (Thailand), most of Asia was subjected to centuries of European colonial occupation. For China, however, World War I also carried a particular twist.

Even though both China and Japan had supported the Triple Entente during the war, by the time of the signing of the Treaty of Versailles, Germany had not returned its former colonial possessions in Shandong to China. Instead they were handed, for a period at least, to Japan. This single act, within a few years of the birth of the Chinese Republic, enraged, radicalized, and mobilized an entire generation of Chinese student activists in what became known as the May the Fourth Movement. This in turn contributed to the formation of the Chinese Communist Party in 1921. By the time the Communist Party united the country in 1949, a central rallying point for party legitimacy was the ability of China to overcome a century of foreign humiliation, starting with the Opium Wars in the 1840s through to the end of the Japanese occupation in the 1940s. This victory continues to be a rallying point of party legitimacy.

If China, as is likely, becomes the world's largest economy within the next decade, it will be the first time since George III was on the British throne that a non-western, non-Anglo Saxon, non-English speaking, nondemocracy will have been so. Thus anyone who assumes that China's growing global economic ascendancy will pass without any impact on the current global rules-based order is a poor student of history. In this context, therefore, it is important to remember that Europe and the idea of "the West" has already cast a long and in large part negative shadow over Asia, in general, and China, in particular.

As for the applicability of the various principles discussed above arising from World War I in Europe to the new, complex political and security circumstances in twenty-first-century Asia, the parallels are at best mixed. Take, for example, the practical utility of the core concept of a balance of power. Both China and the United States approach each other in Asia with a high degree of strategic "realism," drawing from rich domestic traditions of Chinese and Western realism in relation to the possession, deployment, leverage, and actual use of national power. At present, however, there is nothing approaching a balance of power between them. The United States maintains overwhelming military preponderance in the air-sea spaces in the western Pacific and the northern Indian Ocean regions. That preponderance is reinforced by a network of alliances and military cooperation agreements across the region. In other words, even though strategic concepts of military balance, spheres of influence, or (in the case of China) the old Soviet idea of "a correlation of forces" influence the security and foreign policy thinking of both China and the United States, at present the strategic reality is that there is a very large imbalance of power between the two. China, of course, is seeking to close this military gap and the broader correlation of forces over time. And though from Beijing's perspective progress is being made, Chinese analysts conclude that closing this gap will take decades; it also will depend on the relative performance of the two countries' economies and, consequently, their military budgets. Some Chinese analysts anticipate that Chinese military spending, which at present is increasing rapidly while that of the United States is declining, will reach about 70 percent of the United States' by 2023.

The good news for China and the United States is that there is now an open discussion between the two on the challenges to long-term strategic stability posed by the Thucydides Trap, a core conceptual component of balance of power realism. This is the stated reason that the China under Xi Jinping has explicitly proposed "a new type of great power relationship" with the United States.[15] For its part, the United States has initiated a series of annual bilateral working-level summits with an agenda for the future aimed at building strategic trust, step by step, including in a range of sensitive security policy domains. The open question in Washington is the extent to which China will substantively participate in this process, or whether China is primarily attracted to the political symbol and diplomatic prestige of the perceived "parity" offered by regular summitry with the world's only remaining superpower. Or worse, the perception of some in the U.S. foreign policy establishment that China is simply buying time, taking the strategic temperature down in the U.S. relationship at a declaratory level, while operationally continuing its long-term project of maximizing its national power, against that day in the future when China is able to begin to act unilaterally.

Part of the challenge, therefore, is for China to substantively address these concerns, particularly as President Xi Jinping will deal with three U.S. administrations during his term—a new Democratic administration, or a new Republican administration, or possibly both. For this reason, China and the United States must begin now to cooperatively develop regional and global public goods to help sustain and improve the international rules-based order for the future. This cooperation should embrace multiple domains, including cybersecurity; prevention and management of naval incidents at sea; new confidence- and security-building measures across East Asia involving states such as Japan; China's inclusion in any future trans-Pacific partnership on trade and investment in a high-quality, domestically enforceable agreement; and an agreed common approach to climate change between the world's two biggest polluters, if necessary outside any global treaty agreement.

It remains to be seen whether this overall approach succeeds through the planned regular summitry between the two, the first summit having been held in June 2013. It is difficult to support John Mearsheimer's almost a priori assumption, however, that China's peaceful rise is simply impossible.[16] The evidence for such a claim at this stage is thin, particularly given China's long-term strategic need for regional peace for its economic development imperative. At least the two powers publicly recognize that there is a strategic trust deficit and now a mechanism for managing it. This recognition stands in stark contrast to the various governments of Europe, including their royal houses, pretending a century ago that their deep distrust of one another could be kept below the surface, masked by secret undertakings, and somehow papered over by the blood lines linking the Romanovs, the Hohenzollerns, and the House of Hanover (very soon to become Windsor) and the occasional shooting parties on one another's estates. There is a lot to be said for dealing with the problem of strategic trust openly, despite the formidable challenges that must be addressed in reducing it.

More broadly across Asia today, the world is also witnessing what can only be described as a regional arms bazaar, in direct contrast to the real declines in European defense outlays over the last two decades. The danger for broader Asia is that this proliferation of weapons, both nuclear and conventional, which has been developing across the region for some decades, now has the potential to further destabilize the region given the potent cocktail of unresolved territorial disputes that litter the region from north to south. As noted above, territorial disputes between the great powers did not lie at the heart of the Great War, although the aspirations for political sovereignty on the part of the Slavic populations of the Balkans provided the immediate spark for the conflagration that followed. Unlike Europe today, Asia is awash in active, unresolved territorial disputes, compounded by a number of unresolved sovereignty or secessionist claims within states. The most dangerous of these lies on the Korean Peninsula. They also exist, however, between Russia and Japan, between China and Korea, between China and Japan over the East China Sea, between Korea and Japan, between China and four separate states in Southeast Asia over the South China Sea, between Thailand and Cambodia, between China and India, and between India and Pakistan over

Kashmir. Then there are the long-standing Chinese concerns over Taiwan, Tibet, and Xinjiang. Furthermore, many of these interstate disputes involve nuclear weapons states: Russia, China, North Korea, Pakistan, and India. The absence of regional or global mechanisms to deal with these disputes is a major cause of long-term strategic instability.

These disputes are compounded by the capacity for escalation through deep strategic mistrust, an absence of protocols for handling incidents at sea and in the air, and the complex alliance structures that crisscross the region. China has a security relationship with North Korea going back to the Korean War, as does the United States with South Korea. Then there are U.S. security treaties or arrangements with Japan, Taiwan, the Philippines, Thailand, Australia, and New Zealand. Most attention at present is focused on the capacity of the maritime boundary disputes in the East and South China Seas to escalate and to draw in the United States militarily. These two sets of disputes have significant differences: the first involves contested claims between China, Japan, and Korea, with the added complexity of Taiwan; the second involves China, Vietnam, the Philippines, Brunei, and Malaysia, again compounded by the Taiwan factor. I have previously referred to the South China Sea as "a maritime Balkans," reflecting my concerns about the sheer complexity of the overlapping island and maritime claims, the historically belligerent relationship between China and Vietnam, and of course Washington's alliance relationship with Manila. Active diplomacy is being deployed at present to de-escalate these disputes from recent high levels of tension, although the capacity for reigniting them through miscalculation or design remains significant. One of the profound lessons of 1914 is the rapidity with which circumstances can change from utterly benign to utterly catastrophic within the space of months. The region is not experienced in crisis management or in crisis containment, although military and diplomatic networks are slowly evolving.

Then there is the relative sophistication of U.S., Chinese, and Asian diplomacy to deal with any crises in the making, compared to the comprehensive diplomatic failures in Europe leading up to the guns of August. The truth is that the diplomatic networks in Southeast Asia are strong; those between Beijing, Tokyo, and Seoul much less so; and those with North Korea, with the exception of China, virtually nonexistent. Required here is a diplomatic culture of institutional cooperation of the type that belatedly has evolved in Europe.

In Europe, not only did diplomacy fail but so did politics. Here again, the challenge in Asia today is as large as Europe faced a century ago with the rise of nationalism. The most toxic challenge is between China and Japan, compounded by the experience of a brutal Japanese occupation that lasted more than fifteen years. But nationalism, in particular ethnonationalism, is a major challenge across many parts of Asia. The ability of political leaderships to manage these nationalisms, rather than being managed by them, represents a crucial challenge for the future.

Nonetheless, one of the main lessons to be applied from Europe's bloody experience a century ago concerns the thin state of Asian regional architecture and institutionalism to ameliorate interstate tension. Europe, after three major continental wars in the space of two-thirds of a century, finally concluded that it had to embrace fundamental strategic change. The core of this new thinking was Franco-German resolve to build a new Europe based on a common, shared future, rather than one based on mutual suspicion, competing alliances, and a zero-sum game approach to security. Many observers criticize the European Union unfairly, forgetting its formidable strategic achievements. The European Union has constructed an institution based on common security, a common market, and prospectively an economic union. In doing so, Europe has rewritten its history.

This is where Europe has a strategic concept to share with Asia. In 2008 I proposed the establishment of an Asia-Pacific Community—an entity that would have all the principal countries and economies around the region at the same table with an open agenda on political, economic, security, and environmental cooperation. Progress had been made when in 2010 the East Asian Summit, which already had such an open mandate and agenda, expanded from its original sixteen members (the Southeast Asian ten, the Northeast Asian three, together with India, Australia, and New Zealand) to also include the United States and Russia. This expanded East Asia Summit has already begun some forms of soft security cooperation, particularly in counter-disaster management exercises involving most of the region's militaries. There is, however, much more to be done in building the habits, culture, and institutional processes of this vastly divergent region into a framework of common security over time.

Finally, the long-term strategic direction of Asia will be determined between the forces of economic globalization that push the international community toward higher levels of integration and the narrow forces of political nationalism that work in the reverse direction, always seeking to tear the region apart. The forces of economic globalization will not be sufficient to preserve the peace. The value therefore of a program of purposeful regional institution-building is that it is designed to support the forces for integration and to impede those that work against them. It is here that Europe has much to offer, and Germany, as one of the strategic mainstays of the union, has much to offer in particular.

Conclusion

In this year of international reflection about the lessons of a war that tore the world apart, it is important to focus on what the international community should now do together, rather than focus on who was to blame a hundred years ago. Retrospectively establishing intentionality is a difficult historical exercise, particularly when there is a multiplicity of players and the events are now a century removed from our experience. It is even less helpful today, as some have done, to engage in the foreign policy parlor game of trying to identify the twenty-first-century equivalents of these twentieth-century antagonists. Apart from being historically fraught, it is also unhelpful because it is like assigning countries parts in a play whose script we all know and whose story line has already been concluded. This, too, points in the direction of the allocation of blame, rather than the distribution of responsibility for carving out a different future.

In this context, there are five core principles that emerge from the competing historiographies of World War I that are potentially applicable to the present century in Europe, Asia, and beyond. First there is the paramount, some would argue, self-evident need to remain alert to the real possibility that profound change can happen suddenly, and that the international community should not be seduced into a collective complacency that peace has somehow become the permanent condition of humankind simply because it has been that way for some decades. "Deep" strategic factors are already at work across Asia that are potentially destabilizing. There are a number of proximate issues unfolding across the region, including North Korean nuclear and missile tests, the enforcement of air defense information zones, and the political toxicities released by repeated visits of Japanese officials to the Yasukuni Shrine. But as yet, there has been no significant, defining "spark" capable of igniting these many different straws in the wind. The lesson of the Balkans, however, is that catalytic events can occur suddenly. Without established diplomatic processes for managing these, the innate characteristic of a spark is to catch fire, particularly in an environment of sustained political brittleness where natural kindling is in abundance.

A second lesson of the July crisis is the critical importance of creative diplomacy that always seeks actively to solve problems, rather than simply passively to describe them, or worse assume they are insoluble and allow the options for any solution to melt away. This applies particularly to how Beijing and Washington choose to plan their long-term relationship, rather than just react to events as they occur. This will require diplomatic creativity, rather than slavish dependence on old diplomatic playbooks.

Third, there is the responsibility of political leadership, particularly on the profound questions of war and peace, to lead public opinion, not just to follow it. It is also about opening up the domestic political space to keep the channels of political communication open. That is why the critical political and diplomatic relationships within Asia need a new level of ballast, to buffer these relationships against the winds that will inevitably seek to blow these relationships off course in the future.

Fourth, there is the critical learning from the decade leading up to the Great War about the need over time to build the regional institutions that encourage the habits and culture of common security, rather than believing that these habits will somehow naturally evolve out of the ether. Common security is the conceptual opposite to the definition of security through a zero-sum game. This looms now as a critical challenge for Asia.

Finally, in the great challenges that now present themselves for the Asian century ahead, there is a responsibility to work with both China and the United States to forge a common path for a secure, prosperous, and sustainable regional and global future. This is primarily a responsibility for the United States and China, as this is the strategic fulcrum on which these futures will ultimately turn. This in turn will require unprecedented political commitment, transparency, and the building of strategic trust step by step. It is not, however, the responsibility of the great powers alone. As many have speculated in a counterfactual analysis of July and August 1914, what if Britain under Foreign Secretary Sir Edward Grey had decided to stand aside from the conflict erupting between Germany and Russia to play an intermediating role? Instead, adopting a minimalist diplomatic role, concluding that war was inevitable, and Britain becoming a full-blown combatant from the first day of the war rendered any intermediating role impossible. As a direct consequence of this decision and the devastating consequences of the war that followed, British power in the postwar world declined rapidly, as Britain was no longer able to act as the most powerful nation in the world.

As noted above, Australians bring their own perspective to bear, although in the lead-up to World War I, we like others were at best hopeful, rather than purposeful, about how the peace might be preserved. In May 1912, one of my Australian prime ministerial predecessors, Sir George Reid, later high commissioner in London, went to Berlin to address the Reichstag. His words are worth repeating because they reflect the mood of the time. As such, like all those who became combatants, they embraced a sentiment without a strategy. Sir George said:

Forty years ago your country emerged new, born again from a supreme crisis. Her grand federation is only one generation older than the federation of Australia. Already the new Germany wields an immense power among the nations which, with patience and sagacity at the helm, must become infinitely greater still.... The taste for aggressive warfare—once the prevailing fashion—is now opposed to modern sentiment. Preparations for the wars that never come are taking the place of war itself; and the money spent in getting ready to fight is so enormous that it will soon, thank God, be impossible to fight at all. Australia is making vigorous preparations, not for war, but for self-defense. The same—I absolutely assure you—is the position of Great Britain and the whole British Empire. If the other nations will consent to disarm, the first to scrap their Dreadnoughts and to disband their armies would be the British race.

Peace is our supreme aim, it is the one thing we must have even if we have to fight for it.... If Germany and Great Britain would head a European coalition, based on the peaceful settlement of disputes, it would be well for Germany, well for Great Britain, well for Europe and well for all other countries....

As the barriers erected by national ambition or fear or dislike crumble away, more fertile fields for emulation would be opened up to the free play of the combative forces of human nature, in the wider, nobler, more incessant struggles of ability and merit, in the spheres of science, discovery, invention, industry, commerce. By such means advancing confidence, replacing fear, disarming suspicion would breed feelings of friendly rivalry, thus advancing by leaps and bounds human progress and happiness.[17]

Barely two years later, Australia, as part of the British Empire, was at war with Germany on land, at sea, and in the air. Within months of the outbreak of the war, Australian and German cruisers were engaging each other in the Indian Ocean. Then the following year German military advisers, working with the Turks, helped to thwart the allied attack in the Dardanelles, where Australians were now joined fully in the slaughter. Then from 1916 Australians found themselves part of the complete carnage that had become the western front. All before one final, brutal push in the last, great pitched battles of the war in the massive allied offensive of September 1918 across the Hindenburg line, when the Australians, with the Americans, finally broke the German line. And the rest is history.

The question for Australians, and for the other combatants, is how could this have happened among civilized peoples from opposite ends of the earth over such a relatively trivial matter? The answer lies in active policies for the future that are fully mindful of these lessons from the past, when the civilized world seemingly allowed itself to drift into conflict and total war.

14

Contingency as a Cause
(or Little Things Mean a Lot)

Richard N. Rosecrance

T HIS VOLUME SHOWS that World War I was caused by factors that still animate modern international relations: domestic politics, alliances, economic connections or rivalries, repetitive crises, and power relationships.[1] Structure depicts the overarching power and bloc relations within an anarchic system. It changes little if at all during a particular contretemps. In contrast, contingent factors may vary rapidly and shift during a crisis. The authors of this volume have surveyed many factors that contributed to the war. What can we say about them and how might they apply today?

Structure is permanent, contingencies are evanescent. Those who believe that structural features of European international relations caused World War I focus on the rigidity of the balance of power and the intricacy of the alliance system. Beyond this minimal consensus, supporters of the structural explanation tend to disagree. One group sees bipolarity—that is, the offsetting tension between two major powers—as stabilizing, citing the Cold War and its outcome (though conveniently neglecting to mention the Peloponnesian Wars and the struggle between Rome and Carthage).[2] A second group asserts that power transitions between the top two nations in the international system generally lead to conflict, having done so frequently throughout history.[3] In the past, Habsburg kings contended with the (French) Valois. Spain had to contend with a rising Holland seeking unfettered independence. After the Dutch prevailed in that struggle, they faced a challenge from ascending Great Britain. In the eighteenth century, France launched another challenge against Britain. And from 1780 until just short of 1815, France seemed to have prevailed. After 1815, however, Britain took the leadership, but a rising Germany challenged that position in 1914. Britain surmounted the attack but then faced a stronger United States and Russia. The United States subsequently dispatched the Soviet Union in the Cold War. War was involved in every challenge except that of the United States to Britain and Russia to the United States. Unnoticed, Japan peacefully passed the Soviet Union (an admittedly second-ranked power) in 1983.

From 1890 to 1914, the tension in Europe pitted Britain against Germany, each aiming at empire outside Europe. Germany wanted its "place in the sun." Added to that, by 1910 a bipolar split was emerging between Germany and a newly ascendant Russia. In both military and economic terms, Russia had recovered from the revolution of 1905 and was beginning to assert itself in the Balkans and in European politics more generally. In neither case did these partial bipolar relationships produce a standoff leading to peace. Instead, they led to war. In addition, as Thomas Christensen and Jack Snyder demonstrate, after allies of both Britain and Germany became involved, the tensions resulted in "chain-ganging," which dragged every major power into the war.[4] Thus conflicting structural accounts do not adequately explain the outbreak of war in 1914.

The major claim of this book therefore is that "little things"—contingent features of the situation prevailing in Europe on the eve of World War I— were more responsible than enduring structural characteristics of the European or international system. We have looked at multiple causes of the war, not at countries to blame for starting it. Broadly speaking, we conclude that the Great War was by no means inevitable, because there were so many contingencies that might have gone another way. In Sarajevo, Archduke Franz Ferdinand's driver, Leopold Lojka, might not have hesitated at the inter-section of Franz Josef Street and the Quai, having made a wrong turn. It was while Lojka was attempting to back up that Gavrilo Princip fired the shots that killed the archduke and his wife, Duchess Sophie. Without this unprec-edented justification, Vienna could hardly have made demands on Serbia that would have undermined its independence as a state. Russia would not have been involved, and Germany could not have acted. As Joseph Nye points out, domestic politics in Britain over the Irish question might have kept Britain out of the war or delayed its entry. London was more concerned with appeasing Dublin (and Ulster) than pacifying Austria or Serbia. Britain's hesitancy or abstention would have either prevented war or changed its outcome.[5] The United States might not have entered the war if Britain had not been involved, because there would have been no naval blockade of German ports. Germany would then not have had to use submarines to attack the United Kingdom's merchant ships, raising the specter of unrestricted submarine warfare. It was the German proclamation of submarine warfare in January 1917 and Berlin's torpedoing of neutral ships that brought a U.S. declaration of war in April.

Without the United States as a powerful ally, France would have fought alone in the west and probably lost to Germany in a much shorter war.[6] Germany wanted war, but as Stephen Van Evera shows, not a continental or world war. Russia was also hoping to limit its enemies: it wanted to fight Austria alone.

There were also military reasons for hesitation. Russia and France were not fully ready to fight in 1914. Russia had not completed its railway system and therefore could not achieve its goal of rapid mobilization. France had still not fully trained the cohort of troops required by the new three-year conscription law. Given their temporary weakness, Paris and St. Petersburg might have held back. Germany also had military problems. Gen. Helmuth von Moltke, the German commander, was not confident of victory. Even if he had been, he did not have enough troops to fulfill the Schlieffen Plan requirement of a seven to one ratio of forces on the west wing as compared with the rest of the German offensive line. Germany was thereby undertaking an extraordinarily difficult and perhaps impossible task. Given a British blockade, Berlin did not have access to all of the raw materials and oil needed for a prolonged war.

Political factors also played a role. St. Petersburg rushed into war without acknowledging the war's surreptitious—even dubious—origins. If Russian leaders had fully taken into account that their ally, Serbia, was complicit in the murder of Franz Ferdinand,[7] they might have hesitated instead of acting on behalf of "regicides," as Kaiser Wilhelm II pleaded with Tsar Nicholas II not to do.[8] In Germany, Russia, and Austria, weak political leaders were told that an offensive thrust would win the war. Belief in this conclusion proved disastrous. Had leaders with the perception and backbone of Otto von Bismarck, David Lloyd George, Pyotr Stolypin, or Franz Ferdinand himself been in command, they would have been less willing to genuflect before such military bravado. They might have questioned the regnant belief in "offense dominance" that Van Evera correctly impugns as a cause of conflict. Understanding this, Germany might have turned to the defense, which Jack Snyder suggests was more compatible with its location and previous war plans, and achieved a more tolerable outcome. Also as we have seen, countries went to war as much to revivify or honor their alliances as to gain victory over a foe. Finally, most observers believed that war would occur sooner or later; it was seen as an inevitable occurrence in the international scheme of things. Nations then reasoned, "If so, why not fight it now?" As Snyder shows, proper timing thus became the issue, not whether one could surely defeat an adversary.

If these contingencies had been otherwise, the war would not have taken place, or not in the way that it did, and the implications for the future would have been different. As David Richards and Joseph Nye point out, nuclear weapons now deter war between the United States and China as much as they once did between the United States and the Soviet Union. Nuclear retaliation was not possible in 1914. And, as Richard Cooper observes, today's closely knit and largely private economic system has brought the United States and China much closer than the prevailing mercantilism and high tariffs did the progenitors of World War I.

Still, it is worth remembering that China's leader, Xi Jinping, has addressed the potential implications of the Thucydides Trap for the future. As Graham Allison notes, the Chinese president has set the objective of China matching the United States in gross domestic product and after that per capita income by mid-twenty-first century. Xi did not assert that this goal would require the conquest of territory, but the nine-dashed line proclaimed by China over Pacific waters includes a huge swatch of ocean area claimed by other states. These contested waters may contain abundant mineral resources, oil, and natural gas. It is unlikely that Japan, Vietnam, and Korea will stand by while China exploits them unilaterally. As an ally of Japan, South Korea, and the Philippines, the United States could be drawn into disputes surrounding these claims.

Both T.G. Otte and Etel Solingen demonstrate that domestic politics did not prevent international conflict. Otte notes a pervasive "stalemate" within the domestic lives of the five great powers, but not one that would necessarily mandate war. Eckart Kehr's influential dissertation claimed that German leaders thought that a war might bring an end to internal political disputes. Neither Otte nor Solingen accepts this version of events. Solingen argues that "internationalizing coalitions" that favored economic modes of advancement were weak relative to imperialist groups propounding support for a great German navy. Solingen, Richards, and Kevin Rudd maintain that today the sinews of trade and internationalism are much stronger, if not resilient enough to bind the United States and China everlastingly together.

Arthur Stein points to repetitive crises as a cause of war. Germany challenged the French position in Morocco in 1905 and again in 1911; each time Germany conceded French gains. The Austrian annexation of Bosnia in 1908 (without compensation to St. Petersburg at the Dardanelles) caused Russian estrangement, while Russia bided its time, waiting for a chance to redeem its losses. Britain and Germany jousted over sea power but failed to reach agreement. Britain sent Lord Haldane, the most pro-German member of the British establishment, to Berlin in February 1912 to negotiate a naval deal. He returned empty-handed. How many times could the powers challenge each other in games of Chicken confident that the other side would back down?

As Charles Maier and I point out, allies add complexities. They contribute to the national strength of their patron, but they may also involve that partner in war. In the worst of all worlds, they may involve a patron without offering sufficient strength and support to guarantee victory. Neither Serbia nor Austria tipped the scales of power for Russia or Germany in 1914, but they still embroiled them in conflict. Allies can perform a very strong service if they help to create an overbalance of power against a possible foe. If the United States had been firmly committed to Britain's defense in 1914, this stance might have deterred Germany from acting against France, as the power of the Triple Entente would have far outweighed that of the Triple Alliance. During the 1960s and 1970s, the United States built up and sustained its European allies, creating a powerful coalition that in the end amounted to an overbalance against the Soviet Union and brought an end to the Cold War in 1991.

For the future, what kind of overbalance needs to be constructed? Christensen and Snyder argue that chain gangs and passed bucks were the ruling options in 1914 and 1938. The first held sway in 1914 and the second from 1936 to the eve of World War II. Neither was appropriate to the prevailing challenge: the first represented an overresponse, the second an underresponse. In the future, finding a middle position will be difficult, but a system of allied nations that does not drag countries into war is the key answer.

Looking ahead, the tyranny of small things presents a huge problem. The powers of 1914 could not one after another seal off every war-advancing contingency. Will the United States and China have better success in the future? Allies may demand support, thus consigning Washington and Beijing to opposing stances. Repetitive crises are hard to manage even if they start small. Leaders are generally more or less well-equipped for their daunting tasks; yet sometimes strong leaders are in short supply. The European Union strode forward with leaders such as Jean Monnet, Robert Schuman, Jacques Delors, and Helmut Schmidt, but the European coalition has suffered under hesitant leadership since. There is no obvious cohort of future leaders that can manage existing institutions in the detail needed to avoid negative contingencies.

Could the relevant institutions be upgraded? This is the proposal of Kevin Rudd and Alan Alexandroff. Rudd suggests a closer alignment of East Asian countries to improve China's ties with its immediate neighbors. Eventually, other powers could be included. Many East Asian nations, however, are traditional rivals. In an unguarded moment, Japanese Foreign Minister Taro Aso said not too long ago, "China and Japan have hated each other for a thousand years.... Why should things be any different now?"[9] Alexandroff proposes the creation of a worldwide coalition to include China, the United States, and

Europe—a kind of world Concert of Powers. Bismarck or Henry Kissinger would have run such an institution with finesse and balance, never permitting commitments to one nation completely to overwhelm undertakings on behalf of another. In a large and powerful concert, even the strongest member, potentially China, would be subject to restraints drawing from the assembled power of all other members.

These proposals raise two key questions. Would Beijing be allowed to join such an organization? Second, would it wish to do so? The answer to the first question is that China would have to change internally and become a member of institutions such as the Organization for Economic Cooperation and Development (which certifies a country's liberalization) to qualify for membership. Unless China eases economic restrictions and moves to a greater application of the rule of law, other countries would not trust it to participate. The reigning mercantilism in Beijing would have to change to allow outsiders to compete in China on an equal basis. State-owned enterprises now have access to capital on political terms from regional banks. Strictly speaking, they should be granted loans only when their economic performance justifies it and when they can pay them back. Even if China acceded to these requirements, it would still have to renounce further territorial expansion and accept the parceling out of Pacific oil-producing real estate along lines similar to those agreed to in the North Sea by Norway and the United Kingdom. Doing so would be in China's interest, because otherwise its oil rigs would be operating illegally and would be vulnerable given Chinese naval inferiority.

Could new economically based institutions be established that would order events in the Western Pacific as the European Union does for its membership? The European Union has established an *acquis communautaire*—a common agreement—a form of supranationalism to which all members have agreed. Whatever the union's deficiencies, it has at least brought Germany and France together, ending a century and a half of military and political rivalry. A great power union might bring the United States and China together in a similar organization that would protect the security and welfare of both countries.

Alas, such a new concert of power would seem to require more cooperation and even constitutional change than China or the United States is ready to accept. The world may thus be forced to continue dealing with the tyranny of small things and hope that new leadership can control not just major friction but also relatively minor events, and prevent conflict in the future. In the East and South China Seas, the United States will give support to those countries contending with China: the Philippines, Vietnam, and above all Japan. This is not surprising: Beijing has insisted on dealing separately with each regional counter-claimant to East Asian real estate, ruling out a more general settlement. This means that the United States must provide backup for each ally. If, on the other hand, a regional solution could be devised, the United States could be less involved. Resolving these minor but still significant issues one by one is a difficult but necessary task. There is no obvious general solution to the problem of future conflict in world politics.

Sometimes countries must approach the brink of war before they see the overpowering need to devise a more encompassing solution to the problem of conflict. President John F. Kennedy and Premier Nikita Khrushchev found an alternative to war in the 1962 Cuban missile crisis. It is possible that China and the United States will not fully understand the implications of another World War I until they knowingly confront a future crisis, keeping uppermost in their minds Barbara Tuchman's and Christopher Clark's admonitions to avoid sleepwalking into war.[10]

Notes

Introduction: The Sarajevo Centenary—1914 and the Rise of China

1. Keir A. Lieber, for example, challenges long-standing interpretations of German behavior, including the role of the Schlieffen Plan, in Lieber, "The New History of World War I and What It Means for International Relations Theory," *International Security*, Vol. 32, No. 2 (Fall 2007), pp. 155–191.

2. See, for example, Steven E. Miller, Sean M. Lynn-Jones, and Stephen Van Evera, eds., *Military Strategy and the Origins of the First World War*, rev. and exp. ed. (Princeton, N.J.: Princeton University Press, 1991).

3. The bibliography maintained by the International Society for First World War Studies contains hundreds of items on the origins of the war and hundreds more on the course and conduct of the war. The bibliography is available at: http://www.firstworld warstudies.org/bibliography. The approach of the one-hundredth anniversary of 1914 has spawned a new outpouring of work on the outbreak of the war. Notable contributions include Christopher Clark, *The Sleepwalkers: How Europe Went to War in 1914* (New York: HarperCollins, 2013); Margaret MacMillan, *The War That Ended Peace: The Road to 1914* (New York: Random House, 2013); T.G. Otte, *July Crisis: The World's Descent into War, Summer 1914* (Cambridge: Cambridge University Press, 2014); and Max Hastings *Catastrophe 1914: Europe Goes to War* (New York: Alfred A. Knopf, 2013).

4. For more on the beliefs and mentalities that existed in Europe in 1914, see Margaret Macmillan's discussion in *The War That Ended Peace*, pp. 245–284.

5. See T.G. Otte's chapter in this volume, p. 124.

6. See David Richards's chapter in this volume, p. 89.

7. See Richard Rosecrance's chapter in this volume, p. 50.

8. For a particularly emphatic interpretation of the United States' power advantages over China, see Michael Beckley, "China's Century? Why America's Edge Will Endure," *International Security*, Vol. 36, No. 3 (Winter 2011/12), pp. 41–78.

9. Aaron Friedberg, "Ripe for Rivalry: Prospects for Peace in Multipolar Asia," *International Security*, Vol 18, No. 3 (Winter 1993/94), p. 7.

10. See Aaron Friedberg, *A Contest for Supremacy: China, America, and the Struggle for Mastery in Asia* (New York: W.W. Norton, 2012).

11. Robert D. Kaplan, "China's Perilous Tangle of Military and Economic Fortunes," *Financial Times*, July 28, 2014.

12. On this point, see in particular Robert D. Kaplan, *Asia's Cauldron: The South*

China Sea and the End of a Stable Pacific (New York: Random House, 2014). Kaplan cautions that "the South China Sea has become an armed camp." Ibid., p. 12.

13. See Kevin Rudd's chapter in this volume, p. 200.

14. Clark, *The Sleepwalkers*, p. xxxi.

15. Margaret MacMillan, "1914 and 2014: Should We Be Worried?" *International Affairs*, Vol. 90, No. 1 (January 2014), p. 70.

16. Otte, *July Crisis*, p. 1.

Chapter 1. Before the War: Three Styles of Diplomacy

1.   James Joll and Gordon Martel, *The Origins of the First World War*, 3rd ed. (Harlow, U.K.: Pearson Longman, 2007), p. 9.

2.   Woodrow Wilson, "Address Delivered at the First Annual Assemblage of the League to Enforce Peace: 'American Principles,'" May 27, 1916, in Gerhard Peters and John T. Woolley, eds., *The American Presidency Project*, http://www.presidency.ucsb .edu/ws/?pid=65391.

3.   Ibid.

4.   Joll and Martel, *The Origins of the First World War*, p. 3.

5.   Woodrow Wilson, "Address Delivered to Congress," January 8, 1918, http://avalon .law.yale.edu/20th_century/wilson14.asp.

6.   Ibid.

7.   League of Nations, *The Covenant of the League of Nations (Including Amendments Adopted to December, 1924)*, http://avalon.law.yale.edu/20th_century/leagcov.asp.

8.   Lloyd E. Ambrosius, *Wilsonianism: Woodrow Wilson and His Legacy in American Foreign Relations* (New York: Palgrave, 2002), p. 52.

9.   G. John Ikenberry, "The Three Faces of Liberal Internationalism," in Alan S. Alexandroff and Andrew F. Cooper, eds., *Rising States, Rising Institutions: Challenges for Global Governance* (Washington, D.C.: Brookings Institution Press, 2010), pp. 17–47, at p. 26.

10.   Richard Rosecrance, "Transformations in Power," in Ernest R. May, Rosecrance, and Zara Steiner, eds., *History and Neorealism* (Cambridge: Cambridge University Press, 2010), p. 25.

11.   Joll and Martel, *The Origins of the First World War*, p. 55.

12.   Rosecrance, "Transformations in Power," p. 25.

13.   Keith Hamilton and Richard Langhorne, *The Practice of Diplomacy: Its Evolution, Theory, and Administration*, e-Library 2nd ed. (London: Taylor and Francis, 2010), p. 94.

14.   Gordon A. Craig and Alexander L. George, *Force and Statecraft: Diplomatic Problems of Our Time*, 3rd ed. (New York: Oxford University Press, 1995), pp. 27–28.

15.   Margaret MacMillan, *The War That Ended Peace: The Road to 1914* (New York: Random House, 2013), pp. 588–589.

16. Christopher Clark, *The Sleepwalkers: How Europe Went to War in 1914* (New York: HarperCollins, 2013), p. 131.

17. Bernhard von Bülow, speech to the Reichstag on December 6, 1897, in Johannes Penzler, ed., *Furst Bülows Reden nebst urkundlichen Beiträgen zu seiner Politik. Mit Erlaubnis des Reichskanzlers gesammelt und herausgegeben* [Prince Bülow's speeches, together with documented contributions to his policies: Collected and published with the chancellor's permission], Vol. 1: *1897–1903* (Berlin: Georg Reimer, 1907), p. 6, cited in Clark, *The Sleepwalkers*, p. 151.

18. Eyre Crowe, "Memorandum on the Present State of British Relations with France and Germany," January 1, 1907, in G.P. Gooch and Harold Temperley, eds., *British Documents on the Origins of the War, 1898–1914* (London: His Majesty's Stationery Office, 1928), app. A, pp. 397–420.

19. One scholar who does distinguish between the balance of power and a concert system is the diplomatic historian Paul W. Schroeder. See in particular Schroeder, *The Transformation of European Politics, 1763–1848* (Oxford: Oxford University Press, 1994). In addition, a classic analysis of the Bismarck period as a concert system is presented by William L. Langer, *European Alliances and Alignments, 1871–1890* (New York: Vintage, 1950).

20. Two classic studies of the use and abuse of history, especially with respect to U.S. foreign policy, are Ernest R. May, *"Lessons" of the Past: The Use and Misuse of History in American Foreign Policy* (Oxford: Oxford University Press, 1976); and Richard E. Neustadt and Ernest R. May, *Thinking in Time: The Use of History for Decision Makers* (New York: Macmillan, 1986). For Margaret MacMillan's study, see MacMillan, *Dangerous Games: The Uses and Abuses of History* (New York: Random House, 2009).

21. Margaret MacMillan, "The Great War's Ominous Echoes," *New York Times*, December 13, 2013.

22. Ibid.

Chapter 2. Respites or Resolutions?
Recurring Crises and the Origins of War

1. Jay Winter and Antoine Prost, *The Great War in History: Debates and Controversies, 1914 to the Present* (Cambridge: Cambridge University Press, 2005), p. 7. For a chart of the number of works published on World War I, see ibid., p. 17.

2. Ross F. Collins, *World War I: Primary Documents on Events from 1914 to 1919* (Westport, Conn.: Greenwood, 2008), p. 9.

3. As one scholar notes, "Whole books are now written about how the causes of the war have been written about, [and] major academic conferences are staged at every conceivable anniversary of the war's outbreak." See John F.V. Keiger, "The War

Explained: 1914 to the Present," in John Horne, ed., *A Companion to World War I* (Malden, Mass.: Wiley-Blackwell, 2010), p. 19. For relatively recent historiographic discussions, see Annika Mombauer, *The Origins of the First World War: Controversies and Consensus* (London: Longman, 2002); and Samuel R. Williamson Jr. and Ernest R. May, "An Identity of Opinion: Historians and July 1914," *Journal of Modern History*, Vol. 79, No. 2 (June 2007), pp. 335–387. For two characterizations of the competing approaches from an international relations theory perspective, see Dale C. Copeland, *The Origins of Major War* (Ithaca, N.Y.: Cornell University Press, 2000); and Keir A. Lieber, "The New History of World War I and What It Means for International Relations Theory," *International Security*, Vol. 32, No. 2 (Fall 2007), pp. 155–191. Note, however, that both of these works oversell the case that Germany actively sought war.

4. Stephen M. Walt, "Good News: World War I Is Over and Will Not Happen Again," *Foreign Policy*, February 8, 2013.

5. The canonical reference is James D. Fearon, "Rationalist Explanations for War," *International Organization*, Vol. 49, No. 3 (Summer 1995), pp. 379–414. For a recent review, see Matthew O. Jackson and Massimo Morelli, "The Reasons for War: An Updated Survey," in Christopher J. Coyne and Rachel L. Mathers, eds., *The Handbook on the Political Economy of War* (Northampton, Mass.: Edward Elgar, 2011), pp. 34–57. This consensus forms the core of formal models that focus on the decision in favor of war's costly lottery.

6. Arthur A. Stein, *Why Nations Cooperate: Circumstance and Choice in International Relations* (Ithaca, N.Y.: Cornell University Press, 1990), p. 62.

7. One study of enduring rivalries finds that they are more likely to end in war and that they have accounted for almost half of interstate wars. See Paul F. Diehl and Gary Goertz, *War and Peace in International Rivalry* (Ann Arbor: University of Michigan Press, 2000), pp. 61–64.

8. Crises, especially recurring ones, occur only if the power disparity between the countries involved is not so great as to preclude them. Thus crises are more likely to occur between great powers.

9. The standard Win-Stay and Lose-Shift strategy is also known as "Pavlov" in the modeling literature and was dubbed "Simpleton" by Anatol Rapoport and Albert M. Chammah, *Prisoner's Dilemma: A Study in Conflict and Cooperation* (Ann Arbor: University of Michigan Press, 1965). The reason for the modification is that the standard Win-Stay and Lose-Shift strategy shifts to cooperation after a mutual defection outcome. The argument here is that strategy shifts when an outcome has resulted in one's own loss and another's win. For comparisons of Win-Stay and Lose-Shift with other strategies such as Tit-for-Tat, see Lorens A. Imhof, Drew Fudenberg, and Martin A. Nowak, "Tit-for-Tat or Win-Stay, Lose-Shift?" *Journal of Theoretical Biology*, Vol. 247, No. 3 (August 2007), pp. 574–580.

10. In simulation studies of strategies, this is typically operationalized in terms

of some aspiration level that needs to be met for a strategy to be repeated. See, for example, Inkoo Cho and Akihiko Matsui, "Learning Aspiration in Repeated Games," *Journal of Economic Theory*, Vol. 124, No. 2 (October 2005), pp. 171–201.

11. This is referred to as a "grim trigger" strategy, in which an actor initially cooperates but then defects in every move following defection by the other side.

12. For an alternative view, see Robert Jervis, "Bargaining and Bargaining Tactics," in J. Roland Pennock and John W. Chapman, eds., *Nomos XIV: Coercion* (Chicago: Aldine-Atherton, 1972), pp. 272–288. Jervis argues that merely the expectation that one actor will stand firm will lead the other to capitulate. The problem is that this turns out not to be the case empirically in repeated games of Chicken.

13. For the impact of such misperceptions, see Arthur A. Stein, "When Misperception Matters," *World Politics*, Vol. 34, No. 4 (July 1982), pp. 505–526; and Stein, *Why Nations Cooperate*, chap. 3.

14. Stephen D. Krasner, "Global Communications and National Power: Life on the Pareto Frontier," *World Politics*, Vol. 43, No. 3 (April 1991), pp. 336–366.

15. This term was so dubbed by Glenn H. Snyder and Paul Diesing, *Conflict among Nations: Bargaining, Decision Making, and System Structure in International Crises* (Princeton, N.J.: Princeton University Press, 1977). Snyder and Diesing characterize the four crises discussed below as four different games, thus suggesting a change in preference between each crisis.

16. For discussions of this issue, see Stein, "When Misperception Matters"; and Stein, *Why Nations Cooperate*, chap. 3.

17. Eugene N. Anderson, *The First Moroccan Crisis, 1904–1906* (Chicago: University of Chicago Press, 1930), p. vii.

18. Indeed, the formal public title of their agreement was "Declaration between the United Kingdom and France Respecting Egypt and Morocco." The secret protocols they signed at the same time came to be dubbed the "Entente Cordiale."

19. Hew Strachan, *The First World War*, Vol. 1: *To Arms* (New York: Oxford University Press, 2001), pp. 16, 20.

20. A.J.P. Taylor, *The Struggle for Mastery in Europe, 1848–1918* (Oxford: Clarendon, 1954), pp. 440–441.

21. Anderson, *The First Moroccan Crisis, 1904–1906*, p. vii.

22. Strachan, *The First World War*, p. 41.

23. David Schimmelpenninck van der Oye, "Russian Foreign Policy, 1815–1917," in Dominic Lieven, ed., *The Cambridge History of Russia*, Vol. 2: *Imperial Russia, 1689–1917* (Cambridge: Cambridge University Press, 2006), p. 566.

24. Taylor, *The Struggle for Mastery in Europe, 1848–1918*, p. 253.

25. Anderson, *The First Moroccan Crisis, 1904–1906*, p. 405.

26. In the words of historian Hew Strachan, "It is striking in the pre-1914 crises,

particularly both those over Morocco, how Germany would start with a large measure of rightness in her case, but forfeit this legitimacy by her threatening and domineering diplomacy." See Strachan, "The First World War: Causes and Course," *Historical Journal*, Vol. 29, No. 1 (March 1986), p. 235.

27. Margaret MacMillan, "The Rhyme of History: Lessons of the Great War" (Washington, D.C.: Brookings Institution, December 14, 2013), http://www.brookings .edu/research/essays/2013/rhyme-of-history.

28. David Starr Jordan, quoted in Michael S. Neiberg, *Dance of the Furies: Europe and the Outbreak of World War I* (Cambridge, Mass.: Harvard University Press, 2011), p. 59.

29. Ibid.

30. Ibid., p. 57.

31. Paul W. Schroeder, "World War I as Galloping Gertie: A Reply to Joachim Remak," *Journal of Modern History*, Vol. 44, No. 3 (September 1972), p. 321. It should be noted that this is a point of disagreement among scholars. Kenneth N. Waltz, for example, sees recurring crises as a source of stability. Even in a bipolar world, he argues, "if the condition of conflict remains, the absence of crises becomes more disturbing than their recurrence." See Waltz, "The Stability of a Bipolar World," *Daedalus*, Vol. 93, No. 3 (Summer 1964), p. 884.

32. This is the argument made by Joachim Remak, "1914–The Third Balkan War: Origins Reconsidered," *Journal of Modern History*, Vol. 43, No. 3 (September 1971), pp. 354–366.

33. For a description of the dataset, see Daniel M. Jones, Stuart A. Bremer, and J. David Singer, "Militarized Interstate Disputes, 1816–1992: Rationale, Coding Rules, and Empirical Patterns," *Conflict Management and Peace Science*, Vol. 15, No. 2 (Fall 1996), pp. 163–212.

34. There is another sense in which crises may not be independent: if countries and leaders purposely start crises under specific conditions. The case can be made that the triggers for the pre–World War I crises were exogenous to the assertive strategies that originated them. Events in Morocco and the Balkans, as well as elsewhere, repeatedly raised problems that the great powers had to manage. As the Russian foreign minister told the foreign ministers of the other powers in January 1908, "Events do not depend on us." Thus, as historian Dominic Lieven puts it, "Russia could have a crisis imposed on it against its will at any time." See D.C.B. Lieven, *Russia and the Origins of the First World War* (New York: St. Martin's, 1983), p. 33.

35. The same point can be made about the third proffered reason for war: issue indivisibility. If an issue of contention is not divisible and is thus a cause of conflict, it will be just as much so when it first arises as when it arises subsequently.

36. For a broad argument about the role of status and humiliation in international politics, see Joslyn Barnhart, "Prestige, Humiliation, and International Politics," Ph.D. dissertation, University of California, Los Angeles, 2013.

37.   Daryl G. Press contrasts his "current calculus theory" with what he dubs "past actions theory." See Press, *Calculating Credibility: How Leaders Assess Military Threats* (Ithaca, N.Y.: Cornell University Press, 2005).

38.   Jonathan Mercer makes the situational argument in Mercer, *Reputation and International Politics* (Ithaca, N.Y.: Cornell University Press, 1996).

39.   The role of past success and failure has been discussed in different ways. In general, see Robert Jervis, *Perception and Misperception in International Politics* (Princeton, N.J.: Princeton University Press, 1976). Some scholars argue that actors always attempt to fight or prevent the previous war. Others argue that actors try to relive past successes. Still others argue that past failure leads to the adoption of a more coercive strategy. See Russell J. Leng, "When Will They Ever Learn? Coercive Bargaining in Recurrent Crises," *Journal of Conflict Resolution*, Vol. 27, No. 3 (September 1983), pp. 379–419. One can also use such arguments to modify existing ones. For example, prospect theory argues that actors are risk acceptant. The theory can be modified to argue that actors may not make risky choices in the domain of losses the first time around, but will do so having experienced losses in the past. The argument here is that past capitulation and loss result in an unwillingness to again accept a loss as the cost for averting war.

40.   Diehl and Goertz, *War and Peace in International Rivalry*.

41.   Miles Kahler, "Rumors of War: The 1914 Analogy," *Foreign Affairs*, Vol. 58, No. 2 (Winter 1979/80), pp. 374–396.

42.   John J. Mearsheimer, "Back to the Future: Instability in Europe after the Cold War," *International Security*, Vol. 15, No. 1 (Summer 1990), pp. 5–56.

43.   Kevin Rudd, "A Maritime Balkans of the 21st Century?" *Foreign Policy*, January 30, 2013. Ironically, Luxembourg's prime minister saw parallels between modern-day Europe and the Europe of one hundred years ago. See Jean-Claude Juncker, "Interview: The Demons Haven't Been Banished," *Spiegel*, March 11, 2013, http://www.spiegel.de/international/europe/spiegel-interview-with-luxembourg-prime-minister-juncker-a-888021.html.

44.   MacMillan, "The Rhyme of History."

45.   "Stumbling into World War I, Like 'Sleepwalkers': Interview with Christopher Clark," National Public Radio, April 23, 2013. Journalists have made the same point. See Gideon Rachman. "The Shadow of 1914 Falls over the Pacific," *Financial Times*, February 4, 2013; and Richard Gwyn, "Is China Making the Same Mistakes as Kaiser Wilhelm's Germany?" *Toronto Star*, December 9, 2013.

Chapter 3. Better Now Than Later:
The Paradox of 1914 as Everyone's Favored Year for War

1.   L.C.F. Turner, *Origins of the First World War* (New York: W.W. Norton, 1970), p. 105; and Helmuth von Moltke, quoted in Helmut Haessler, *General William Groener*

and the Imperial German Army (Madison: State Historical Society of Wisconsin, 1962), p. 50.

2.   Margaret MacMillan, *The War That Ended Peace: The Road to 1914* (New York: Random House, 2013), pp. 561–562.

3.   Geoffrey Blainey, *The Causes of War* (New York: Free Press, 1973), pp. 114–124.

4.   William C. Wohlforth, "The Perception of Power: Russia in the Pre-1914 Balance," *World Politics*, Vol. 39, No. 3 (April 1987), p. 377.

5.   James D. Fearon, "Rationalist Explanations for War," *International Organization*, Vol. 49, No. 3 (Summer 1995), pp. 379–414. See also Arthur A. Stein, "Respites or Resolutions? Recurring Crises and the Origins of War," in *The Next Great War? The Roots of World War I and the Risk of U.S.-China Conflict*, Richard N. Rosecrance and Steven E. Miller, eds. (Cambridge, Mass.: MIT Press, 2015), pp. 13–23.

6.   Blainey, *The Causes of War*, pp. 53–56.

7.   Wohlforth, "The Perception of Power," p. 376; and Risto Ropponen, *Die Kraft Russlands: Wie beurteilte die politische und militarische Fuhrung der Europaischen Grossmachte in der Zeit von 1905 bis 1914* [Russia's strength: How the European great powers' leadership evaluated it] (Helsinki: Turun Sanomalehti, 1968).

8.   Wohlforth, "The Perception of Power," p. 380.

9.   Gerhard Ritter, *The Schlieffen Plan: Critique of a Myth* (New York: Praeger, 1958), p. 66.

10.   Wohlforth, "The Perception of Power," p. 377.

11.   Stephen Van Evera, "Why Cooperation Failed in 1914," *World Politics*, Vol. 38, No. 1 (October 1985), pp. 101–102.

12.   Fearon, "Rationalist Explanations for War," pp. 393–395.

13.   Dan Reiter, *How Wars End* (Princeton, N.J.: Princeton University Press, 2009).

14.   David G. Herrmann, *The Arming of Europe and the Making of the First World War* (Princeton, N.J.: Princeton University Press, 1996), p. 217.

15.   William C. Fuller Jr., *Strategy and Power in Russia, 1600–1914* (New York: Free Press, 1992), p. 437; and Herrmann, *The Arming of Europe and the Making of the First World War*, p. 202.

16.   Herrmann, *The Arming of Europe and the Making of the First World War*, p. 218.

17.   MacMillan, *The War That Ended Peace*, pp. 559–560.

18.   Ibid., p. 563.

19.   Ibid., p. 560. For the Austrians' "better now than later" attitude, see Samuel R. Williamson Jr., "Aggressive and Defensive Aims of Political Elites? Austro-Hungarian Policy in 1914," in Holger Afflerbach and David Stevenson, eds., *An Improbable War: The Outbreak of World War I and European Political Culture before 1914* (New York: Berghahn, 2007), p. 70.

20.   Stig Förster, "Russische Pferde: Die Deutsche Armeeführung und die Julikrise 1914" [Russian horses: The German army leadership and the July crisis of 1914], in Christian

Th. Müller and Matthias Rogg, eds., *Das ist Militärgeschichte! Probleme - Projekte - Pers-pektiven. Festschrift für Bernhard R. Kroener zum 65. Geburtstag* [That's military history! Problems - projects - perspectives. *Festschrift* for Bernhard R. Kroener on his sixty-fifth birthday] (Paderborn, Germany: Verlag Ferdinand Schöningh GmbH, 2013), pp. 63–82.

21.   Holger H. Herwig, "Imperial Germany," in Ernest R. May, ed., *Knowing One's Enemies: Intelligence Assessment before the Two World Wars* (Princeton, N.J.: Princeton University Press, 1986), p. 94.

22.   Marc Trachtenberg, "French Foreign Policy in the July Crisis, 1914: A Review Article," *H-Diplo/ISSF*, No. 3, December 1, 2010, p. 8, http://www.h-net.org/~diplo/ISSF/PDF/3-Trachtenberg.pdf; and Stefan Schmidt, *Frankreichs Aussenpolitik in der Julikrise 1914* [France's foreign policy during the July crisis of 1914] (Munich: Olden-bourg, 2009), pp. 209–210.

23.   John C. Cairns, "International Politics and the Military Mind: The Case of the French Republic, 1911–1914," *Journal of Modern History*, Vol. 25, No. 3 (September 1953), p. 276.

24.   *Mezhdunarodrye Otnosheniia v Epokhu Imperializma*, series 3, Vol. 2, pp. 266–268, cited in D.C.B. Lieven, "Towards the Flame: Imperial Russia on the Road to War and Revolution," University of Cambridge, 2014, chap. 7.

25.   Jack Snyder, *The Ideology of the Offensive: Military Decision Making and the Disasters of 1914* (Ithaca, N.Y.: Cornell University Press, 1984), pp. 48–50, 130–132, 162.

26.   Herwig, "Imperial Germany," p. 70.

27.   David Stevenson, *Armaments and the Coming of War: Europe, 1904–1914* (Oxford: Clarendon, 1996), pp. 359–360.

28.   D.C.B. Lieven, *Russia and the Origins of the First World War* (London: Macmillan, 1983), p. 114.

29.   Herrmann, *The Arming of Europe and the Making of the First World War*, pp. 191–192.

30.   Herwig, "Imperial Germany," p. 72. For additional information on German intel-ligence, see ibid., pp. 70–72; for further analysis of the Germans' strategic framework, see ibid., pp. 70–97, especially pp. 77, 91. See also Holger H. Herwig, "Germany and the 'Short-War' Illusion: Toward a New Interpretation?" *Journal of Modern History*, Vol. 66, No. 3 (July 2002), pp. 681–693, especially p. 688.

31.   Bruce W. Menning, "The Offensive Revisited: Russian Preparation for Future War, 1906–1914," in David Schimmelpenninck van der Oye and Bruce W. Menning, eds., *Reforming the Tsar's Army: Military Innovation in Imperial Russia from Peter the Great to the Revolution* (Cambridge: Cambridge University Press, 2004), p. 226.

32.   Zara S. Steiner, *Britain and the Origins of the First World War* (New York: St. Martin's, 1977); and Dale C. Copeland, *The Origins of Major War* (Ithaca, N.Y.: Cornell University Press, 2000), pp. 60–64, 79, 84–85, 92–93, 111–112, 116.

33.   Van Evera, "Why Cooperation Failed in 1914," pp. 103–106.

34.   Sean McMeekin, *The Russian Origins of the First World War* (Cambridge, Mass.:

Belknap, 2011), chaps. 1–2; and Christopher Clark, *The Sleepwalkers: How Europe Went to War in 1914* (New York: HarperCollins, 2013), chaps. 9, 11–12. On Van Evera's side, see Stephen Van Evera, "European Militaries and the Origins of World War I," in Rosecrance and Miller, *The Next Great War?* pp. 149–174; and Annika Mombauer, *Helmuth von Moltke and the Origins of the First World War* (New York: Cambridge University Press, 2001), pp. 185, 203–207, 211.

35.   Mombauer, *Helmuth von Moltke and the Origins of the First World War*, pp. 6, 159, 285–286; and Snyder, *The Ideology of the Offensive*, pp. 116–119.

36.   David Stevenson, "The European Land Armaments Race," in Afflerbach and Stevenson, *An Improbable War*, p. 139.

37.   Stevenson, *Armaments and the Coming of War*, p. 374.

38.   Glenn H. Snyder, *Alliance Politics* (Ithaca, N.Y.: Cornell University Press, 1997), p. 337.

39.   Fearon, "Rationalist Explanations for War," p. 392.

40.   Ibid., pp. 392–393.

41.   Bayes's theorem expresses how prior estimates of probability can be continually revised based on experience.

42.   Alfred Vagts, *Defense and Diplomacy: The Soldier and the Conduct of Foreign Relations* (New York: King's Crown, 1956).

43.   Sean McMeekin, *July 1914: Countdown to War* (New York: Basic Books, 2013), pp. 145–152; and Clark, *The Sleepwalkers*, pp. 190–197, 295–313, 438–505. On the role of alliances in moderating relations between allies, with a discussion of World War I, see Patricia A. Weitsman, *Dangerous Alliances: Proponents of Peace, Weapons of War* (Redwood City, Calif.: Stanford University Press, 2004), pp. 137–164.

44.   Fearon, "Rationalist Explanations for War," p. 408.

45.   Reiter, *How Wars End*, pp. 42–47.

46.   This possibility is what Fearon says the declining state fears after the power transition.

47.   Fearon, too, appears to be thinking along these lines. He notes that German leaders thought that Russia might accept Austrian demands, and suggests that this shows that the war may have been caused by private information, perhaps in conjunction with the preventive logic of a commitment problem. See Fearon, "Rationalist Explanations for War," pp. 407–408.

48.   Blasius Schemua, Austria's chief of the General Staff, quoted in Herrmann, *The Arming of Europe and the Making of the First World War*, p. 178.

49.   Stevenson, *Armaments and the Coming of War*, pp. 352–356; Wohlforth, "The Perception of Power," p. 364; Herrmann, *The Arming of Europe and the Making of the First World War*, p. 207; and Paul W. Schroeder, "Romania and the Great Powers before 1914," *Revue Roumaine d'Histoire*, Vol. 14, No. 1 (1975), pp. 40–53, especially p. 46.

50.   Thomas C. Schelling, *Arms and Influence* (New Haven, Conn.: Yale University Press, 1966); and Kurt Riezler [J.J. Ruedorffer, pseud.], *Grundzüge der Weltpolitik*

in der Gegenwart [The primary features of contemporary world politics] (Stuttgart: Deutsche Verlags-Anstalt, 1914).

51. Paul Kennedy, "Tirpitz, England, and the Second Navy Law of 1900: A Strategical Critique," *Militärgeschichtliche Mitteilungen*, Vol. 2 (1970), pp. 33–58.

52. Clark, *The Sleepwalkers*, pp. 266, 269.

53. Samuel R. Williamson Jr., "Military Dimensions of Habsburg-Romanov Relations during the Era of the Balkan Wars," in Bela K. Kiraly and Dimitrije Djordjevic, eds., *War and Society in East Central Europe*, Vol. 18: *East Central European Society and the Balkan Wars* (New York: Columbia University Press, 1987), pp. 317–337.

54. Lieven, *Russia and the Origins of the First World War*; and Lieven, "Towards the Flame," chap. 7.

55. Lieven, "Towards the Flame," chap. 7, citing *Mezhdunarodnye Otnosheniia v Epokhu Imperializma*, series 3, Vol. 1, pp. 266–268, Benckdorff to Sazonov, January 15/28, 1914.

56. Herwig, "Imperial Germany," p. 93.

57. Fearon, "Rationalist Explanations for War," p. 382; and Stacie E. Goddard, *Indivisible Territory and the Politics of Legitimacy: Jerusalem and Northern Ireland* (Cambridge: Cambridge University Press, 2010), chap. 2.

58. Lieven, "Towards the Flame," chap. 7, p. 7.

59. Stevenson, *Armaments and the Coming of War*, pp. 348–349. As it turned out, the British impounded one of the battleships for their own use just before it was ready for delivery at the outset of the war.

60. Ibid., p. 348; and Ronald Park Bobroff, *Roads to Glory: Late Imperial Russia and the Turkish Straits* (London: I.B. Tauris, 2006), p. 94.

61. McMeekin, *The Russian Origins of the First World War*, p. 25.

62. Ibid., p. 40.

63. Richard E. Nisbett and Lee Ross, *Human Inference: Strategies and Shortcomings of Social Judgment* (Englewood Cliffs, N.J.: Prentice Hall, 1980).

64. Robert Jervis, "Cooperation under the Security Dilemma," *World Politics*, Vol. 30, No. 2 (January 1978), pp. 167–214, especially pp. 181–182.

65. Robert Jervis, *Perception and Misperception in International Politics* (Princeton, N.J.: Princeton University Press, 1976), pp. 319–328.

66. Jonathan Mercer, *Reputation and International Politics* (Ithaca, N.Y.: Cornell University Press, 1996).

67. Mombauer, *Helmuth von Moltke and the Origins of the First World War*, pp. 6, 159, 285–286. On Germany's "polycratic chaos," see John C.G. Röhl, "The Curious Case of the Kaiser's Disappearing War Guilt: Wilhelm II in July 1914," in Afflerbach and Stevenson, *An Improbable War*, p. 77.

68. Snyder, *The Ideology of the Offensive*, pp. 165–188. Bruce W. Menning presents an updated version of this argument, with nuanced archival information. See Menning,

"Pieces of the Puzzle: The Role of Iu. N. Danilov and M.V. Alekseev in Russian War Planning before 1914," *International History Review*, Vol. 25, No. 4 (December 2003), pp. 775–798. See also Menning, "The Offensive Revisited," pp. 224, 230, which exploits archival sources, concluding that "the ideology of the offensive," decentralized military planning, and weaknesses in implementing reforms all contributed to the emergence of war plans that "failed to deal adequately with issues of time, mass, and space." In contrast, Fuller, *Strategy and Power in Russia, 1600–1914*, p. 443, acknowledges that the multiple offensives of 1914 stretched Russia's capacity to its limits. He blames their failure, however, on poor implementation rather than on any inherent flaw in the plans, and he warns against exaggerating the role of bureaucratic politics in determining the outcome.

69. McMeekin, *The Russian Origins of the First World War*, pp. 58–59, 95–97; Clark, *The Sleepwalkers*, pp. 271–272, 473–474; and Lieven, "Towards the Flame."

70. Barry R. Posen, *The Sources of Military Doctrine: France, Britain, and Germany between the World Wars* (Ithaca, N.Y.: Cornell University Press, 1984), pp. 47–48.

71. Fuller, *Strategy and Power in Russia, 1600–1914*, p. 450.

72. Herrmann, *The Arming of Europe and the Making of the First World War*, p. 214.

73. Lieven, *Russia and the Origins of the First World War*, p. 114.

74. Wohlforth, "The Perception of Power," p. 368; Stevenson, *Armaments and the Coming of War*, pp. 238–239; and McMeekin, *The Russian Origins of the First World War*, p. 404. On the alliance dimension of the readiness question, and for hard-to-prove speculations about hidden motives behind Sukhomlinov's claims, see Ernest R. May, "Cabinet, Tsar, Kaiser," in May, *Knowing One's Enemies*, p. 23.

75. Snyder, *The Ideology of the Offensive*, pp. 197–198.

76. Copeland, *The Origins of Major War*, chap. 4.

77. Isabel V. Hull, *Absolute Destruction: Military Culture and the Practices of War in Imperial Germany* (Ithaca, N.Y.: Cornell University Press, 2005).

78. Herwig, "Germany and the 'Short-War' Illusion," p. 688.

79. Stig Förster, "Dreams and Nightmares: German Military Leadership and the Images of Future Warfare, 1871–1914," in Manfred F. Boemeke, Roger Chickering, and Förster, eds., *Anticipating Total War: The German and American Experiences, 1871–1914* (Cambridge: Cambridge University Press, 1999), p. 360.

Chapter 4. Allies, Overbalance, and War

1. See Stephen Van Evera's chapter in this volume.

2. See Eric Hobsbawn, *Industry and Empire: The Making of Modern English Society, 1750 to the Present Day* (Harmondsworth, U.K.: Penguin, 1969).

3. See Daniel Ellsberg, "The Crude Analysis of Strategic Choices" (Santa Monica, Calif.: RAND Corporation, 1961).

4.   In 1891 at Kronstadt the Russians entertained a French naval squadron and Tsar Alexander III stood bare-headed as the band played the revolutionary hymn "La Marseillaise."

5.   See, inter alia, Henry Kissinger, *Diplomacy* (New York: Simon and Schuster, 1994); and Richard Rosecrance, "Kissinger, Bismarck, and the Balance of Power," *Millennium: Journal of International Studies*, Vol. 3, No. 1 (March 1974), pp. 45–52.

6.   See Kenneth N. Waltz, *Theory of International Politics* (Reading, Mass.: Addison-Wesley, 1979); and F.H. Hinsley, *Power and the Pursuit of Peace: Theory and Practice in the History of Relations between States* (London: Cambridge University Press, 1963).

7.   See A.F.K. Organski, *World Politics* (New York: Alfred A. Knopf, 1959); and A.F.K. Organski and Jacek Kugler, *The War Ledger* (Chicago: University of Chicago Press, 1980). Robert Gilpin and George Modelski have speculated that "power transitions" usually create conflict between rising and static countries. See Gilpin, *War and Change in World Politics* (Cambridge: Cambridge University Press, 1981); and Modelski, *Long Cycles in World Politics* (Seattle: University of Washington Press, 1985). See also Graham Allison's chapter in this volume; and Richard Rosecrance, *The Resurgence of the West: How a Transatlantic Union Can Prevent War and Restore the United States and Europe* (New Haven, Conn.: Yale University Press, 2013), chap. 5.

8.   See John A. Vasquez, "The Realist Paradigm and Degenerative vs. Progressive Research Programs: An Appraisal of Neotraditional Research on Waltz's Balancing Proposition," *American Political Science Review*, Vol. 91, No. 4 (December 1997), pp. 899–912.

9.   See Robert Powell, *In the Shadow of Power: States and Strategies in International Politics* (Princeton, N.J.: Princeton University Press, 1999).

10.   See Gilpin, *War and Change in World Politics*.

11.   See Thomas J. Christensen and Jack Snyder, "Chain Gangs and Passed Bucks: Predicting Alliance Patterns in Multipolarity," *International Organization*, Vol. 44, No. 2 (Spring 1990), pp. 137–168.

12.   U.S. gross domestic product exceeded Germany's and Britain's combined in 1914. It is possible, however, that some in Berlin would have thought that U.S. power would not be brought to bear in time to prevent the Schlieffen Plan's envelopment of France.

13.   Glenn H. Snyder, *Alliance Politics* (Ithaca, N.Y.: Cornell University Press, 1997).

14.   A.J.P. Taylor, *The Course of German History: A Survey of the Development of German History since 1815* (London: Hamish Hamilton, 1954) p. 68.

15.   Britain and Russia forged the Triple Entente's third link in 1907.

16.   See Stephen Van Evera, "The Cult of the Offensive and the Origins of the First World War," *International Security*, Vol. 9, No. 1 (Summer 1984), pp. 58–107.

17.   Zara Steiner, *The Triumph of the Dark: European International History, 1933–1939* (Oxford: Oxford University Press, 2011).

18.   See Niall Ferguson, "Realism and Risk in 1938: German Foreign Policy and the Munich Crisis," in Ernest R. May, Richard Rosecrance, and Zara Steiner, eds., *History*

and Neorealism (Cambridge: Cambridge University Press, 2010), pp. 155–184.

19. Steiner, *The Triumph of the Dark*, pp. 781ff.

20. Steiner writes, "[The outbreak of] war did not bring any change in the [U.S.] president's determination to avoid military involvements abroad." See Steiner, *The Triumph of the Dark*, p. 1054. See also Alan Alexandroff and Richard Rosecrance, "Deterrence in 1939," *World Politics*, Vol. 29, No. 3 (April 1977), pp. 404–424; and Richard Rosecrance and Zara Steiner, "British Grand Strategy and the Origins of World War II," in Rosecrance and Arthur A. Stein, eds., *The Domestic Bases of Grand Strategy* (Ithaca, N.Y.: Cornell University Press, 1993), especially pp. 135–136.

21. See, inter alia, Frank Harary, Robert Z. Norman, and Dorwin Cartwright, *Structural Models: An Introduction to the Theory of Directed Graphs* (New York: Wiley, 1965); and Patrick Doreian and Andrej Mrvar, "Partitioning Signed Social Networks," *Social Networks*, Vol. 31, No. 1 (January 2009), pp. 1–11.

22. See H. Brooke McDonald and Richard Rosecrance, "Alliance and Structural Balance in the International System: A Reinterpretation," *Journal of Conflict Resolution*, Vol. 29. No. 1 (March 1985), pp. 57–82.

23. In the Mediterranean Agreement of 1887.

24. In a territorial dispute between China and Japan, the United States would want to act as an intermediary, bringing the two sides together.

25. James K. Sebenius, "Sequencing to Build Coalitions: With Whom Should I Talk First?" in Richard J. Zeckhauser, Ralph L. Keeney, and Sebenius, eds., *Wise Choices: Decisions, Games, and Negotiations* (Boston: Harvard Business Review Press, 1996), pp. 324–348; and James K. Sebenius, "The Law of the Sea," in Howard Raiffa, ed., *The Art and Science of Negotiation: How to Resolve Conflict and Get the Best out of Bargaining* (Cambridge, Mass.: Harvard University Press, 1982), pp. 275–287.

26. See the work of Emma L. Belcher on agglomeration and the Proliferation Security Initiative, which was negotiated among the United States and other powers. The United States first convinced Britain, Australia, and New Zealand to join the Proliferation Security Initiative, only later approaching the more difficult targets of Russia and China. See Belcher, "The Proliferation Security Initiative: Lessons for Using Nonbinding Agreements" (New York: Council on Foreign Relations, July 2011).

27. See Sean M. Lynn-Jones, "Détente and Deterrence: Anglo-German Relations, 1911–1914," *International Security*, Vol. 11, No. 2 (Fall 1986), pp. 121–150; and Charles Maier's chapter in this volume.

28. See Richard Cooper's chapter in this volume.

29. Or in Britain's case, the de facto associate, Belgium, whose neutrality Britain was committed to protect.

30. The weaker ally might even require more assistance than it could provide.

Chapter 5. Economic Interdependence and War

1.   Norman Angell, *The Great Illusion: A Study of the Relation of the Military Power in Nations to Their Economic and Social Advantage* (London: William Heinemann, 1910).
2.   Paul Bairoch and Susan Burke, "European Trade Policy, 1815–1914," in Peter Mathias and Sidney Pollard, eds., *Cambridge Economic History of Europe*, Vol. 8: *The Industrial Economies: The Development of Economic and Social Policies* (Cambridge: Cambridge University Press, 1989), pp. 1–160.
3.   Barry R. Chiswick and Timothy J. Hatton, "International Migration and the Integration of Labor Markets," in Michael D. Bordo, Alan M. Taylor, and Jeffrey G. Williamson, eds., *Globalization in Historical Perspective* (Chicago: University of Chicago Press, 2003), p. 69.
4.   Niall Ferguson, *The Pity of War* (New York: Basic Books, 1999).
5.   Christopher Clark, *The Sleepwalkers: How Europe Went to War in 1914* (New York: HarperCollins, 2013); Ferguson, *The Pity of War*; William L. Langer, ed., *An Encyclopedia of World History*, 4th ed. (Boston: Houghton Mifflin, 1968); Sean McMeekin, *July 1914: Countdown to War* (New York: Basic Books, 2013); Sean McMeekin, *The Russian Origins of the First World War* (Cambridge, Mass.: Harvard University Press, 2011); A.J.P. Taylor, *War by Timetable: How the First World War Began* (London: Macdonald, 1969); and L.C.F Turner, *Origins of the First World War* (New York: W.W. Norton, 1970).
6.   Clark, *The Sleepwalkers*, pp. 330–332; and Patrick J. McDonald, *The Invisible Hand of Peace: Capitalism, the War Machine, and International Relations Theory* (New York: Cambridge University Press, 2009), pp. 209–212.
7.   Taylor, *War by Timetable*.
8.   McMeekin, *July 1914*, p. 401.
9.   Angus Maddison, *The World Economy: A Millennial Perspective* (Paris: Organization for Economic Cooperation and Development, 2001), p. 262; cf. Angus Maddison, *Historical Statistics for the World Economy, 1–2003 A.D.* (Paris: Organization for Economic Cooperation and Development, 2004), http://www.ggdc.net/maddison/. See also McDonald, *The Invisible Hand of Peace*, p. 205.
10.   Olga Crisp, *Studies in the Russian Economy before 1914* (New York: Macmillan, 1976); and Margaret S. Miller, *The Economic Development of Russia, 1905–1914* (London: P.S. King and Son, 1926).
11.   McDonald, *The Invisible Hand of Peace*; and McMeekin, *The Russian Origins of the First World War*.
12.   McDonald, *The Invisible Hand of Peace*.
13.   Nicholas A. Lambert, *Planning Armageddon: British Economic Warfare and the First World War* (Cambridge, Mass.: Harvard University Press, 2012).

Chapter 6. The Thucydides Trap

1. Xi Jinping, presentation, "Understanding China" conference, Berggruen Institute on Governance, Beijing, November 4, 2013.
2. Ibid.
3. Ezra Vogel, *Deng Xiaoping and the Transformation of China* (Cambridge, Mass.: Belknap, 2011).
4. Robert D. Blackwill and Graham Allison, "Seek the Wisdom of Lee Kuan Yew," www.politico.com/story/2013/02/seek-the-wisdomof-lee-kuan-yew-87620.html.
5. Graham Allison and Robert D. Blackwill, with Ali Wyne, eds., *Lew Kuan Yew: The Grand Master's Insights on China, the United States, and the World* (Cambridge, Mass.: MIT Press, 2013).
6. Ibid., p. 16.
7. Ibid., p. 2.
8. Ibid., p. 3.
9. Ibid., p. 4.
10. Ibid., p. 3.
11. Ibid., p. 42.
12. Ibid., p. 12.
13. Thucydides, *History of the Peloponnesian War*, trans. Rex Warner (New York: Penguin, 1972), p. 49.
14. Christopher Clark, *The Sleepwalkers: How Europe Went to War in 1914* (New York: HarperCollins, 2013), p. 562.

Chapter 7. Thucydides Dethroned:
Historical Differences That Weaken the Peloponnesian Analogy

1. Thucydides, *History of the Peloponnesian War*, trans. Rex Warner (New York: Penguin, 1972), p. 162.
2. See Stephen Van Evera's chapter in this volume.
3. Ibid.
4. Christopher Clark, *The Sleepwalkers: How Europe Went to War in 1914* (New York: HarperCollins, 2013).
5. Arthur J. Grant, *Greece in the Age of Pericles* (London: John Murray, 1893), chap. 7, p. 169.

Chapter 8. Thucydides, Alliance Politics, and Great Power Conflict

1. See Graham Allison's chapter in this volume.

2.   Thucydides, *History of the Peloponnesian War*, trans. Rex Warner (New York: Penguin, 1972), p. 49.

3.   Robert Gilpin, "The Theory of Hegemonic War," in Theodore K. Rabb and Robert Rotberg, eds., *The Origin and Prevention of Major Wars* (Cambridge: Cambridge University Press, 1989), p. 1539.

4.   Thucydides, *History of the Peloponnesian War*, pp. 74–75.

5.   Ibid., pp. 400–408.

6.   Arnold Wolfers, *Britain and France between Two World Wars: Conflicting Strategies of Peace since Versailles* (New York: Harcourt Brace, 1945).

Chapter 9. War, Revolution, and the Uncertain Primacy of Domestic Politics

1.   See John W. Langdon's appropriately named study, *July 1914: The Long Debate, 1918–1990* (Oxford: Berg, 1991).

2.   Eckart Kehr, *Schlachtflottenbau und Parteipolitik, 1894–1901* (Berlin: E. Ebering, 1930). For discussions of Kehr's work, see Hans-Ulrich Wehler, "Einleitung" [introduction] to Eckart Kehr, *Primat der Innenpolitik* (Berlin: Walter de Gruyter, 1965), pp. 1–29; Hans-Ulrich Wehler, "Eckart Kehr," in Hans-Ulrich Wehler, ed., *Deutsche Historiker*, Vol. 1 (Göttingen: Vandenhoeck and Ruprecht, 1971), pp. 100–113; and Arthur Lloyd Skop, "The Primacy of Domestic Politics: Eckart Kehr and the Intellectual Development of Charles A. Beard," *History and Theory*, Vol. 13, No. 2 (May 1974), pp. 119–131.

3.   Quotes from Arno J. Mayer, "Internal Crises and War since 1870," in Charles L. Bertrand, ed., *Revolutionary Situations in Europe, 1917–1922: Germany, Italy, Austria-Hungary* (Montreal: Interuniversity Centre for European Studies, 1977), p. 231; and Arno J. Mayer, *The Persistence of the Old Regime: Europe to the Great War* (New York: Pantheon, 1981), pp. 305–306. See also Arno J. Mayer, "Internal Causes and Purposes of War in Europe, 1870–1956," *Journal of Modern History*, Vol. 41, No. 3 (September 1969), pp. 291–303.

4.   For a thoughtful discussion, see Wolfgang J. Mommsen, "Domestic Factors in German Foreign Policy before 1914," *Central European History*, Vol. 6, No. 1 (March 1973), pp. 3–43; and Michael R. Gordon, "Domestic Conflict and the Origins of the First World War: The British and German Cases," *Journal of Modern History*, Vol. 46, No. 2 (June 1974), pp. 191–226.

5.   See the essays in William Mulligan and Brendan Simms, eds., *The Primacy of Foreign Policy: How Strategic Concerns Shaped Modern Britain* (Basingstoke, U.K.: Palgrave, 2010).

6.   For a further discussion, see Thomas G. Otte, "'Outdoor Relief for the Aristocracy?' European Nobility and Diplomacy, 1850–1914," in Markus Mösslang and Torsten Riotte, eds., *The Diplomat's World: A Cultural History of Diplomacy, 1815–1914* (Oxford: Oxford University Press, 2008), pp. 23–57; and Zara S. Steiner, *The Foreign*

Office and Foreign Policy, 1898–1914 (Cambridge: Cambridge University Press, 1969).

7.   Eyre Crowe, October 19, 1909, on Spring-Rice to Grey (No. 152), October 16, 1909, FO 371/707/38606, National Archives, Kew, United Kingdom. A reference to the emergence of rifle clubs affiliated with the Social Democratic Party triggered Crowe's comment.

8.   Eyre Crowe, June 17, 1914, on Kidston to Grey (No. 33), June 11, 1914, FO 371/1962/26783, National Archives, Kew, United Kingdom. Crowe was commenting on the constitutional crisis in Denmark.

9.   Hohenlohe-Schillingsfürst diary, June 18, 1890, in F. Curtius, ed., *Denkwürdigkeiten des Fürsten Clodwig zu Hohenlohe-Schillingsfürst*, Vol. 2 (Stuttgart Leipzig: Deutsche Verlagsanstalt, 1907), p. 470.

10.   See the arguments advanced by Hans-Ulrich Wehler, *Deutsche Gesellschaftsgeschichte*, Vol. 3: *1849–1914* (Munich: C.H. Beck, 1995), pp. 1000–1001; John C.G. Röhl, *The Kaiser and His Court: Wilhelm II and the Government of Germany* (Cambridge: Cambridge University Press, 1996), pp. 70–109; and Geoff Eley, "Capitalism and the Wilhelmine State: Industrial Growth and Political Backwardness in Recent German Historiography, 1890–1918," *Historical Journal*, Vol. 21, No. 3 (September 1978), pp. 737–750.

11.   John C.G. Röhl, *Germany without Bismarck: The Crisis of Government in the Second Reich, 1890–1900* (London: Batsford, 1967), pp. 241–270; Katherine A. Lerman, *The Chancellor as Courtier: Bernhard von Bülow and the Governance of Germany, 1900–1909* (Cambridge: Cambridge University Press, 1990), pp. 210–247; and Eric Dorn Brose, *Christian Labor and the Politics of Frustration in Imperial Germany* (Washington, D.C.: Catholic University of America Press, 1985), pp. 195–214.

12.   Carl E. Schorske, *German Social Democracy, 1905–1917: The Development of the Great Schism* (Cambridge, Mass.: Harvard University Press, 1955), pp. 226–241.

13.   Goschen to Grey (No. 184), June 24, 1910, FO 371/905/22942, National Archives, Kew, United Kingdom. For discussions of Bethmann, see Konrad H. Jarausch, *Enigmatic Chancellor: Bethmann Hollweg and the Hubris of Imperial Germany* (New Haven, Conn.: Yale University Press, 1973); and Eberhard von Vietsch, *Bethmann Hollweg: Staatsmann zwischen Macht und Ethos* (Boppard am Rhein, Germany: Harald Boldt, 1969).

14.   See H.G. Zmarlzik, *Bethmann Hollweg als Reichskanzler, 1909–1914: Studien zu Möglichkeiten und Grenzen seiner innerpolitischen Machtstellung* (Düsseldorf: Droste, 1957); and Wolfgang J. Mommsen, "Die Regierung Bethmann Hollweg und die öffentlich Meinung, 1914–1917," *Vierteljahreshefte für Zeitgeschichte*, Vol. 27, No. 2 (April 1969), pp. 118–119.

15.   The literature on the subject is vast. For a representative sample, see Paul M. Kennedy, *The Rise of the Anglo-German Antagonism, 1860–1914* (London: George Allen and Unwin, 1981). The modern *locus classicus* for the domestic aspects of the German naval program is Volker R. Berghahn, *Der Tirpitzplan: Genesis und Verfall einer innenpolitischen Krisenstrategie unter Wilhelm II* (Düsseldorf: Droste, 1971).

16.   Goschen to Nicolson (private), March 3, 1911, FO 371/1123/11853, National

Archives, Kew, United Kingdom.

17. Peter-Christian Witt, *Die Finanzpolitik des Deutschen Reiches von 1903 bis 1913: Eine Studie zur Innenpolitik des Wilhelminischen Deutschland* (Lübeck, Germany: Matthiesen, 1970), pp. 303–305; and Peter-Christian Witt, "Reichsfinanzen und Rüstungspolitik," in Herbert Schottelius and Wilhelm Deist, eds., *Marine und Marinepolitik im kaiserlichen Deutschland, 1871–1914* (Düsseldorf: Droste, 1972), pp. 146–177. In the period between 1900 and 1913, Reich debt had more than doubled, from Mk 2,418,517 to Mk 4,922,242. See Kaiserliches Statistisches Amt, ed., *Statistisches Jahrbuch für das Deutsche Reich 1913* (Berlin: Puttkammer and Mühlbrecht, 1913), p. 343. Most of the princely states, though not the three mercantile republics of Hamburg, Bremen, and Lübeck, were equally indebted. See ibid., p. 346.

18. Corbett to de Bunsen (private), January 20, 1914, box 14, De Bunsen MSS, Bodleian Library, Oxford; and Corbett to Grey (No. 3), January 16, 1914, FO 371/1986/2529, National Archives, Kew, United Kingdom.

19. Wehler, *Deutsche Gesellschaftsgeschichte*, Vol. 3, pp. 1015–1016. Support for the National Liberals and Conservatives remained strong at the local and provincial levels. See Dan S. White, *The Splintered Party: National Liberalism in Hessen and the Reich, 1867–1918* (Cambridge, Mass.: Harvard University Press, 1976), pp. 190–198; Brett Fairbairn, "Interpreting Wilhelmine Elections: National Issues, Fairness Issues, and Electoral Mobilization," in Larry Eugene Jones and James Retallack, eds., *Elections, Mass Politics, and Social Change in Modern Germany: New Perspectives* (Cambridge: Cambridge University Press, 1992), pp. 17–48; and Hartmut Pogge von Strandmann, "The Liberal Monopoly in the Cities of Imperial Germany," in Jones and Retallack, *Elections, Mass Politics, and Social Change in Modern Germany*, pp. 93–118.

20. Jagow to Pourtalès, January 16, 1914, GFM 25/3, Nachlass Pourtalès, National Archives, Kew, United Kingdom.

21. Bethmann Hollweg to Eisendecher, June 4, 1911, GFM 25/10, Nachlass Eisendecher, National Archives, Kew, United Kingdom. See also Wolfgang J. Mommsen, *Der autoritäre Nationalstaat: Verfassung, Gesellschaft und Kultur des deutschen Kaiserreiches* (Frankfurt: Fischer, 1990), p. 304.

22. Lerchenfeld to Hertling (No. 328), June 4, 1914, in Pius Dirr, ed., *Bayerische Dokumente zum Kriegsausbruch und zum Versailler Schuldspruch* (Munich: R. Oldenbourg, 1922), n. 1. Hence Bethmann's attempt to bind the SPD leadership into the decision to go to war. See Egmont Zechlin, *Krieg und Kriegsrisiko: Zur deutschen Politik im Ersten Weltkrieg: Aufsätze* (Düsseldorf: Droste, 1979), pp. 75–78; and Hagen Schulze, *Otto Braun, oder Preussens demokratische Sendung: Eine Biographie* (Frankfurt: Propyläen, 1977), pp. 172–175.

23. Ludwig Frank, quoted in Peter-Christian Witt, *Friedrich Ebert: Parteiführer, Reichskanzler, Volksbeauftragter, Reichspräsident*, 2nd ed. (Bonn: J.H. Dietz, 1988), p. 64. Frank volunteered for the army and was killed in September 1914.

24. T.G. Otte, *July Crisis: The World's Descent into World War, Summer 1914* (Cambridge: Cambridge University Press, 2014).

25. Joachim Remak, "The Healthy Invalid: How Doomed Was the Habsburg Empire?" *Journal of Modern History*, Vol. 41, No. 2 (June 1969), pp. 127–143; Richard George Plaschka, Horst Haselsteiner, and Arnold Suppan, *Innere Front: Militärassistenz, Widerstand, und Umsturz in der Donaumonarchie 1918*, 2 Vols. (Munich: R. Oldenbourg, 1974); and István Deák, *Beyond Nationalism: A Social History of the Habsburg Officer Corps, 1848–1918* (Oxford: Oxford University Press, 1990).

26. For a succinct explanation, see Goschen to Grey (No. 22), March 8, 1907 (= Annual Report 1906), FO 881/8916, National Archives, Kew, United Kingdom.

27. Lewis B. Namier, *Vanished Supremacies: Essays on European History, 1812–1918* (London: Penguin, 1962), p. 147. For detailed examinations, see C.A. Macartney, "The Compromise of 1867," in Ragnhild Hatton and M.S. Anderson, eds., *Studies in Diplomatic History: Essays in Memory of David Bayne Horn* (Harlow, U.K.: Longmans, 1970), pp. 287–300; and József Galántai, *Der österreichisch-ungarische Dualismus, 1867–1918* (Vienna: Österreichischer Bundesverlag, 1985), pp. 42–49, 108–141.

28. See Arthur J. May, *The Habsburg Monarchy, 1867–1914* (1951; repr. New York: W.W. Norton, 1968), pp. 343–361; and Norman Stone, "Constitutional Crises in Hungary, 1903–1906," *Slavonic and East European Review*, Vol. 45, No. 104 (January 1967), pp. 163–182.

29. Kasimir Badeni, quoted in Gunther Rothenberg, *The Army of Francis Joseph* (West Lafayette, Ind.: Purdue University Press, 1976), p. 128.

30. Czernin to Buquoy, April 7, 1897, quoted in Paul Molisch, ed., *Briefe zur deutschen Politik in Österreich von 1848 bis 1918* (Vienna: Braumüller, 1934), p. 346; and Paul Vyšný, *Neo-Slavism and the Czechs, 1898–1914* (Cambridge: Cambridge University Press, 1977).

31. Berthold Sutter, *Die Badenische Sprachenverordnung von 1897, ihre Genesis und ihre Auswirkungen vornehmlich auf die innerösterreichischen Alpenländer*, 2 Vols. (Graz, Austria: Bülow, 1960–65).

32. See A. Wandruszka, "Die Habsburgermonarchie von der Gründerzeit bis zum Ersten Weltkrieg," in H. Kühnel, ed., *Das Zeitalter Franz Josephs*, Vol. 2: *1880–1916, Glanz und Elend* (Vienna: Niederösterreichische Landesmuseum, 1987), p. 8.

33. Min. Craigie, July 31, 1913, on Cartwright to Grey (No. 108), July 22, 1913, FO 371/1575/34037, National Archives, Kew, United Kingdom; Jörg K. Hoensch, *Geschichte Böhmens: Von der slavischen Landnahme bis ins 20. Jahrhundert*, 2nd ed. (Munich: C.H. Beck, 1992), pp. 402–405; and Gary B. Cohen, *The Politics of Ethnic Survival: Germans in Prague, 1861–1914*, 2nd ed. (West Lafayette, Ind.: Purdue University Press, 2006), pp. 172–200.

34. Thun to brother Jaroslav, February 28, 1914, quoted in Jan Galandauer, *Franz Fürst Thun: Statthalter des Königreiches Böhmen* (Vienna: Böhlau, 2014), pp. 298–299.

35. Min. Craigie, August 28, 1913, on Cartwright to Grey (No. 123), FO

371/1575/38015, National Archives, Kew, United Kingdom.

36. Max Müller to Grey (No. 27), December 8, 1913, FO 371/1576/57517, National Archives, Kew, United Kingdom.

37. See Cartwright to Grey (No. 23), February 15, 1913, FO 371/1575/7514, National Archives, Kew, United Kingdom.

38. Max Müller to Grey (No. 21), September 1, 1913, FO 371/1575/42324, National Archives, Kew, United Kingdom.

39. Freeman [consul at Sarajevo] to Grey (Nos. 5 and 6, Political), May 17 and October 6, 1913, FO 371/1575/23238 and FO 371/1575/46057, National Archives, Kew, United Kingdom (quote from latter); Josef Brauner, "Bosnien und Herzegovina: Politik, Verwaltung und leitende Personen vor Kriegsausbruch," *Berliner Monatsheft zur Kriegsschuldfrage*, Vol. 7, No. 4 (1929), pp. 319–320; and Noel Malcolm, *Bosnia: A Short History* (London: Papermac, 1994), pp. 151–155.

40. Max Müller to Edward Grey (No. 9), March 10, 1914, FO 371/1898/11682, National Archives, Kew, United Kingdom.

41. John W. Boyer, *Political Radicalism in Late Imperial Vienna: Origins of the Christian Social Movement, 1848–1897* (Chicago: University of Chicago Press, 1981); Andrew G. Whiteside, *The Socialism of Fools: Georg Ritter von Schönerer and Austrian Pan-Germanism* (Berkeley: University of California Press, 1975); Johannes Hawlik, *Der Bürgerkaiser: Karl Lueger und seine Zeit* (Vienna: Herold, 1985); and Helmut Konrad, *Nationalismus und Internationalismus: Die österreichische Arbeiterbewegung vor dem Ersten Weltkrieg* (Vienna: Europa, 1976).

42. John W. Boyer, "The End of an Old Regime: Visions of Political Reform in Late Imperial Austria," *Journal of Modern History*, Vol. 58, No. 1 (1986), pp. 159–193.

43. Cartwright to Grey (No. 23), February 15, 1913.

44. See de Bunsen to Grey (Nos. 9 and 42), January 8 and March 3, 1914, FO 371/1898/2491 and FO 371/1898/11508, National Archives, Kew, United Kingdom; and Galandauer, *Franz Fürst Thun*, pp. 297–304.

45. Grant Duff to Grey (No. 12), March 27, 1913, FO 371/1575/14650, National Archives, Kew, United Kingdom; and István Schlett, *A szociáldemokrácia és a magyar társadalom 1914-ig* (Budapest: Gondolat, 1982).

46. Max Müller to Grey (No. 5), February 7, 1914, FO 371/1898/6952, National Archives, Kew, United Kingdom.

47. R.J.W. Evans, "The Habsburg Monarchy and the Coming of War," in Evans and H. Pogge-von Strandmann, eds., *The Coming of the First World War* (Oxford: Oxford University Press, 1991), p. 35. For an authoritative study of Franz Ferdinand, see Robert A. Kann, *Erzherzog Franz Ferdinand Studien* (Munich: R. Oldenbourg, 1976).

48. Franz Ferdinand to Berchtold, February 1, 1913, quoted in Hugo Hantsch, *Leopold Graf Berchtold, Grand Seigneur und Staatsmann*, Vol. 1 (Graz, Austria: Styria

Verlag, 1963), pp. 388–391.

49.   Carl Freiherr von Bardolff, *Soldat im alten Österreich: Erinnerungen aus meinem Leben* (Jena, Germany: Eugen Diederichs, 1938), p. 177; Samuel R. Williamson Jr., "Austria-Hungary and the Coming of the First World War," in Ernest R. May, Richard Rosecrance, and Zara Steiner, eds., *History and Neorealism* (Cambridge: Cambridge University Press, 2010), pp. 103–128; and François Fejtö, *Requiem pour un empire défunt: Histoire de le destruction de l'Autriche-Hongrie* (Paris: Seuil, 1993), pp. 174–182.

50.   Storck to Berchtold (No. Z 98/P A-B, strictly confidential), June 30, 1914, HHStA PA I/810, Liasse XX Attentat auf Erzherzog Franz Ferdinand, Österreichisches Staatsarchiv, Vienna. See also Otte, *July Crisis*, pp. 41–43.

51.   Verneuil to Pichon, November 10, 1913, in Ministère des Affaires Étrangères, ed., *Documents Diplomatiques Français*, 3rd series, 11 Vols. (Paris: Impr. nationale, 1929–36), p. viii, n. 469; and René Girault, *Emprunts russes et investissement français en Russie, 1887–1914* (Paris: Librairie Armand Colin, 1973).

52.   For some statistics, see A.P. Korelin (for Rossiskaya Akademi'ia Rossiskoi Istori'i), ed., *Rossiʾa 1913 god: Statistisko-dokumentalʾnyi Spravochnik* (St. Petersburg: BLITS, 1995), especially pp. 152–165; Paul R. Gregory, *Russian National Income, 1895–1913* (Cambridge: Cambridge University Press, 1982), pp. 153–165; W.E. Mosse, *An Economic History of Russia, 1856–1914* (London: I.B. Tauris, 1996), pp. 249–265; and T.G. Otte, "'A Formidable Factor in European Politics': Views of Russia in 1914," in Jack S. Levy and John A. Vasquez, eds., *The Outbreak of the First World War* (Cambridge: Cambridge University Press, 2014), pp. 87–112.

53.   Richard Pipes, *The Russian Revolution, 1899–1919* (London: Fontana, 1992), p. 191. For the notion of "pseudo-constitutionalism," see Max Weber, "Russlands Übergang zum Scheinkonstitutionalismus," in Johannes Winckelmann, ed., *Gesammelte Politische Schriften*, 5th ed. (Tübingen: J.C.B. Mohr [Paul Siebeck], 1988), pp. 69–111; David MacLaren Macdonald, *United Government and Foreign Policy in Russia, 1907–1914* (Cambridge, Mass.: Harvard University Press, 1992); and Peter Waldron, *Between Two Revolutions: Stolypin and the Politics of Renewal in Russia* (London: UCL, 1998).

54.   Quotes from min. Nicolson, n.d. [February 12, 1914], on telegram from Buchanan to Grey (No. 46R), February 11, 1914, FO 371/2091/6329, National Archives, Kew, United Kingdom; Czernin to Berchtold (No. 8B), January 31/February 14, 1914, PA X/139, Österreichisches Staatsarchiv, Vienna; Raymond Pearson, *The Russian Moderates and the Crisis of Tsarism, 1914–1917* (London: Macmillan, 1977), pp. 11–12; and Dominic Lieven, *Nicholas II: Emperor of All the Russias* (London: John Murray, 1993), pp. 184–185.

55.   Memo. Pares, January 14, 1914, enclosed in Boswell to Grey, January 20, 1914, FO 371/2090/3312, National Archives, Kew, United Kingdom.

56.   Ibid.

57.   See Heinz-Dietrich Löwe, *Antisemitismus und reaktionäre Utopie: Russischer*

Konservatismus im Kampf gegen den Wandel von Staat und Gesellschaft (Hamburg: Hoffmann und Campe, 1978), pp. 30–39; and Hans Rogger, *Jewish Policy and Right-Wing Politics in Imperial Russia* (London: Macmillan, 1986), pp. 1–24.

58. Buchanan to Grey (No. 60), March 4, 1914, FO 371/2092/10333, National Archives, Kew, United Kingdom; Hans Rogger, "The Beilis Case: Anti-Semitism and Politics in the Reign of Nicholas II," *Slavic Review*, Vol. 25, No. 4 (December 1966), pp. 615–629; and Michael F. Hamm, *Kiev: A Portrait, 1800–1917* (Princeton, N.J.: Princeton University Press, 1993), pp. 131–133.

59. Szápáry to Berchtold (No. 58), February 19, 1914, HHStA PA X/140; I.V. Bestuzhev, "Bor'ba v Rossii po voprosam vneshnei politici nakanune pervoi mirovoi voiny, 1910–1914," *Istoricheskie Zapiski*, Vol. 75 (1965), pp. 62–64; and Robert Edelman, *Gentry Politics on the Eve of the Russian Revolution: The Nationalist Party, 1907–1917* (New Brunswick, N.J.: Rutgers University Press, 1980), pp. 193–201.

60. Dietrich Geyer, *Russian Imperialism: The Interaction of Domestic and Foreign Policy, 1860–1914*, trans. Bruce Little (New Haven, Conn.: Yale University Press, 1987), pp. 299–300.

61. Buchanan to Grey (No. 60), March 4, 1914.

62. Pipes, *The Russian Revolution, 1899–1919*, p. 192; and Leopold Haimson, "The Problem of Social Stability in Urban Russia, 1905–1917, Part One," *Slavic Review*, Vol. 23, No. 4 (December 1964), pp. 634–636.

63. Pourtalès to Bethmann Hollweg (No. 34), January 31, 1914, Russland 61, Allgemeine Angelegenheiten, Bd. 121, Politisches Archiv des Auswärtigen Amts, Berlin.

64. Buchanan to Grey (No. 60), March 4, 1914.

65. Kohlhaas to Bethmann Hollweg (No. 6365), September 16, 1912, Allgemeine Angelegenheiten, Russland 61, Bd. 120, Politisches Archiv des Auswärtigen Amts, Berlin. The kaiser commented in a margin: "This will end badly."

66. Geyer, *Russian Imperialism*, p. 306; and Pearson, *The Russian Moderates and the Crisis of Tsarism, 1914–1917*, pp. 10–19.

67. Pourtalès to Bethmann Hollweg (No. 118), April 12, 1913, Allgemeine Angelegenheiten, Russland 61, Bd. 121, Politisches Archiv des Auswärtigen Amts, Berlin.

68. Pipes, *The Russian Revolution, 1899–1919*, p. 194.

69. Mendelssohn to Bethmann Hollweg (private), April 10, 1913, Allgemeine Angelegenheiten, Russland 61, Bd. 121, Politisches Archiv des Auswärtigen Amts, Berlin. Mendelssohn's informant was Iakov Isaakovich Utin, director of the St. Petersburg Discount Bank.

70. Dominic Lieven, "Bureaucratic Authoritarianism in Late Imperial Russia: The Personality, Career, and Opinions of P.N. Durnovo," *Historical Journal*, Vol. 26, No. 2 (1983), pp. 391–402; Mark Aldanov, "P.N. Durnovo: Prophet of War and Revolution," *Russian Review*, Vol. 2, No. 1 (Autumn 1942), p. 31–45; and Geoffrey A. Hosking, *The Russian Constitutional Experiment: Government and Duma, 1907–1914* (Cambridge:

Cambridge University Press, 1973), p. 222.

71.   The exodus from the countryside expedited this political process. See Philippe Ariès, *Histoire des populations françaises et de leurs attitudes devant la vie depuis le XVIIIe siècle* (Paris: Seuil, 1971), pp. 290–300; and G. Le Béguec and J. Prévotat, "1898–1914: L'éveil à la modernité," in Jean-François Sirinelli, ed., *Les droites françaises: De la Révolution à nos jours* (Paris: Gallimard, 1992), pp. 383–393, 498–503.

72.   Jean-Marie Mayeur, *La vie politique sous la Troisième République* (Paris: Seuil, 1984), pp. 220–224; and Zeev Sternhell, *La droite révolutionnaire: Les origines françaises du fascisme, 1885–1914* (Paris: Seuil, 1978), pp. 385–400. See also the essays in D.M. Shapiro, ed., *The Right in France, 1890–1919: Three Studies* (London: Chatto and Windus, 1962).

73.   Eric Cahm, *The Dreyfus Affair in French Society and Politics* (London: Longman, 1996), pp. 182–194; R. Pernoud, *Histoire de la bourgeoisie en France*, Vol. 2: *Les temps modernes* (Paris: Seuil, 1981), pp. 471–472; and Béatrice Philippe, *Les Juifs à Paris à la Belle Epoque* (Paris: Albin Michel, 1992), pp. 169–174.

74.   Telegram from Bertie to Grey, June 12, 1914, FO 371/1980/26487, National Archives Kew, United Kingdom; Peter Campbell, *French Electoral Systems and Elections since 1789* (London: Faber and Faber, 1958), pp. 85–90; and G. Krumeich, *Armaments and Politics in France on the Eve of the First World War: The Introduction of Three-Year Conscription, 1913–1914* (Leamington Spa, U.K.: Berg, 1984), pp. 103–117, 181–193.

75.   Poincaré diary, August 3, 1914, bnfr 16027, Papiers de Poincaré, Bibliotheque Nationale, Paris; also in M.B. Hayne, *The French Foreign Office and the First World War, 1898–1914* (Oxford: Clarendon, 1993), p. 274, but misdated.

76.   See Paléologue diary, July 23, 1914, M. Paléologue, *La Russie des Tsars pendant la grande guerre*, Vol. 1 (Paris: Plon-Nourrit, 1921), p. 17.

77.   Telegram from Viviani to Paléologue (No. 318, very confidential), July 10, 1914, in Ministère des Affaires Etrangères, *Documents Diplomatiques Français*, 3rd series, p. x, n. 491; and David G. Herrmann, *The Arming of Europe and the Making of the First World War, 1904–1914* (Princeton, N.J.: Princeton University Press, 1995), pp. 191–195.

78.   Poincaré diary, July 29 and 31, 1914.

79.   Raymond Poincaré, quoted in Pierre Miquel, *Poincaré* (Paris: Fayard, 1984), p. 333. See also M.B. Hayne, "The Quai d'Orsay and Influences on the Formation of French Foreign Policy, 1898–1914," *French History*, Vol. 2, No. 4 (1988), pp. 431–432.

80.   David B. Ralston, *The Army of the Republic: The Place of the Military in the Political Evolution of France, 1871–1914* (Cambridge, Mass.: MIT Press, 1967), pp. 319–371.

81.   See Poincaré's official announcements on assuming the seals of the foreign ministry, Maurice Poincaré, *Au Service de la France: Neuf Annés de Souvenirs* (Paris: Plon, 1926), Vol. 1, pp. 23–25; and John F.V. Keiger, *France and the Origins of the First World* (London:

Macmillan, 1983), pp. 55–56.

82. Poincaré's journals give an impression of the tense and claustrophobic atmosphere. See Poincaré diary, July 26–31, 1914.

83. Telegrams from Szécsen to Berchtold (Nos. 97 and 103), July 1 and 9, 1914, in Ludwig Bittner et al., eds., *Österreich-Ungarns Aussenpolitik von der Bosnischen Krise bis zum Kriegsausbruch*, Vol. 8 (Vienna: Osterreichischer Bundesverlag, 1926–1931), nn. 9970, 10159 ; and Gerd Krumeich, "Raymond Poincaré et l'affairs du 'Figaro,'" *Revue Historique*, Vol. 264, No. 3 (1980), pp. 365–373.

84. Michael Bentley, *Politics without Democracy, 1815–1914: Perception and Preoccupation in British Government* (London: Fontana, 1984), p. 346.

85. See George Dangerfield's classic, *The Strange Death of Liberal England, 1910–1914* (New York: Capricorn, 1935). For a nuanced assessment of the period, see Martin Pugh, *The Making of Modern British Politics, 1867–1939* (repr. Oxford: Blackwell, 1987), pp. 136–182.

86. Nicolson to Goschen, May 5, 1914, Nicolson MSS, TNA (PRO), FO 800/374, National Archives, Kew, United Kingdom; and Keith Robbins, "Britain in the Summer of 1914," in Robbins, ed., *Politicians, Diplomacy, and War in Modern British History* (London: Hambledon, 1994), pp. 175–188.

87. Murray diary, December 16, 1911, MS 8814, Elibank MSS, National Library of Scotland, Edinburgh. Capt. the Hon. A.C. Murray was Edward Grey's parliamentary private secretary.

88. Vernon Bogdanor, *The Monarchy and the Constitution* (repr. Oxford: Oxford University Press, 1997), pp. 113–122; and Bruce K. Murray, *The People's Budget, 1909–10: Lloyd George and Liberal Politics* (Oxford: Oxford University Press, 1980), pp. 232–240.

89. Memo. Balfour, "Constitutional Question, 1913," n.d., quoted in Bogdanor, *The Monarchy and the Constitution*, p. 123; and E.A. Smith, *The House of Lords in British Politics and Society, 1815–1911* (London: Longman, 1992), pp. 174–184.

90. For a detailed discussion of the Welsh and Irish disestablishments, see P.M.H. Bell, *Disestablishment in Ireland and Wales* (London: S.P.C.K., 1969), pp. 226–259.

91. Memo. Birrell, "Impressions of Ulster," June 15, 1914, TNA (PRO), CAB 37/120/70, National Archives, Kew, United Kingdom; Robert Blake, *The Unknown Prime Minister: The Life and Times of Andrew Bonar Law* (London: Eyre and Spottiswoode, 1955), pp. 173–175; Leon Ó Broin, *The Chief Secretary: Augustine Birrell in Ireland* (London: Chatto and Windus, 1969), pp. 99–102; and Nicholas Mansergh, *The Unresolved Question: The Anglo-Irish Settlement and Its Undoing, 1912–1972* (New Haven, Conn.: Yale University Press, 1991), pp. 41–78.

92. David Dutton, *"His Majesty's Loyal Opposition": The Unionist Party in Opposition, 1905–1915* (Liverpool: Liverpool University Press, 1992), pp. 226–237; Patricia Jalland, *The Liberals and Ireland: The Ulster Question in British Politics to 1914* (Brighton, U.K.:

Harvester, 1980), chap. 7; and Patricia Jalland and John Stubbs, "The Irish Question after the Outbreak of War in 1914: Some Unfinished Party Business," *English Historical Review*, Vol. 96, No. 4 (October 1981), pp. 778–780.

93. Asquith to George V, July 24, 1914, CAB 41/35/19, National Archives, Kew, United Kingdom; and Michael G. Ekstein and Zara Steiner, "The Sarajevo Crisis," in F.H. Hinsley, ed., *British Foreign Policy under Sir Edward Grey* (Cambridge: Cambridge University Press, 1977), pp. 397–410.

94. P.F. Clarke, "The Electoral Position of the Liberal and Labour Parties, 1910–1914," *English Historical Review*, Vol. 90, No. 4 (1975), pp. 829–835.

95. James R. MacDonald, *Socialism and Government*, Vol. 1 (London: Independent Labour Party, 1909), p. xxvi; and Henry Pelling, "The Politics of the Osborne Judgment," *Historical Journal*, Vol. 26, No. 4 (December 1982), pp. 889–909.

96. Murray diary, August 17, 1911; Roy Gregory, *The Miners and British Politics, 1906–1914* (Oxford: Oxford University Press, 1968), pp. 29–31, 79–82; Walter Kendall, *The Revolutionary Movement in Britain, 1900–1921: The Origins of British Communism* (London: Weidenfeld and Nicolson, 1969), pp. 34–45, 142–149; and George L. Bernstein, "Liberalism and the Progressive Alliance in the Constituencies, 1900–1914," *Historical Journal*, Vol. 26, No. 3 (September 1983), pp. 617–640.

97. Hobhouse to Harcourt, January 15, 1914, Harcourt MSS, Ms. Harcourt, dep. 444, Bodleian Library, Oxford. See also Ian Packer, "Land-Reform and By-elections, 1885–1914: Do By-elections Matter?" in T.G. Otte and Paul Readman, eds., *By-elections in British Politics, 1832–1914* (Woodbridge, U.K.: Boydell, 2013), especially pp. 211–224; and H.V. Emy, *Liberals, Radicals, and Social Politics, 1892–1914* (Cambridge: Cambridge University Press, 1973), pp. 189–280.

98. For a discussion of the "Holt Cave," see D.J. Dutton, ed., *Odyssey of an Edwardian Liberal: The Political Diary of Richard Denning Holt* (Gloucester, U.K.: Record Society of Lancashire and Cheshire, 1989).

99. Murray diary, May 6, 1914; and Martin Pugh, *Electoral Reform in Peace and War, 1906–1918* (London: Routledge and Keegan Paul, 1978), pp. 17–44.

100. Masterman to Ponsonby, May 30, [1914], Ponsonby MSS, Ms. Eng. hist. c. 660, Bodleian Library, Oxford.

101. "Lloyd George Speech at the Mansion House, July 17, 1914," *Times*, July 18, 1914; Kendall, *The Revolutionary Movement in Britain, 1900–1921*, pp. 148–149; and J. White, "1910–1914 Reconsidered," in James E. Cronin and Jonathan Schneer, eds., *Social Conflict and the Political Order in Modern Britain* (London: Croom Helm, 1982), pp. 73–95.

102. Mair to Scott, July 22, 1914, as quoted in Cameron Hazlehurst, *Politicians at War, July 1914 to May 1915: A Prologue to the Triumph of Lloyd George* (London: Jonathan Cape, 1971), p. 27; and Paul Readman and Luke Blaxill, "Edwardian By-elections," in Otte and Readman, *By-elections in British Politics, 1832–1914*, especially pp. 246–248.

103. Nicolson to Rodd, November 30, 1912, Rennell of Rodd MSS, box 14, Bodleian Library, Oxford.

104. Dillon [Irish Nationalist member of Parliament] to Browne [professor of Persian, Cambridge University], November 28, 1911, author's possession. For the speech, see *Parliamentary Debates*, 5th series, Vol. 33 (November 27, 1911), cols. 43–65. A.J.P. Taylor, *The Troublemakers: Dissent over Foreign Policy, 1792–1939* (London: Hamish Hamilton, 1957) remains the *locus classicus* for a discussion of this subject.

105. Charles Silvester Horne, *Pulpit, Platform, and Parliament* (London: Hodder and Stoughton, 1913), p. 122. Horne was a Congregationalist minister-turned-member of Parliament for Ipswich from 1910 to 1914. For an instructive description of Radical thinking, see also G.H.S. Jordan, "Pensions Not Dreadnoughts: The Radicals and Naval Retrenchment," in A.J.A. Morris, ed., *Edwardian Radicalism, 1900–1914: Some Aspects of British Radicalism* (London: Routledge and Keegan Paul, 1974), pp. 162–179.

106. Arnold Stephenson Rowntree to wife (Mary Katherine Rowntree), July 30, 1914, in Ian Packer, ed., *The Letters of Arnold Stephenson Rowntree to Mary Katherine Rowntree, 1910–1918* (Cambridge: Cambridge University Press, 2002), p. 153. Rowntree, a Quaker businessman, was the member of Parliament for York from 1910 to 1918.

107. [Viscount] Elibank [Arthur C. Murray] to the editor, *Observer*, November 30, 1958.

108. Carl von Clausewitz, *On War*, ed. and trans. Michael Howard and Peter Paret (Princeton, N.J.: Princeton University Press, 1990), p. 517 (emphasis in original).

109. See the Organization for Economic Cooperation and Development (OECD) statistics in Angus Maddison, *The World Economy: A Millennial Perspective* (Paris: O ECD, 2006), pp. 261–263.

Chapter 10. Domestic Coalitions, Internationalization, and War: Then and Now

1.   Richard Rosecrance, *The Rise of the Trading State: Commerce and Conquest in the Modern World* (New York: Basic Books, 1986); Richard Rosecrance, *The Rise of the Virtual State: Wealth and Power in the Coming Century* (New York: Basic Books, 1999); Alexander Gerschenkron, *Bread and Democracy in Germany* (Ithaca, N.Y.: Cornell University Press, 1989); Jack Snyder, *Myths of Empire: Domestic Politics and International Ambition* (Ithaca, N.Y.: Cornell University Press, 1991); Arthur A. Stein and Richard Rosecrance, eds., *The Domestic Bases of Grand Strategy* (Ithaca, N.Y.: Cornell University Press, 1993); Etel Solingen, *Regional Orders at Century's Dawn: Global and Domestic Influences on Grand Strategy* (Princeton, N.J.: Princeton University Press, 1998); Patrick J. McDonald and Kevin Sweeney, "The Achilles' Heel of Liberal IR Theory? Globalization and Conflict in the Pre–World War I Era," *World Politics*, Vol. 59, No. 3 (April 2007), pp. 370–403; and Steve Chan, *China, the U.S., and Power Tran-

sition Theory: A Critique (London: Routledge, 2013). Space constraints limit references to massive literatures on Word War I, interdependence, Germany, China, and other relevant topics discussed throughout this piece.

2.   Edward A. Hill, ed., *Max Weber on the Methodology of the Social Sciences* (Glencoe, Ill.: Free Press, 1949), pp. 105–107; and John G. Ruggie, *Constructing the World Polity: Essays on International Institutionalism* (New York: Routledge, 1998).

3.   A fuller theoretical rationale and empirical foundation for the argument can be found in Solingen, *Regional Orders at Century's Dawn*; and Etel Solingen, *Comparative Regionalism: Economics and Security* (London: Routledge, 2014).

4.   Albert O. Hirschman, *National Power and the Structure of Foreign Trade* (Berkeley: University of California Press, 1945).

5.   David Lloyd George, prime minister of Great Britain in 1916, described the outbreak of World War I as accidental: "How was it that the world was so unexpectedly plunged into this terrible conflict? Who was responsible? . . . The nations slithered over the brink into the boiling cauldron of war without any trace of apprehension or dismay." Lloyd George, *War Memoirs*, Vol. 1 (London: Odhams, 1924), p. 32.

6.   Jack Snyder and Karen Ballentine, "Nationalism and the Marketplace of Ideas," *International Security*, Vol. 21, No. 2 (Fall 1996), pp. 5–40.

7.   Karl Polanyi, *The Great Transformation: The Political and Economic Origins of Our Time* (Boston: Beacon, 1944).

8.   As Ernst B. Haas warns, "Even to assert a simple causal connection between international interdependence and international violence is to skate on theoretical ice that is too slippery for comfort." See Haas, "War, Interdependence, and Functionalism," in Raimo Vayrynen, ed., *The Quest for Peace: Transcending Collective Violence and War among Societies, Cultures, and States* (Beverly Hills, Calif.: Sage, 1987), p. 109. On contingency in World War I, see Richard Ned Lebow, *Forbidden Fruit: Counterfactuals and International Relations* (Princeton, N.J.: Princeton University Press, 2010).

9.   Ruggie, *Constructing the World Polity*, p. 31.

10.   Recent scholarship includes Lebow, *Forbidden Fruit*; Margaret MacMillan, *The War That Ended Peace: The Road to 1914* (New York: Random House, 2013); and Christopher Clark, *The Sleepwalkers: How Europe Went to War in 1914* (New York: HarperCollins, 2013).

11.   *Kaiserreich* institutions reflected fiercely conservative Prussian resistance to rising Social Democracy. The Reichstag (parliament) was responsible for approving the *Kaiserreich's* budget but could not control the government's executive branch. Furthermore, various institutional barriers obstructed universal male suffrage. See Gerschenkron, *Bread and Democracy in Germany*; Stephen Van Evera, "The Cult of the Offensive and the Origins of the First World War," *International Security*, Vol. 9, No. 1 (Summer 1984), pp. 58–107; and Snyder, *Myths of Empire*.

12. The Kolonialverein (Colonial League) was formed in 1882, the ultranationalist Alldeutscher Verband (Pan-German League) in 1891, the Flottenverein (Navy League) in 1898, and the Wehrverein (Army League) in 1912.

13. Fritz Fischer, *War of Illusions: German Policies from 1911 to 1914* (New York: W.W. Norton, 1975), pp. 6–12.

14. Eckart Kehr, *Economic Interest, Militarism, and Foreign Policy: Essays on German History* (Berkeley: University of California Press, 1977), p. 43. On internal dissent within the Industrialists League regarding proposed 1902 tariffs, U.S. export growth, and Mitteleuropa, see "Germans Discuss the 'American Danger'; Industrial League Favors the Proposed Tariff Bill. Thinks This Country Can Be Coerced by It—Wants Plan for European Anti-American Union Considered," *New York Times*, October 22, 1901. On left-of-center parties' support for lower tariffs and international cooperation, see Paul M. Kennedy, *The Rise of the Anglo-German Antagonism, 1860–1914* (London: George Allen and Unwin, 1980), p. 305.

15. Peter Gourevitch, *Politics in Hard Times: Comparative Responses to International Economic Crises* (Ithaca, N.Y.: Cornell University Press, 1986), p. 99.

16. Chemical, paper, and other industries opposing protection left the Industrialists League in 1900. Prominent Hansa League banks—Deutsche Bank, Bleichröder, and Discontogesellschaft—had more moderate foreign policy positions than the core parties to the AIMC. See Kennedy, *The Rise of the Anglo-German Antagonism, 1860–1914*.

17. Although a Prussian banking consortium and other banks benefited from government borrowing at high interests beginning in the late 1890s, internationalizing financiers were concerned about the effects of international crises and the prospect of war on their external networks. See Kennedy, *The Rise of the Anglo-German Antagonism, 1860–1914*, pp. 302–305; and Hans-Ulrich Wehler, *The German Empire, 1817–1918* (London: Bloomsbury Academic, 1985), p. 141.

18. Kehr, *Economic Interest, Militarism, and Foreign Policy*.

19. "Morocco Crisis: Berlin Excited—Paris Calm," *New Zealand Herald*, October 24, 1911, http://paperspast.natlib.govt.nz/cgi-bin/paperspast?a=d&d=NZH19111024.2.98; and Fischer, *War of Illusions*, pp. 75, 81.

20. Forces friendlier than the AIMC to internationalization favored a different conception of Mitteleuropa, one closer to a voluntary customs union than an entity created by forceful annexation. Among these forces were the Internationalist League's president, Deutsche Bank's directors (Arthur von Gwinner and Karl Helfferich), and the chairman of the electrical engineering company Allgemeine Elektrizitätsgessellschaft, Walther Rathenau. Bethmann ignored Rathenau's advice not to join Austria in war or annex France and to accept a "voluntary peace." Gwinner opposed "blind" annexation and urged accommodation with Britain, as did international trade financier Max Warburg. Asked by Kaiser Wilhelm in June 1914 what he thought of preventive

war against Russia, Warburg responded that Germany could only become stronger economically and militarily with every year of peace; therefore it could only benefit from waiting. Export-oriented shipping magnate Albert Ballin opposed war, insisting that Germany could not afford a naval race with Britain. Although Ballin occasionally succumbed to more hard-line positions, in a 1915 letter to Foreign Secretary Gottlieb von Jagow, he accused Jagow of shared responsibility for "staging" a war that cost Germany generations of splendid men. See Luigi Albertini, *The Origins of the War of 1914*, Vol. 1., trans. Isabella M. Massey (Oxford: Oxford University Press, 1965), pp. 325, 334; Niall Ferguson, *The Pity of War* (New York: Allen Lane, 1998), p. 33; Fritz Fischer, *Germany's War Aims in the First World War* (New York: W.W. Norton, 1967), pp. 10, 28, 91; and Fischer, *War of Illusions*, pp. 75, 134, 327, 457, 520–522.

21. Cornelius Torp, "The 'Coalition of "Rye and Iron"' under the Pressure of Globalization: A Reinterpretation of Germany's Political Economy before 1914," *Central European History*, Vol. 43, No. 3 (2010), p. 413. Alexander Gerschenkron describes the effects of Junker power as follows: "Preservation of the Junkers means autarchy, and autarky in Germany means war." See Gerschenkron, *Bread and Democracy in Germany*, p. 183. On German decisionmakers' emphasis on self-reliance and their development of *Weltpolitik* to appeal to domestic audiences, see Clark, *The Sleepwalkers*, p. 152.

22. Wehler, *The German Empire, 1817–1918*, p. 98. Chief of the General Staff Helmuth von Moltke argued that "things must be so built up that war will be seen as a deliverance from the great armaments, the financial burdens, the political tensions." See Ferguson, *The Pity of War*, p. 140. The concept of the *Machtstaat* alluded to a repressive, militarized state that projected power beyond its borders.

23. David E. Kaiser, "Germany and the Origins of the First World War," *Journal of Modern History*, Vol. 55, No. 3 (September 1983), p. 453; Wolfgang J. Mommsen, "Domestic Factors in German Foreign Policy before 1914," *Central European History*, Vol. 6, No. 1 (March 1973), p. 24; and Kehr, *Economic Interest, Militarism, and Foreign Policy*, pp. 22, 11–12. In a 1905 letter, the kaiser instructed Bülow, "First shoot down the Socialists, behead them and render them harmless— if necessary by a bloodbath— and then [fight a] war against the foreign foe! But not beforehand and not a tempo [at the same time]." See John C.G. Röhl, *The Kaiser and His Court: Wilhelm II and the Government of Germany* (Cambridge: Cambridge University Press, 1995), pp. 416–417.

24. Kehr, *Economic Interest, Militarism, and Foreign Policy*, p. 12; Annika Mombauer, *Helmuth von Moltke and the Origins of the First World War* (Cambridge: Cambridge University Press, 2001); and Clark, *The Sleepwalkers*, pp. 329–332.

25. In July 1914, the kaiser declared several times: "This time I shall not give in." See MacMillan, *The War That Ended Peace*, Kindle line 10577. Jagow, Undersecretary of State Arthur Zimmermann, Bethmann's personal assistant (Kurt Riezler), and Foreign Office Political Director Wilhelm von Stumm, among others, acknowledged war to be

a calculated and deliberate choice. Jagow publicly admitted that Russia, France, and Britain were not interested in war; asked whether Germany really wanted the war, he responded with an unequivocal "yes, we wanted it." See Fischer, *War of Illusions*, pp. 478, 31–38. Riezler admits in his diaries that the *Kaiserreich*'s policies were to both provoke and obstruct Russia, France, and Britain in an effort to obtain small prestige victories, appeal to public opinion, and respond to nationalist parties' efforts to strengthen their popularity through foreign policy. See Kurt Riezler, *Tagebücher, Aufsätze, Dokumente* [Diaries, essays, documents] (Göttingen: Vandenhoeck and Ruprecht, 2008), p. 188.

26. Riezler, *Tagebücher, Aufsätze, Dokumente*; and Snyder, *Myths of Empire*.

27. Richard Rosecrance, *The Resurgence of the West: How a Transatlantic Union Can Prevent War and Restore the United States and Europe* (New Haven, Conn.: Yale University Press, 2013), p. 100; Michael R. Gordon, "Domestic Conflict and the Origins of the First World War: The British and German Cases," *Journal of Modern History*, Vol. 46, No. 2 (June 1974), p. 217; Albertini, *The Origins of the War of 1914*, Vol. 2, p. 431; and Kaiser, "Germany and the Origins of the First World War," pp. 463–470.

28. It is a sign of the *Kaiserreich*'s political center of gravity that Mommsen considers Bülow—committed to nationalism, imperial expansion, war on Russia, and a weak Reichstag—a moderate. See Mommsen, "Domestic Factors in German Foreign Policy before 1914," p. 18. Bülow understood the costs of protection and regressive taxation better than he did the risks of war. See Albertini, *The Origins of the War of 1914*, Vol. 2, p. 163; and Fischer, *War of Illusions*, pp. 45, 523. In 1919 Bülow's nephew and namesake removed from official archives documents reportedly proving German responsibility for World War I. See Holger H. Herwig, *The Outbreak of World War I: Causes and Responsibilities* (Boston: Houghton Mifflin, 1997); and Holger H. Herwig, "Clio Deceived: Patriotic Self-Censorship in Germany after the Great War," *International Security*, Vol. 12, No. 2 (Fall 1987), pp. 5–44.

29. Van Evera, "The Cult of the Offensive and the Origins of the First World War"; and Snyder, *Myths of Empire*.

30. On counterfactuals and World War I, see Gary Goertz and Jack S. Levy, eds., *Explaining War and Peace: Case Studies and Necessary Condition Counterfactuals* (New York: Routledge, 2007); and Lebow, *Forbidden Fruit*.

31. Kennedy, *The Rise of the Anglo-German Antagonism, 1860–1914*, p. 358; and Ferguson, *The Pity of War*, pp. 135–140.

32. China's government revenue has grown 20 percent annually since the 1990s—in sharp contrast to the *Kaiserreich*'s stagnant revenues and fiscal deficits. See Hongying Wang, "China's Long March toward Economic Rebalancing," Policy Brief No. 38 (Waterloo, Canada: Center for International Governance Innovation, April 2014).

33. Jessica Chen Weiss, *Powerful Patriots: Nationalist Protest in China's Foreign Relations* (Oxford: Oxford University Press, 2014).

34. Margaret M. Pearson, "China's Foreign Economic Relations and Policies," in Saadia Pekkanen, John Ravenhill, and Rosemary Foot, eds., *The Oxford Handbook of the International Relations of Asia* (Oxford: Oxford University Press, 2014).

35. Trade openness is here a consequence, not the driver, of an internationalizing model.

36. Susan L. Shirk, *China: Fragile Superpower* (New York: Oxford University Press, 2007); Thomas J. Christensen, "The Advantages of an Assertive China: Responding to Beijing's Abrasive Diplomacy," *Foreign Affairs*, Vol. 90, No. 2 (March/April 2014), pp. 54–67; and Beijie Tang, "Internationalization's Discontents: Domestic Coalitions and the Future of China's Peaceful Rise," Ph.D. dissertation, University of California, Irvine, 2014.

37. The "Chongqing model," associated with Bo Xilai, involved increased control and activity by state security agencies. It was ostensibly designed to combat corruption and organized crime, but also to tighten Chongqing authorities' political control. The model entailed increased reliance on propaganda to restore New Left themes reminiscent of Maoism or a "red culture," urging the masses to "sing red songs" from the revolutionary Maoist era.

38. "Everybody Who Loves Mr. Xi, Say Yes," *Economist*, November 16, 2013, p. 49; and Xu Lin, "Experience, Attitudes, and Social Transition—A Sociological Study of the Post-'80s Generation," January 9, 2014, http://www.womenofchina.cn/html/womenof china/report/168821-1.htm.

39. Pearson, "China's Foreign Economic Relations and Policies."

40. Even Bo Xilai warned nationalists against irrationally boycotting Japanese goods. See Weiss, *Powerful Patriots*; and Alastair Iain Johnston, "How New and Assertive Is China's New Assertiveness?" *International Security*, Vol. 37, No. 4 (Spring 2013), pp. 7–48.

41. "Xi: There Is No Gene for Invasion in Our Blood," *China Daily*, May 16, 2014, http://usa.chinadaily.com.cn/china/2014-05/16/content_17511170.htm. Riots in Vietnam ensued after China deployed a deep-sea oil rig in waterways claimed by both China and Vietnam. See "Vietnam Detains Hundreds after Riots Targeting Chinese Businesses," *Guardian*, May 22, 2014.

42. Nuclear weapons are often cited as another major difference between the two eras, but a discussion of their role is beyond my focus here. See Etel Solingen, *Nuclear Logics: Contrasting Paths in East Asia and the Middle East* (Princeton, N.J.: Princeton University Press, 2007).

43. John Ravenhill, "The Economics-Security Nexus in the Asia-Pacific Region," in William T. Tow, ed., *Security Politics in the Asia-Pacific: A Regional-Global Nexus?* (Cambridge: Cambridge University Press, 2009), pp. 188–207. See also Christina L. Davis and Sophie Meunier, "Business as Usual? Economic Responses to Political Tensions," *American Journal of Political Science*, Vol. 55, No. 3 (July 2011), pp. 628–646.

44. Länder and localities funded social expenditures with revenues that spared wealthy landowners.

45. Clark, *The Sleepwalkers*. From 1894 to 1913, military expenditures rose by 164 percent for the Central Powers and 57 percent for the Entente. See Ferguson, *The Pity of War*, p. 106.

46. From 1909 to 1914, trade openness levels averaged 33 percent for Germany; 27 percent for France; 22 percent for Austria-Hungary; 12 percent for Russia; and lower in Serbia and the Ottoman Empire. From 2007 to 2012, by contrast, trade level openness averaged 118 percent for Taiwan; 101 percent for South Korea; and 30 percent for Japan. China's trade openness level averaged 68 percent in 2008. See Stephen N. Broadberry and Kevin H. O'Rourke, *The Cambridge Economic History of Modern Europe*, Vol. 2: *1870 to the Present* (Cambridge: Cambridge University Press, 2010); and Erik Gartzke and Yonatan Lupu, "Trading on Preconceptions: Why World War I Was Not a Failure of Economic Interdependence," *International Security*, Vol. 36, No. 4 (Spring 2012), pp. 115–150.

47. Sean M. Lynn-Jones, "Détente and Deterrence: Anglo-German Relations, 1911–1914," *International Security*, Vol. 11, No. 2 (Fall 1986), pp. 142–145; Kennedy, *The Rise of the Anglo-German Antagonism, 1860–1914*, p. 303; Gourevitch, *Politics in Hard Times*, p. 114; and Gordon, "Domestic Conflict and the Origins of the First World War."

48. Wehler, *The German Empire, 1817–1918*. The kaiser labeled Britain "that filthy nation of grocers." A significant contingent of *Kaiserreich* academics called for a German imperial challenge against Britain and the "Muscovite yoke." See Fischer, *Germany's War Aims in the First World War*, p. 83; and Fischer, *War of Illusions*, p. 32.

49. Although initially tempted to ride the wave of nationalist protests against China, Vietnamese officials concerned with threats to FDI later punished those involved in violent riots.

50. Kevin H. O'Rourke and Jeffrey G. Williamson, *Globalization and History: The Evolution of a Nineteenth-Century Atlantic Economy* (Cambridge, Mass.: MIT Press, 1999).

51. Arvind Subramanian and Martin Kessler, "The Hyperglobalization of Trade and Its Future," Working Paper No. 13-6 (Washington, D.C.: Peterson Institute for International Economics, July 2013), http://www.iie.com/publications/wp/wp13-6.pdf; and Edward D. Mansfield and Helen V. Milner, *Votes, Vetoes, and the Political Economy of International Trade Agreements* (Princeton, N.J.: Princeton University Press, 2012). Sino-U.S. interdependence, which is much higher than the interdependence between pre–World War I Germany and Britain, is a crucial part of this broader and unparalleled global economic landscape.

52. Rosecrance, *The Rise of the Trading State*. Foreign-invested firms account for more than half of China's total trade; exports represent 40 percent of GDP. These exports, in turn, rely heavily on imported components that account for 60–80 percent of the value of all exports; more sophisticated manufactured exports increasingly rely on technologies imported from China's relevant strategic cluster. See Ravenhill, "The Economics-Security Nexus in the Asia-Pacific Region." China's FDI to GDP ratio reached 35 percent

in 2002. Germany experienced reduced French and British capital inflows after 1900.

53. Stephen G. Brooks, "Economic Actors' Lobbying Influence on the Prospects for War and Peace," *International Organization*, Vol. 67, No. 4 (Fall 2013), pp. 863–888.

54. Bethmann told Riezler in July 1914 that action against Serbia could lead to a world war, yet such a "leap into the dark" would be justified. See Riezler, *Tagebücher, Aufsätze, Dokumente*, p. 185; and Volker R. Berghahn, *Imperial Germany 1871–1918: Economy, Society, Culture, and Politics* (New York: Berghahn, 1994), p. 267.

55. At the same time, Kennedy argues that blaming all other powers "equally" is "an historical evasion" given that "at the end of the day, virtually all tangled wires of causality led back to Berlin." See Kennedy, *The Rise of the Anglo-German Antagonism, 1860–1914*, p. 457.

56. Etel Solingen, "Pax Asiatica versus Bella Levantina: The Foundations of War and Peace in East Asia and the Middle East," *American Political Science Review*, Vol. 101, No. 4 (November 2007), pp. 757–780.

57. Marc Trachtenberg, "French Foreign Policy in the July Crisis, 1914: A Review Article," *H-Diplo/ISSF*, No. 3, December 1, 2010, http://www.h-net.org/~diplo/ISSF/PDF/3-Trachtenberg.pdf implies that war might have been avoided had appropriate neorealist calculations prevailed. On the danger of accepting politicians' claims of strategic "vulnerability" at face value, see Snyder, *Myths of Empire*.

58. On spirals, see Robert Jervis, *Perception and Misperception in International Politics* (Princeton, N.J.: Princeton University Press, 1976).

Chapter 11. European Militaries and the Origins of World War I

1. Samuel P. Huntington, by contrast, argues that the Wilhelmine military largely confined itself to the military sphere. See Huntington, *The Soldier and the State: The Theory and Politics of Civil-Military Relations* (Cambridge, Mass.: Harvard University Press, 1957), pp. 100–102. The overwhelming consensus of historians, however, is that Wilhelmine German officers played a large role in shaping German ideas and foreign policies before 1914.

2. Wilhelm Deist, "Kaiser Wilhelm II in the Context of His Military and Naval Entourage," in John C.G. Röhl and Nicolaus Sombart, eds., *Kaiser Wilhelm II: New Interpretations* (Cambridge: Cambridge University Press, 1982), pp. 169–192, at p. 177.

3. Gasser's views are summarized in John A. Moses, *The Politics of Illusion: The Fischer Controversy in German Historiography* (London: George Prior, 1975), pp. 84, 87.

4. Friedrich Meinecke, quoted in Huntington, *The Soldier and the State*, p. 105.

5. Isabel V. Hull, *The Entourage of Kaiser Wilhelm II, 1888–1918* (Cambridge: Cambridge University Press, 1982), pp. 236–237.

6. Louis L. Snyder, *From Bismarck to Hitler: The Background of Modern German*

Nationalism (Williamsport, Pa.: Bayard, 1935), p. 121.

7.   Gordon A. Craig, *The Politics of the Prussian Army: 1640–1945* (London: Oxford University Press, 1955), p. 252. For a concurring assessment, see Alfred Weber, quoted in ibid., p. xvi. Many contemporary observers also saw the dominance of the military in German society. British journalist Wickham Steed warned in early 1914 that "in Prussia the army is supreme, and through Prussia the army rules Germany." This was the first lesson "for those who lightly imagine the German Empire to be even as other states." Steed, quoted in Hans Kohn, *The Mind of Germany: The Education of a Nation* (New York: Charles Scribner's, 1960), p. 292.

8.   Lamar Cecil, *Wilhelm II: Prince and Emperor, 1859–1900* (Chapel Hill: University of North Carolina Press, 1989), pp. 58–59, 62, 66.

9.   In 1900, Friedrich von Holstein, quoted in Gerhard Ritter, *The Schlieffen Plan: Critique of a Myth* (Westport, Conn.: Greenwood, 1979), p. 91.

10. Jehuda L. Wallach, "Misperceptions of Clausewitz' *On War* by the German Military," *Journal of Strategic Studies*, Vol. 9, Nos. 2 and 3 (June/September 1986), pp. 213–239, at p. 230.

11. S.E. Finer, *The Man on Horseback: The Role of the Military in Politics*, 2nd ed. (Harmondsworth, U.K.: Penguin, 1976), p. 42.

12. Ibid.

13. Hans Speier, *Social Order and the Risks of War* (New York: George W. Stewart, 1952), p. 283. The civilian secretary of war saw the kaiser only once a week. See ibid.

14. Samuel R. Williamson and Russel Van Wyk, *July 1914: Soldiers, Statesmen, and the Coming of the Great War: A Brief Documentary History* (Boston: Bedford/St. Martin's, 2003), pp. 18–30; and Mark Cornell, "Serbia," in Keith Wilson, ed., *Decisions for War, 1914* (New York: St. Martin's, 1995), pp. 55–96, at pp. 55–58.

15. Michael Howard, *War in European History* (London: Oxford University Press, 1976), p. 110.

16. Margaret MacMillan, *The War That Ended Peace: The Road to 1914* (New York: Random House, 2013), p. 275. MacMillan notes that "a century later the only political leaders routinely appearing in uniforms were military dictators such as Saddam Hussein and Muammar Gaddafi." See ibid.

17. Stig Förster, "Dreams and Nightmares: German Military Leadership and the Images of Future Warfare, 1871–1914," in Manfred F. Boemeke, Roger Chickering, and Förster, eds., *Anticipating Total War: The German and American Experiences, 1871–1914* (New York: Cambridge University Press, 1999), pp. 343–376, at p. 351.

18. Ibid.; and Imanuel Geiss, *German Foreign Policy, 1871–1914* (London: Routledge and Kegan Paul, 1976), p. 56.

19. Annika Mombauer, *Helmuth von Moltke and the Origins of the First World War* (New York: Cambridge University Press, 2001), p. 5.

20. Hull, *The Entourage of Kaiser Wilhelm II, 1888–1918*, p. 212.

21. Förster, "Dreams and Nightmares," p. 373.

22. Mombauer, *Helmuth von Moltke and the Origins of the First World War*, pp. 114–115.

23. Ibid, pp. 122–124.

24. Helmuth von Moltke in a letter to his wife, August 19, 1911, quoted in ibid., p. 124.

25. Annika Mombauer, ed. and trans., *The Origins of the First World War: Diplomatic and Military Documents* (New York: Manchester University Press, 2013), p. 86.

26. John C.G. Röhl, "Germany," in Wilson, *Decisions for War, 1914*, pp. 27–54, at p. 44.

27. Ibid.

28. Helmuth von Moltke, on May 12, 1914, quoted in Mombauer, *The Origins of the First World War*, p. 131.

29. Mombauer, *The Origins of the First World War*, p. 137.

30. Ibid., p. 140.

31. Ibid., p. 141.

32. Fischer, *War of Illusions*, p. 493. Bavarian Military Plenipotentiary Gen. Karl Ritter von Wenninger reported on the same day: "[Moltke]…now insists that the situation has never been more favorable and should be used to start the fight." See ibid.

33. Luigi Albertini, *The Origins of the War of 1914*, Vol. 3, trans and ed. Isabella M. Massey (Westport, Conn.: Greenwood, 1980), pp. 6–7. For context and back story, see ibid., pp. 1–5, 8–18.

34. On Schlieffen, see Hull, *The Entourage of Kaiser Wilhelm II, 1888–1918*, p. 258. On Einem and Groener, see Imanuel Geiss, ed., *July 1914: The Outbreak of the First World War: Selected Documents* (New York: W.W. Norton, 1967), p. 40. On Ludendorff and Goltz, see Alfred Vagts, *Defense and Diplomacy: The Soldier and the Conduct of Foreign Relations* (New York: Kings Crown, 1956), p. 294. On the General Staff, see Geiss, *German Foreign Policy, 1871–1914*, p. 101; and Geiss, *July 1914*, p. 60.

35. Hull, *The Entourage of Kaiser Wilhelm II, 1888–1918*, p. 259; and Mombauer, *Helmuth von Moltke and the Origins of the First World War*, p. 45.

36. Hull, *The Entourage of Kaiser Wilhelm II, 1888–1918*, p. 259.

37. Ibid. Gen. Gustav von Kessel (an old friend of Kaiser Wilhelm) and Gen. Adjutant Alfred von Löwenfeld probably pressed for war as well in 1911. See ibid., p. 260.

38. In September 1911, in Mombauer, *The Origins of the First World War*, p. 54.

39. Hull, *The Entourage of Kaiser Wilhelm II, 1888–1918*, p. 261; and Mombauer, *Helmuth von Moltke and the Origins of the First World War*, p. 45.

40. Report by Baron Karl von Bienerth, Austro-Hungarian military attaché in Berlin, quoted in Röhl, "Germany," p. 42.

41. Belgian attaché Bevens, November 1913, quoted in Mombauer, *The Origins of the First World War*, p. 104n. France's ambassador to Germany, Jules Cambon, noted in 1913 that this lobbying was gaining "a greater hold over [the emperor's] mind." See

Craig, *Politics of the Prussian Army*, p. 291.

42. Röhl, "Germany," p. 44.

43. Hugo Philipp Graf von und zu Lerchenfeld-Koefering, Bavarian envoy in Berlin, June 4, 1914, quoted in Mombauer, *The Origins of the First World War*, p. 142.

44. Gen. Traugott Freiherr von Leuckart von Weissdorf, Saxon military plenipotentiary in Berlin, reporting to the Saxon minister of war, July 3, 1914, quoted in Mombauer, *Helmuth von Moltke and the Origins of the First World War*, p. 187.

45. Report by Hugo Philipp Graf von und zu Lerchenfeld-Koefering, Bavarian envoy in Berlin, on July 6, 1914, quoted in Geiss, *July 1914*, p. 68n. German civilian and military views on policy diverged during June 28–July 6: while the military favored war, German civilians aimed toward a peaceful resolution of the Serbo-Austrian conflict, until the kaiser agreed to a belligerent policy during July 5–6. See Geiss, *July 1914*, p. 61.

46. Albertini, *The Origins of the War of 1914*, Vol. 2, p. 141.

47. Ibid.

48. In an undated response to a letter of July 18, 1914. Quoted in Mombauer, *The Origins of the First World War*, p. 280n.

49. Albertini, *The Origins of the War of 1914*, Vol. 2, p. 491.

50. Ibid., Vol. 3, pp. 17–18.

51. Reported by Eugen Fischer, quoted in ibid., p. 23.

52. Report by Bavarian Military Attaché Gen. Karl Ritter von Wenninger, quoted in Röhl, "Germany," p. 39. Stig Förster notes that "after 1911 the General Staff became a hotbed of warmongers." See Förster, "Dreams and Nightmares," p. 361.

53. For example, during the July crisis Moltke favored waiting until Russia gave Germany a pretext before launching German mobilization. But he sought to begin war under the best conditions, not to avoid it. War was clearly his goal.

54. Albertini, *The Origins of the War of 1914*, Vol. 3, p. 16.

55. Lawrence Sondhaus, *Franz Conrad von Hötzendorf: Architect of the Apocalypse* (Boston: Brill, 2000), pp. 89, 105–107.

56. Mombauer, *The Origins of the First World War*, p. 42; and Hew Strachan, *The First World War*, Vol. 1: *To Arms* (New York: Oxford University Press, 2001), p. 69.

57. Vagts, *Defense and Diplomacy*, p. 301.

58. Berchtold suggested that "we send Serbia a demand to dissolve certain societies, relieve the Minister of Police of his post, etc." See "Conversation between Berchtold and Conrad, 29 June, 1914," in Geiss, *July 1914*, p. 64.

59. Ibid.

60. Max Hastings, *Catastrophe 1914: Europe Goes to War* (New York: Alfred A. Knopf, 2013), p. 29. During the war, Austrian politician Josef Redlich told journalist Theodor Wolff that in his view "the two General Staffs [German and Austrian] had made the war, the governments were then sucked in." Josef Redlich, quoted in Röhl,

"Germany," pp. 27–54, at p. 49n.

61.   On Krobatin, see Richard F. Hamilton and Holger H. Herwig, *Decisions for War, 1914-1917* (New York: Cambridge University Press, 2004), p. 53. On Potiorek, see Samuel R. Williamson, "Aggressive and Defensive Aims of Political Elites? Austro-Hungarian Policy in 1914," in Holger Afflerback and David Stevenson, eds., *An Improbable War? The Outbreak of World War I and European Political Culture before 1914* (New York: Berghahn, 2007), pp. 61–74, at p. 69.

62.   Williamson, "Aggressive and Defensive Aims of Political Elites?" p. 69.

63.   Christopher Clark, *The Sleepwalkers: How Europe Went to War in 1914* (New York: HarperCollins, 2013), p. 220. Russian military representatives also supported war if necessary in late 1913, agreeing that war was "fully permissible" over the Liman von Sanders affair. See Mombauer, *The Origins of the First World War*, p. 108n.

64.   Bernadotte E. Schmitt, *The Coming of the War, 1914*, Vol. 2 (New York: Charles Scribner's Sons, 1930), p. 31n.

65.   Geiss, *July 1914*, p. 266.

66.   Nicolson to Grey, 24 February 1913, quoted in Mombauer, *The Origins of the First World War*, p. 97.

67.   Moltke pointed to French and Russian premobilizations as he argued for German mobilization on July 30: "If we hesitate with mobilization, our situation will be worsening day by day and can lead to the most fateful results for us if our opponents can continue to prepare themselves undisturbed." See Helmuth von Moltke, quoted in Albertini, *The Origins of the War of 1914*, Vol. 3, p. 25. Bethmann agreed that French and Russian premobilizations required a quick German response: "Germany cannot wait very long before deciding [about mobilization], for we should otherwise fall behindhand in respect of Russia and France." Theobald von Bethmann Hollweg, quoted in ibid., p. 17. See also ibid., Vol. 2, p. 491.

68.   On July 30, Moltke persuaded or coerced Bethmann to agree to support a decision for German mobilization, to be taken the next day, as discussed above. The German government decided to mobilize at around noon on July 31. Germany then ordered *Kriegsgefahrzustand* (preliminary mobilization) at 1:00 p.m. on July 31, and full mobilization at 5:00 p.m. on August 1. France ordered full mobilization at 3:55 p.m. on August 1. See Schmitt, *The Coming of the War, 1914*, Vol. 2, pp. 263–265, 323–324, 336. When they ordered *Kriegsgefahrzustand*, German leaders firmly intended to promptly follow with full mobilization and war. See Albertini, *The Origins of the War of 1914*, Vol. 3, p. 38. Thus Germany's key leaders decided for war on July 30; its government decided for war on July 31. France independently decided for mobilization on August 1.

69.   Guillaume to Davignon, July 30, quoted in Mombauer, *The Origins of the First World War*, p. 467.

70.   Sean McMeekin, *July 1914: Countdown to War* (New York: Basic Books, 2013), p. 200.

71. Mombauer, *The Origins of the First World War*, p. 139.

72. Lt. Cmdr. J.M. Kenworthy, quoted in Zara S. Steiner, *Britain and the Origins of the First World War* (New York: St. Martin's, 1977), p. 193.

73. Mombauer's excellent *Helmuth von Moltke and the Origins of the First World War* and her annotations to *The Origins of the First World War* are signal exceptions.

74. Marc Trachtenberg, *History and Strategy* (Princeton, N.J.: Princeton University Press, 1991), p. 96.

75. On the origins of the cult of the offensive, see Jack Snyder, *The Ideology of the Offensive: Military Decision Making and the Disasters of 1914* (Ithaca, N.Y.: Cornell University Press, 1984). On the failure of Europeans to learn defensive lessons from the wars of 1860–1914, see Jay Luvaas, *The Military Legacy of the Civil War: The European Inheritance* (Chicago: University of Chicago Press, 1959); and T.H.E. Travers, "Technology, Tactics, and Morale: Jean de Bloch, the Boer War, and British Military Theory, 1900–1914," *Journal of Modern History*, Vol. 51 (June 1979), pp. 264–286. Another valuable source on military offense-mindedness before 1914 is Bernard Brodie, *Strategy in the Missile Age* (Princeton, N.J.: Princeton University Press, 1965), pp. 42–52.

76. Ritter, *The Schlieffen Plan*, p. 100.

77. Alfred von Schlieffen, quoted in Snyder, *The Ideology of the Offensive*, p. 139.

78. Friedrich von Bernhardi, *How Germany Makes War* (New York: George H. Doran, 1914), pp. 153, 155.

79. Geiss, *July 1914*, p. 357; and Wallace Notestein and Elmer E. Stoll, eds., *Conquest and Kultur: Aims of the Germans in Their Own Words* (Washington, D.C.: U.S. Government Printing Office, 1917), p. 43.

80. Notestein and Stoll, *Conquest and Kultur*, pp. 43–44.

81. Gerhard Ritter, *The Sword and the Scepter: The Problem of Militarism in Germany*, Vol. 2 (Coral Gables, Fla.: University of Miami Press, 1972), p. 117.

82. Martin Kitchen, *The German Officer Corps, 1890–1914* (Oxford: Oxford University Press, 1968), p. 102. The German navy was also infused with offensive ideas. See Holger H. Herwig, *Politics of Frustration: The United States in German Naval Planning, 1889–1941* (Boston: Little, Brown, 1976), pp. 42–66, outlining the navy's far-fetched prewar schemes for invading the United States. Germany's Chief of Admiralty Staff Adm. Otto von Diederichs explained that "our only means of defense lies in an offense." See ibid., p. 52.

83. B.H. Liddell Hart, *Through the Fog of War* (New York: Random House, 1938), p. 57.

84. Luvaas, *The Military Legacy of the Civil War*, p. 165.

85. Ibid.

86. Joseph Joffre in 1913, quoted in John Ellis, *The Social History of the Machine Gun* (New York: Pantheon, 1975), pp. 53–54.

87. Theodore Ropp, *War in the Modern World*, rev. ed. (New York: Collier, 1962), p. 222. De Grandmaison declared that all victorious armies have "an unmitigated

offensive spirit." See Snyder, *The Ideology of the Offensive*, p. 91.

88. Maj. Emile Driant, quoted in Alfred Vagts, *A History of Militarism: Civilian and Military*, rev. ed. (New York: Free Press, 1959), p. 350; 1913 French field regulations, quoted in Barbara W. Tuchman, *The Guns of August* (New York: Dell, 1962), p. 51; and Ferdinand Foch, quoted in ibid., p. 264.

89. Tuchman, *The Guns of August*, p. 51.

90. Emile Driant, in 1912, quoted in John M. Cairns, "International Politics and the Military Mind: The Case of the French Republic, 1911–1914," *Journal of Modern History*, Vol. 25, No. 3 (September 1953), p. 282.

91. Nöel Edouard de Castelnau, in 1913, quoted in L.C.F. Turner, *Origins of the First World War* (London: Edward Arnold, 1970), p. 53.

92. On the offensive in French prewar thought, see B.H. Liddell Hart, "French Military Ideas before the First World War," in Martin Gilbert, ed., *A Century of Conflict, 1850–1950: Essays for A.J.P. Taylor* (London: Hamilton Hamish, 1966), pp. 135–148.

93. Richard D. Challener, *The French Theory of the Nation in Arms, 1866–1939* (New York: Columbia University Press, 1955), p. 81. Likewise, Joffre later explained that Plan XVII, his battle plan for 1914, was less a plan for battle than merely a plan of "concentration....I adopted no preconceived idea, other than a full determination to take the offensive with all my forces assembled." See Ropp, *War in the Modern World*, p. 229.

94. R.C.B. Haking, in 1913 and 1914, quoted in Travers, "Technology, Tactics, and Morale," p. 275.

95. Vladimir Sukhomlinov in 1909, quoted in D.C.B. Lieven, *Russia and the Origins of the First World War* (New York: St. Martin's, 1983), p. 113.

96. Bruce W. Menning, "The Offensive Revisited: Russian Preparation for Future War, 1906–1914," in David Schimmelpenninck van der Oye and Menning, eds., *Reforming the Tsar's Army: Military Innovation in Imperial Russia from Peter the Great to the Revolution* (Cambridge: Cambridge University Press, 2004), pp. 215–231, at p. 219.

97. Snyder, *The Ideology of the Offensive*, pp. 160–162.

98. Belgium could field only six army divisions against thirty-four opposing German army divisions in 1914. See Tuchman, *The Guns of August*, pp. 39, 41.

99. Ibid., pp. 127–128. See also Albertini, *The Origins of the War of 1914*, Vol. 3, p. 461.

100. Stig Förster has argued that the cult of the offensive was not widespread among German military officers, and specifically that German General Staff officers lacked confidence in Germany's planned offensive against France. See Förster, "Dreams and Nightmares." Most observers have concluded otherwise, however, and most evidence indicates otherwise.

The most reliable picture of German General Staff views probably comes from diplomatic observers who reported regularly on General Staff thinking and from top German officials who used General Staff judgments to make policy. These observers consistently reported that the German General Staff was confident of victory over

France in 1914. For example, in 1914 Hugo Philipp Graf von und zu Lerchenfeld-Koefering, the long-time Bavarian envoy in Berlin, and Gen. Ludwig von Gebsattel, the Bavarian military attaché in Berlin, reported that German General Staff officers were confident that the German offensive against France would succeed. As mobilization was ordered on July 31, Lerchenfeld telegrammed: "Prussian General Staff anticipates war with France with great confidence, reckons will be able to defeat France in 4 weeks; in the French army no good spirit, few mortars and worse guns." See Mombauer, *The Origins of the First World War*, p. 487. Gebsattel, whose brother was an active-duty general with good contacts in Berlin, reported on August 2: "Chances better than in two or three years hence and the General Staff is reported to be confidently awaiting events." See Fritz Fischer, *War of Illusions: German Policies from 1911 to 1914*, trans. Marian Jackson (New York: W.W. Norton, 1975), p. 403. A third observer, the British military attaché, noted a mood of "supreme confidence" that "reigns in military circles in Berlin" as the war began. See Albertini, *The Origins of the War of 1914*, Vol. 3, p. 171. A fourth observer, Bethmann's deputy, Kurt Riezler, recorded in retrospect: "The General Staff declared the war would be over in 40 days." See Röhl, "Germany," p. 33. These observers talked directly with General Staff officers, giving them good insight into the views of the General Staff community as a whole.

There is also direct testimony from German military and civilian leaders. The vast majority express confidence in the German offensive against France. For example, the *Post*, a German newspaper that reflected the views of German military leaders, argued on February 24, 1914, that prospects for an aggressive war by Germany were favorable: "France is not yet ready to fight," and "with a determined offensive we could take charge of European policy and safeguard our future." See Fischer, *War of Illusions*, p. 372. See also the confidence of the kaiser, Generals Waldersee and Loebell, and officers Häsler and Hochberg, in Stephen Van Evera, *Causes of War: Power and the Roots of Conflict* (Ithaca, N.Y.: Cornell University Press, 1999), pp. 19, 204; and Moltke in Fischer, *War of Illusions*, p. 227. Finally, there are the many statements by German officers and civilians that indicate faith in the general power of the offense. See, for example, statements by Generals Bernhardi and Keim, a 1902 General Staff study, and Martin Kitchen's summary quoted above.

Förster apparently gives this evidence no weight—he leaves it undiscussed—but I see no basis for dismissing it. Overall, a large preponderance of evidence indicates that German officers and civilians were deeply imbued with faith in the offense before 1914. Mark Hewitson reviews this issue and concludes that "German leaders were confident that they could win a continental war" in 1914. See Hewitson, *Germany and the Causes of the First World War* (New York: Berg, 2004), pp. 3, 137.

101. These propositions are drawn from offense-defense theory. Elaborations of offense-defense theory include Robert Jervis, "Cooperation under the Security Dilemma," *World*

Politics, Vol. 30, No. 2 (January 1978), pp. 167–214; and Van Evera, *Causes of War,* pp. 117–160.

102. These and other war-causing effects of the cult of the offensive in 1914 are detailed in Stephen Van Evera, "The Cult of the Offensive and the Origins of the First World War," *International Security,* Vol. 9, No. 1 (Summer 1984), pp. 58–107.

103. Georg von Müller in 1896, in a memorandum to the kaiser's brother, quoted in J.C.G. Röhl, ed., *From Bismarck to Hitler: The Problem of Continuity in German History* (London: Longman, 1970), pp. 56–57, 59.

104. Friedrich von Bernhardi, *Germany and the Next War,* trans. Allen H. Powles (London: Edward Arnold, 1914, first published in Germany in 1912), pp. 21, 82–83; and Ferdinand Foch, *The Principles of War,* trans. J. de Morinni (New York: Fly, 1918), pp. 36–37.

105. Centralverband deutscher Industrieller and Emil Kirdorf, quoted in Fischer, *War of Illusions,* pp. 75, 81. Another forecast: "If we do not soon acquire new territory, a frightful catastrophe is inevitable." See Alexander Wirth, quoted in William Archer, ed., *501 Gems of German Thought* (London: T. Fisher Unwin, 1916), p. 53. Similar views were expressed elsewhere in Europe: Joseph Chamberlain warned the British that "if we were to cut adrift from the great dependencies which now look to us for protection and which are the natural markets for our trade...half at least of our population would be starved." Chamberlain, in 1888, quoted in Bernard Porter, *The Lion's Share: A Short History of British Imperialism 1850–1970* (New York: Longman, 1975), p. 80.

106. Basserman, quoted in Volker R. Berghahn, *Germany and the Approach of War in 1914* (London: Macmillan, 1973), p. 95.

107. Theodor Schiemann, quoted in Fischer, *War of Illusions,* p. 39. More examples can be found in Jonathan Steinberg, *Yesterday's Deterrent: Tirpitz and the Birth of the German Battle Fleet* (London: Macdonald, 1965), p. 57; and Notestein and Stoll, *Conquest and Kultur,* pp. 89, 136.

108. Arthur Dix, in 1912, quoted in Fischer, *War of Illusions,* p. 31.

109. Quoted in Ritter, *The Schlieffen Plan,* pp. 100–101. A more reliable summary of Entente intentions is Geiss, *July 1914,* pp. 26–33.

110. Quoted in Fischer, *War of Illusions,* p. 118; and Bernhardi, *Germany and the Next War,* pp. 76, 92. Similarly, Admiral Tirpitz warned that the Anglo-French Entente "*de facto* has the character of an offensive alliance." General Moltke declared, "War with France is inevitable" and "war must come...between Germandom and Slavdom." See Helmuth von Moltke, quoted in Fischer, *War of Illusions,* pp. 125 (in 1912), p. 227 (in 1913); and Helmuth von Moltke, quoted in Hull, *The Entourage of Kaiser Wilhelm II, 1888–1918,* p. 241. For more examples, see Geiss, *German Foreign Policy, 1871–1914,* pp. 122, 152; Notestein and Stoll, *Conquest and* Kultur, pp. 99, 115, 119; and Paul M. Kennedy, "Tirpitz, England, and the Second Navy Law of 1900: A Strategic Critique," *Militärgeschichtliche Mitteilungen,* No. 2 (1970), pp. 33–57, at p. 39.

111. In 1914 Britain, France, and Russia all favored the status quo—not from magnanimity but from self-interest: the status quo served them well. They had no aggressive designs on Germany. Britain viewed German power with concern but had no plan to undermine it. France had once dreamed of recovering Alsace-Lorraine, but this dream had largely been forgotten. Russia accepted the status quo almost everywhere. It considered seizing the Turkish Straits if, but only if, the Ottoman Empire collapsed and another power seemed poised to take them. Russia's activities in the Balkans were generally focused on containing Austrian expansion, not on expanding Russia's own power. On France and Alsace-Lorraine, see Eugen Weber, *The Nationalist Revival in France, 1905–1914* (Berkeley: University of California Press, 1959). On Russia and the Balkans, see Lieven, *Russia and the Origins of the First World War*, pp. 33–46; on Russia and the straits, ibid., pp. 45–46. Lieven summarizes: "Russia was much less aggressive than Germany before 1914." See ibid., p. 153. British strategy toward Germany before 1914 was framed in Eyre Crowe's 1907 memorandum, "Present State of British Relations with France and Germany," which argued for cooperation with Germany unless Germany behaved aggressively. For excerpts, see Geiss, *July 1914*, pp. 28–33.

112. Vagts, *Defense and Diplomacy*, p. 297.

113. A.A. Kersnovskii, quoted in Snyder, *The Ideology of the Offensive*, p. 168. See also William C. Fuller Jr., "The Russian Empire," in Ernest R. May, ed., *Knowing One's Enemies: Intelligence Assessment before the Two World Wars* (Princeton, N.J.: Princeton University Press, 1986), pp. 98–126, at pp. 109–110. Fuller also notes that Russian diplomats generally saw a less threatening world. See ibid., p. 123.

114. Charles E. McClelland, *The German Historians and England: A Study in Nineteenth-Century Views* (Cambridge: Cambridge University Press, 1971), p. 208.

115. In 1914, quoted in Archer, *501 Gems of German Thought*, p. 113. For more examples, see Abraham Ascher, "Professors as Propagandists: The Politics of the Kathedersozialisten," *Journal of Central European Affairs*, Vol. 23 (October 1963), pp. 282–302, at p. 293; McClelland, *The German Historians and England*, pp. 182, 203, 209; Archer, *501 Gems of German Thought*, p. 115; and Louis L. Snyder, *German Nationalism: The Tragedy of a People* (Harrisburg: Stackpole, 1952), p. 146.

116. Walter Consuelo Langsam, "Nationalism and History in the Prussian Elementary Schools," in Edward Mead Earle, ed., *Nationalism and Internationalism: Essays Inscribed to Carlton J.H. Hayes* (New York: Columbia University Press, 1950), pp. 241–260, at p. 259; and Edward H. Reisner, *Nationalism and Education since 1789* (New York: Macmillan, 1922), p. 209.

117. *Hamburger Nachrichten*, December 31, 1912, *Kolnische Zeitung*, March 2, 1914, and *Das neue Deutschland*, August 1, 1914, all quoted in Fischer, *War of Illusions*, pp. 94, 374, 244; and *Der Tag*, April 1913, quoted in Berghahn, *Germany and the Approach of War in 1914*, p. 170. See also I.F. Clarke, *Voices Prophecying War, 1763–1984* (London: Oxford

University Press, 1966), pp. 49, 122, 143, which reports that European bookshelves were flooded with novels that conveyed a Darwinistic image of international relations.

118. Wilhelm II, quoted in Anonymous [William Roscoe Thayer?], ed., *Out of Their Own Mouths: Utterances of German Rulers, Statesmen, Savants, Publicists, Journalists, Poets, Businessmen, Party Leaders, and Soldiers* (New York: D. Appleton, 1917), p. 3; and Wilhlem II, quoted in Fischer, *War of Illusions*, p. 221. For similar statements, see Schmitt, *The Coming of the War, 1914*, Vol. 1, p. 102; Geiss, *German Foreign Policy, 1871–1914*, p. 121; and James Joll, "1914: The Unspoken Assumptions," in H.W. Koch, ed., *The Origins of the First World War: Great Power Rivalry and German War Aims* (London: Macmillan, 1972), pp. 307–328, at p. 322.

119. Izvolsky, December 20, 1911, quoted in Schmitt, *The Coming of the War, 1914*, Vol. 1, p. 55. For more examples, see Schmitt, *The Coming of the War, 1914*, p. 370; and Lieven, *Russia and the Origins of the First World War*, p. 96.

120. Porter, *The Lion's Share*, p. 124; and Frederick Greenwood, in ibid., p. 125.

121. In 1913, quoted in Kitchen, *The German Officer Corps, 1890–1914*, p. 141.

122. In 1914, quoted in Notestein and Stoll, *Conquest and Kultur*, p. 43.

123. In 1911, in Bernhardi, *Germany and the Next War*, pp. 18, 20. Other examples can be found in ibid., pp. 23, 37; and Kitchen, *The German Officer Corps, 1890–1914*, p. 96. Bernhardi also believed that even defeat in war could be a healthy experience, bearing "a rich harvest" for the defeated. "[Defeat] often, indeed, passes an irrevocable sentence on weakness and misery, but often, too, it leads to a healthy revival, and lays the foundation of a new and vigorous constitution." See ibid., p. 28. Thus Bernhardi argued that the Boers had benefited from their encounter with British arms in the Boer War: they had made "inestimable moral gains" and won "glorious victories," by which they had "accumulated a store of fame and national consciousness." See ibid., p. 44.

124. Dr. Schmidt-Gibichenfels, publisher of the *Politisch-Anthropologische Revue*, November 8, 1912, quoted in Fischer, *War of Illusions*, p. 194; *Alldeutscher Blatter*, in 1911, quoted in Snyder, *German Nationalism*, p. 241; and *Das neue Deutschland*, August 1, 1914, quoted in Fischer, *War of Illusions*, p. 244.

125. *Berliner Neuest Nachrichten*, December 24, 1912, quoted in Fischer, *War of Illusions*, p. 194. Another observer wrote, "War is the great chiming of the world clock...the expulsion of stagnation by progress; the struggle of the stronger and more vigorous, with the chance to create new cultural values of a richer existence; a necessity that cannot be eliminated." See Philipp Stauff, in 1907, quoted in Roger Chickering, *Imperial Germany and a World without War: The Peace Movement and German Society, 1892–1914* (Princeton, N.J.: Princeton University Press, 1975), p. 395. Historian Heinrich Treitschke declared, "War is both justifiable and moral," and "the ideal of perpetual peace is not only impossible but immoral as well," while the "corroding influence of peace" should be deplored. See Treitschke, quoted in Chickering, *Imperial Germany*

and a World without War, p. 395; and Notestein and Stoll, *Conquest and* Kultur, p. 41. For more examples, see Chickering, *Imperial Germany and a World without War*, pp. 394–395; Archer, *501 Gems of German Thought*, pp. 60, 62, 69; Fischer, *War of Illusions*, p. 33; Notestein and Stoll, *Conquest and* Kultur, pp. 34, 39, 41; Snyder, *From Bismarck to Hitler*, p. 28; and Paul M. Kennedy, "The Decline of Nationalistic History in the West, 1900–1970," *Journal of Contemporary History*, Vol. 8, No. 1 (January 1973), p. 79.

126. Quoted in Roland N. Stromberg, *Redemption by War: The Intellectuals and 1914* (Lawrence: Regents Press of Kansas, 1982), p. 180.

127. Kennedy, "Decline of Nationalistic History in the West, 1900–1970," p. 82. Likewise, Sidney Low wrote that wars are "bracing tonics to the national health"; and Lord Lansdowne declared that warfare would benefit society by "strengthening the moral fibre of the nation." See Porter, *The Lion's Share*, p. 129; and Bernard Brodie, *War and Politics* (New York: Macmillan, 1973), p. 266. See also Michael Howard, "Empire, Race, and War in Pre-1914 Britain," in Hugh Lloyd-Jones, Valerie Pearl, and Blair Worden, eds., *History and Imagination: Essays in Honour of H.R. Trevor-Roper* (London: Duckworth, 1981), pp. 340–355.

128. General Cherfils, quoted in Cairns, "International Politics and the Military Mind," p. 283.

129. *Hamburger Nachrichten*, June 1910, quoted in Notestein and Stoll, *Conquest and* Kultur, p. 113; and *Die Post*, in August 1911, quoted in Fischer, *War of Illusions*, p. 83.

130. General Lynker reportedly favored war in 1909, because he saw "war as desirable in order to escape from difficulties at home and abroad." Bernhardi wrote, "A great war will unify and elevate the people and destroy the diseases which threaten the national health." See Lynker, quoted in Hull, *The Entourage of Kaiser Wilhelm, 1888–1918*, p. 259; and Friedrich von Bernhardi, quoted in Notestein and Stoll, *Conquest and* Kultur, p. 38. This idea also had detractors high in the German government, however, and emphasis placed on it should be qualified accordingly. For examples, see Berghahn, *Germany and the Approach of War in 1914*, pp. 82, 97; Geiss, *German Foreign Policy, 1871–1914*, pp. 125–126; Turner, *Origins of the First World War*, p. 76; and David E. Kaiser, "Germany and the Origins of the First World War," *Journal of Modern History*, Vol. 55, No. 3 (September 1983), pp. 442–474, at p. 470. See also Arno J. Mayer, "Domestic Causes of the First World War," in Leonard Krieger and Fritz Stern, eds., *The Responsibility of Power* (London: Macmillan, 1968), pp. 286–300, especially p. 297.

131. On August 7, 1914, quoted in Stromberg, *Redemption by War*, p. 42. Max Weber wrote, "No matter what the outcome will be, this war is great and wonderful," while one poet declared that the war had "swept like a purifying storm into our close and fetid atmosphere." See ibid., p. 52; and Ludwig Schueller, quoted in Leon W. Fuller, "The War of 1914 as Interpreted by German Intellectuals," *Journal of Modern History*, Vol. 14, No. 2 (June 1942), pp. 145–160, at p. 152.

132. Stromberg, *Redemption by War*, pp. 43, 51.

133. Joll, "Unspoken Assumptions," p. 318.

134. On bandwagoning versus balancing, the landmark study is Stephen M. Walt, *The Origins of Alliances* (Ithaca, N.Y.: Cornell University Press, 1987), pp. 17–33, 147–180, 263–266, 274–280. Walt argues that balancing prevails over bandwagoning. He corroborates his argument with evidence from the modern Middle East. His argument is also corroborated by the persistent formation of powerful countervailing coalitions against every real or perceived aspirant for European dominion during the past five hundred years. Specifically, the Habsburg Empire, France under Louis XIV, revolutionary and Napoleonic France, Russia in the 1850s, Wilhelmine Germany, Nazi Germany, and the Soviet Union were all contained or destroyed by countervailing coalitions that formed to check their expansion.

135. Ropp, *War in the Modern World*, p. 212; and Ritter, *The Schlieffen Plan*, p. 163.

136. Ludwig Dehio, *Germany and World Politics in the Twentieth Century*, trans. Dieter Pevsner (New York: W.W. Norton, 1967), p. 20.

137. In October, 1913, quoted in Geiss, *German Foreign Policy, 1871–1914*, pp. 136–137.

138. In February 1914, Jagow declared: "We have not built our fleet in vain, and in my opinion, people in England will seriously ask themselves whether it will be just that simple and without danger to play the role of France's guardian angel against us." See Jagow, quoted in Geiss, *German Foreign Policy, 1871–1914*, p. 25. Similarly, Chancellor Bethmann Hollweg later confessed that he had believed before the war that Germany could intimidate Britain into abandoning its traditional commitment to maintain the continental balance of power. Moltke expressed similar views. See Fischer, *War of Illusions*, pp. 69, 227. For more examples, see Wayne C. Thompson, *In the Eye of the Storm: Kurt Riezler and the Crises of Modern Germany* (Iowa City: University of Iowa Press, 1980), p. 50; and Fischer, *War of Illusions*, p. 133.

139. During the July crisis, Jagow argued: "The more determined Austria shows herself, the more energetically we support her, so much the more quiet will Russia remain." See Geiss, *July 1914*, p. 123. Bethmann Hollweg similarly believed that the Austrian attack on Serbia might shatter the Entente by forcing Russia or France to publically abandon its ally. See Geiss, *German Foreign Policy, 1871–1914*, p. 166; and Schmitt, *The Coming of the War, 1914*, Vol. 1, p. 399.

140. *Die Post*, December 1912, interpreting a Bethmann Hollweg speech, quoted in Fischer, *War of Illusions*, p. 241.

141. Joseph L. Reimer, in 1905, quoted in Notestein and Stoll, *Conquest and* Kultur, p. 57.

142. Karl von Winterstetten warned in 1914 that Austria, the Scandinavian states, Romania, Bulgaria, and Turkey would all be lost to Germany "if Russia should gain control over one of them, and thus be able to exert pressure on the others"; hence Germany should seek to control the whole bloc. Winterstetten, quoted in Notestein and Stoll, *Conquest and*

Kultur, p. 60. For another example, see Thayer, *Out of Their Own Mouths*, p. 74.

143. On the social isolation and contempt for civilians of the Wilhelmine German military, see Hull, *The Entourage of Kaiser Wilhelm II, 1888–1918*, pp. 199–201; and Kitchen *The German Officer Corps, 1890–1914*, pp. 49–63, 115–118.

144. Some scholars have doubted that inadvertent wars ever happen. Bernard Brodie, using the term "accidental" as a synonym for inadvertent, writes: "I know of no war in modern times that one could truly call accidental in the sense that it came about despite both sides having a strong aversion to it, through not seeing where their diplomatic moves were taking them." Brodie, quoted in Scott D. Sagan, "Accidental War in Theory and Practice," Stanford University, February 28, 2000, p. 3. After surveying the causes of wars from 1300 to 1985, Evan Luard did not find a single case of "a war started accidentally; in which it was not, at the time when war broke out, the deliberate intention of at least one party that war should take place." See ibid. Michael Howard writes that the initiation of war "is almost by definition a deliberate and carefully considered act…if history shows any record of 'accidental' wars, I have yet to find them." See ibid. F.H. Hinsley argues more specifically that World War I was not inadvertent: "Those who took the decisions [that brought about the war] did not underestimate the risk of a general war." See Hinsley, "The Origins of the First World War," in Wilson, *Decisions for War*, pp. 1–8, at p. 4. Marc Trachtenberg argues that World War I was not inadvertent, but he uses a narrower definition of "inadvertent" than mine, one more focused on military factors alone. See Trachtenberg, *History and Strategy*, pp. 47–99. It is unclear if Trachtenberg would deem World War I inadvertent if he used my broader definition.

145. Germany briefly had false hopes of a sixth outcome, eastern war (EW), in which Russia and Serbia would fight Germany and Austria. German leaders wrongly thought that Britain was offering such an outcome on August 1. An EW scenario was very unlikely, however, as France had compelling security reasons to fight Germany if Germany fought Russia.

146. That Bethmann preferred CW over ADS as well as SDBH is suggested by his many references in conversation and writing to Russia's ominously rising power. CW would address that threat, but ADS and SDBH would not, so Bethmann should logically have favored CW over ADS and SDBH. For examples of Bethmann's gloom, see Fischer, *War of Illusions*, p. 224; Konrad H. Jarausch, "The Illusion of Limited War: Chancellor Bethmann Hollweg's Calculated Risk, July 1914," *Central European History*, Vol. 2, No. 1 (March 1969), pp. 48–76, at pp. 48, 57; Richard Ned Lebow, *Between Peace and War: The Nature of International Crisis* (Baltimore, Md.: Johns Hopkins University Press, 1981), p. 258n; and Volker R. Berghahn and Martin Kitchen, eds., *Germany in the Age of Total War* (Totowa, N.J.: Barnes and Noble, 1981), p. 45.

147. The kaiser was also averse to CW. He indicated his aversion to both CW and WW when, on July 28, he moved to end the crisis by restraining Austria. His decision was a choice for SDBH over WW and CW, as those were the live alternatives at that point. The

kaiser's full preference order during the crisis was probably ADS > SDBH > CW/SQAB (the priority is not clear) > WW, although he was mercurial and hard to pin down. On the kaiser and the crisis, see John C.G. Röhl, "The Curious Case of the Kaiser's Disappearing War Guilt: Wilhelm in July 1914," in Afflerbach and Stevenson, *An Improbable War*, pp. 75–92. Röhl believes that the kaiser's views were somewhat more hawkish than my summary indicates.

148. As Moltke insisted that Germany move to mobilization and war on July 30, he clearly knew this would bring world war, telling Hans von Haeften: "This war will turn into a world war in which England will also intervene." See Helmuth von Moltke, quoted in Mombauer, *The Origins of the First World War*, p. 459.

149. On Russian decisions, see Albertini, *The Origins of the War of 1914*, Vol. 2, pp. 290–294, 297–309; and Mombauer, *The Origins of the First World War*, pp. 321–328, 331–334, 340–345.

150. Mombauer, *The Origins of the First World War*, p. 333.

151. Sazanov took several steps during the July crisis that indicated a desire to avoid war. He advised Serbia on July 24 to observe "extreme moderation" in its reply to the Austrian ultimatum. See Mombauer, *The Origins of the First World War*, pp. 309, 322. He advised Serbia on July 24 that it should not resist an Austrian invasion, and should instead peacefully allow an Austrian occupation while appealing to the powers for help. Ibid., pp. 309, 321, 332. He advised Serbia on July 25 to ask Britain to mediate the Austro-Serbian dispute, and asked his ambassadors in Belgrade and London to support such British mediation "energetically." See ibid., p. 345. Also, he endorsed a solution to the crisis on July 30 that was in line with an SDBH formula. See ibid., p. 464.

152. Albertini, *The Origins of the War of 1914*, Vol. 2, p. 309.

153. Ibid., pp. 22–23. See also Moltke's and Bethmann's statements in note 67 above.

154. I thank M. Taylor Fravel for educating me on Chinese civil-military relations. Studies on the topic include David M. Finkelstein and Kristen Gunness, eds., *Civil-Military Relations in Today's China* (London: M.E. Sharpe, 2007); and Nan Li, ed., *Chinese Civil-Military Relations* (New York: Routledge, 2006).

155. See Jane K. Cramer, *National Security Panics and U.S. Foreign Policy Shifts* (New York: Routledge, 2014).

156. The administration of President Richard Nixon also was deeply complicit in this massacre. See Gary Bass, *The Blood Telegram: Nixon, Kissinger, and a Forgotten Genocide* (New York: Alfred A. Knopf, 2013).

157. Carlotta Gall, *The Wrong Enemy: America in Afghanistan, 2001–2014* (New York: Houghton Mifflin, 2014), pp. 248–249, 253–255.

158. Ibid., pp. 180, 259. Unlike pre-1914 European militaries, the Pakistani military has spiced its belligerence and expansionism with a religious twist. It infuses its officers and wider Pakistani society with a hateful, xenophobic version of Islam, which it exploits

to win support for itself and its belligerent policies. The result is pre-1914 European-style militarism with a heavy Islamist/jihadist flavor. See Husain Haqqani, *Pakistan: Between Mosque and Military* (Washington, D.C.: Carnegie Endowment for International Peace, 2005).

Chapter 12. Inevitability and War

1.   Bernhard von Bülow, *Memoires of Prince von Bülow, 1909–1919* (Boston: Little, Brown, 1932), pp. 165–166.

2.   Niall Ferguson, *The Pity of War* (New York: Basic Books, 1999), p. xxxvi.

3.   Martin Wolf, "China Must Not Copy the Kaiser's Errors," *Financial Times*, December 4, 2013.

4.   Margaret MacMillan, "The Great War's Ominous Echoes," *New York Times*, December 14, 2013. See also Margaret MacMillan, *The War That Ended Peace: The Road to 1914* (New York: Random House, 2013).

5.   "Look Back with Angst," *Economist*, December 21, 2013, p. 17.

6.   John J. Mearsheimer, "The Gathering Storm: China's Challenge to U.S. Power in Asia," Michael Hintze Lecture, University of Sydney, August 5, 2010, www.usyd.edu.au/news/84.html?Newstoryid=5351.

7.   See Joseph S. Nye Jr., "As China Rises, Must Others Bow?" *Economist*, June 27, 1998, p. 23.

8.   Richard E. Neustadt and Ernest R. May, *Thinking in Time: The Uses of History for Decision Makers* (New York: Free Press, 1986).

9.   See the chapters by Graham Allison, Charles Maier, and David Richards in this volume.

10.   Thucydides, *History of the Peloponnesian War* (London: Penguin, 1972) p. 57.

11.   Ibid., p. 62.

12.   Robert Axelrod, *The Evolution of Cooperation*, rev. ed. (New York: Basic Books, 2006), p. 124.

13.   Donald Kagan, *The Outbreak of the Peloponnesian War* (Ithaca, N.Y.: Cornell University Press, 1969), p. 354. For an alternative interpretation of the realities of Athenian expansion, see G.E.M. de Ste. Croix, *The Origins of the Peloponnesian War* (Ithaca, N.Y.: Cornell University Press, 1972), pp. 60, 201–203.

14.   The classic approach is Kenneth N. Waltz, *Man, the State, and War* (New York: Columbia University Press, 1959).

15.   A.J.P. Taylor, *The Struggle for Mastery in Europe, 1848–1918* (Oxford: Oxford University Press, 1954), p. xxxi.

16.   Christopher Clark, *The Sleepwalkers: How Europe Went to War in 1914* (New York: HarperCollins, 2013), p. 123.

17.   See Arthur Stein's chapter in this volume.

18. See T.G. Otte's chapter in this volume.

19. Sidney Bradshaw Fay, *The Origins of the World War*, Vol. 2 (New York: Macmillan, 1929), pp. 185–186.

20. See Etel Solingen's chapter in this volume.

21. See Stephen Van Evera's chapter in this volume.

22. MacMillan, *The War That Ended Peace*, p. 584.

23. Clark, *The Sleepwalkers*, p. 416.

24. See MacMillan, *The War That Ended Peace*, p. 613.

25. Bernadotte Everly Schmitt, *Interviewing the Authors of the War* (Chicago: Chicago Literary Club, 1930), p. 41.

26. Ernest R. May, *The World War and American Isolation, 1914–1917* (Cambridge, Mass.: Harvard University Press, 1959), p. 428.

27. Clark, *The Sleepwalkers*, pp. 362–363.

28. John E. Mueller, *Retreat from Doomsday: The Obsolescence of Major War* (New York: Basic Books, 1988).

29. Winston S. Churchill, *The World in Crisis, 1911–1918* (New York: Free Press, 2005), p. 92.

30. MacMillan, *The War That Ended Peace*, p. 63.

31. National Intelligence Council, *The World in 2030* (Washington, D.C.: National Intelligence Council, 2013).

Chapter 13. Lessons from Europe 1914 for Asia 2014: Reflections on the Centenary of the Outbreak of World War I

1. Drew Faust, *Death and the American Civil War* (New York: Vintage, 2009).

2. "Peaceful End to Germany's Problems Seen" *Christian Science Monitor*, January 1, 1914.

3. "Noteworthy Events in the World's Progress in 1913" *New York Times*, December 31, 1913.

4. "The Old Year and the New," *Economist*, January 3, 1914, p. 3.

5. See Joseph Nye's chapter in this volume.

6. "The July 1914 Crisis—Sleepwalking Diplomats?" http://london.diplo.de/Vertretung/london/en/092-WWI/Sleepwalking.html.

7. Christopher Clark, *The Sleepwalkers: How Europe Went to War in 1914* (New York: HarperCollins, 2013), p. 20.

8. Graham Allison, "2014: Good Year for a Great War?" *National Interest*, January 1, 2014, http://nationalinterest.org/commentary/2014-good-year-great-war-9652. See also Graham Allison, "Thucydides Trap Has Been Sprung in the Pacific," http://www.ft.com/intl/cms/s/0/5d695b5a-ead3-11e1-984b-00144feab49a.html#axzz38xpLQVsF;

and James R. Holmes, "Beware the 'Thucydides Trap' Trap: Why the U.S. and China Aren't Necessarily Athens and Sparta or Britain and Germany before WWI," http://thediplomat.com/2013/06/beware-the-thucydides-trap-trap/.

9.   "Stumbling into World War I, Like 'Sleepwalkers': Interview with Christopher Clark," National Public Radio, April 23, 2013.

10.   Quoted in Barbara Tuchman, *The Guns of August: The Outbreak of World War I* (New York: Macmillan, 2009), p. 81.

11.   "Which War to Mention? Germany's Russia Policy," *Economist*, March 22, 2014, p. 25. See also "The July 1914 Crisis—Sleepwalking Diplomats?"

12.   Clark, *The Sleepwalkers*, p. xxix.

13.   Andrew Carnegie, "New Year Greeting 1914," *Independent*, January 5, 1914.

14.   See Richard Cooper's chapter in this volume.

15.   Jackie Calmes and Steven Lee Myers, "Obama and Xi Tackle Cybersecurity as Talks Begin in California" *New York Times*, June 7, 2013.

16.   John Mearsheimer, "Can China Rise Peacefully?" *National Interest*, April 8, 2014, http://nationalinterest.org/commentary/can-china-rise-peacefully-10204.

17.   George Reid, speech to the Reichstag, Berlin, May 1912.

Chapter 14. Contingency as a Cause (or Little Things Mean a Lot)

1.   Regarding the title of this conclusion, see, for example, the statement of former Deputy Assistant Secretary of Defense for South and Southeast Asia Vikram Singh: "Wars start from small things, often by accident and miscalculation—like dangerous maneuvers by aircraft that result in collision or aggressive moves that lead to an unexpected military response." Quoted in Helene Cooper and Jane Perlez, "U.S. Sway in Asia Is Imperiled as China Challenges Alliances," *New York Times*, May 30, 2014.

2.   See Kenneth N. Waltz, *Theory of International Politics* (Reading, Mass.: Addison-Wesley, 1979). Of the authors in the present volume, Graham Allison finds the Thucydides Trap worrisome. Charles Maier, Joseph Nye, and David Richards argue that it was not a decisive factor in 1914 and urge caution when applying it to potential future conflicts.

3.   See Graham Allison's chapter in this volume; and Richard Rosecrance, *The Resurgence of the West: How a Transatlantic Union Can Prevent War and Restore the United States and Europe* (New Haven, Conn.: Yale University Press, 2013), chap. 5.

4.   Thomas J. Christensen and Jack Snyder, "Chain Gangs and Passed Bucks: Predicting Alliance Patterns in Multipolarity," *International Organization*, Vol. 44, No. 2 (Spring 1990), pp. 137–168.

5.   As Niall Ferguson shows, even a delay in sending British troops to France might have led to a quick German victory. See Ferguson, *The Pity of War* (New York: Basic Books, 1999).

6.   See ibid., chap. 14.

7.   According to Christopher Clark, "It is virtually certain that [Serbian leader Nikola] Pašić was informed of the plan [to kill Franz Ferdinand] in some detail." See Clark, *The Sleepwalkers: How Europe Went to War in 1914* (New York: HarperCollins, 2013), p. 56.

8.   Ibid.

9.   Quoted in Bill Emmot, *Rivals: How the Power Struggle between China, India, and Japan Will Shape Our Next Decade* (Boston: Mariner, 2009), p. 96.

10.   See Barbara Tuchman, *The Guns of August* (New York: Macmillan, 1962); and Clark, *The Sleepwalkers*.

Contributors

Alan Alexandroff is Director of the Global Summitry Project at the Munk School of Global Affairs at the University of Toronto and Director of Online Research. His work focuses on the contemporary global governance architecture and the influence and role of rising states, particularly China, in the global economy. Alexandroff is Founder and Senior Editor of the *Global Summitry Journal* with Donald Brean, and has long authored the blog *Rising BRICSAM*. Alexandroff received his B.A., cum laude with distinction in all subjects from Cornell University, an M.A. and Ph.D. in government from Cornell University, an M.A. in international history from the London School of Political Science and Economics, and an L.L.B. from the McGill University Law School.

Graham Allison is Director of the Belfer Center for Science and International Affairs and Douglas Dillon Professor of Government at the John F. Kennedy School of Government at Harvard University. The "founding dean" of the modern Kennedy School, Allison has served as a special adviser to the secretary of defense under President Ronald Reagan and as an assistant secretary of defense under President Bill Clinton. His first book, *Essence of Decision: Explaining the Cuban Missile Crisis*, ranks among the all-time best-sellers with more than 450,000 copies in print. His latest book, *Lee Kuan Yew: The Grand Master's Insights on China, the United States, and the World*, coauthored with Robert D. Blackwill, has been a best-seller in the United States and abroad.

Richard N. Cooper is Maurits C. Boas Professor of International Economics at Harvard University. He is a member of the Trilateral Commission, the Council on Foreign Relations, the Executive Panel of the U.S. Chief of Naval Operations, and the Brookings Panel on Economic Activity. He has served as chairman of the National Intelligence Council, undersecretary of state for economic affairs, deputy assistant secretary of state for international monetary affairs, and senior staff economist at the Council of Economic Advisers. He was chairman of the Federal Reserve Bank of Boston and vice chairman of the Global Development Network. As a Marshall Scholar, he studied at the London School of Economics and earned his Ph.D. at Harvard. Most recently, he coauthored *Boom, Crisis, and Adjustment: The Macroeconomic Experience of Developing Countries*; *Macroeconomic Management in Korea, 1970-1990*; *Environment and Resource Policies for the World Economy*; and *What the Future Holds: Insights from Social Science*.

Charles S. Maier received his bachelor's and doctoral degrees from Harvard University, where he is Leverett Saltonstall Professor of History. He specializes in the history of modern Europe, international relations, and global history. He is a member of the American Academy of Arts and Sciences and the Council on Foreign Relations, and has been decorated by the German and Austrian governments for his cultural contributions. His most recent books include *Among Empires: American Ascendancy and Its Predecessors* and *Leviathan 2.0: Inventing Modern Statehood.*

Steven E. Miller is Director of the International Security Program at the Belfer Center for Science and International Affairs at the John F. Kennedy School of Government at Harvard University, Editor-in-Chief of the quarterly journal *International Security*, and coeditor of the International Security Program's book series, Belfer Center Studies in International Security. Previously, he was a senior research fellow at the Stockholm International Peace Research Institute and taught Defense and Arms Control Studies in the Department of Political Science at the Massachusetts Institute of Technology. He is coauthor of the monographs *War with Iraq: Costs, Consequences, and Alternatives* and *Nuclear Collisions: Discord, Reform, and the Nuclear Nonproliferation Regime.* Miller is editor or coeditor of more than two dozen books, including, most recently, *Do Democracies Win Their Wars?* and *Contending with Terrorism: Roots, Strategies, and Responses.*

Joseph S. Nye Jr. is University Distinguished Service Professor and former dean of the John F. Kennedy School of Government at Harvard University. He received his bachelor's degree summa cum laude from Princeton University, won a Rhodes Scholarship to the University of Oxford, and earned a Ph.D. in political science from Harvard. He has served as an assistant secretary of defense for international security affairs, chair of the National Intelligence Council, and as a deputy undersecretary of state. His most recent books include *Soft Power: The Means to Success in World Politics, The Powers to Lead,* and *The Future of Power.* He is a fellow of the American Academy of Arts and Sciences, the British Academy, and the American Academy of Diplomacy. In a recent survey of international relations scholars, he was ranked as the most influential scholar on U.S. foreign policy, and in 2011 *Foreign Policy* named him one of the top 100 Global Thinkers.

T.G. Otte is Professor of Diplomatic History at the University of East Anglia. He is the author or editor of fifteen books. Among his latest publications are *The China Question: Great Power Rivalry and British Isolation, 1894–1905; The Foreign Office Mind: The Making of British Foreign Policy, 1865–1914; July 1914: Europe's Descent into World War*, and *An Historian in Peace and War: The Diaries of Harold Temperley, 1900–1939*, ed. From 2007 to 2010, he was an adviser to the British government's Foreign and Commonwealth Office.

David K. Richards is a private investor based in Santa Monica, California. Previously he was a professional investment manager of mutual funds, pension funds, and endowments. He is a graduate of Harvard College; Wadham College at the University of Oxford; and the Harvard Business School. He serves on Harvard's Committee on University Resources, the Campaign Executive Committee, the Dean's Council of the Faculty of Arts and Sciences, the Dean's Council of the John F. Kennedy School of Government, and the International Council of the Kennedy School's Belfer Center for Science and International Affairs. He is a foundation fellow of Wadham College and a member of the chancellor's Court of Benefactors of the University of Oxford. He is a trustee of the RAND Corporation and serves on the board of advisers of RAND Health and the Center for Middle East Public Policy.

Richard N. Rosecrance, a high honors graduate from Swarthmore College, received his Ph.D. from Harvard University. He has held professorships in political science and international politics at Cornell University; the University of California, Berkeley; and the University of California, Los Angeles (UCLA). He directed the Burkle Center for International Relations at UCLA. He is currently Adjunct Professor in the John F. Kennedy School of Government at Harvard University and Director of the U.S.-China Relations Project at the Belfer Center for Science and International Affairs at the Kennedy School. Most recently, he authored *The Resurgence of the West: How a Transatlantic Union Can Prevent War and Restore the United States and Europe* and served as coeditor of *History and Neorealism*. He previously served on the Policy Planning Council at the U.S. Department of State.

Kevin Rudd served as the twenty-sixth prime minister of Australia from 2007 to 2010, as foreign minister from 2010 to 2012, and again as prime minister in 2013. As prime minister, he was a co-founder of the Group of Twenty as the central institution of global economic governance. He also was a primary advocate of expanding the East Asian Summit in 2010 to include the United

States. In 2008 he launched a proposal to build an Asia Pacific Community as a central element for the future political, economic, and strategic architecture of the Asia-Pacific region. A first-class honors graduate in Chinese language and history from the Australian National University and a former Australian diplomat, Rudd has been a senior fellow at the Belfer Center for Science and International Affairs at the John F. Kennedy School of Government at Harvard University and a visiting scholar in the Department of International Relations at Tsinghua University.

Jack Snyder is Robert and Renée Belfer Professor of International Relations in the Department of Political Science and the Saltzman Institute of War and Peace Studies at Columbia University. His books include *Electing to Fight: Why Emerging Democracies Go to War*; *The Ideology of the Offensive: Military Decision Making and the Disasters of 1914*; *Myths of Empire: Domestic Politics and International Ambition*; *From Voting to Violence: Democratization and Nationalist Conflict*; and *Power and Progress: International Politics in Transition*.

Etel Solingen is Thomas T. and Elizabeth C. Tierney Chair in Peace Studies at the University of California, Irvine, and recent Chancellor's Professor and President of the International Studies Association. Her book *Nuclear Logics: Contrasting Paths in East Asia and the Middle East* received the American Political Science Association's Woodrow Wilson Foundation Award and the Robert Jervis and Paul Schroeder Award. She is also author of *Regional Orders at Century's Dawn: Global and Domestic Influences on Grand Strategy*; *Comparative Regionalism: Economics and Security*; and *Industrial Policy, Technology, and International Bargaining: Designing Nuclear Industries in Argentina and Brazil*. Among her edited volumes is *Sanctions, Statecraft, and Nuclear Proliferation*.

Arthur A. Stein is Professor of Political Science at the University of California, Los Angeles. He received an A.B. from Cornell University and a Ph.D. from Yale University. Stein is author of *The Nation at War* and *Why Nations Cooperate: Circumstance and Choice in International Relations*, and coeditor of *The Domestic Bases of Grand Strategy* and *No More States? Globalization, National Self-Determination, and Terrorism*. He is a former coeditor of the *American Political Science Review* and has been an international affairs fellow of the Council on Foreign Relations and a guest scholar at the Brookings Institution. He previously served on the Policy Planning Staff of the U.S. Department of State.

Stephen Van Evera is Ford International Professor of Political Science at the Massachusetts Institute of Technology (MIT). He holds a Ph.D. in political science from the University of California, Berkeley. His publications include books on the causes of war and on social science methods, and articles on U.S. foreign policy, U.S. defense policy, nationalism and the causes of war, the origins of national identity, the origins of World War I, U.S. intervention in the developing world, Europe's future international relations, the Israel-Arab conflict, and U.S. strategy in the war on terror. He teaches courses on U.S. foreign policy and on the causes and prevention of war. He is a member of the MIT Security Studies Program and chair of the Tobin Project working group on national security.

Index

Belfer Center for Science and International Affairs

Graham Allison, Director
John F. Kennedy School of Government, Harvard University
79 JFK Street, Cambridge MA 02138
Tel: (617) 495-1400 | Fax: (617) 495-8963
http://www.belfercenter.org | belfer_center@hks.harvard.edu

The Belfer Center is the hub of the Harvard Kennedy School's research, teaching, and training in international security affairs, environmental and resource issues, and science and technology policy.

The Center has a dual mission: (1) to provide leadership in advancing policy-relevant knowledge about the most important challenges of international security and other critical issues where science, technology, environmental policy, and international affairs intersect; and (2) to prepare future generations of leaders for these arenas. Center researchers not only conduct scholarly research, but also develop prescriptions for policy reform. Faculty and fellows analyze global challenges from nuclear proliferation and terrorism to climate change and energy policy.

The Belfer Center's leadership begins with the recognition of science and technology as driving forces constantly transforming both the challenges we face and the opportunities for problem solving. Building on the vision of founder Paul Doty, the Center addresses serious global concerns by integrating insights and research of social scientists, natural scientists, technologists, and practitioners in government, diplomacy, the military, and business.

The heart of the Belfer Center is its resident research community of more than 150 scholars, including Harvard faculty, researchers, practitioners, and each year a new, international, interdisciplinary group of research fellows. Through publications and policy discussions, workshops, seminars, and conferences, the Center promotes innovative solutions to significant national and international challenges.

The Center's International Security Program, directed by Steven E. Miller, publishes the Belfer Center Studies in International Security, and sponsors and edits the quarterly journal, *International Security*.

The Center is supported by an endowment established with funds from Robert and Renée Belfer, the Ford Foundation, and Harvard University, by foundation grants, by individual gifts, and by occasional government contracts.

Belfer Center Studies in International Security

Published by The MIT Press
Sean M. Lynn-Jones and Steven E. Miller, series editors
Karen Motley, executive editor
Belfer Center for Science and International Affairs
John F. Kennedy School of Government, Harvard University

Acharya, Amitav, and Evelyn Goh, eds., *Reassessing Security Cooperation in the Asia-Pacific: Competition, Congruence, and Transformation* (2007)

Agha, Hussein, Shai Feldman, Ahmad Khalidi, and Zeev Schiff, *Track-II Diplomacy: Lessons from the Middle East* (2003)

Allison, Graham, and Robert D. Blackwill, with Ali Wyne, *Lee Kan Yew: The Grand Master's Insights on China, the United States, and the World* (2013)

Allison, Graham T., Owen R. Coté Jr., Richard A. Falkenrath, and Steven E. Miller, *Avoiding Nuclear Anarchy: Containing the Threat of Loose Russian Nuclear Weapons and Fissile Material* (1996)

Allison, Graham T., and Kalypso Nicolaïdis, eds., *The Greek Paradox: Promise vs. Performance* (1997)

Arbatov, Alexei, Abram Chayes, Antonia Handler Chayes, and Lara Olson, eds., *Managing Conflict in the Former Soviet Union: Russian and American Perspectives* (1997)

Bennett, Andrew, *Condemned to Repetition? The Rise, Fall, and Reprise of Soviet-Russian Military Interventionism, 1973–1996* (1999)

Blackwill, Robert D., and Paul Dibb, eds., *America's Asian Alliances* (2000)

Blackwill, Robert D., and Michael Stürmer, eds., *Allies Divided: Transatlantic Policies for the Greater Middle East* (1997)

Blum, Gabriella, and Philip B. Heymann, *Laws, Outlaws, and Terrorists: Lessons from the War on Terrorism* (2010)

Brom, Shlomo, and Yiftah Shapir, eds., *The Middle East Military Balance, 1999–2000* (1999)

Brom, Shlomo, and Yiftah Shapir, eds., *The Middle East Military Balance, 2001–2002* (2002)

Brown, Michael E., ed., *The International Dimensions of Internal Conflict* (1996)

Brown, Michael E., and Sumit Ganguly, eds., *Fighting Words: Language Policy and Ethnic Relations in Asia* (2003)

Brown, Michael E., and Sumit Ganguly, eds., *Government Policies and Ethnic Relations in Asia and the Pacific* (1997)

Carter, Ashton B., and John P. White, eds., *Keeping the Edge: Managing Defense for the Future* (2001)

Chenoweth, Erica, and Adria Lawrence, eds., *Rethinking Violence: States and Non-State Actors in Conflict* (2010)

de Nevers, Renée, *Comrades No More: The Seeds of Change in Eastern Europe* (2003)

Elman, Colin, and Miriam Fendius Elman, eds., *Bridges and Boundaries: Historians, Political Scientists, and the Study of International Relations* (2001)

Elman, Colin, and Miriam Fendius Elman, eds., *Progress in International Relations Theory: Appraising the Field* (2003)

Elman, Miriam Fendius, ed., *Paths to Peace: Is Democracy the Answer?* (1997)

Falkenrath, Richard A., *Shaping Europe's Military Order: The Origins and Consequences of the CFE Treaty* (1995)

Falkenrath, Richard A., Robert D. Newman, and Bradley A. Thayer, *America's Achilles' Heel: Nuclear, Biological, and Chemical Terrorism and Covert Attack* (1998)

Feaver, Peter D., and Richard H. Kohn, eds., *Soldiers and Civilians: The Civil-Military Gap and American National Security* (2001)

Feldman, Shai, *Nuclear Weapons and Arms Control in the Middle East* (1996)

Feldman, Shai, and Yiftah Shapir, eds., *The Middle East Military Balance, 2000–2001* (2001)

Forsberg, Randall, ed., *The Arms Production Dilemma: Contraction and Restraint in the World Combat Aircraft Industry* (1994)

George, Alexander L., and Andrew Bennett, *Case Studies and Theory Development in the Social Sciences* (2005)

Gilroy, Curtis, and Cindy Williams, eds., *Service to Country: Personnel Policy and the Transformation of Western Militaries* (2007)

Hagerty, Devin. T., *The Consequences of Nuclear Proliferation: Lessons from South Asia* (1998)

Heymann, Philip B., *Terrorism and America: A Commonsense Strategy for a Democratic Society* (1998)

Heymann, Philip B., *Terrorism, Freedom, and Security: Winning without War* (2003)

Heymann, Philip B., and Juliette N. Kayyem, *Protecting Liberty in an Age of Terror* (2005)

Howitt, Arnold M., and Robyn L. Pangi, eds., *Countering Terrorism: Dimensions of Preparedness* (2003)

Hudson, Valerie M., and Andrea M. Den Boer, *Bare Branches: The Security Implications of Asia's Surplus Male Population*

Kayyem, Juliette N., and Robyn L. Pangi, eds., *First to Arrive: State and Local Responses to Terrorism* (2003)

Kokoshin, Andrei A., *Soviet Strategic Thought, 1917–91* (1998)

Lederberg, Joshua, ed., *Biological Weapons: Limiting the Threat* (1999)

Mansfield, Edward D., and Jack Snyder, *Electing to Fight: Why Emerging Democracies Go to War* (2005)

Martin, Lenore G., and Dimitris Keridis, eds., *The Future of Turkish Foreign Policy* (2004)

May, Ernest R., and Philip D. Zelikow, eds., *Dealing with Dictators: Dilemmas of U.S. Diplomacy and Intelligence Analysis, 1945–1990* (2007)

Phillips, David L., *Liberating Kosovo: Coercive Diplomacy and U.S. Intervention* (2012)

Rosecrance, Richard N., and Steven E. Miller, eds., *The Next Great War? The Roots of World War I and the Risk of U.S.-China Conflict* (2015)

Shaffer, Brenda, *Borders and Brethren: Iran and the Challenge of Azerbaijani Identity* (2002)

Shaffer, Brenda, ed., *The Limits of Culture: Islam and Foreign Policy* (2006)

Shields, John M., and William C. Potter, eds., *Dismantling the Cold War: U.S. and NIS Perspectives on the Nunn-Lugar Cooperative Threat Reduction Program* (1997)

Tucker, Jonathan B., ed., *Toxic Terror: Assessing Terrorist Use of Chemical and Biological Weapons* (2000)

Utgoff, Victor A., ed., *The Coming Crisis: Nuclear Proliferation, U.S. Interests, and World Order* (2000)

Weiner, Sharon K., *Our Own Worst Enemy? Institutional Interests and the Proliferation of Nuclear Weapons Expertise* (2011)

Williams, Cindy, ed., *Filling the Ranks: Transforming the U.S. Military Personnel System* (2004)

Williams, Cindy, ed., *Holding the Line: U.S. Defense Alternatives for the 21st Century* (2001)

Zoughbie, Daniel E. *Indecision Points: George W. Bush and the Israeli-Palestinian Conflict* (2014)